MW00527294

REVISITING THE EMPTY TOMB
THE EARLY HISTORY OF EASTER

DANIEL A. SMITH

FORTRESS PRESS
MINNEAPOLIS

For my teachers, especially

John P. Egan, S.J.†
John S. Kloppenborg
Richard N. Longenecker

REVISITING THE EMPTY TOMB
The Early History of Easter

Translations of biblical and other ancient texts are the author's own unless otherwise noted.

"Side with the Seeds," written by Jeff Tweedy and Mikael Jorgenson © 2007 WORDS AMPERSAND MUSIC (BMI) AND JORGENSTORMUSIC (ASCAP)/Administered by BUG MUSIC. All rights reserved. Used by permission.

Cover image: Ivory relief about 400 A.D. Bayerisches Nationalmuseum.
Cover design: Laurie Ingram
Book design: Michelle L. N. Cook

Smith, Daniel Alan, 1963-
  Revisiting the empty tomb : the early history of Easter / Daniel A. Smith.
    p. cm.
  Includes bibliographical references (p.   ) and indexes.
  ISBN 978-0-8006-9701-3 (alk. paper)
    1. Jesus Christ—Resurrection—Biblical teaching. 2. Holy Sepulcher—Biblical teaching. 3. Bible. N.T—History of Biblical events. I. Title.
  BT482.S65 2010   2009044518

The paper used in this publication meets the minimum requirements of American National Standard for Information Sciences—Permanence of Paper for Printed Library Materials, ANSI Z329.48-1984. Manufactured in the U.S.A.

14   13   12   11   10   1   2   3   4   5   6   7   8   9   10

Tires type black
Where the blacktop cracks
Weeds spark through
Dark green enough to be blue
When the mysteries we believe in
Aren't dreamed enough to be true
Some side with the leaves
Some side with the seeds

—Wilco, "Side With The Seeds"
(written by Jeff Tweedy and Mikael Jorgensen)

What you sow is not brought to life unless it dies. And that
which you sow—you do not sow the body that is to come,
but a naked seed, perhaps of wheat, or of something else.
But God gives to that seed a body exactly as he wishes—and
he gives to each of the seeds its own particular body.

—1 Corinthians 15:36-38

Contents

Preface

Over the course of this project, from its inception to its completion, many individuals have offered important support and encouragement in various ways, and I wish to offer them my thanks. First, I want to thank those who kindly agreed at various stages of this project to read individual chapters and to provide feedback, in particular John Kloppenborg, Agnes Choi, Darrell Reimer, and Timothy Connor. I am especially grateful to those who agreed to read the book as it was being prepared for publication: Dale Allison, Wendy Cotter, John Kloppenborg, and Amy-Jill Levine.

Some of the material contained in this book was presented, at earlier stages and in very different forms, at annual meetings of the Canadian Society of Biblical Studies. I am especially grateful to the CSBS, not only for the feedback and advice I received from those who patiently endured my several papers on the empty tomb stories, but especially for the generous and collegial forum the Society provides.

I also wish to express my gratitude to the library staff at Huron University College, in particular Bice Schmitz du Moulin, who was always willing to rush a new volume through the cataloging process so that I could use it. Thanks are also due to the Huron University College Faculty of Theology, particularly to Rev. Dr. William Danaher (Dean of Theology), and to Rt. Rev. Dr. John Chapman (former Dean), for support given to my work; I also wish to thank Jennifer Martin for the help she gave me as my research assistant during the summer of 2008.

I am also grateful to the Venerable Dr. Timothy Connor and the wardens at St George's Anglican Church in London, Ontario, for their permission to use the image of the stained-glass window that appears in the introduction. I also thank Evan Agnew, who took the picture.

I am very grateful to the editorial staff at Fortress Press, in particular Neil Elliott, who took an interest in this project and was very supportive and helpful in the process of bringing the book to publication.

Above all, I thank my wife, Patricia, and our sons, Matthew and James. My family was a great source of encouragement especially in the final stages of this project, when I was not often absent, but often absentminded; without their loving support I could not have completed this book.

Finally, I wish to express my indebtedness to my teachers, in particular Fr. John Egan, John Kloppenborg, and Richard Longenecker, who invested their time and energy in my formation as a student of Christian origins, not only during my doctoral program, but also in the years since, whether by their example or direct involvement. More than any method, hypothesis, or fact, what I learned particularly from these three was careful devotion to the study of the texts of early Christianity. This book is dedicated to them with gratitude and admiration.

Abbreviations

AB	Anchor Bible
ABD	*Anchor Bible Dictionary.* Edited by D. N. Freedman. 6 vols. New York: Doubleday, 1992.
ABRL	Anchor Bible Reference Library
AGJU	Arbeiten zur Geschichte des antiken Judentums und des Urchristentums
AnBib	Analecta biblica
ANF	*Ante-Nicene Fathers*
AR	*Archiv für Religionswissenschaft*
BAR	*Biblical Archaeology Review*
BBR	*Bulletin for Biblical Research*
BDAG	W. Bauer, F. W. Danker, W. F. Arndt, and F. W. Gingrich. *Greek-English Lexicon of the New Testament and Other Early Christian Literature.* 3rd ed. Chicago: University of Chicago Press, 1999.
BDF	F. Blass, A. Debrunner, and R. W. Funk. *A Greek Grammar of the New Testament and Other Early Christian Literature.* Chicago: University of Chicago Press, 1961.
BETL	Bibliotheca ephemeridum theologicarum lovaniensium
BNTC	Black's New Testament Commentaries
BR	*Biblical Research*
BZNW	Beihefte zur Zeitschrift für die neutestamentliche Wissenschaft
CBQ	*Catholic Biblical Quarterly*
CCSL	Corpus Christianorum, series latina
CEJL	Commentaries on Early Jewish Literature
CH	*Church History*
CIG	*Corpus inscriptionum graecarum.* Edited by A. Böckh. 4 vols. Berlin: G. Reimer, 1828–77.
ConBNT	Coniectanea biblica, New Testament Series
CSCO	Corpus scriptorum christianorum orientalium
CSHJ	Chicago Studies in the History of Judaism
CTR	*Criswell Theological Review*
CW	*Classical World*

CWS	Classics of Western Spirituality
Ebib	*Etudes bibliques*
EKKNT	Evangelisch-katholischer Kommentar zum Neuen Testament
ESCJ	Etudes/Studies in Christianity and Judaism
ETL	*Ephemerides theologicae lovanienses*
ExpT	*Expository Times*
GBS	Guides to Biblical Scholarship
HSCP	*Harvard Studies in Classical Philology*
HTR	*Harvard Theological Review*
HTS	Harvard Theological Studies
HUT	Hermeneutische Untersuchungen zur Theologie
HZAG	*Historia: Zeitschrift für Alte Geschichte*
ICC	International Critical Commentary
IEJ	*Israel Exploration Journal*
IG	*Inscriptiones graecae, consilio et auctoritate Acadaemiae Litterarum Borussicae editae*. Edited by F. H. von Gaertringen et al. Berlin: de Gruyter, 1873–.
JBL	*Journal of Biblical Literature*
JHS	*Journal of Hellenic Studies*
JRS	*Journal of Roman Studies*
JSNT	*Journal for the Study of the New Testament*
JSNTSup	Journal for the Study of the New Testament Supplement Series
JSSS	Journal of Semitic Studies Supplement Series
JTS	*Journal of Theological Studies*
LCL	Loeb Classical Library
LD	Lectio divina
LNTS	Library of New Testament Studies
LSJ	H. G. Liddell, R. Scott, and H. S. Jones. *A Greek-English Lexicon*. 9th ed. with revised supplement. Oxford: Clarendon, 1996.
MdB	Le Monde de la Bible (Labor et Fides)
NA²⁷	*Novum Testamentum Graece*, Nestle-Aland, 27th ed.
NCB	New Century Bible
Neot	*Neotestamentica*
NICNT	New International Commentary on the New Testament
NIGTC	New International Greek Testament Commentary
NovT	*Novum Testamentum*
NovTSup	Novum Testamentum Supplements
NTAbh	Neutestamentliche Abhandlungen
NTL	New Testament Library
NTS	*New Testament Studies*
NTTS	New Testament Tools and Studies
OTP	*Old Testament Pseudepigrapha*. Edited by J. H. Charlesworth. 2 vols. New York: Doubleday, 1983–85.
ProEccl	*Pro ecclesia*

Proof	*Prooftexts: A Journal of Jewish Literary History*
PVTG	Pseudepigrapha Veteris Testamenti Graece
RevPhil	*Revue de philologie*
RGRW	Religions in the Graeco-Roman World
RHPR	*Revue d'histoire et de philosophie religieuses*
SANT	Studien zum Alten und Neuen Testament
SBB	Stuttgarter biblische Beiträge
SBLDS	Society of Biblical Literature Dissertation Series
SBLSCS	Society of Biblical Literature Septuagint and Cognate Studies
SBLSP	*Society of Biblical Literature Seminar Papers*
SBLSS	Society of Biblical Literature Symposium Series
SBLTT	Society of Biblical Literature Texts and Translations
SBLWGRW	Society of Biblical Literature Writings from the Greco-Roman World
SBS	Stuttgarter Bibelstudien
SBT	Studies in Biblical Theology
SC	Sources chrétiennes
SemeiaSt	Semeia Studies
SJT	*Scottish Journal of Theology*
SNTSMS	Society for New Testament Studies Monograph Series
SP	Sacra pagina
SPHS	Scholars Press Homage Series
SR	*Studies in Religion*
SVTQ	*St Vladimir's Theological Quarterly*
TDNT	*Theological Dictionary of the New Testament.* Edited by G. Kittel and G. Friedrich. Translated by G. Bromiley. 10 vols. Grand Rapids: Eerdmans, 1964–76.
TQ	*Theologische Quartalschrift*
TRE	*Theologische Realenzyklopädie.* Edited by G. Krause and G. Müller. Berlin: de Gruyter, 1977–.
TUGAL	Texte und Untersuchungen zur Geschichte der altchristlichen Literatur
TynBul	*Tyndale Bulletin*
WBC	Word Biblical Commentary
WUNT	Wissenschaftliche Untersuchungen zum Neuen Testament
ZNW	*Zeitschrift für die neutestamentliche Wissenschaft und die Kunde der älteren Kirche*
ZRGG	*Zeitschrift für Religions- und Geistesgeschichte*

Introduction
Not Here but Risen: Seeing and Not Seeing the Easter Jesus

On the north side of the nave in St. George's Anglican Church in London, Ontario, not far from where I usually sit, there is a stained-glass window that depicts a resurrection scene. In this scene, Jesus is standing outside the tomb with his hand raised in blessing, and Mary Magdalene is in the foreground turning around and looking over her shoulder at him. The window represents an incident narrated in the Fourth Gospel, in which Mary, alone outside the tomb, turns around as she recognizes the risen Jesus (John 20:14-16). Only John tells the story of this private encounter. At the bottom of the stained-glass window there is a line of text that reads, "He is not here, but is risen." This line is not from John, but from Luke 24:5, although similar words are also found in Matthew and Mark. The speakers in Luke are two men in clothes as bright as lightning (Luke

24:4), but these angelic speakers are not shown in the window. In the context of the window, these words seem intended as a supporting testimony to the fact that God raised Jesus from the dead, although there is some dissonance between text and image. It is quite common to find ideas, images, or words from different Gospels combined like this. Readers interested in the Gospels because of their faith commitments are often eager to make sure that conflicting details from the different accounts can be harmonized, and this is especially so when it comes to pivotal episodes like the resurrection of Jesus.

Often the urge to conflate is unconscious, for it is very deep in the Christian interpretive tradition: the tendency to read one version of the story into another is evident in the very earliest Christian texts that comment on the resurrection narratives. The result is that instead of having four (more than four, actually) accounts of what the followers of Jesus experienced after his execution, in the church people tend to speak about "the Easter story" (singular). When we look closely at the canonical Gospels and other early Christian texts and hear how they tell the story of the discovery of the empty tomb, however, we almost immediately notice how different the successive uses or deployments of the story are. These differences in detail and in perspective are opportunities for us to discern "the early history of Easter," as the subtitle of this book suggests: the history of how the Easter story developed. Those who received and retold the traditions about the resurrection of Jesus told not only the story of Jesus and his earliest followers, but their own story as well. Each new retelling arose out of (and was spoken into) a different set of historical circumstances and theological concerns that gave shape and contemporary meaning to the received traditions. This process is what lies behind the differences and divergences in the story's successive deployments. The details in the Gospels simply make the best sense when we read them in the narrative contexts for which they were intended, rather than seeing them as facts that must be reconciled in one way or another into a bigger narrative on whose cogency the Christian claim that God raised Jesus from the dead depends.

So when I first noticed the Easter window at St George's, I was not really surprised to see details from Luke and John combined in this way. But I was interested—and, truthfully, a little bothered—to notice that the window juxtaposes an image of Jesus appearing at the tomb with a text that explains his absence, or his disappearance, from the tomb. My first reaction was to ask myself, "Well, is he here or isn't he?" In some ways, the window's mistake is quite forgivable, because according to the Gospel stories, Jesus' tomb is empty and he appears to Mary and to others because God raised him from the dead. He is present "here" outside the tomb and appearing to Mary and to others because he is absent, not "there" inside the tomb. In other words, the picture of Jesus present with Mary and the text about his absence from the tomb both point, though in different ways, to one idea: Jesus was raised from the dead.

Two Independent Traditions: The Disappearance and the Appearances of Jesus

Yet when we consider the two early convictions that after Jesus' death (1) he was gone, in particular, gone from the tomb, and (2) he was appearing to his followers, we find that they might not have been understood originally as two expressions of the one belief that Jesus had risen from the dead. From the letters of Paul, we know of very early traditions about the appearances of the risen Jesus, but none of these traditions locates the appearances; and from the Gospel of Mark, we have the earliest version of the empty tomb story, a story in which the risen Jesus does not appear. Only gradually and incrementally did the empty tomb stories become stories about the risen Jesus appearing at the tomb. The earliest evidence suggests that traditions that described Jesus' absence from the tomb circulated at the earliest times separately from traditions that he had appeared to his followers.[1] Willi Marxsen noted that these two traditions are depicted sequentially in the Gospel resurrection stories—the empty tomb is discovered, and then the risen Jesus appears—although the evidence suggests they originally were independent of one another.[2] As James Dunn remarks, "Though interdependent in terms of the earliest conceptualization of Jesus' resurrection, the traditions themselves seem to have emerged from and kept alive independent memories."[3] We will find reason to challenge Dunn's view that the empty tomb tradition can only be understood as part of "the earliest conceptualization of Jesus' resurrection," that is, that the empty tomb was always seen as signifying a bodily resurrection out of the tomb. However, he is correct that because "Paul could virtually ignore [the empty tomb], and the earliest accounts of the empty tomb make no mention of any appearance at the tomb itself," it is difficult to see how one tradition could have given rise to the other.

Very early in the process of literary narration, however, these two traditions began to be merged in various ways. This original separation and then gradual combination of the two traditions has led some to identify the appearance tradition as oriented to the validation of male figures, while the empty tomb tradition is a women's tradition (although there are good reasons to dispute this dichotomization).[4] Others think that the empty tomb story originated as a way of narrating what early Christians must have concluded from the proclamation of Jesus' resurrection—that is, if Jesus' followers were saying that he appeared to them after his death, and that he had appeared because he had risen from the dead, then the tomb must have been empty.[5] As we will see, however, there are good reasons to think that the empty tomb story did not originate as a way of explaining how it was that God raised Jesus from the dead.

The empty tomb story and the appearance reports are *traditions* in the sense that each is a confessional or narrative piece that circulated orally among early members of the Jesus movements and was handed down (Lat., *traditio*) in the context of instruction or proclamation. Paul, in the earliest source of information about the resurrection of Christ (1 Cor. 15:3b-7), repeats and adapts a tradition that claims that Jesus "appeared" to Cephas (Peter) and the Twelve, to more than five hundred believers, and to James and all the apostles. Paul adapts this tradition by adding his own name to the list (15:8). The Greek term translated "appeared" here is *ōphthē*, which literally means "was seen," or even "was caused to be seen."[6] In a different letter, Paul talks about his life-changing experience of the living Jesus as God "revealing" the Son in him (Gal. 1:15-16). Paul thought that these revelatory experiences of the risen Jesus that he and others experienced were important signs of God's commissioning and the authority that came with it: in 1 Corinthians 9:1 he writes, "Am I not free? Am I not an apostle? Have I not seen Jesus our Lord?" Paul believed that God vindicated Jesus after his death by raising him to new life and allowing him to appear—allowing him to be present—to certain of his followers. Because Christ did not appear to everyone, those who claimed such an experience could also claim that they were validated by God in Christ for mission and leadership in the movement. In contrast to Paul's emphasis on the appearances of Jesus, he has almost nothing to say about Jesus' absence: nowhere in his letters does Paul mention the empty tomb of Jesus. This demands an explanation, particularly if (as Dunn argues) the two traditions are to be considered interdependent aspects of a single conceptualization of what it meant that "Jesus was raised."[7] To claim, as many scholars do, that Paul simply took the empty tomb for granted is to sidestep the problem, especially since the empty tomb of Jesus might have been good evidence for the bodily resurrection of the dead, an idea evidently in dispute in Paul's Corinthian congregation (1 Cor. 15:12, 35).[8] Or perhaps he knew about traditions to the effect that Jesus' tomb was discovered empty but avoided using this as part of his argument, knowing the idea would be problematic for the Corinthians. In any event, the tradition Paul handed on to the Corinthians did not contain any reference to the women's discovery that Jesus' tomb was empty on the third day, and this silence is something that deserves careful consideration.

On the other hand, there are also some indications that the people who put together and used the Sayings Gospel Q (the source, now lost, of certain sayings of Jesus now found in Matthew and Luke) were thinking along different lines, that is, more in terms of absence than presence.[9] An important text for establishing this view is a Q saying now found at Matthew 23:39 and Luke 13:35 in which Jesus says, "You will not see me." This "not seeing" language is the precise opposite of what we find in Paul, and it has striking similarities to the story about the disappearance (ascension/assumption) of Elijah in 2 Kings 2. Just as Paul was silent on the subject of the empty tomb, so also Q does not reflect on the postmortem significance of Jesus using the category of resurrection, even though resurrection is part of the document's eschatology. Mark also used source material that talked about the disappearance of Jesus from the tomb, but neither that source material nor the Gospel of Mark directly narrates an appearance of the risen Jesus (Mark 16:1-8). What is more, a first-century person (Jewish or Greek) would have interpreted an inexplicably disappearing body or an unaccountably empty tomb as evidence not of "resurrection" but of "assumption." This is the idea found in almost every ancient culture that in certain special cases God (or some divine being or beings) could take a person immediately and bodily into the divine realm. The language and implications of assumption are very different from resurrection, although both can imply "postmortem vindication." Is it possible that some of Jesus' early followers expressed their convictions about his vindication by God in terms different from resurrection?[10]

The different language originally used to express the basic conviction that God had vindicated Jesus after his death clarifies how early understandings of his ongoing and future existence—risen, ascended, present as Spirit, coming as Son of Man—may have originated. As Gerhard Lohfink suggests, there were three possible ways that early followers of Jesus could have expressed convictions about his divine vindication: (1) God had exalted him in heaven (as in Isaiah 52); (2) God had taken him directly into heaven (as with Enoch and Elijah and others); and (3) God had raised him from the dead as the beginning of the eschatological resurrection.[11] All three expressions have left their traces in the early Christian traditions, but they quickly and finally were merged into resurrection as the dominant paradigm, as the window in St George's demonstrates. In many ways this fusing of paradigms was facilitated by the fact that there was some overlap, whether in perceived applicability to Jesus or in theological conception. In any event, studying the traces these three conceptions have left in our texts allows us to arrive at a clearer picture of the diversity and creativity of the early Christian movements as different groups sought to make sense not only of Jesus' death but also of the validity of his teachings about the kingdom of God and the meaning of the spiritual experiences they had when they gathered in his name.

Only in this sense is this book an early history of Easter. Although many have considered it a worthwhile venture to try to prove (or to disprove) the historicity of the resurrection of Jesus, or of the empty tomb, this kind of "historical" (or apologetic or anti-apologetic) approach is not taken in this book. As Mary Rose D'Angelo has observed, there are serious problems involved in approaching the resurrection of Jesus as an object of historical inquiry, not least because the early texts that refer to it—whether the more overtly theological reflections of Paul or the more concretely narrative depictions at the end of the canonical Gospels—see it as an event that transcends history. For these texts "never treat the fate of Jesus as a return to life (like that of Lazarus in John 11:1-44 or of the daughter of Jairus in Mark 5:21-43), but always describe it as a transformation of the world."[12] Although at times our discussion will take us into inquiries as to the relative age or origin of traditions about Jesus' postmortem vindication and about the experiences of his followers, there are other, more immediate questions posed by the Gospel writings than questions about historicity, and these are questions of meaning and interpretation. How did the authors of the Gospels (and their forebears in the developing tradition) think about the resurrection of Jesus? What did it mean for their understanding of his significance? What did it mean for their understanding of God's purposes for humankind? These theological questions arise from the narratives themselves, and they are the questions these narratives were designed to answer. As careful and interested readers we do well to attend to them.

Yet this book does have a historical objective, as the subtitle claims. In particular, this book attempts to explain how and why the story that we now find in Mark 16 was adapted and retold in different settings, and to describe what such adaptations and retellings indicate about the unique interests and problems of the retellers. When we compare Luke with Mark, for instance, we find that some significant differences result from Luke's adaptation of Mark, probably the most important of which is the addition of Peter's visit to the tomb (Luke 24:12). Luke's version of the story is not merely another perspective on the historical events. According to such a view, the author of Luke was trying to give as complete and authentic a report as possible, and so he included a detail omitted or overlooked by Mark's author or unknown to him. While this in fact could be the case, that is not all there is to it. The authors of the Gospels, Luke included, were not simply recorders of history or even of tradition, but careful, creative editors and composers of sayings and narrative material. When one of the Gospels (e.g., Luke) differs from its source material (Mark or Q), we are justified in asking, "Where did this come from?" and "Why was it composed (or included) and to what end?" Such questions are the focus of this book. So, although this book does not address questions of historicity, it does have a historical objective: to study the empty tomb stories in their original contexts and to account historically, culturally, and theologically for the developments we find in them.

Of course, we cannot revisit the empty tomb in the same way that Peter does in Luke's narrative. The differences between the tomb stories clearly indicate that we are not dealing with "history" straightforwardly recorded, but with narratives having distinctive features and purposes. Our sources simply do not permit us to revisit the tomb in a "historical" way. We can, however, revisit the empty tomb stories by asking why, for example, it was important for the author and original readers of Luke that they tell a story in which Peter sees the empty tomb for himself. In this way at least, we as readers may revisit the empty tomb to see if somehow we missed something on our initial visit. It is the aim of this book to try to make sense of what we as readers can see narratively in these stories and to show how a new approach to these stories can illuminate the beginnings of Christian thinking about the vindication of Jesus and about its significance to the development of early Christology.

When we turn to the empty tomb stories themselves, we see that it is only gradually and by degrees that disappearance/absence and appearance/presence come together, as the story was told in different settings for different audiences. Mark, as just noted, claims that the missing body of Jesus means that he has been raised from the dead, and the young man at the tomb says exactly that: "He has been raised; he is not here" (Mark 16:6). Notice here that the announcement of the resurrection precedes the demonstration of the empty tomb. But in Mark, Jesus is seen by his followers only in an ending not written by the author of Mark but appended to the Gospel by a much later scribe (whose "longer ending" can be designated Pseudo-Mark 16:9-20). There is good evidence for concluding that the author of Mark thought the Gospel was finished at the end of Mark 16:8: "And they said nothing to anyone, for they were afraid." This original ending is probably why Mark's alternate endings (for there are two) were written.[13] The later canonical Gospel writers similarly made adjustments and additions to the story they received, adjustments and additions that made it clear that the empty tomb meant Jesus was appearing to his followers. Luke has Peter inspect the tomb after the apostles disbelieve the initial report of the women (Luke 24:12); Matthew depicts the risen Jesus appearing to the women as they run to tell the others (Matt. 28:9-10); and the Fourth Gospel has both of these narrative developments (John 20:3-10, 14-18).

The additional features found in Luke, Matthew, and John are important because, like the later additions to the ending of Mark, they demonstrate that many early readers of Mark were not comfortable with the idea of Jesus' absence unless it was combined with some description of his presence after the resurrection. As John Dominic Crossan has written:

> The intracanonical tradition of the empty tomb is . . . a single stream of redacted and expanded transmission from Mark 16:1-8 as its only source. From the women at the tomb in Mark 16:1-8 comes, genetically, not only the women at the tomb in Matthew 28:1-8, Luke 24:1-11, John 20:1, 11-13, but also, redaction-ally, Jesus at the tomb in Matthew 28:9-10, John 20:14-18, and the disciple(s) at the tomb in Luke 24:12 and John 20:2-10.[14]

Given some important qualifications, Crossan's observation seems, in substance, to be correct: what the later evangelists drew from Mark is clear; other details can mainly be understood as points at which the story has undergone narrative or literary development (and not necessarily on the basis of traditional sources). Not everyone shares this perspective, of course. Pheme Perkins writes that "the divergence of detail surrounding the stories of the tomb suggests there was no unified tradition about the empty tomb in early Christianity. . . . It is impossible to harmonize them in such a way as to produce a single, simpler tradition that has then been redacted by the narrators."[15] Harmonizing, as we have seen, does not move the interpreter in the direction of a more primitive tradition, but rather conflates more or less conflicting narratives into one story in which these conflicts have been resolved.[16] More recently, N. T. Wright has insisted that the differences should be put down simply to the "different ways in which the original astonished participants told the stories," and that the Gospel texts as we have them show little evidence of narrative development or editorial creativity.[17] But what if we took Mark's version to be the earliest textual version of the empty tomb story and understood subsequent versions—in Matthew, Luke, John, and beyond—as responses to Mark? The stories, as the studies here will bear out, do show clear evidence of literary interdependence and editing, and many (or even most) of the differences should be assigned not to the level of oral tradition deriving from eyewitness accounts but to the narrative creativity and theological ingenuity of those who told and retold, then wrote and rewrote, the story of the empty tomb.

When we look at the developments in the individual narratives after Mark, what we find is a tendency to bring the empty tomb story more and more completely into agreement with the appearance traditions. This tendency is evident in different ways when we move from Mark to Matthew and Luke and John and finally to narratives of the empty tomb in later or extracanonical sources, as in, for instance, the *Gospel of Peter* or in the alternative endings early Christian scribes added to Mark's Gospel. But although the empty tomb story is—if not already in Mark, then certainly in Matthew, Luke, and John—essentially a resurrection story, efforts to accommodate the empty tomb to the appearance tradition could never really efface the narrative and theological impact that the disappearance/assumption tradition had on the development of early reflection on Jesus' post-mortem vindication by God and significance for humankind. Discerning this impact is what makes revisiting the empty tomb a worthwhile endeavor.

A short explanation of the image on the cover may illustrate this helpfully. An ivory panel dated to around 400 CE and now in the Bavarian National

Museum in Munich, it depicts both the women attending the tomb and two men (apostles, one assumes) witnessing the ascension.[18] One commentator suggests that the image would have been a fine example of the influence of late pagan "nostalgia" on Christian art, since the women "approach [the tomb] in measured step and restrained pathos" in "some sacred grove," approximating the depiction of priestesses in other pieces of the same era—but "the innate Christian urge to pack the image with content" led to the introduction of the ascension scene in the upper part of the panel.[19] Kurt Weitzmann suggests that the ascension scene reflects knowledge of the *Apocryphon of James*, a Nag Hammadi Gnostic text that reports James and Peter as the only two witnesses of the ascension.[20] I am not really in a position to dispute this, but I would still offer an alternative interpretation of the panel as a whole: the proximity of the closed tomb (attended by the women, guarded by sleeping soldiers, and interpreted by a wingless angel) to the ascending Jesus suggests not a forty-day delay as in Luke-Acts, but a rising Jesus going directly into the divine realm as, I would argue, in Mark and Matthew, or John and the *Gospel of Peter* (although after a brief hiatus in these last two texts).[21] Maurice Goguel, in his study of the resurrection in early Christianity, suggested that this understanding of the resurrection as assumption persisted well into the fourth century.[22] Given how early Christian literary sources tended to conflate elements from the various versions of the empty tomb story, the wingless angel could be interpreted as the "young man" of Mark 16:5-7; he seems ready to interpret the empty tomb to the women (Mark 16:6), but he has not opened it yet (16:3-4). In other early depictions of this scene, the tomb is already open. The guards in our ivory panel, of course, come from Matthew, and they sleep on as the scene unfolds. Could the two figures witnessing Christ's ascension into heaven be Peter (cowering) and the Beloved Disciple (believing), ready to inspect the empty tomb as in John 20:3-10? On this reading, the ivory panel illustrates just what I intend to argue in this book, that the influence of the disappearance/assumption tradition, though already in Mark subjugated to the resurrection/appearance tradition, can still be perceived, and not only in the earliest texts but in later ones as well.

Four Basic Reminiscences

To say that all the literary versions of the empty tomb story must be traced genetically back to Mark, however, is not to claim that a purely literary approach can explain the origin of all the details in all the stories. To be sure, many details may in fact go back to earlier oral traditions or recollections, whether about the empty tomb or about the appearances. In some cases it will be possible to distinguish what is "traditional" from what comes from an author's own hand, and that will sometimes be illuminating—not because it gets us any closer to "what really happened," but because it helps us say something concrete about how the author interpreted the tradition to his audience. Four of these core traditions or reminiscences are listed and discussed briefly here, if only to present a basic survey of the core elements of the narratives under discussion in this book. I list these not in order of their origin or importance, but in the narrative order in which they appear. I also make no judgments as to the historicity of what these traditions or reminiscences report.

1. *Jesus was buried in a tomb that was attended by female disciples.* It is sometimes claimed that because the standard Roman practice was to leave the bodies of crucifixion victims on their crosses, on display as a warning, this is what happened to Jesus.[23] The discovery of the remains of a crucified man in a Judean ossuary—a small box in which an individual's bones would be collected for a secondary burial—indicates that with any such general practice there may be exceptions.[24] Regardless of the historical likelihood of either scenario, the earliest tradition about the death and resurrection of Jesus indicates that he was buried (1 Cor. 15:4) and not left unburied. The narrative sources about the death and burial of Jesus (Mark 15:42-47 and parallels) indicate that his body was attended to by Joseph of Arimathea, who is described as someone friendly to Jesus' movement or even as a disciple, but nevertheless a member of the Judean ruling council (Mark 15:43 and parallels). The development of Joseph as a character in successive formulations of the burial account makes it difficult to determine much about him; on the other hand, Acts 13:29 is strikingly at odds with the picture we get in the Gospels: "Now when they had completed everything that had been written about him, they took him down from the tree and put him into a tomb."[25]

Byron McCane argues that "based on what we know of Roman practice and Jewish custom, one or more members of the Sanhedrin obtained the body of Jesus from Pilate and arranged for a dishonorable interment."[26] The fact that the Gospel narratives refrain from indicating that he was buried in a family tomb and publicly mourned might reflect an old reminiscence that Jesus was given a shameful burial, in keeping with his execution as a criminal. McCane also points out that a new tomb (as described in Matt. 27:60; Luke 23:53; John 19:41) "would be the only culturally acceptable alternative to a criminals' burial place, for it would be the only other way to preserve the boundary of shame that separated Jesus from his people."[27] Yet even this might be a development of the tradition. The expediency of a tomb near to the crucifixion site (John 19:41-42) makes good narrative sense, but it would be difficult to show that this has a traditional basis. Although in the ancient cultures of the Mediterranean it would be typical to depict women attending a tomb, the placement of female disciples both at the crucifixion and at the grave site seems also to have been part of the pre-Markan passion narrative.

2. *Jesus' tomb was discovered empty by the women.* Some scholars also propose that Mark 16:1-8, which is the earliest version of the empty tomb story, has no basis in pre-Markan tradition and was composed by Mark's author, either as a narrative depiction of the aftereffects of the resurrection (that is, if he was raised from the dead, his tomb must have been empty) or as a response to circles that emphasized appearances as the validation of authority figures as in Paul's reports (1 Cor. 15:5-8).[28] To anticipate somewhat the argument of chapter 3 below, there are good grounds for suggesting that the empty tomb story, as a *disappearance* story, did not originate as a conclusion drawn from the resurrection

proclamation, because "resurrection" was not a self-evident (religious) inter-pretation an ancient person would give to an empty tomb or a missing body. Besides, the story is always treated ambivalently—by the canonical authors as well as by later Christian writers—and it was rarely used as an apologetic device to prove resurrection of the flesh, even in early Christian settings in which such issues were in dispute.[29] Several of the adjustments to the story made by the post-Markan authors are best understood as apologetic additions to the story, made in order to solve some of the problems the story presented. In addition, there is strong evidence to suggest that the author of Mark was editing a story he had received from the tradition, a story in which female disciples discover the tomb empty, encounter a mysterious figure (possibly) who speaks to them about Jesus, and flee in fear.[30]

3. *Jesus appeared to (was seen by) some of his followers after his death.* That there was a traditional basis for the appearance reports given by Paul (1 Cor. 15:5-8) is not in doubt. The phrasing is formulaic and stereotypical, and Paul introduces these reports as traditional material: "I handed over to you among the things of primary importance [the tradition] which I had also received, that Christ died for our sins according to the Scriptures, and that he was buried, and that he was raised on the third day according to the Scriptures, and that he appeared to Cephas and then to the Twelve . . ." (1 Cor. 15:3-5). Paul him-self makes the claim that the risen Christ appeared to him (1 Cor. 9:1; 15:8). From Paul's list it appears that such claims evidently were fairly widespread. As will be seen below (chap. 2), the language Paul (and the traditional formula he is citing) uses for "he appeared" suggests the visionary nature of these experi-ences. In some circles—and again Paul himself is the clearest example because he speaks for himself—the interpretation given to these experiences was that they were moments of revelation and commissioning for proclamation (1 Cor. 15:8-11; Gal. 1:15-16).[31]

4. *Diverging accounts include both prominent male and female figures.* Paul's list does not include any women, but both Matthew and John (Matt. 28:9-10; John 20:14-18) narrate appearances of the risen Jesus to a woman (or women) at the tomb; Mary Magdalene is the only person mentioned in John 20:14-18, and she figures prominently in Matthew (see Matt. 27:61; 28:1). Although both these stories show evidence of authorial composition (as will be discussed below), there are also indications that an older tradition lies behind the stories in the Gospels. One of the clues lies in how the author of Matthew narrates the Christophany at the tomb: because Jesus simply repeats what the angel says, this appearance report has no real narrative content except that the risen Jesus appeared to the women as they were leaving the tomb (Matt. 28:9-10). This suggests that Matthew had knowledge of a tradition about an appearance to women including Mary, but knew (and so could narrate) little more.[32] Many scholars think John had more by way of traditional material to work with.[33] In addition, Mary's first-person report in John 20:18 is remarkably similar to what Paul says about his own experience of the risen Christ in 1 Corinthians 9:1. All this, together with the prominence of Mary as a visionary in second-century apocryphal writings,[34] suggests that the

accounts in Matthew and John were not simply invented. This raises questions as to whether Paul may have suppressed appearance reports involving women, or whether he is citing a tradition that was in competition with such reports. It also raises questions about Mark. Mark 16:7 seems aware of a tradition that Peter had experienced a resurrection encounter, but this is not narrated in Mark; had Mark known of a tradition of an appearance to Mary and others at the tomb, he probably would have suppressed that as well in order to emphasize the absence of Jesus (on this, see chap. 5 below). On the other hand, it may be that the placement of the appearance to Mary and others at the tomb is a redactional creation of Matthew.

I leave it to my readers, and to other scholars, to draw their own conclusions as to how these traditions originated or what their historical value may be for reconstructing what "happened" after the end of Jesus' life. These traditions, however, are extremely important to other (answerable!) historical questions about the origins of Christianity. For the purposes of this study, it is sufficient to claim these four elements as the basis of what, as the result of a variety of literary, historical, and theological processes, would become the Easter story. In the end, however, our main concern will be not these core traditions but the finished forms of the story in its various literary expressions, for which of course the individual authors ultimately were responsible. In tracing the development and relationship of these two traditions, as far as possible from their emergence to their use and reuse in various narrative depictions and theological arguments in the second century and beyond, we will get a glimpse not only of their importance to the resurrection narratives, but also of their influence on Christian theological reflection on the vindication of Jesus, his corporate or even universal significance (whether as the Son of Man or as the New Adam), and his role in God's plan for the future of humankind.

1. When the Dead and/or Gone Appear to the Living

Have I not seen our Lord Jesus?
—1 Corinthians 9:1

And when they saw him they worshipped him, although some doubted. And Jesus drew near to them and said, "All authority, in heaven and on earth, has been given to me."
—Matthew 28:17-18

Thus, then, a certain man of the patricians, nobly born and of the most esteemed character . . . Julius Proculus by name, went into the agora . . . and bound himself by oath and said before all that Romulus appeared to him while walking on the road . . . great and beautiful to be seen, as never before, adorned in bright, flaming armor; and he was overwhelmed by the vision. . . . And Romulus said, "It seemed fitting to the gods, O Proculus, for us to be with humankind in this way only for a time, and now after having founded a city destined for the greatest rule and glory, to dwell in heaven again. But farewell . . . and I will be to you the benevolent deity Kyrinos."
—Plutarch, *Romulus* 28.1-2

Our study of how the two traditions of disappearance/absence and appearance/presence came to be so fully integrated in early Christian tradition and literature begins with what Paul says about his experience of the risen Jesus: "God was pleased . . . to reveal his son in [or to] me" (Gal. 1:15-16); "Have I not seen Jesus our Lord?" (1 Cor. 9:1); "He appeared to Cephas . . . and last of all . . . he also appeared to me" (1 Cor. 15:5, 8). In this last citation just given, Paul is quoting a traditional formula that outlines the basic proclamation, or *kerygma*, taken up by some forms of the Jesus movement.[1] This formula will be examined in detail in the following chapter, but for now we simply note that Paul includes himself among those to whom the risen Jesus appeared, and that he does not see any distinction between his own experience and those of others (such as Cephas/Peter and James). Paul says that he saw the risen Jesus, although it is not entirely clear what he meant by that. Importantly, neither Paul nor the traditional kerygmatic formula he cites in 1 Corinthians 15:3b-7 refers to the empty tomb, that is, the "disappearance" tradition (as I will be calling it). His interest is entirely in the "appearance" tradition. Some scholars take this as an indication that the empty tomb tradition had not yet originated,[2] but this is to conclude too much from Paul's silence. At the very least, the writings of Paul provide evidence of a religious context in which the empty tomb tradition was not found to be useful. As we will see in the next chapter, while one might think that the empty tomb story would have been a useful ingredient in Paul's argument for the resurrection of the dead (1 Cor. 15:12-58), the difficulty the Corinthians had with resurrection may have been precisely the kind of view of embodied immortality that disappearance stories normally would imply. For the present, however, our concern is what "he appeared" could have meant to Paul and to the other followers of Jesus who used this kind of language, as well as to the members of Paul's group in Corinth.

Here we do well to distance ourselves as readers of Paul from our knowledge of the Easter narratives in the canonical Gospels. There Jesus "appears" because he is not in the tomb and is alive again outside of it. This naturally implies that there is a one-to-one correspondence, a direct continuity, between the body that was buried and the embodied form that appears, despite the obvious distinctions the narratives make between the body of the risen Jesus and human bodies as normally experienced. On the one hand, the risen Jesus does things that human beings normally do with their bodies: he can occupy space physically, walk, talk, eat, and touch and be touched. But he also suddenly appears or disappears, goes about unrecognized, and raises questions and doubts in those who see him.[3] In contrast with the Gospels, what Paul has to say about the resurrection appearances does not really clarify what the risen Jesus was like, although Paul would affirm that his experience was of a risen Jesus who was "bodily," at least in some sense. Therefore, we cannot simply assume that Paul has in mind the same kind of physical correspondence or continuity the Gospel narratives describe, although he would say that the risen Jesus in his spiritual body corresponded in some respects to the premortem Jesus in his natural body (1 Cor. 15:42-49). Nor can we assume that the unusual embodiedness of the risen Jesus in the Gospels is essentially a narrative expression of what Paul meant when he wrote about the resurrection body as "spiritual" (Gk., *pneumatikon*) in 1 Corinthians 15. In fact, Luke has the risen Jesus explicitly deny that he is a "spirit" (Luke 24:39). What Paul meant by "spiritual body" will be investigated in the following chapter; for now, we look at Paul's language about the "appearances" of Jesus to see what it could be taken to mean.

While Galatians 1:16 suggests a personal, even internal, revelatory experience, in 1 Corinthians 9:1 Paul says simply, "Have I not seen (*ouchi . . . heoraka*) our Lord Jesus?" and in 1 Corinthians 15:8 he says that "last of all, he appeared (*ōphthē*) also to me." We should not be misled by our English translations here. The connotations of "I have seen him" and "he appeared" are potentially somewhat different: the former stresses Paul as the percipient, and the latter, Christ as the active party; the former could connote "normal" seeing, and the latter could connote "visionary" seeing. However, Paul uses different forms of the same verb, *horaō*, in 1 Corinthians 9:1 as in 1 Corinthians 15:8: in the former, he uses the perfect active, "I have seen," and in the latter, the aorist passive, "he was seen [by]," or, as it is commonly translated, "he appeared [to]." This is also the same verb the appearance tradition (1 Cor. 15:5 et al.; see also Luke 24:34) uses for the appearances to Peter and the others. This indicates that Paul thought his experience was consistent with theirs. This is a different picture than we get from Luke, who separates Paul's experience from the resurrection appearances that occurred during the forty days.[4] So we must ask what exactly *ōphthē* ("he appeared," or more literally, "he was seen") could have signified for the tradition, for Paul, and for the Corinthians to whom he was writing.

Outside the biblical writings, passive forms of the verb *horaō* (such as *ōphthē*) can denote appearances of ordinary people or things, or of supernatural people or things, sometimes with the implication in the context that the sight would be visible to any observer.[5] In the Septuagint, the ancient Greek translation of the Hebrew Bible, *ōphthē* denotes the appearance sometimes of ordinary phenomena and sometimes of supernatural phenomena.[6] It is, with a dative direct object, the Septuagint's usual word for theophanies, that is, appearances of God or the Angel of Yahweh (as in Gen. 12:7 LXX: "The LORD appeared to Abram").[7] Although the theophanies in which this verb is used are diffuse in type and character— for instance, Jacob's dream about the ladder is interpreted as a theophany using *ōphthē* in Genesis 31:13 LXX—the consistent emphasis is on the unique presence of the divine and the revelatory effect of the appearance.[8] In the New Testament, *ōphthē* is used for the appearance of supernatural figures or phenomena, such as angels (Luke 1:11; Acts 7:30, 35) or other figures from the heavenly realm (Moses and Elijah in Mark 9:4 and parallels), or the fiery tongues at Pentecost (Acts 2:3), or the various omens and portents in the book of Revelation (Rev. 12:1, 3). Most frequently this verb is used for appearances of the risen or exalted Jesus, and the obvious conclusion is that this usage deliberately imitates the Septuagint's language for theophanies.[9] When 1 Corinthians 15:5-8 uses the same language, it seems appropriate to infer from the way theophanies are described in the Septuagint that the risen Jesus was thought of as belonging to that realm from which theophanies and angelophanies originate.

Thus the language suggests that the risen Jesus appeared from heaven, although we should be careful not to read the earth-bound perspective of the Gospel appearance narratives into this language—this is simply not made clear. In both the Septuagint and the New Testament, however, *ōphthē* is used in contexts in which it is not specified that what (or who) was seen would have been considered "really there" or "just a vision." The texts simply do not seem to be interested in that kind of distinction. As Reginald Fuller pointed out, "the emphasis rests on the revelatory initiative" of the one who appears, rather than on questions about the nature or "reality" of the experience.[10] Ultimately, therefore, the verb *ōphthē*, when used for a theophany or Christophany, is not exclusive to either ecstatic seeing or normal vision, but the primary sense is always "seeing." Interpreters have long been aware of how this verb is connected in certain texts with commissioning by God (or the risen Jesus). Some who understand the function of the verb in 1 Corinthians 15:5-8 as legitimating the authority of certain individuals tend to think this is the primary sense intended and exclude the normal sense of seeing; others who think *ōphthē* is principally revelatory speak in terms of an experience of presence but not in terms of "seeing" in the usual sense.[11] Ulrich Wilckens, however, was correct to insist that in 1 Corinthians 15:5-8 seeing and testifying are both necessary to the consequence of legitimation, for the verb itself is mainly focused on the fact that something was seen (rather than the consequence of the apparition, and much less its nature or "reality").[12] First Corinthians 9:1 confirms this: "Have I not seen our Lord Jesus?" For Paul, and for whatever pre-Pauline tradition lies beneath 1 Corinthians 15:3-7, the appearances result from God's action in raising Jesus from the dead.

Apparitions of the Dead and/or Gone in Greco-Roman Literature

Although there were numerous ways to talk about the dead "appearing" (most prominently, *phainomai* and *epiphainō*), *ōphthē* was sometimes used in Greek literature for dead people (or their souls, shades, or phantoms) when they were seen by the living.[13] Ghosts are depicted in literary sources in various ways and in varying degrees of embodied states.[14] Generally, the ancients thought that when the ghosts of dead people appeared to the living, it was because their souls were not at rest: they had returned, after a fashion, in order to finish business that was cut short by untimely or violent death, or to seek vengeance or proper burial, or to bring a message from the beyond.[15] It was also thought that such ghosts, particularly the ghosts of persons who died by violence, were susceptible to the control of necromancers, who would use them as assistants; ancient magical texts, such as the Greek magical papyri, and other literary sources describe the various rituals and incantations necessary to bring such malevolent and dangerous entities under a magician's control.[16] Narrative texts describe the sort of apparitions that could result from this kind of activity (normally considered aberrant behavior).

Today the phenomenon of postmortem apparitions[17] is well documented by the social sciences and may provide a limited comparative context for understanding the experiences of the early followers of Jesus.[18] As Dale Allison explains, such apparitions are normally recounted by their percipients in terms very similar to the Gospel appearance stories: they are auditory and visual experiences, in which the recently deceased can seem "real" or "solid" and can appear or disappear suddenly; they are sometimes experienced by more than one person; they can provide comfort or occasion doubt or a radical change for the percipient(s).[19] However, Paul, the early tradition he cites, and other early Christians evidently considered that the appearances demonstrated, or resulted from, God's raising of Jesus, and this suggests that they distinguished between seeing a postmortem apparition and seeing Jesus.[20] For such an apparition, whether in antiquity or today, never leads to the conclusion that the dead person is alive again. To cite one example: A story is told in the *Book of Marvels* by Phlegon of Tralles (c. 140 CE) of a young woman who returns from the dead in order to sleep with a house guest (*Mirab.* 1).[21] Despite the physicality of her presence—she is able to walk, talk, even have sex—and despite a search of the tomb, which shows that her body is missing, neither her parents nor her new lover concludes that she is alive again, for she had been dead six months. Clearly Paul and other early followers of Jesus thought the resurrection appearances were in an entirely different category of apparition. This, as we shall see, has everything to with the interpretive context in which Jesus' followers sought to understand these experiences.

A closer analogy, possibly, can be found elsewhere in the Greco-Roman background. Celsus, an opponent of Christianity who wrote during the second century, noted the similarity between Jesus' resurrection appearances and the appearances or epiphanies (Gk., *epiphaniai*) of heroes and other figures (Origen, *Cels.* 2.55).[22] In the ancient Greek milieu, heroes were archetypal human beings, long dead or legendary, but who were considered to have some sort of ongoing existence and influence, so that the pious would venerate them in order to procure their favor or appease their anger.[23] Their divine or semidivine status could be understood and accounted for in a variety of ways.[24] As Walter Burkert explained, a hero was thought of as a "deceased person who exerts from his grave a power for good or evil and who demands appropriate honour."[25] Thus heroes normally were thought of as having influence only in certain locales, and scholars accordingly have conjectured an original connection between the cult of the hero and the cult of the dead. Heroes were therefore chthonic (underworld) deities and were venerated accordingly.[26] Although in earlier times cultic veneration was reserved for heroes of the epic past, in Hellenistic times more recently deceased persons were frequently viewed as heroes as well.[27] Heroes were sometimes described as appearing for various reasons, but mainly to exert their influence, positively or otherwise, on the living. These epiphanies normally took place in the vicinity of the tomb where the hero's relics were contained, that is, near the cultic site associated with their veneration and within their locale of influence.

In Philostratus's *Heroikos* (or *On Heroes*), an apology for hero worship written around 225 CE,[28] one of the characters, a vinedresser, describes for his conversation partner (a Phoenician) how the Trojan War hero Protesilaos would appear to him in a palpable but transformed bodily form (*Her.* 10.1–11.6) to offer advice, to protect his property, even to help with the gardening (2.6-11).[29] Evidently when not appearing to the vinedresser, Protesilaos made his residence sometimes in Hades, sometimes in Phthia, and sometimes in Troy (*Her.* 11.7-8). In the theology of Philostratus, "heroes have a higher status than souls of the dead because of a special *anabiōsis* (lit., 'a return to life again'), and they enjoy direct association or communion (*sunousia*) with the gods."[30] Exactly how this *anabiōsis* occurred was, evidently, part of the hero's mysteries— that is, information disseminated only to those formally initiated into the cult.[31]

The Phoenician, who at first has doubts about heroes, says at the end: "But now, since you have filled us with heroic stories, I would no longer ask how he had returned to life, since you say that he treats this tale as sacred and not to be spoken" (*Her.* 58.2). Apart from this "return to life," at least for Philostratus, the ongoing appearances and influence of Protesilaos would be impossible. The pious hero worshipper could also experience communion with the hero, as the vinedresser did with Protesilaos, though the kind of ongoing direct and individual contact that Philostratus has in mind was not typical in other hero cults. Ordinarily, communion with heroes took place within the context of their cultic veneration, that is, in the attendance at sacred sites, sacrificial rituals, and festal meals in their honor. Thus the veneration of the hero, and the hero's influence, was normally limited to the vicinity of their cultic sites.

The Corinthian congregation would also have been familiar with the appearances of another figure, Asklepios, who in varying accounts and legends was described "as a human being with therapeutic skills, as a hero, and as a god."[32] Supplicants would seek healing in temples devoted to Asklepios, called Asklepieia, which could be found in many of the major urban centers of the Roman Empire. There was an Asklepieion on the outskirts of Corinth during Paul's time.[33] Commonly, the ill or afflicted person would fall asleep in the Asklepieion; this practice, known as incubation (or *enkoimēsis* in Greek), was intended to bring about an appearance of Asklepios in a dream, in which the god would prescribe the cure. A stele found at the Asklepieion in Epidauros, which was held to be Asklepios's place of origin, recounts forty-three healings and the ways that the god conveyed the method of healing to the dreaming supplicant.[34]

It is difficult to say whether Paul's original readers in Corinth, hearing or reading about the appearances of the risen Jesus, would have thought them any different from appearances of Asklepios, or indeed of heroes or similar figures. As we have seen, the term *ōphthē*, as used by Paul and by the tradition he cites in 1 Corinthians 15, does not specify how the appearances were experienced/ perceived, whether in a dream or visionary state, or in normal perception. If the Corinthians were familiar with the various angelophanies and theophanies in the Septuagint, they may have understood the Hellenistic Jewish religious connotations of the verb, including the fact that such language sometimes described theophanies that occurred in dreams (Gen. 31:13; 35:1 LXX).[35] One difference is that apparitions of Asklepios and other heroes were experienced at a cultic site and in a cultic setting, and supplicants would prepare for and invite such apparitions. There is no indication from 1 Corinthians 15:5-8 of a cultic setting or preparations for the resurrection appearances.[36]

The similarities between Jesus and various heroes and other figures venerated in Greco-Roman cult practices—exaltation after suffering (Gk., *pathos*), renewed life despite death, apparitions to the pious, ongoing communion with the living through veneration and festal meals—have caused some scholars of Christian origins to think that early Christologies were at some primitive stage patterned after the heroic model.[37] David Aune has attributed these similarities to "the more general tendency of [ancient] traditions about great personalities to conform to the morphology of Greco-Roman heroes through the folkloristic process of the communal re-creation of tradition."[38] In other words, this was how such stories were told, and we must allow for the possibility of literary influence on the Gospels from the wider culture, an influence that would partly explain their narrative focus on the mighty deeds and resolute suffering of Jesus.

Yet there are also significant differences, which Hans Dieter Betz understands as evidence that "the gospel writers are opposed to a heroic kind of Christology."[39] First, the resurrection appearances were understood as chronologically limited, at least in some circles; this was not the case with appearances of heroes.[40] Second, the influence of the risen Christ was not thought of as limited to a particular locale: thus, Christ was considered not "a chthonic hero whose presence was bound up with the grave" but "ruler of the cosmos."[41] His appearances are narrated in the Gospels as occurring in the Jerusalem area and in the Galilee, although Paul nowhere says where he saw the risen Jesus.[42] Third, the worship of Christ was not connected with his tomb or his relics, as often hero worship was.[43] These critical differences aside, however, the similarities between apparitions of heroes and the appearances of the risen Jesus that Paul mentions in 1 Corinthians 15 probably would have been obvious to the letter's original recipients.

As Dieter Zeller suggests, probably the closest analogy to the early Christian narratives and traditions about the resurrection appearances of the risen Jesus may be found in the classical and Hellenistic Greek stories about human beings who were taken directly into the divine realm and divinized.[44] Some figures venerated as heroes were thought to have received this honor.[45] In some cases, legends told about the mysterious ways that the earthly lives of these figures concluded: Herakles, Romulus, and Aristeas, according to a variety of sources, all disappeared—that is, they were taken away by divine agency—and thus were thought of as having been accepted into the divine realm and elevated to a higher plane of existence. The technical term for this is "assumption," and the aftereffect for human beings is called "apotheosis" or deification. Similar stories are also found in the Jewish literary tradition. Because such stories describe the disappearance of the person taken away by divine agency, there are some obvious similarities with the stories about the disappearance of Jesus' body from the tomb (or rather, about the discovery of that disappearance).[46] Our focus here, however, is on the idea that sometimes persons taken away into the divine realm would reappear on earth again.

Epiphanies of such figures are narrated sometimes as occurring shortly after their acceptance into the divine realm, or sometimes even centuries thereafter, whether to confirm their apotheosis or to stipulate how they should be venerated.[47] In one such story, Apollonius of Tyana, a philosopher and wonder-worker, appears to a would-be follower who doubted his teachings on the immortality of the soul (Philostratus, *Vit. Apoll.* 8.31). In this appearance, which occurs sometime after Apollonius's purported disappearance (8.29-30), the wise man is not visible to all present, but the one who sees him reports his majestic declamation on the human soul. "'Do you not see Apollonius the wise?' he said. 'For he is present with us, listening to the discussion, and holding forth wondrously concerning the soul!' 'But where is he?' the others said. 'He is not visible to us anywhere, though we would wish this more than the wealth of all humankind'" (Philostratus, *Vit. Apoll.* 8.31). This private epiphany confirms for the incredulous disciple not only Apollonius's apotheosis, but also his ongoing presence and the validity of his teachings (cf. Matt. 28:16-20; Luke 24:36-49). The reappearance of Romulus is perhaps a better-known example.[48] According to the stories, Romulus disappeared mysteriously, with various heavenly portents reported in different versions of the story; a search for his remains was unsuccessful (Plutarch, *Rom.* 27–28).[49] However, shortly thereafter, it was told, he appeared to a prominent citizen of inscrutable character. As Plutarch tells the story, the nobility were urging the common folk "to honor and revere Romulus, since having been caught up to the gods he had become for them a benevolent god instead of a good king" (*Rom.* 27.7). While some remained in doubt, there came forward a certain Julius Proculus, a member of the nobility, who swore an oath that while he was traveling along the road, Romulus appeared to him, confirming that he had returned to the gods and was deserving of honor as such. Plutarch attributes the Romans' acceptance of Proculus's testimony, and their subsequent veneration of Romulus as a god, to a divine influence (Gk., *enthousiasmos*, *Rom.* 28.3).

Interestingly, in this context Plutarch uses exactly the same verb "to be seen" or "to appear" (Gk., *ophthēnai*) as found in the biblical writings and in Paul's resurrection tradition. As already shown, this verb need not connote an appearance from the divine realm, for it is also used of ghosts appearing from the realm of the dead. However, the similarity between Romulus and the risen Jesus is clear: the thinking is such apparitions are considered to be the appearances from the divine realm of dead and/or gone human beings who have already been deified (or, in the language used by the New Testament for Jesus, exalted).[50] This is very different from the apparition of a ghost: in the view of Zeller, the verb *ōphthē* in 1 Corinthians 15:5-8 and elsewhere connotes "a becoming-visible of Jesus that shows that the crucified one is alive, but because he appears as one from beyond this world, no longer lives on this earth."[51] Therefore an appearance in this category would have been viewed as something quite different from the apparitions of the souls or shades (or ghosts) of those who have died.[52] It is also interesting that when the exalted Romulus appears to Julius Proculus, he commissions him to tell the Romans that their city is destined for the pinnacle of human power, and that Romulus will henceforth be their beneficent deity (Gk., *daimōn*) Quirinius. The connection between epiphany and commissioning is the same as that found in Paul's letters and in the conclusions of the canonical Gospels.

Apparitions of the Dead and/or Gone in Early Jewish and Christian Literature

In early Jewish and Christian literature, stories about epiphanies are relatively common, although typically it is an angel who appears to a human observer, and it is clear throughout the biblical and extrabiblical writings that angels are not exalted human beings but intermediaries between humankind and a transcendent God.[53] Stories about encounters with angels are told not only in novelistic or biographical works such as Tobit and the canonical Gospels, but also in apocalyptic writings, such as Daniel, Revelation, and *1 Enoch*. In the apocalyptic tradition, with which Paul was intimately familiar, specially qualified seers would sometimes be allowed a glimpse into the normally unseen transcendent realm of God and his agents, and would see not only exalted heavenly beings (God, angels, other figures), but also the departed righteous. These sightings normally are described as occurring in ecstatic visionary experiences in which, for instance, John of Patmos or Paul or the characters in pseudepigraphical literature are present in the heavens (or under the earth), one way or another, to receive special revelation (Gk., *apokalypsis*). As Paul himself said, "Whether this happened in the body or outside the body, I do not know, but God knows" (2 Cor. 12:2). In Daniel 7, for instance, the seer has a dream vision (Dan. 7:1) of "one like a human being" receiving dominion from an enthroned figure called "Ancient of Days" (Dan. 7:13-14). Similar visions of exalted heavenly figures occur throughout Jewish and early Christian apocalyptic literature, although it is rarely clear that actual visionary experiences like the one Paul describes in 2 Corinthians 12 lie behind the literary texts (since the literary expressions tend to be so formulaic).[54]

In some texts, the figure seen by the visionary was an exalted human being. *First Enoch* 71 describes how Enoch, after several visions of the heavenly realm, and after his final journey to heaven (see Gen. 5:21-24; Heb. 11:5; Sir. 44:16), comes before the Ancient of Days and learns that he himself is "that Son of Man" whom he had been seeing in his visions (71:9-17). In the Wisdom of Solomon, an individual known only as "the righteous one" stands exalted before his erstwhile oppressors, those who engineered his wrongful death, in a judgment scene (Wisd. 5:1-2). While the Wisdom of Solomon is not an apocalyptic writing, lacking the apocalyptic literary device of the (pseudonymous) seer, here it uses stock imagery from apocalyptic texts—a vision of an exalted figure—to describe God's vindication of the paradigmatic suffering righteous one.[55] A third example is found in the vision of "one like a Son of Man" in Revelation 1:9-20, a vision that James Robinson calls the second of the only two first-person accounts of resurrection appearances in the New Testament.[56] The author of Revelation combines the descriptions of "the Ancient of Days" and "one like a human being" from the vision in Daniel 7 to depict the seer's apocalyptic experience of the risen and exalted Jesus. In all of these instances, the exalted figure functions representatively, being almost a supernatural personification of the community of the elect, symbolizing (or better, embodying) the community's future but presently hidden vindication.[57]

Our interest is in the fact that Paul, just as the seer in the book of Revelation (John of Patmos), may not have distinguished between a "resurrection appearance" and an "apocalyptic vision of the exalted Christ" in the way that eventually became customary in Christian tradition. This distinction is based at least in part in the different genres in which such appearances are narrated (recall that Paul himself only reports his experience; he does not narrate it). But it is also due to the chronological framework presented in Luke-Acts, whose author carefully differentiated between the appearances of the risen Jesus to his apostolic witnesses in the forty days between Easter and the Ascension, and the experiences of Paul and others of the post-ascension exalted Christ (e.g., Acts 7:55-56; 9:3-9). For modern/postmodern readers, however, this distinction becomes one between "real" and "visionary" experiences, although neither Paul nor Luke would have drawn such a line. Even for Luke, Paul's Damascus Road experience was no less "real" than the experiences of the Eleven, although Luke puts it in a different narrative category. In 2 Corinthians 12:1-4, Paul speaks of a person (probably himself) who was taken up to the third heaven, but he does not disclose what was seen there. In fact, he only says that what was heard cannot be disclosed. He classifies this incident as an instance of "visions and revelations [Gk., *optasiai kai apokalypseis*] of the Lord" (2 Cor. 12:1). It would be difficult to maintain that Paul (or others) would not have counted his formative experience of seeing the risen Lord as one of these apocalyptic revelations.

Not many stories in early Jewish and Christian literature describe appearances of the dead and/or gone in an earthly setting, however; but the story of Jesus' transfiguration (Mark 9:2-8 and parallels) is one example. In this story, Jesus is glorified or metamorphosized, and he has a bright, shining appearance, just as angels and denizens of the heavenly realm are often described as having in early Jewish literature. Elijah and Moses appear (Gk., *ophthēsan*) with him, and the three converse together as Peter, James, and John look on. Nothing in any of the three versions of this story suggests that these were apparitions from the realm of the dead, the ghosts of Moses and Elijah; rather, Moses and Elijah appear as exalted heavenly beings.[58] This is possible because, as Adela Yarbro Collins explains, "in the cultural context of Mark, [Elijah and Moses were] believed to have been taken up to heaven and made immortal."[59] In other words, Elijah and Moses appear with Jesus just as figures like Romulus—deified (or exalted, as one might say about such figures in the Jewish tradition) through their reception into the heavenly realm—would sometimes appear afterward to human observers. Collins says this foreshadows for Mark's reader the transformation of Jesus' body and its translation into heaven in Mark 16:1-8, an idea to which we will return in a later chapter.

The Appearances of (the Risen) Jesus and the Origins of Belief in Jesus' Resurrection

Compared with the appearance stories in the Gospels, which demonstrate a tendency to materialize/concretize the body in which the risen Jesus appears, and with Paul himself, who defines resurrection bodies as "spiritual," the tradition that Paul cites in 1 Corinthians 15:3b-7 is strikingly vague.[60] The connotations of *ōphthē* as it occurs in the Septuagint probably influenced the original tradition and probably were recalled by Paul and others as they heard and used this tradition. In other words, "Christ appeared" in a way analogous to the Old Testament accounts of appearances of angels or of God *from* the divine realm to a particular human person. Possibly Paul also may have considered all the appearances apocalyptically, as revelatory visionary encounters *within* the divine realm, although there is room for debate on that point. This is partly because the apocalyptic genre, because of its narrative emphasis on the transcendence of the divine realm, can tend to locate and to depict its revelatory encounters there (see Daniel 7; Rev. 4:1).[61] Would the Corinthians, being Gentiles, and perhaps having a limited or indirect knowledge of the scriptures and traditions of Judaism, have picked up on either of these interpretive possibilities when they heard the resurrection kerygma in Paul's preaching and read it in his letter? Although Paul is not at his most exegetical with the Corinthians, in places in his correspondence with them, he seems fairly comfortable citing Scripture for them (see 1 Cor. 3:19-20; 15:45; et al.) and using complex scriptural argumentation to make a point (see 1 Cor. 10:1-11). Thus it is not impossible that they were familiar with the use of *ōphthē* in the Septuagint. His later letter also clarifies that he was a recipient of apocalyptic visions (2 Cor. 12:1-4).

On the other hand, within their home environment, the Corinthians would also have been abundantly familiar with stories about apparitions of various types of figures, whether from the realm of the dead or from the divine realm. In the context of 1 Corinthians 15, the logic would exclude the possibility that Jesus had appeared to Cephas and to Paul and the others from the realm of the dead, for the proclamation they accepted ran as follows: he died, was buried, *was raised*, and then appeared. Yet Paul's focus on the redemptive death of Jesus and his subsequent resurrection and appearances probably would have evoked for the Corinthians associations with various hero cults with which they would have been familiar. Thus, while other interpretive options evidently would have been ready at hand, those who saw Jesus after his death concluded that the appearances were the result of God raising him, and that the raising of Jesus meant not only his personal return to life, vindication, and exaltation, but also that the eschatological resurrection of the dead had begun.[62] The similarities to other appearances in the wider Greco-Roman religious world are clear: the appearances of Jesus, like the appearances of heroes like Protesilaos, signify, as Zeller puts it, that he "no longer lives on this earth" because he appeared "as one from beyond this world."[63] Yet for Paul, Jesus' return to life had a universal/cosmic significance, which he explains in 1 Corinthians 15:24-28: "All things have been made subject under his feet" (v. 27, citing Ps. 8:6 LXX).[64] So as to their cause (God raised Jesus from the dead) and to their implication (God will make all things subject to him at the end of the age, which is now inevitable owing to Jesus' resurrection), the postmortem appearances of Jesus were, according to the individuals involved, worlds apart from the appearances of other figures. But why did they think this?

This, in fact, is a huge question and one that is not easily answered through "historical" arithmetic, as follows:

     Jesus' body was missing from the tomb
+   Jesus appeared to some of his followers after his execution
     _____

     God raised Jesus from the dead

There are a couple of problems with this line of thinking. First, neither the two data listed above nor the conclusion below is directly accessible to us as history.[65] Only the claims themselves are open to historical analysis, but *only as claims*. This means that one could argue that the two claims (1) that Jesus' tomb was found empty and (2) that he was seen after his death by his followers are simply variant implications of the single claim that God had raised Jesus from the dead. Then, however, we no longer have an argument about the origins of belief in Jesus' postmortem divine vindication, but one about the development of linguistic expressions of that belief. Even here the task is complicated by the fact that both the appearances and the empty tomb, as will be explained more fully in the following chapters, can lead to other conclusions or be explained by other ways of thinking about Jesus' ongoing postmortem significance. In other words, we must be careful not to take the end point of the early Christian narrative tradition (Jesus was present with the disciples because he was no longer in the tomb, or vice versa) as definitive for that narrative tradition's development. This is so because, as suggested earlier, the literary evidence shows that these two traditions—one about the appearances of Jesus and another about the discovery of the empty tomb—did not always go hand in hand.

If we must ask about the origins of Christian belief in the divine postmortem vindication of Jesus, whether in the mode of "God raised him and he appeared" or in the mode of "God took him away and he was exalted," we are at something of an impasse. On the one hand, if we focus only on the language they used, especially when we consider other applications of similar language in Second Temple Judaism or in the Greco-Roman world, we could conclude that Jesus' followers were simply experimenting with different ways of saying that God declared Jesus right (or Messiah, or God's Son, etc.) despite the way he died.[66] But this is to overlook the formative role that experience played in arriving at this conclusion, as well as the fact that when Paul, Luke, and others said, "Jesus has been raised from the dead," they thought they were talking about something that really happened to Jesus, and when they said, for instance, "He appeared to Cephas" or "to me," they were talking about something they thought really happened to them. This is still true even though they might have disagreed about what it all meant. On the other hand, focusing on the experiences of Jesus' followers (i.e., they saw him after his death, or found an empty tomb) can lead us to overlook the interpretive matrix in which belief in Jesus' continuing life and presence originated.[67] Interpreting the appearances of Jesus after his death as *resurrection* appearances requires, as Henk de Jonge argues, acceptance "that Christ *is* a living reality," just as "the assumption of the reality of God . . . underlies the theophanies of the Old Testament."[68] This involves a basic conviction that God would vindicate, either by resurrection or by exaltation, those who die faithful to his cause, and that God had done so for Jesus. Allison points out that this conviction must be interpreted in relation to the way that the teaching of Jesus shaped his followers' religious worldview, in particular, their "eschatological expectations."[69] Apart from this interpretive matrix, the experiences would have led to other interpretations (such as, they saw his ghost, or somebody moved the body), as indeed they apparently did among outsiders. In my opinion, neither the interpretive matrix (or matrices) nor the experience(s) of Jesus' followers can sufficiently explain the origin of these beliefs; both are absolutely necessary in order to make sense of the evidence.

The focus of this book, however, is not primarily the origins of the "appearance" and "disappearance" traditions, but how the mutual influence of these traditions shaped the way the empty tomb stories were told and interpreted. The literary evidence suggests that these traditions originally had separate trajectories of development until they were combined into the one "Easter story," for neither the appearance tradition in its formulaic versions (1 Cor. 15:3b-7; Luke 24:34) nor the disappearance tradition in its earliest forms (Q 13:34-35, and the tradition behind Mark 16:1-8) refers to the other. It is true that both traditions, for the early Christians who took Jesus' resurrection as a central component of their proclamation, faith, and future hope, pointed to the conviction that "God raised Jesus from the dead." On the other hand, as we have seen, appearances of the dead and/or gone were open to a number of possible interpretations; a missing body can similarly lead to a variety of different conclusions. The early Christians themselves eventually took the appearances and the empty tomb together as resulting from the single cause of Jesus' resurrection, and this is a conviction that is mainly expressed in narrative form. But in order to understand the narrative products, we must first understand the traditions that shaped them. So, to begin, we turn to Paul and the pre-Pauline tradition in 1 Corinthians 15.

2. Paul: "Last of All, He Appeared Also to Me"

For I handed down to you, among the things of primary impor-
tance, what I in turn had received: that Christ died for our sins
according to the Scriptures, and that he was buried, and that
he was raised on the third day according to the Scriptures,
and that he appeared to Cephas, then to the Twelve; next he
appeared to upwards of five hundred believers at once, most
of whom remain to this day, though some have fallen asleep;
next he appeared to James, then to all the apostles; and last of
all, he appeared also to me, as to someone untimely born.

—1 Corinthians 15:3-8

Even though neither the pre-Pauline tradition that is preserved in 1 Corinthians 15:3b-5, 7 nor Paul himself (anywhere in his surviving letters) mentions the empty tomb, our investigation of the empty tomb stories begins with Paul. This is for two reasons. First, the tradition he refers to is the earliest source that offers any substantial information about belief in Jesus' resurrection, and so it demands our attention. Elsewhere in Paul's letters, and elsewhere in the early Christian writings, pieces of preexisting traditions referring to the resurrection can often be found embedded and redeployed in new literary contexts. These traditions may have originated in settings of communal worship in which believers con-fessed or proclaimed their faith. Some of these traditional pieces only assert that "God raised Jesus from the dead" (1 Thess. 1:10 et al.).[1] Others that have more to say are of interest not for information they offer about the resurrection of Jesus itself (because they offer none at all), but for the theological meaning they ascribe to it. Romans 1:3-4, for instance, offers very little information about Jesus' resur-rection, or about the origins of belief in it. It says neither that he appeared to his followers nor that he left behind an empty tomb, but it does claim that on the basis of "the resurrection of the dead" he was "confirmed" or "designated" as "Son of God" (Rom. 1:4). In 1 Corinthians 15:3-7, on the other hand, Paul cites a very primitive kerygmatic tradition that offers a considerable amount of detail, at least about those to whom the risen Christ appeared.

Second, we begin with this piece of tradition *because* it makes no reference to the empty tomb, despite the fact that it clearly states that Christ died, was buried, rose on the third day, and appeared to Cephas (Peter, that is)[2] and others. As already noted, Paul himself makes no reference to the empty tomb anywhere in his letters, so here in 1 Corinthians 15 we have to do with resurrection conceived of in terms of appearances of the risen Jesus, but not explicitly or necessarily as involving a disappearance of Jesus' body from the tomb. Thus Paul marks the beginning of (or at least the earliest accessible point on) the trajectory of the "appearance" tradition, and it is this tradition that becomes a major controlling influence in later narratives about the empty tomb.

It is a bit of a puzzle why Paul does not use empty tomb language or refer to an empty tomb tradition. One approach commonly taken by scholars is to argue that Paul (or the tradition cited by him) assumes, or takes for granted, that the tomb was empty, or that an empty tomb is implied in the connection the tradition makes between burial and resurrection. N. T. Wright, for instance, thinks that Paul's silence "is not significant: the mention here of 'buried, then raised' no more needs to be amplified [with a reference to the empty tomb] than one would need to amplify the statement 'I walked down the street' with the qualification 'on my feet.'"[3] Wright's opinion is based on his view that "resurrection" was only ever understood in the ancient world in terms of revivification of the physical body.[4] This is, however, a hotly debated point, and a different appraisal of the textual evidence for ancient views of resurrection will lead to an opposing approach to the problem of Paul and the empty tomb. Besides, since members of his Corinthian congregation—a congregation made up largely of Gentile believers, it would seem—doubted that there could be a "resurrection of the dead," would not an empty tomb tradition have helped Paul as he constructed his argument? We will return to this question below.

Other scholars insist, particularly on the basis of 1 Corinthians 15:35-57, that Paul simply did not think in terms of a "physical" resurrection, and so would have had little use for a tradition or story about an empty tomb. Paul understood the individual resurrection of Jesus as the beginning of the eschatological resurrection of the dead, and he took for granted that "resurrection" is an embodied kind of postmortem existence. Thus he answers questions he thinks will arise, or perhaps have arisen, about what a resurrection body is like (1 Cor. 15:35). However, in 1 Corinthians 15:42-49 Paul also talks about this "body" as "spiritual" (Gk., *pneumatikos*) and not "physical" or "natural" (*psychikos*, which literally means "ensouled" or "soulish"), arguing that "flesh and blood cannot inherit the kingdom of God, and what is corruptible does not inherit incorruptibility" (1 Cor. 15:50). Paul did seem to think of both the resurrection of Jesus and the future resurrection of the dead as being "bodily" but not "physical," an idea we will need to explore in detail in this chapter. Some scholars conclude from this that Paul would not have been interested in a story or tradition about an empty tomb had he known of one, and that he would not have needed to think that Jesus' tomb was empty in order to talk about his vindication and ongoing presence using "resurrection" language.

Willi Marxsen famously wrote that "the empty tomb would even be an inconvenience," given Paul's "spiritual" understanding of resurrection bodies. According to Marxsen's reading of Paul, the physical body "mortifies" just as a seed dies and decays in the earth (1 Cor. 15:36-38), and the resurrection body is raised by God as spiritual (15:44-46); therefore resurrection, for Paul at least, occurs on another plane of existence.[5] As we will see below, there is evidence (not entirely unambiguous, however) that not all understandings of "resurrection" in early Judaism involved the resuscitation or reconstitution of the physical body. In light of this, some suggest that the empty tomb story was invented, whether by Mark or by early Christians before that Gospel was written, as a narrative expression of belief in the resurrection of Jesus along lines opposed to (and even secondary to) Paul's "spiritual" view.[6] Gerd Lüdemann has argued that the empty tomb story arose as a conclusion drawn from the kerygma about the resurrection of Jesus: "The story is first inferred from the 'dogma.'"[7] This solution, however, would only hold for those who believed that "resurrection" had to involve the body in such a way that the risen Jesus must have left the tomb—and from Paul's letters it is not entirely clear that all early Christians would have viewed resurrection in such a way.[8] This view also depends on the idea that the empty tomb tradition is best explained as a narrative expression of a certain kind of resurrection theology, but as we will see in the next chapter, the "disappearance" tradition may originally have had more to do with another understanding of Jesus' postmortem vindication.

Nevertheless, Paul's use of this kerygmatic tradition and his failure to mention the empty tomb raise important questions for our discussion, questions about how Paul and his Corinthian readers understood the nature of "resurrected" bodies as well as questions about what Paul and his congregations did and did not know. In the end, the evidence requires a position more nuanced than those of Wright or Marxsen. However the problem of Paul and the empty tomb is resolved, the focus of the pre-Pauline kerygmatic tradition (and of Paul himself) is not the empty tomb but the appearances, and especially what they signify.

Paul and the Resurrection Kerygma

Fundamental to Paul's argument in favor of "the resurrection of the dead" (Gk., *anastasis nekrōn*), against certain members of the Corinthian church who questioned this feature of his eschatological message (1 Cor. 15:12), is his appeal to the traditional kerygmatic formula referred to above. This formula functions as a basic statement of shared belief, and it stands at the beginning of his argument just as a narrative of the facts of the case would introduce a piece of judicial rhetoric. The agreed-upon facts are then, in the argument that follows, analyzed according to their proper significance and implications.[9] Paul is able to argue for the resurrection of the dead at the end of the age (15:23; 15:51-52) because, he says, the Corinthians have already believed in the resurrection of Jesus (15:1-2; 15:12). He uses the sacrificial imagery of "firstfruits" to argue this: just as the first sacrificial offering represents the whole harvest or flock, so also the resurrection of Jesus is determinative for the resurrection of the dead at the end of the age (15:20-23). Paul introduces the formula with customary language about "receiving" and "handing over" traditional material (15:3a), as he did earlier in the letter in relation to a tradition about the Lord's Supper (11:23a). The language and structure of verses 3b-5 also set it off as traditional, as shown here:[10]

...	that he died	for our sins	according to the scriptures,
and	that he was buried,		
and	that he was raised	on the third day	according to the scriptures,
and	that he appeared	to Cephas,	
		then to the twelve ...	

We should also note that verse 7 has the same structure as verse 5:

Next	he appeared	to James,
		then to all the apostles.

Interestingly, this introduces a distinction between "the apostles" and "the Twelve," but it still probably belonged to the original tradition.[11] On the other hand, verses 6 and 8, in which Paul mentions the five hundred believers and himself, were likely not part of the original tradition, but appear to be additions by Paul himself for his purposes in this literary context. Structurally speaking, they simply do not fit. So what are we left with? The parallel structure of the core tradition indicates that the second and fourth lines are to be read as consequences of the first and third lines (respectively), each of which is elaborated with two modifying phrases. Thus "he was buried" should be connected with "he died" as its consequence, and equally "he appeared" should be connected with "he was raised" as its consequence.

Although these observations lead me to conclude that the basic tradition was originally a single unit, a different approach has been proposed by Stephen Patterson, based partly on earlier work by Reginald Fuller.[12] Patterson argues that the "resurrection tradition" and the "appearance tradition" were originally separate but were combined here by Paul.[13] Patterson makes this distinction for several reasons, and not only because verses 3b-4 and verses 5-7 differ in content (the former is about the resurrection of Jesus, and the latter about his postmortem appearances). Formally, Patterson claims, verses 3b-4 are more like the "resurrection" traditions discussed above (such as 1 Thess. 4:14), and verses 5-7 also have analogues elsewhere in the early Christian writings (e.g., 1 Cor. 9:1). He also notes that when Paul talks about his experience of the risen Jesus (such as in Gal. 1:15-16), he does not talk about this using language of "resurrection," and when Paul talks at length about the resurrection (such as in Romans 6), he does not mention the appearances.[14] Patterson also thinks that 1 Corinthians 15:3b-4 had its origin in the interpretation of Scripture but that verses 5-7 originated in missionary circles in which an individual's call or commissioning as an apostle needed the specific authorization only an appearance of Jesus could provide.[15]

Despite these observations, the original unity of the tradition (15:3b-5 + 7) can still be maintained on good grounds. First of all, although there are examples of traditional formulations that focus either on the resurrection or on the appearances, it is not out of the question that an original formulation could have combined them. Paul evidently thought that resurrection and appearances belonged together, since they are together here in 1 Corinthians 15:3-8. When Paul does write at length about the resurrection of Jesus and its theological significance (as in Romans 6), he does not mention the appearances of the risen Jesus because he is writing not about the origins of resurrection faith, but about the meaning of the resurrection of Jesus for those who are, in his language, "in Christ." In Galatians 1:15-16, on the other hand, when he writes about his commissioning as an apostle, he speaks about "God revealing the Son in me," but not about the resurrection of Jesus (strictly speaking, he does not use the language of appearance here either). Yet in the opening salutation of the letter, Paul claims that his status as an apostle comes from "God who raised Jesus from the dead" (Gal. 1:1), thus linking his divine authorization with the resurrection (but not explicitly with an appearance). Furthermore, it is somewhat artificial to distinguish between the first part as exegetical and the second as experiential, when "he was buried" cannot be claimed to have originated exegetically. Finally, to attribute the parallelism between verses 3b-4 and verse 5 to Paul's editorial work, as Patterson must, is not justified when the pieces that do appear to be editorial in this section interrupt rather than improve the flow (vv. 6, 8).[16] Yet Patterson is also correct that "he was raised" and "he appeared" are two different claims and that their meanings should not be conflated.[17]

The fact that "died . . ." is connected with "was buried," and "was raised . . ." with "appeared," is important for a second reason. Sometimes "he was buried" is read together with "he was raised" as a way of finding an implied reference to the empty tomb traditions in this kerygmatic formulation, whether for the tradition itself or for Paul, who clearly cites it favorably. William Lane Craig, for example, states that "in saying that Jesus died—was buried—was raised—appeared, one automatically implies that the empty grave has been left behind."[18] Martin Hengel argues along a somewhat different line that from the beginning kerygmatic proclamation and community confession were inseparable from the narration of the facts concerning Jesus' death and resurrection, so that the exegete is right to discern the empty tomb story (as found in the canonical Gospels) behind the connection "was buried" and "was raised."[19] He also argues that "the chronological notice ['on the third day'] is related to the discovery of the empty tomb."[20] This phrase occurs in other formulaic references to Jesus' resurrection (see also Matt. 16:21; Acts 10:40), and it need not rest upon knowledge of a narrative tradition about the discovery of the empty tomb on "the first day of the week" (such as preserved in Mark 16:1-8 et al.). Some see in "the third day" an allusion to the Greek version of Hosea 6:2, "He will restore us after two days; on the third day, we will be raised and we will live in his presence,"[21] even though this passage does not become a "proof text" for the resurrection until a couple of centuries later.[22] In any case, this early tradition, like the Gospel narratives, sees only a very short interval between the death of Jesus and the beginnings of belief in his divine vindication by resurrection.[23]

In its original setting, this kerygmatic tradition could have been understood to mean that Jesus was raised by God in such a way that he left the tomb in a renewed physical body. However, this does not mean that all early Christians who used this tradition, Paul included, would have naturally thought along similar lines, nor that the core tradition was formulated on the basis of knowledge of a story about the discovery of the empty tomb. Furthermore, contrary to what Craig and Wright assert, what Paul says explicitly about resurrection bodies does cause problems for any straightforward argument that his implicit meaning was "he was raised *so that the tomb was empty.*" For there is considerable ambiguity concerning what Paul may have thought happened to the body of Jesus when "he was raised."[24]

Observing the parallel structure is important, finally, because it demonstrates that the logic in the second part runs in the direction given: "he appeared" should be connected with "he was raised" as its consequence, but not necessarily as its proof. In other words, the tradition gives evidence of the belief that "he appeared" because "he was raised," so that the line of thinking is that the appearances resulted from the resurrection and therefore confirmed or demonstrated it, but not that it was concluded that "he was raised" because "he appeared."[25] As we saw in the previous chapter, in the ancient world (just as today) the appearance of someone who had died could lead to any of a variety of conclusions, "resurrection" being rather further on down the list. Thus for Paul the resurrection of Jesus is fundamentally part of the proclamation of the good news, and it is therefore something to be preached and believed, rather than proven and given intellectual assent. The persons and groups he lists in 1 Corinthians 15:5-8, then, testify to the resurrection of Jesus as believers to whom the risen Jesus appeared, and most of them (but not the five hundred) testify as those whom the risen Jesus authorized for a particular role of leadership in particular sectors of the early Christian movement.

It is impossible to be precise about the age of this traditional formula, though many scholars think it can be dated to within a few years of Jesus' death.[26] One consideration arises from Paul's introduction: he says the tradition is "among the things of primary importance," and possibly this indicates that he became aware of it soon after his own experience of the risen Jesus. It is also interesting how the formula highlights Peter and James "the brother of the Lord," apostles whom Paul considered "pillars" of the Judean community of believers (Gal. 1:18-19; 2:6-10). This particular James does not figure at all in the Synoptic Gospels or in the Jesus traditions therein; and just as with Peter, there is no narrative record (nor any other mention) of an appearance to James.[27] Yet three years after Paul's call, he visited Jerusalem to inquire of Cephas (Peter) and the apostle James (Gal. 1:18-19). It is unclear how James could have risen to prominence in the Judean communities (Galatians 1–2; see also Acts 15:12-21) unless it was widely known that he had experienced an appearance of the risen Jesus, even though in Paul's words he was "the brother of the Lord" (Gal. 1:19). This detail in itself is not sufficient grounds to date the tradition, but taken together with the formulaic language and structure, we do have enough to conclude that 1 Corinthians 15:3b-5 + 7 is a very early tradition.

It is also difficult to determine whether Paul knew of other appearances that he or the tradition he cites does not mention. For it is immediately apparent that some of the appearances described in the Gospels are not included in 1 Corinthians 15:5-8: the appearance to Mary Magdalene and/or other women (Matt. 28:9-10; John 20:11-18); the appearance to two unnamed disciples (Luke 24:13-32); and other appearances in which one or two followers figure prominently (John 20:24-29; 21:1-23). Not only that, but some of the appearances mentioned in 1 Corinthians 15 are not narrated (the appearance to Cephas/Peter) or even mentioned (the appearances to James and to the five hundred) anywhere else.[28] Paul probably is not listing here all the appearances known to him, and it is also possible that he omitted some appearances from the tradition.[29] It may be that he preferred not to mention, for political or polemical reasons, certain appearances of which he was aware.

Since Paul was concerned, for instance, to limit the prophetic activities of certain women in the Corinthian group (1 Cor. 14:33b-36), he might have avoided referring to an appearance to female disciples or to Mary Magdalene specifically, had the original tradition included such an appearance (as Matt. 28:9-10 and John 20:11-18 narrate).[30] However, there were also difficulties of factionalism in the Corinthian community, with one group claiming allegiance to Cephas (1 Cor. 1:12). Paul clearly did not pass over the reference to Cephas in the kerygmatic tradition in order to remove support for a pro-Petrine faction in Corinth. That Paul did not leave out the appearance to Peter indicates that it was integral to the tradition he is citing, and likely also to the body of traditions about the appearances of the risen Jesus—even though no such story about Peter has survived. Peter is first on this list, and historically he perhaps was the first to claim to have seen the risen Jesus.[31] Though Paul could not leave the reference to Cephas out of the tradition, it seems the opposite was true, however, for the appearances to the women. That is, Paul apparently—if he knew of any traditions concerning such appearances—did not feel constrained by their prominence, either in this particular tradition or in others, to include them here. Or, as Ann Graham Brock points out, it may be that competing traditions about appearances to both Peter and Mary go back to the earliest times, and Paul simply has received a tradition that gives the primacy to Peter and to Judean circles within the early Jesus movements.[32]

All this is not only about verifying the appearances by determining the sum total of witnesses mentioned in various formulae and narrative traditions. If Paul did leave out the appearances to the women because of troubles he perceived in Corinth, this is because legitimation of leadership status and authority was an accepted function of claims about appearances of the risen Jesus. This function resides deep in the kerygmatic tradition and deep in the narrative tradition as well: those who proclaim the Gospel as apostles claim they have "seen the Lord" (1 Cor. 9:1; 15:5-8), and in the Easter stories the risen Jesus usually appoints those to whom he appears to a particular commission (Matt. 28:10, 16-20; Luke 24:44-49; Acts 1:6-8; John 20:16-18, 19-23; 21:15-19).[33] As to the tradition behind 1 Corinthians 15:3-8, Ulrich Wilckens noted its probable use in proclamation and in instruction within the community of faith, but he also argued that appearance claims such as those in 1 Corinthians 15:5-8 meant "not merely that [one] thereby became a witness to the event of the raising of Jesus, but at the same time that as such a witness [one] also received special authority within the Church."[34] An appearance of Jesus, testimony to it, and legitimation and commissioning as its results all went together as "a single whole." Wilckens also noticed that Peter and James are mentioned (in vv. 5, 7) in connection with groups in which they functioned as authority figures. In the same way, Paul's apostolic legitimacy among the Gentiles hinges on his claim that his experience of the risen Jesus was authentic.[35] The mention of the appearance to the five hundred does not seem to have this legitimating function,[36] and this is one reason for thinking verse 6 was added to the tradition by Paul as relevant support for the resurrection of Jesus in his argument for the resurrection of the dead.

This explains why Paul, especially in this letter to this congregation, is eager to ensure that he is included among those who experienced appearances of the risen Jesus. In the Corinthian correspondence, the issue of apostolic authority is never far from Paul's mind, so that he even refers to it at great length (1 Corinthians 9) in order to make a point in relation to another question, that of eating meat sacrificed in cult centers (dealt with in chapters 8 and 10).[37] Paul's apostolic digression in 15:9-11 is similarly purposeful. He clarifies, in a characteristically backhanded way, how his apostolic status is not diminished even though he was the "last of all" (or possibly the "least of all")[38] to receive an appearance of the risen Jesus. For "the grace of God," which was harder at work in him than in the other apostles, overcame Paul's past as a persecutor of the Jesus movements, to the end that the gospel was proclaimed and the Corinthians came to believe (vv. 10-11). With this in view, Paul's digression here concerning his apostolic status is very appropriate to the original purpose of the traditional formula he cites in 15:3b-5 + 7, as Wilckens argued.

Paul thinks his apostolic call is just as legitimate as the call of the other apostles, since it is based on an appearance of the risen Jesus to him (1 Cor. 9:1). The language he uses in 1 Corinthians 15:8 for his experience—its chronological abnormality aside—is the same as the language the tradition uses for those of the others (Gk., *ōphthē* + dative). As noted above, this indicates that Paul does not distinguish between the nature of his experience and the others. As well, leading figures in other early Christian groups apparently likewise considered his experience (as borne out by the exercising of his call: Gal. 2:7-10) sufficient for him to be considered "apostle to the Gentiles." Perhaps they, like him, did not distinguish between his experience and theirs. We should draw this inference with some caution, however, because Paul has an apologetic interest in depicting his experience as the same as those of the others. As already noted, Paul's apostolic status was an ongoing issue for him in Corinth, and (as 2 Corinthians attests) it would become even more of an issue despite his various letters and appeals in person and through emissaries. Paul employs similar rhetoric in Galatians with believers who were, in his view, being led astray to think that his gospel—which they had originally accepted—was aberrant at points where it diverged from that of Judean Christian communities (Gal. 2:11-14) and derivative at points where it agreed (Gal. 1:11-12).

On the other hand, we ought similarly to avoid judging this issue along the lines presented by the author of Luke-Acts, who limited the physically tangible appearances (as in Luke 24:36-43) to the forty days before Jesus' ascension into heaven (Acts 1:1-4a, 9-11) and who consequently depicted Paul's experience along more visionary lines (Acts 9:3-9; 22:6-11; 26:12-18).[39] As we will see in a later chapter, Luke distinguishes narratively and chronologically between the resurrection appearances "the apostles" experienced and what he says happened to Paul, with the result that he effectively demotes Paul from the office of resurrection witness and apostle. Paul does not make any such distinction, and indeed may not have conceived of (any of) the appearances of the risen Jesus along the physically tangible lines presented in Luke 24, for he could speak of his own experience as one in which God "revealed his Son in me" (Gal. 1:16). This could mean Paul is thinking of how his fulfillment of his apostolic calling reveals the Son. However, in Galatians 1:1 he claims that this apostolic calling originates from "Jesus Christ and God the Father who raised him from the dead," making the same connection between the resurrection and commissioning that other early leaders were also making. This suggests he is thinking here about the resurrection appearance he claims he had experienced (1 Cor. 9:1; 15:8); and in another context Paul claims (in a roundabout way) to have had visionary experiences with significant revelatory content (2 Cor. 12:1-9). The question of how Paul conceived of his own experience of the risen Christ is one we can answer, possibly, with a clearer understanding of what Paul thought about resurrection bodies. For this we must turn to the rest of his argument in 1 Corinthians 15.

The Resurrection of the Dead and the Finer Points of Greek Anthropology

In 1 Corinthians 15:12, Paul asks his readers, "How is it that some among you are saying that there is no resurrection of the dead?" The idea that God, at the end of the age, would raise up human beings (whether only the righteous and chosen or all humankind) from the dead, was a relatively new one for early Judaism: the earliest textual evidence for the idea is probably *1 Enoch* 24:2–27:5, a passage that perhaps is reflected already in Daniel 12:2.[40] According to George Nickelsburg, belief in the resurrection of the dead developed in the Hellenistic era out of a concern for divine justice: while the wicked prospered in this world, some looked ahead to an age to come in which all humankind would be judged (and rewarded or punished) for their deeds during their earthly life, or to one in which only the righteous and chosen would have a share in the final restoration of all things.[41] Not all Jews believed it, and those who did not (notably, the Sadducees) were probably conservatives resisting a theological innovation.[42] The Corinthians who did not believe there was going to be a resurrection of the dead, on the other hand, probably had other reasons for resisting the idea.

According to one line of thinking, the problem was not exactly that the Corinthians disagreed with the idea of a restoration of humankind per se. The problem was the eschatology. Does God need to restore all things through some final, cataclysmic intervention, or has this already taken place in Christ? C. K. Barrett wrote that for the Corinthians it was "as if the age to come were already consummated. . . . For them there is no 'not yet' to qualify the 'already' of realized eschatology."[43] In other words, they thought everything they needed they already had, in Christ, and that included the restoration of their very selves. A critical support for this position is 1 Corinthians 4:8, in which Paul says, with obvious sarcasm, "Already you have become satisfied, already you have become rich, and apart from us you have become kings!" Does this mean that the Corinthians thought "resurrection" had already taken place in their redemption and regeneration, and that this was why "some" were saying, "There is no resurrection of the dead"? In Fuller's opinion, the problem was that "the Corinthians interpreted Christ's resurrection not as an anticipation of the future resurrection of the believers at the end, but as the opening up of a new existence into which by baptism they were completely initiated."[44] Some of the things Paul says in his various letters might be taken to imply this (see, e.g., 2 Cor. 5:17; Rom. 6:4-11; see also Col. 2:12-13; 3:1).

However, Dale Martin points out that there is no solid evidence that the Corinthians had transferred an originally eschatological idea (resurrection) to their present experience (spiritual transformation).[45] On the other hand, there is evidence that at least some of the Corinthians—those who considered themselves to be "wise" and "strong" (1 Cor. 1:26-27; 3:18-20; 4:10) and having "knowledge" (8:1, 7, 10-11) and who made status claims on those grounds—had been influenced by popular philosophy. The status claims they were making led to various kinds of trouble within the congregation: for instance, the factionalism and abuses at the communal meal (11:18-22). Martin is probably correct that the practice of baptizing on behalf of the dead (15:29) indicates that the Corinthian resurrection doubters expected some sort of an afterlife, though not everyone in the Greco-Roman world did.[46] So if the problem was not the idea of an afterlife, it must have been the application of "afterlife" to "body." Through popular Greek philosophy, the Corinthian "strong" faction had learned to devalue the body and therefore could not believe that the body had a future beyond this present life.[47] In addition, the lengths to which Paul goes to explain what a resurrected body would be like (1 Cor. 15:35-57) also suggests that the problem was mainly philosophical, specifically anthropological.

According to many scholars, there was a considerable range of opinion among early Jewish proponents of the eschatological resurrection on the question of what "resurrection" would be like. Some texts—for instance, the tale of the seven brothers in 2 Maccabees—clearly envisage a physical, bodily resurrection in which martyrs receive back body parts mutilated by their persecutors (2 Macc. 7:10-11), "as a remedy for their bodily tortures."[48] Luke's narrative of the appearance of the risen Jesus to the Twelve (Luke 24:36-43) similarly describes a "flesh and bones" resurrection body.[49] Other writings, Daniel 12:2-3, for example, are not as unambiguous: "And many of those who sleep in the land of dust will awake, some to endless life, and some to disgrace and endless contempt. And the wise shall shine like the splendor of the sky, and those who vindicate the many [or lead the many to righteousness], like the stars forever and ever" (Dan. 12:2-3). Some scholars take this as a veiled association of resurrection with astral immortality, an idea found in various ancient milieus, to the effect that special human individuals live on after their death as stars.[50] Most scholars, on the other hand, think this refers to bodily resurrection.[51] Taking a different approach, the book of *Jubilees* (c. 170–150 BCE) uses resurrection language together with the idea that the bones of the righteous rest in the earth while their spirits rejoice (*Jub.* 23:30-31).[52] And according to *1 Enoch* 103:4:

> The souls of the pious who have died will come to life,
> and they will rejoice and be glad;
> their spirits will not perish,
> nor their memory from the presence of the Great One
> for all the generations of eternity.[53]

In addition, some early Christian writings also talk about Jesus' resurrection as being noncorporeal—quite in contrast to the perspective offered by the canonical Gospels.[54]

Not everyone agrees on this point, however: others insist that resurrection is always "bodily." Wright defines resurrection as "life after 'life after death,'" by which he means a renewed existence in a renewed physical body after an interim period after death, during which the righteous dead are in some sense "safe in God's keeping."[55] His survey concludes with the following observation: "Nothing in the entire Jewish context warrants the suggestion . . . that the Jewish literature of the period 'speaks both of a resurrection of the body and a resurrection of the spirit without the body.'"[56] Not everyone is as certain as Wright, particularly given the texts outlined above, that resurrection always meant renewed existence in a physical (or, in Wright's language, "transphysical") body.[57] Nickelsburg, for instance, reflecting recently on his 1967 dissertation on resurrection in early Judaism, states that he saw "more variety [than Wright and others are inclined to see] in Jewish teachings on resurrection, immortality, and eternal life."[58] Some scholars think Paul's view represents the earliest interpretation of Jesus' resurrection, rather than the more tangible "flesh and bones" presentation of the canonical Gospels.[59]

Ultimately, most of these disputed passages are really not clear whether resurrection is a "bodily" or "nonbodily" affair. Some texts appear to use "resurrection" language in a metaphorical sense, while others merge "resurrection" expressions with the beliefs about the immortality of the soul. If it is correct that some early Jews could think of resurrection as being more applicable to the soul or spirit than to the body, a possibility some of the texts mentioned above at least allow, then it is remarkable that in the face of anthropological questions about resurrection, Paul would write to the Corinthians affirming the resurrection of the body. Why not simply say that "the resurrection of the dead" has to do with their souls and not their bodies? Clearly, whatever others could say about resurrection, for Paul resurrection could not be a nonembodied phenomenon. Nowhere does he talk about a "resurrection" of the individual's soul or spirit. What he does do to answer the Corinthians' objections, however, is even more surprising: he redefines the notion of "body" in such a way that the Corinthians could accept that a body could be raised.

In his helpful discussion of the problem the Corinthians had with "the resurrection of the dead,"[60] Martin points out that for many in the Greco-Roman world, particularly the uneducated, the idea of the dead coming back to life again was not a problem. There were many stories about corpses being reanimated, about people being taken bodily into the divine realm at the end of their earthly lives, and so forth. For the educated, or those who considered themselves philosophically sophisticated, on the other hand, such ideas were hard to swallow—and not because they required a belief in "the supernatural" (as the objection has normally been since the Enlightenment).[61] In Martin's words, the problem was "purely physiological."[62] How could the human body, which by its essence belongs to the earth, have any part in the divine realm? Perhaps the Corinthians had problems with this idea, just as Plutarch had problems with traditional stories about the holus-bolus deification of human beings:

> One must by no means, contrary to nature, think that the bodies of the good can be sent up into heaven; but one must think absolutely that it is their virtues and their souls which, according to nature and to divine justice, are elevated as they progress from human beings to heroes (Gk., *eis hērōas*), from heroes to demigods (*eis daimonas*), and from demigods to gods (*eis theous*), but only once they have finally been purified and sanctified (just as in a sacred initiation) so as to escape from everything that is mortal and sensible, not merely by means of a civic decree, but by means of truth and according to right reason, thus receiving the finest and most blessed fate. (*Rom.* 28.8)[63]

The issue, explains Martin, is not that the body is material and the soul (and the divine realm) immaterial, for that is a later Western philosophical distinction. The soul, according to the ancients, was not immaterial, because it was composed of *something*; the problem with the body is that it, unlike the soul, is not composed of the right kind of something to share in the divine realm.[64] Various ancient philosophical schools had different theories about the nature and composition of the human soul. Most schools of thought took for granted a basic Platonic dualism of body and soul, though there was wide disagreement as to other related issues: for instance, what a soul released from the body was composed of, and whether a soul released from the body remained "individual" (so to speak). As to its composition, according to most ancient schools of thought, it was composed of the same sort of stuff that heavenly bodies were composed of (such as fire or air/wind—that is, *pneuma*); and like heavenly bodies, the soul was considered by some schools of thought to have an "embodied" form (even though separable from the actual physical body).

The problem was more that the body is not composed of the stuff of the divine realm: it is composed of the stuff of the mortal realm. As Cicero wrote concerning the apotheosis of Heracles and Romulus, "[Their] bodies, I say, were not taken away into heaven: such is not in fact permitted by nature, since what originates from the earth must remain with the earth."[65] The soul, which, on the other hand, comes from the gods, can be immortal or dwell among the gods, and only when "pure, fleshless [*asarkos*], and undefiled" (Plutarch, *Rom.* 28.7).[66] Thus, according to Martin, "the reason why the normal human body cannot experience immortality is that it occupies a relatively low place on the spectrum of stuff, which ranges from fine, thin, rarified stuff, down to gross, thick, heavy stuff."[67] Or, as Jeffrey Asher explains, the normal human body quite simply belongs to the earth. In 1 Corinthians 15:38-41, Paul argues from the relative status of certain kinds of "stuff," arranging in order of status, higher to lower, the "flesh" of certain kinds of terrestrial beings (humans, animals, birds, fish), and then listing the "bodies" of celestial beings (the sun, the moon, the stars).[68] This contrast between "flesh" and "body" is crucial to Paul's argument. The resurrection body, he explains in 1 Corinthians 15:42-50, is a body, but not like the regular human body: it is not composed of "flesh and blood" (Gk., *sarx kai haima*), and unlike a "regular" or "natural" (*psychikon*) body, it is not characterized and animated by "soul" (*psychē*), but is "spiritual" (*pneumatikon*), that is, characterized and animated by "spirit" (*pneuma*).

We have difficulty today understanding what Paul meant by the term "spiritual body," because we take it for granted that a body is material, and hence not spiritual, and that a soul is immaterial, and hence spiritual. But a "body" characterized by or even composed of "spirit" would not be a conceptual problem for the Corinthians, at least not because of the matter/nonmatter dualism we presume today. In fact, Paul's explanation should solve the problem, since such a body essentially (that is, by virtue of its very essence as "spirit") can be immortal and incorruptible and can be raised from the dead. This is why Martin says that the more "sophisticated" Corinthians, like Plutarch, had "physiological" questions about such views, questions about the composition of the human person.[69] More than that, however, Plutarch shows that there is a theological side to this as well, for he writes against those who "unreasonably deify the mortal aspects of [human] nature, as well as the divine" (*Rom.* 28.6). The soul can share in the divine realm because it has its origin there (28.6-7).

Well-educated and sophisticated ancients, such as Plutarch, seeking to salvage the old tales from their unsophisticated anthropology, found new ways of reading or explaining stories that described special human individuals becoming immortal through the divine removal of the person, body and all. As the above citation shows, Plutarch wanted to affirm that in special cases human beings can be elevated to another plane of existence in the divine realm—only that the "virtues and souls" of such individuals, and not their bodies, are subject to such an elevation.[70] Along similar lines, Ovid retold the old tales about the apotheosis of Heracles and Romulus by describing the dissolution of their mortal bodies but the elevation of their souls (*Metam.* 9.266-71; 14.816-28; also Philostratus, *Her.*

7.3). Philo, a Hellenistic Jewish contemporary of Paul, described Moses' death/apotheosis as follows: "The Father transposed entirely his natural dyad of body and soul into a single reconstituted nature, into mind, just like the sun" (*Mos.* 2.288).[71] In *2 Enoch* 22:8, Enoch's ascent into heaven requires his "extraction" from the clothing of his body, which is replaced with the clothing of the Lord's glory.[72] Even *1 Enoch* 71 describes the final ascension of Enoch as a being taken away "in the spirit" (71:1, 5). Yet this passage also suggests that once he is in the presence of the Head of Days, Enoch is transformed out of his body, or at least out of his flesh: "And I fell on my face, and all my flesh was melted, and my spirit was transformed" (71:11). All these sources, both non-Jewish and Jewish, display the typical Hellenistic reticence to see the physical body, which to all observable indications will always decay and rot, have any part to play in the celestial realm. Consequently, most authors imagine a transformation out of the body, but not Paul. The resurrection transformation of the believer involves the corruptible and mortal body putting on incorruptibility and immortality (1 Cor. 15:53-54), which is to say, spirit: body is retained, but not in its mortal and corruptible aspects or components. "Flesh and blood cannot inherit God's kingdom" (v. 50).[73]

We should probably understand this not only in light of ancient ideas about earthly and heavenly bodies but also in light of Paul's dualistic understanding of "flesh" and "spirit" as conditions of life in the earthly body.[74] Galatians 5:19-21 can help illuminate what Paul says in 1 Corinthians 15:50: following a table of the "deeds of the flesh" (Gal. 5:19-21a), Paul writes that "those who do such things will not inherit God's kingdom" (v. 21b). As James Dunn explains, "The negative factor was not . . . bodily existence itself but the ephemeral character of human existence as existence in desiring, decaying flesh which, as it is focused on and clung to, subverts that existence as existence before and for God."[75] For Paul, "flesh" (Gk., *sarx*) often signifies that which is weak and corruptible about human existence. It is through the flesh that sin exercises its dominion over human persons (Rom. 7:5, 25; cf. Rom. 6:12), and flesh symbolizes that part of the human person that is opposed to the work of God (Rom. 8:6-7; Gal. 5:16-26). Paul therefore speaks of an embodied life in which the believer experiences, albeit partially and incompletely, the indwelling and empowerment of the divine Spirit as the positive side of a transformation that negatively involves the crucifixion of the flesh through the believer's identification with Christ (Gal. 5:24-25; cf. Rom. 6:1-14). This embodied life is the beginning of God's re-creative work in the human person, a work that is to be completed in the resurrection of the dead. Then, according to Paul, Spirit will overwhelm flesh and blood entirely, in just the same way that "the last Adam became a life-giving Spirit" (1 Cor. 15:45) in the first and paradigmatic instance of resurrection.

Paul and the Empty Tomb

In 1 Corinthians 15, Paul argues from the received tradition about the resurrection of Jesus to the disputed teaching of the resurrection of the dead; he explains resurrection as a process of eschatological transformation whose end result is a spiritual body. We have already seen that others who, like Paul, wrote about the exaltation or transformation of individual human beings tended not to extend such transformation to the body, since that was culturally or philosophically problematic. Paul himself, as suggested above, seems to have envisioned such a transformation as one in which the body of flesh and blood would be somehow transformed or resolved into one of spirit. Whether such a transformation would leave any remainder (corpse, bones, dust) is uncertain: Paul in 1 Corinthians 15 simply does not comment, neither in relation to the resurrection of Jesus nor in relation to the eschatological resurrection of the dead. Philippians 3:20-21 similarly does not address this question. "But our citizenship is in the heavens, whence we expect a savior, the Lord Jesus Christ, who will transform the body of our humiliation so that it will be conformed to the body of his glory, in accordance with the power which enables him to make all things to submit to himself." Paul does not explain the "mechanics" of this eschatological transformation, simply because his rhetorical (theological and pastoral) interests lie elsewhere: for instance, the believer's conformity to the paradigm of the risen Christ, and Christ's expected reception of his full power and authority (as also in 1 Cor. 15:24-28; Phil. 2:9-11; et al.). Notice also that Paul emphasizes a corporate understanding of this transformation when he speaks of the body (singular) of our (plural) humiliation; perhaps this is influenced by his customarily corporate view of the body of Christ. These interests focus not on mundane concerns about bodily remains but on transmundane concerns about eschatological fullness, as this will come about for those who are "in Christ," whose "citizenship is in the heavens."

Two other texts are sometimes read as clues to Paul's view. One is the image of the sown seed in 1 Corinthians 15:36-38. As already noted, some scholars have found in that image an indication that in Paul's understanding the physical body remains in the earth at the resurrection, just as the husk of the seed is left to decompose in the ground.[76] Yet that perhaps is to infer too much from the image. The seed dies and the plant comes to life (v. 36), but the focus of the analogy is not the husk that remains. Though the seed and the plant appear to be different, the seed is related to the plant both as to *genos* (kind) and as to *telos* (goal): one plants a grain of wheat and one gets a wheat plant. Paul also emphasized that this is God's doing, indeed, God's will (v. 38), as is the resurrection transformation. The analogy calls to mind what Paul says much earlier in the letter, in a different connection: "I planted, Apollos watered, but God caused it to grow" (3:6). Interestingly, here Paul calls the plant that grows a "body," evidently thinking of how he will apply the analogy. The second possible clue is found in 2 Corinthians 5:1-10. In the context of his extended argument about his suffering as proof of the validity of his apostolic authority (which was in dispute among the Corinthians, evidently because of outside influence), Paul explains how the corruptible earthly tent, the physical body, will be exchanged for an eternal heavenly house—presumably, the transformed resurrection body.[77] Paul is arguing that the eternal state that God intends for the believer is one in which "we will not be found naked" (v. 3), that is, in a disembodied state, but rather "clothed with our heavenly dwelling"

(v. 2). As John Gillman has shown, although the language is anthropological in 1 Corinthians and metaphorical in 2 Corinthians, the argument in 1 Corinthians 15:50-57 about the transformation of what is earthly into what is heavenly is developed further here in 2 Corinthians 5.[78] In this passage Paul also contrasts being "in the body" with being "at home with the Lord" (2 Cor. 5:6-8), which seems to suggest that Paul imagines an "intermediate" postmortem state in which the believer is with the Lord but still awaiting being clothed with the transformed (resurrection) body, although the immediate transformation of the living believer at the coming of Christ is to be preferred (2 Cor. 5:2; 1 Cor. 15:51-57).[79] In any event, with these passages we are no closer to an answer to the question of whether Paul would have concluded that Jesus' tomb had to be empty.

Another approach to the question has been to seek, as Hengel has done, to demonstrate indirectly that Paul could not have been ignorant of an empty tomb story or tradition. Hengel asserts that Paul must have known the details now found in the Gospel passion and resurrection narratives (including a tradition about an empty tomb) because, he claims, proclamation and confession were supported by narration from the very beginning. Hengel repeatedly appeals to the "Urgemeinde," the putative earliest core community of Jesus' followers, as the origin of both this narrating trend and the details it transmitted.[80] Although the traditional formula in 1 Corinthians 15:3-7 probably was supported with narration, it is problematic to equate that narration, as Hengel does, with the contents of the canonical passion narratives, which themselves are the products of considerable theological reflection and literary development.[81] On the other hand, in Galatians 1:18 Paul admits that he conferred with Peter for two weeks at an early stage in his ministry. The Greek word he uses to describe this meeting is *historēsai*, which can mean "inquire" or "consult," even though it is often translated as simply "visit."[82] The empty tomb tradition could have been among the things they discussed if it was in circulation at that point. The problem is that there is no independent evidence for the existence of the empty tomb tradition outside of the canonical resurrection stories, which themselves are literary products not nearly as old as Paul's letters. Moreover, the earliest version of the story seems to include a justification for its late acceptance. Mark's Gospel concludes with the admission that the women "told no one" about their experience (Mark 16:8), and this should be read as part of their astonished reaction to being confronted with the result of divine power[83] or as a narrative device inviting the readers to examine their own discipleship.[84] But this admission also raises a historical question about how widely known the empty tomb tradition was, because it sounds like an explanation for its limited circulation. The Sayings Gospel Q includes a saying of Jesus, Q 13:34-35,[85] that displays certain affinities with the empty tomb story, and although (as we will see) the disappearance tradition's origins are equally unclear, it seems unlikely that the empty tomb story began to be told as a narrative invention based on the kind of kerygmatic formula found in 1 Corinthians 15:3-7.[86]

To try another approach, if we assume that Paul knew a tradition concerning the empty tomb, we can see, given what can be inferred from the argument of 1 Corinthians 15 about the position of those who denied the resurrection of the dead, why Paul probably would not have mentioned it. As explained above, Paul was operating in a context in which such a tradition probably would not have been useful and may even have caused more problems for the philosophically minded Corinthian believers than it could have solved. If Paul had said that Jesus rose out of the grave leaving no remainder, would his readers have thought he meant that "flesh and blood" were to inherit the divine realm (which would contradict his own argument in 15:50), or to be merged into the *pneumatikon* body, or to be consumed by the process of transformation? It is impossible to say anything except that Paul himself did not consider precision about this to be germane to the argument. Paul's main concerns in 1 Corinthians 15 seem to be to show (1) that accepting Jesus' specific vindication by resurrection required one to accept the eschatological resurrection of the dead, (2) that this resurrection will be bodily, involving a transformation of the natural body into a spiritual body, and (3) that it will happen when Christ returns in his God-given authority over all things.

Paul and the Two Traditions

Alan Segal explains that Paul did not argue for a "physically present Jesus" as an apologetic response to questions about the resurrection.[87] As we look deeper into the origins of the empty tomb story in the "disappearance tradition," we will see that initially it did not emphasize the physical presence of Jesus, but the physical absence of Jesus and his ongoing presence elsewhere. Paul's understanding of the appearances of the risen Christ, evidently, had not been influenced by the narrative trend seen in the later canonical Gospels that emphasizes the physicality of the resurrection appearances by narrating them in relation to the empty tomb. Ultimately, the most significant result of the resurrection for Paul was not an interim period of Jesus' physical presence, but the continuing spiritual presence of Christ, which signified for Paul the beginning of the extension of resurrection to those who are in Christ. The narrative Gospels use the tangible resurrection appearances to emphasize the continuity between the mission of Jesus and the mission(s) of his followers (as in Matt. 28:18-20; Luke 24:44-49), but Paul finds his mission authenticated first of all by his calling by God, experienced when Christ appeared to him, and by the continuing influence of the risen Christ as Spirit in his congregations. Since he had no personal connection to the pre-Easter mission of Jesus, his own commissioning comes about through his experience of the risen Christ as Spirit. His letters indicate by their lack of interest in traditions about Jesus' own message or activities that Paul does not validate his own mission as a direct continuation of the mission of the earthly Jesus.

Paul refers to and affirms the kerygmatic tradition about the appearances of the risen Jesus for a number of reasons. As indicated by the traditional formula in 1 Corinthians 15:3-5 + 7, others claimed that the risen Jesus had appeared to them, and Paul wished to align himself with them, at least in terms of the origin of his authority. Christ's appearance to Paul provided for him (as it did for the others) a validation of his mission, which was especially important given that its authenticity was coming under fire in some circles (see, e.g., Gal. 1:1, 15-17). As far as his purposes in 1 Corinthians 15 are concerned, the appearance tradition could function as a demonstration of the raising of Christ by God, and therefore as a support for his argument for the eschatological resurrection of the dead, which had come into question among the Corinthian believers. But the resurrection of Christ was not only a "given" in his argument for the resurrection of the dead; it was also fertile conceptual ground for his christological thinking. For Paul, the resurrection demonstrated Jesus' identity as God's Son (Rom. 1:4), and this has anti-imperial implications. It would scarcely be missed by the readers of the letter that the one who was "of David's seed according to the flesh" was "designated as Son of God by resurrection from the dead," and not *divi filius* (son of the divine one) by virtue of senatorial decree or imperial funeral rite.

In 1 Corinthians 15, it becomes clearer what Paul means by saying the resurrection marked out Jesus as the Son of God. There Paul argues that the risen Christ is a universal paradigmatic figure along the same lines as Adam: just as everyone related to Adam will die, so also everyone related to Christ will be raised (1 Cor. 15:21-22); and when that happens, Paul writes:

> Then comes the end, when he will hand over the kingdom to God the Father, when he will destroy every ruler and every authority and power. For he must rule until he puts all his enemies under his feet. Death is the last enemy to be destroyed. . . . And when all things have been put in submission to him, then the Son himself will submit to the one who put all things in submission to him, in order that God may be all in all. (1 Cor. 15:24-26, 28)

For Paul, only Christ is deserving of the title "Son of God," and this is by virtue of the resurrection from the dead; this must be seen in contrast with the Roman imperial figures who claimed the same title for themselves, on the basis of the apotheosis of their predecessor (which would be established through funeral ceremonies and through public acclaim and Senate decree). Paul's digression here is reminiscent of Daniel 7:2-14, in which the "one like a human being" in Daniel's vision receives from "the Ancient One" the dominion, kingship, and authority that have been taken away from four beasts (which represent four empires).[88] As in Daniel 7, here the Son remains subject to the authority of God the Father. Paul does not allude directly to Daniel but references Psalm 110:1 and Psalm 8:6 as the basis of the idea that the Son will put his enemies under his feet.[89] But his readers would probably also have been familiar with Roman imperial imagery in which emperors were depicted triumphing over conquered peoples, sometimes depicted as women stripped and groveling at their feet.[90] Examples of such depictions have been discovered in the Sebasteion at Aphrodisias, a large sanctuary complex devoted to Aphrodite and the Julio-Claudian emperors. Here in 1 Corinthians, however, "every ruler and every authority and power" would undoubtedly include the current imperial power. The anti-imperial implications of Paul's resurrection theology (and of the Christology he bases on it) are clear.

Beyond influencing Paul's Christology, the resurrection of Christ also provided him with a conceptual basis for thinking about inclusion in the community (Rom. 4:24-25), initiation and identity therein (Rom. 6:1-11; Gal. 2:19b-20), and eschatology (1 Corinthians 15), among other things. In the end, however, Paul referred to the appearance tradition in 1 Corinthians 15 because he believed Christ had appeared to him. Evidently this formative experience, as well as Paul's ongoing experience of Christ as the spiritually present Lord in congregations such as the one in Corinth, shaped the way Paul thought about the nature of resurrection, including "in what sort of bodies" the dead will be raised (1 Cor. 15:35-57).

We cannot be certain why Paul does not affirm or acknowledge the disappearance tradition. As we have seen, even if he had known of a tradition about the resurrection of Jesus out of the grave, he still would have had reasons for not making this part of his argument in 1 Corinthians 15. Paul writes in a number of places about the transformation of normal bodily existence into immortal bodily existence, with the resurrection of Christ being both paradigm and source of this transformation. And yet nowhere does he indicate that his claim that "Christ was raised on the third day in accordance with the Scriptures, and appeared to Cephas" (1 Cor. 15:5) needed a story about an empty tomb as the basis for that conclusion. For the purposes of this study, one important insight we gain from Paul's use of the appearance tradition is that the earliest source of any detail about the resurrection of Jesus, the pre-Pauline formula in 1 Corinthians 15:3b-5 + 7, does not mention the empty tomb at all. This indicates that the appearance tradition originally traveled separately from the disappearance tradition. It is also important to note that when Paul does speak about the appearances of the risen Christ, he does not necessarily have in mind the same kind of physical presence the canonical Gospels emphasize in their narrative descriptions/depictions of the risen Jesus. This much is clear from the way he describes the resurrection body (*pneumatikon*, spiritual, but not "flesh and blood") and the risen Christ (a life-giving *pneuma*).

3. Empty Tombs and Missing Bodies in Antiquity

Now the grave robbers shut the tomb carelessly, since they were hurrying in the night; but Chaereas, after waiting that night till morning, came to the tomb on the pretext of bringing wreaths and libations, but really intending to take his own life there. When he arrived, he found the stones moved away and the entrance open, and seeing this, he was dumbfounded, seized by an anxious fear on account of what had happened. A report of the mystery came quickly to the residents of Syracuse, who all ran together to the tomb; but no one dared go inside until Hermocrates ordered it. The man who was sent inside reported everything accurately: incredibly, the dead girl was not lying there! Then Chaereas himself thought he should go in, wanting to see Callirhoe one more time, even though she was dead; but searching the tomb, he could not find anything either. . . . All kinds of explanations were offered by the crowd, but Chaereas, looking up to heaven and stretching up his hands, said, "Which of the gods has become my rival and carried off Callirhoe and now has her instead of me, against her will but constrained by a better fate? . . . Or did I not know that I had a goddess as a wife, and so her end was to be better than ours? But even so, she should not have left us so swiftly or for such a cause. . . . I will search for you over land and sea, and, if I could, I would even rise up into the air!"

—Chariton, *Chaereas and Callirhoe*, 3.3.1-7

This passage from the novel *Chaereas and Callirhoe*, written by the Greek author Chariton of Aphrodisias sometime in the first half of the first century CE, describes the discovery of an empty tomb and illustrates how such a discovery would be interpreted. Earlier in the novel, the young husband Chaereas flies into a jealous rage and kicks his wife, Callirhoe, and to all indications she dies. She is given a fabulous funeral and is buried with great treasures in a tomb much like the one described in the Gospel narratives. During the night, pirates come to pillage the tomb, and they break in just as Callirhoe revives, for she was not really dead. This is a classic example of the narrative device of apparent death, which, as G. W. Bowersock has remarked, "allows for all the excitement and tragedy of extinction and resurrection without unduly straining the credulity of the reader."[1] The pirates decide to take the girl along with the treasure. When the grief-stricken Chaereas arrives at the tomb, planning to commit suicide, he finds the tomb open and empty.

Had the tomb robbers been more careful about replacing the stones, of course, Chaereas would have carried out his plan and the story could not proceed. As readers of the canonical Gospels know, empty tombs must be seen to be empty (this is why the stone needs to be rolled away: see Matt. 28:2-6). The reader of *Chaereas and Callirhoe* would not confuse Callirhoe's resuscitation with anything like resurrection, so what happens to Callirhoe is not really a fitting parallel to what the Gospels claim happened to Jesus.[2] But Chaereas does not know Callirhoe is alive, so the religious conclusions he draws from the missing body are very important. In fact, Sjef van Tilborg has recently observed that this "is a text which prototypically determines how . . . the disappearance of a body from a grave was interpreted religiously."[3]

The similarities between this story and the empty tomb stories in the canonical Gospels are immediately striking: an early morning visit to the tomb, a stone moved away from the mouth of the tomb, a reaction of fear, a hesitant entry, an unsuccessful search for the body, and a reason given for its absence. It is possible, as some have suggested, that these similarities result from Chariton's awareness of stories or rumors of Jesus' empty tomb, though it is hard to say precisely when Chariton wrote the novel or how far and wide such stories or rumors had circulated by the time he did.[4] Perhaps Justin Martyr (d. c. 165 CE), by the time he wrote his *Dialogue with Trypho*, was acquainted with a rumor that the disciples had stolen the body (*Dial.* 108); but we cannot be certain that Justin was not simply repeating what he learned from Matthew 28:13-15.[5] Matthew 27–28 probably reflects a more local controversy over Jesus' resurrection, rather than a story that could have reached Chariton in Aphrodisias (in Asia Minor) by the time he wrote his novel. In any event, the fact that the stories share narrative devices in common suggests either influence (one way or the other) on the literary level, or that there was a standard way such stories were told in antiquity. But what is more significant than the similarities or their origin is the way that the two missing bodies in the two different stories lead to two different conclusions. In the Gospels, the reader is led to the conclusion that God has raised Jesus from the dead—led, of course, by Jesus' own predictions and by the interpretive help of those encountered at the tomb. In Chariton's novel, the conclusion is "assumption," the bodily removal of a human being (living or dead) directly into the divine realm, as (or at) the end of that person's earthly life.[6]

According to the canonical Gospels, of course, Jesus' body is missing because he has risen from the dead, whereas Chaereas thinks Callirhoe's body has been taken away by the gods.[7] It is interesting that it does not occur to him that she was not really dead but revived while in the tomb, much less that she has risen from the dead. This is not because the idea of resurrection was unknown to Greek readers. In fact, even apart from the "apparent death" motif, there are several instances in Greek literature of dead people becoming alive again, at least in terms of bodily revivification. A noteworthy example is Euripides' story of Alcestis, who is brought back from the dead by Herakles. Plato knew of this story and allowed it as one of only a handful of examples of souls brought back from the dead into living bodies.[8] Stories were also told of corpses being reanimated ("revenants"), but such were more along the lines of "zombies."[9] In the story, Chareas thinks of none of these possibilities, and indeed, the obvious conclusion (that Callirhoe was not really dead but was abducted) does not occur to him, even though the tomb has been emptied not only of the body but also of the treasure. This is a minor glitch in the story, but it illustrates that the more common view was that people whose bodies disappeared were taken away by the gods, rather than walking around alive again on earth. In guessing what had happened to Callirhoe, Chaereas refers to other similar instances either of people who were taken away and made divine, or of gods who appeared as humans and whose sudden removal showed that they were divine (Chariton, *Chaer.* 3.3.4-6).

This story is also very important for another reason, since it helps us see some significant similarities and differences between how Greek people and Jewish people thought about the idea of humans being taken bodily into the divine realm. In the Greek way of thinking, it was possible for a dead person to be taken away by the gods and deified, or made worthy of veneration as a hero.[10] As seen in the previous chapter, most sophisticated Greeks balked at the idea of the baser components of the human person having a share in divinity. For Jews, on the other hand, assumption was considered the way that God rescued certain extraordinarily faithful individuals from experiencing death. Thus it is almost always a living person who is blessed by God in this way, although, possibly under the influence of Greek view, there are a couple of important instances in later Hellenistic Jewish sources where assumption is not an escape from death. As we will see, even in those instances, assumption still signifies an unusual display of divine favor. And whereas Greeks associated divine removal with apotheosis, Jews thought instead that those rescued from death were waiting in heavenly places for their special role in the eschatological drama.[11]

Assumption in the Hebrew Bible, the Ancient Near East, and Early Jewish Apocalypticism

In the genealogy in Genesis 5, Enoch stands out: where all the other ancestors of Noah are said to have died, Genesis 5:24 reads, "Enoch walked with God and then was no more, because God took him" (Heb., *kî-lāqaḥ ʾōtô ʾĕlōhîm*). As Gerhard Lohfink has observed, the Hebrew verb *lqḥ* (take) is standard Hebrew terminology for assumption.[12] On first blush, it seems that Enoch's "walking with God" was the reason for Enoch's assumption. It is hard to see how "walking with God" is a criterion for the special honor of assumption unless it is understood as connoting an extraordinary level of intimacy with God (or with the divine realm and its inhabitants).[13] This elliptical reference to Enoch's assumption is expanded in the Septuagint, which reads instead that "Enoch pleased God, and he was not found, because God transferred him to another place." Here the reason for Enoch's divine removal is clarified: he pleased God. The "not finding" language is typical of Hellenistic references to assumption, though the motif of an unsuccessful search is also present in the biblical story of the assumption of Elijah, the only other character in the Hebrew Bible whose assumption is described (2 Kings 2:1-18).

In comparison with the brief note about Enoch in Genesis 5, the account of Elijah's assumption is a complete story, and it contains many of the elements that were also standard motifs in Hellenistic assumption stories.[14] Elijah knows beforehand that God is going to take him directly into heaven, and Elisha and the company of prophets know as well (see 2 Kings 2:3, 5, 9-10). The assumption itself is accomplished by God by means of a whirlwind, though "the chariots of Israel and its horsemen" are also involved (2:1, 11-12). Because the story is narrated from Elisha's perspective, the removal of Elijah is expressed with "not seeing" language: "when he could no longer see him" (2:12). Finally, even though Elisha is not keen to verify Elijah's removal, the company of prophets searches for him and does not find him (2:16-18). This assumption story gives no hint that Elijah was taken into heaven to be kept for a special eschatological role, but the later text Malachi 4:5-6 indicates that Elijah was expected to return before the Day of the Lord (see also Mark 9:11).

Similar stories about the assumption of notable figures are also found in earlier sources from elsewhere in the ancient Near East. One of the earliest myths about a human being taken into the divine realm is found in the Akkadian story of Adapa (the longest account is dated to the fourteenth century BCE). In this story, Adapa is taken up into heaven by the god Anu and is offered, but refuses, the gift of immortality.[15] In different versions of the Mesopotamian flood story, the protagonist is taken away by the gods and is granted immortality in a distant land. In the Epic of Gilgamesh, Utnapishtim is made to dwell far away, at the mouths of the rivers, and he and his wife are said to become "like unto us gods."[16] In the earlier Sumerian version of the flood story, Ziusudra is given divine life and eternal breath in Dilmun, the land of crossing.[17] A later Hellenistic version of the story, from the "History of Babylonia" of Berossos, has an expanded description:

> When he saw that the boat had run aground on a certain mountain, Xisouthros got out, with his wife and daughter and with the helmsman, and he kissed the ground and dedicated an altar and sacrificed to the gods. Then he and those who had disembarked with him disappeared. Those who had remained on the boat and did not get out with Xisouthros then disembarked and searched for him, calling out for him by name; but Xisouthros himself was no more to be seen by them. Then a voice came from up in the air, commanding that they should honor the gods. For Xisouthros had gone to dwell with the gods on account of his piety; and his wife and daughter and the helmsman had shared in the same honor. (Syncellus, *Ecloga Chronographica* 55)[18]

Several of the motifs here are familiar from the biblical texts about Enoch and Elijah: disappearing (or ceasing to be seen on earth) as a way of describing a removal or translation by a divine agent; an unsuccessful search for the person or their remains; and the sense that assumption is both a mark of divine favor and a mark of a new status from the perspective of those who remain on earth.

In early Jewish apocalyptic literature such as *1 Enoch*, divine favor and new postmundane status—normally a privileged role in the unfolding of the end of the age—are accorded to those whom God takes away. In an important little study, Günter Haufe concluded that "the only way a historical person could receive a special eschatological function is to be received into the heavenly realm by means of a bodily assumption."[19] Thus, if someone was taken away alive into heaven, it was because God's eschatological designs included a special role for that individual, and not (as was the case in other ancient Near Eastern texts and in the Greco-Roman literary tradition) because they had been made like the gods. These figures, according to Haufe, are limited to Enoch, Elijah, Moses, Ezra, and Baruch; other human beings who are accorded a special role in apocalyptic literature or traditions are never identified with specific "historical" individuals and so are not accorded the honor of a bodily removal into the divine realm.[20] The roles imagined for these figures range from seer or witness to exalted heavenly judge.

Malachi 4:5-6, for instance, predicts that Elijah would come as a precursor to the Day of the Lord, in order to turn the hearts of parents to children and the hearts of children to parents; a similar role for Elijah is in view in Sirach 48:9-10, where it is also said that he will "restore the tribes of Judah." These texts are in the background of the idea that according to "the scribes," Elijah must come first (that is, before the Day of the Lord and the resurrection of the dead).[21] Probably the clearest example of an apocalyptic text in which someone is taken up into heaven and exalted and given a special function as judge is found at the conclusion to the Similitudes (or Parables) of Enoch (*1 Enoch* 37–71), a text written "sometime around the turn of the era."[22] In the three Similitudes, which are really a combination of revelatory discourses and apocalyptic vision reports, Enoch sees on a number of occasions an exalted figure who goes by a variety of names, in particular "the Chosen One" and "that Son of Man." This figure "combines the titles, attributes, and functions of the one like a son of man in Daniel 7:13-14, the Servant of the Lord in Second Isaiah, the Davidic Messiah, and pre-existent heavenly Wisdom (Proverbs 8)."[23] This Chosen One, sometimes also called "that Son of Man," is endowed by the "Lord of Spirits" with authority and "the spirit of righteousness," so that he may preside over the eschatological judgment of "the kings and the mighty and the exalted and those who possess the earth" (*1 Enoch* 62:1-2). The kings and mighty ones tremble in fear at the sight of this figure, but the chosen will stand in his presence (62:3-8). However, the narrator describes this Chosen One as one who was hidden, preserved, and finally revealed: "For from the beginning the son of man was hidden, and the Most High preserved him in the presence of his might, and he revealed him to the chosen" (62:7).

This language of preservation suggests that the Chosen One was a human figure who was kept from death by God, perhaps through assumption, and then kept hidden until the time came for his role in the eschatological drama to be played out. Even so, nothing quite prepares the reader of the Similitudes of Enoch for the conclusion of the book, in which it is revealed, once Enoch has made his final journey into the divine presence, that he himself is "that Son of Man." "And that angel came to me and greeted me with his voice and said to me, 'You are that son of man who was born for righteousness, and righteousness dwells on you, and the righteousness of the Head of Days will not forsake you'" (1 Enoch 71:14). As already noted, an earlier passage in the Similitudes describes how the Chosen One (Son of Man) was endowed with righteousness for the task of judgment (62:1-2). Scholars disagree about whether chapter 71 was originally part of the Similitudes or was added later.[24] However, other texts also identify Enoch with the Son of Man, although possibly under the influence of 1 Enoch 71 (3 Enoch; Tg. Ps.-J. Gen. 5:26).

Enochic materials that predate the Similitudes do not focus on his assumption and postearthly career, but mostly on the revelations he received in a series of heavenly journeys during his lifetime. It is impossible to say decisively why this development took place in the Enochic literature, but it probably had something to do with the way he is described in Genesis 5:24: "Enoch walked with God" (as the Hebrew reads), or "Enoch pleased God" (as the Septuagint reads). In the Book of the Watchers (1 Enoch 1–36), for instance, Enoch is commanded to execute judgment on the "Watchers," that is, fallen angels, and he petitions on their behalf (1 Enoch 12–16; see also 87:3-4). These texts show evidence of a belief that after his assumption he would have had a special role as a scribe or recorder of the misdeeds of fallen angels or of humankind. So in the book of Jubilees, a rewriting of Genesis and Exodus from the second century BCE, it is said:

> He was taken from human society, and we led him into the Garden of Eden for (his) greatness and honor. Now he is there writing down the judgment and condemnation of the world and all the wickedness of humankind. Because of him the flood water did not come on any of the land of Eden because he was placed there as a sign and to testify against all people in order to tell all the deeds of history until the day of judgment. (Jub. 4:23-24)[25]

In later apocalyptic writings, this task of seeing and writing revelations concerning the end of the age and concerning the blessings and rewards of humankind was accorded such importance that other scribes to whom apocalyptic writings were attributed (namely, Ezra and Baruch) were also described as being taken into heaven at the end of their lives. With Enoch, a reference to his assumption (Gen. 5:24) led to speculation about the revelations he had received, which came to expression in the Enochic writings; however, with Ezra and Baruch, their scribal role in the biblical tradition gave rise to the literature, which credited them with the special eschatological role of seer and ultimately with the special honor of assumption. In the seventh and final vision in 4 Ezra, a Jewish apocalyptic text from the late first century CE, God tells Ezra to make preparations for the end: "And now I tell you: Store up within your heart the signs that I have shown, the dreams that you have seen, and the interpretations that you have heard, for you shall be taken away from humankind, and you will be changed to reside with my Son and with those who are like you, until the times are completed" (*4 Ezra* 14:7-9).

However, Ezra is also given the task of instructing the people (14:13), and over the course of forty days he writes down all the revelations he had received. These revelations filled ninety-four books, of which seventy remained secret, only for the wise among the people (14:23-26, 37-47). Then, in an ending that does not survive in all versions of the text, Ezra's assumption is described: "At that time Ezra was caught up, and taken to the place of those who are like him, after he had written all these things. And he was called the scribe of the knowledge of the Most High for ever and ever."[26] A similar pattern—prediction of assumption, intermediate period for instruction, assumption—is also evident in material about Enoch and Baruch (*1 Enoch* 81:6 and *2 Bar.* 76:1-5)[27] as well as in Luke-Acts.[28] Despite the description of Moses' death in Deuteronomy 34:1-8, traditions about his assumption were evidently in circulation, as were traditions about his role in the end of the age, although these are not as explicit as those just discussed.[29]

Assumption in Greco-Roman Writings, Hellenistic Judaism, and Early Christianity

There are some significant similarities in language and associated motifs between Greek and Hellenistic Jewish stories about humans being taken bodily into the divine realm. Standard terminology includes "taking up" language (Gk., *analambanō*), "rapture" or "taking away" language (*harpazō*), "translation" or "transferral" language (*metatithēmi*), and "disappearing" (*aphanizō*) or "not seeing/finding" language (*ou* + *horaō* or *heuriskō*); and standard motifs, after the fact, include unsuccessful search for remains, and worship (whether of the person taken away or of God).[30] Many of these features are evident in the above excerpts about Elijah (from 2 Kings 2) and about Xisouthros (from Berossos). But one important point separates Greek and Jewish thinking about assumption, and that had to do with whether a person had to be taken into the divine realm while still alive. According to ancient Greek sources, people could be taken alive into the presence of the gods and sometimes reappeared to confirm their apotheosis, as we saw above in chapter 1.[31] But if a corpse disappeared from a tomb, a bier, or a funeral pyre, this would be interpreted, as in the story about Callirhoe, as proof that the person had been taken bodily (and after his or her death) to the gods.[32] Sometimes such a narrative was meant to explain how a human being had become a god (as with Herakles) or worthy of veneration as a hero (as with Aristeas), or to account for the end of the earthly career of a god who had been sojourning among humans (as was hinted about Romulus).[33] This last idea is found in Josephus, who—writing for a non-Jewish audience—hinted that Moses was taken away by God but sought to conceal this so that it would not be thought that he had "returned to the divinity" (that is, whence he had come).[34] As seen in the citation at the beginning of this chapter, Chaereas concluded from Callirhoe's empty tomb that either (a) she had been taken away by some deity or deities, or (b) she had been a goddess all along and had simply left the earth by disappearing.

A hero cult would be located at a shrine called a *herōon*, typically associated with a grave site thought to contain the hero's remains.[35] However, in narrative sources, the motif of disappearance or assumption was a common way to describe the end of a hero's life, although such an idea would not be integrated into the hero cult.[36] Different ancient sources appear to offer conflicting interpretations of the missing body motif, particularly as to whether a cult was justified if the body had disappeared and there were no remains to situate the hero at the site of his memorial. Lawrence Wills comments, however, that "the variety of reactions to the missing-body problem, then, indicates not a lack of tangible evidence of divinization, but an indeterminacy of status for the hero that is meant to be provocative and suggestive."[37] Often, however, the *anabiōsis*, or return to life, which was always assumed if a hero was thought to have any ongoing influence, was not tied to a removal like this: "Divinization of a dead hero in Greek culture is accomplished by the burial of the body and the ascension of the spirit."[38] In Philostratus's *Heroikos*, however, the process by which Protesilaos received his *anabiōsis* was a secret teaching (*Her.* 58.2).

In any case, the connection in Greek thinking between postmortem disappearance and apotheosis was so strong that there are numerous examples of individuals conspiring before they died to hide their remains in order to promote their postmortem veneration. Arrian, for instance, told about Alexander the Great contriving to effect his own bodily disappearance so that he would thereafter be revered as a god.[39] Examples of the contrived disappearance were well known and numerous, so that Celsus (c. 180 CE), in an interesting turn on the rumor that the disciples of Jesus had stolen the body, could refer to such examples as arguments against the resurrection of Jesus.[40] Sometimes, however, the "logic" of this connection could work in the opposite direction. The Ptolemaic queen Arsinoë II Philadelphos (316–270 or 268 BCE), during her lifetime, was revered with her brother and husband, Ptolemy II Philadelphos (309–246 BCE), as one of the *theoi adelphoi* (sibling gods); but after her death, the poet Callimachus wrote an elegy entitled "The Deification of Arsinoë," which evidently described how she was taken away by the Dioscouroi (the twin gods Castor and Pollux).[41] The text is fragmentary, and no narration of the assumption survives; but the poem does describe the smoke from her funeral pyre, which might be an accommodation of the idea to the Herakles myth. It would seem that her veneration as a god during her lifetime led to the idea that she had been taken away by the gods at or after her death.[42]

Even under the influence of Hellenism, Jewish writers continued to think of assumption as an escape from death, although sometimes they made use of assumption language and associated ideas to talk about someone who had died, thinking of an assumption not of the body but of the soul. This understanding of apotheosis had become fairly standard in Greco-Roman thought, especially since it did not conflict with more elevated anthropologies. More commonly, as seen in the previous chapter, apotheosis was thought to coincide with the dissolution of the physical body, rather than with its removal into the divine realm. About Enoch, for instance, Philo of Alexandria wrote: "When he was sought, he was invisible, not merely rapt from their eyes. . . . He is said (to have moved) from a sensible and visible place to an incorporeal and intelligible form" (*Quaest. in Gen.* 1.86).[43] This is an elevation to another plane of existence, but one outside the body. What Philo said about the end of Moses clarifies this somewhat: "The Father transposed entirely his natural dyad of body and soul into a single reconstituted nature, into mind, just like the sun" (*Mos.* 2.288). As we saw in the previous chapter, Plutarch wrote that the soul, and only the soul, ascends to the divine realm because inherently it belongs there. Of course, Plutarch represents a host of Greek writers who thought that it was "natural" (Gk., *kata phusin*) for the soul to ascend to a higher plane of existence after death frees it from the body, because of its immortality.[44] Some authors reconciled older stories about "disappearance" with this anthropology by claiming that the soul had shed the body, or that the body had melted away.

The idea of the assumption of the soul developed from this anthropology. As Lohfink noted, the apotheosis of the Roman emperor was reinterpreted as an assumption of the soul, even though it was originally patterned after the assumption of Romulus and according to some sources incorporated a manufactured "disappearance" in the funeral ceremony (the wax effigy of the emperor would melt on the pyre).[45] Hellenistic Jewish writers took over this view of the entrance into the afterlife and applied it to notable figures. Arie Zwiep explains that a "crude cosmology" underlies belief in assumption, and "the more refined 'assumption of the soul' lent itself much more to integration into the OT-Jewish context of belief."[46] Texts that describe assumptions of the soul characteristically use variations on the "taking up" language but not disappearance language, since the body of the person does not disappear from the mortal realm. Abraham's soul was taken up in this way, according to the *Testament of Abraham*, a text that survives in heavily Christianized forms.[47]

> And immediately Michael the archangel stood alongside him with a multitude of angels, and they took up his precious soul in their hands, in a divinely woven linen; and they attended to the body of the upright Abraham with divine ointments and spices until the third day after his death, and then they buried it in the promised land, at the Oak of Mamre; but the angels escorted his precious soul in a procession, going up into heaven singing the thrice-holy hymn to God, the ruler of all, and they set [Abraham's soul] there for the worship of the God and Father. (*T. Abr.* [Longer Recension] 20:10-12)[48]

Notice that the body is buried but the soul is escorted by angels into heaven. Similar stories are also told about Adam, Moses, and Job.[49]

Something different from soul assumption is found in Wisdom of Solomon 2–5. Language drawn from Genesis 5:24 LXX, about how Enoch pleased God and then was taken away, is applied in Wisdom 4:10-15 to a paradigmatic "Righteous One" who dies an unjust death. This almost euphemistic use of assumption language—similar to the way English speakers today sometimes talk about someone being "taken" to describe a sudden or unexpected death—draws on language and ideas found in Greek consolation literature and epitaphs.[50] In those sources, assumption language is often used to express the grief of parents at the untimely death of a child. Sometimes the early death is rationalized in terms of a malevolent deity stealing the child. For instance, in the following epitaph, Hades is accused of undue haste and of robbing the parents of their child: "Insatiable Hades, why did you snatch away my child so suddenly? Why did you hasten? Do we not all belong to you?" (Rome, second or third century CE).[51] And yet early death was often seen as an indication of divine favor, as in the following epitaph:

> Fifteen years old, you were snatched away by the cruel thread of the Fates,
> Attalos, the delight of your most noble mother, Tyche;
> You practiced wisdom and . . . into all good things,
> Attalos, your life was well-blessed by Fate.
> Do not be overly sorrowful: for though you are young, as some say,
> If one is friend to the gods, he has a swift death. (Gythium, c. 75 BCE)[52]

This use of assumption language may be behind Callimachus's poem about Arsinoë, which refers to the queen as "stolen by the gods," and whose fragmentary conclusion runs somewhat as follows: "intense lamentations . . . this single voice . . . [our] Queen, departed."[53] This is exactly the sense in which assumption language is used of the Righteous One in Wisdom 4. "He became well pleasing to God, and was beloved by him, and while living among sinners, he was taken up; he was snatched away so that evil would not alter his understanding, or deceit lead his soul astray" (Wisd. 4:10-11). The untimely death of the Righteous One is interpreted as a kind of "taking away," just as in the Greek consolation literature and in the epitaphs cited above. Note also that his early death is considered God's rescue of his soul from sin and deceit. What is striking about this text from Wisdom of Solomon is that the idea of heavenly exaltation or eschatological function, typical in the Jewish tradition but not found in Greek consolation materials, is retained. For in what seems to be a postmortem judgment scene, the wicked who condemned the Righteous One to an unjust death (Wisd. 2:12-20) see him standing with great confidence: they are amazed at his salvation and repent of their misdeeds (4:16-20; 5:1-13).

One extraordinary example of postmortem assumption is found in the *Testament of Job*. In this writing, assumption language is used to explain what happened to the bones of Job's dead children—and so it describes their physical removal by God after death. Sitidos, Job's wife, implores Eliphas to search through the ruins of their house in order to recover the children's bones (*T. Job* 39:8-11). Job recalls:

And they went off to dig, but I stopped them, saying, "Do not fatigue yourselves without a cause; for you will not find my children, because they were taken up into heaven by the Creator, their King." So they answered me again and said, "Who would not say that you have lost your mind and are raving mad, because you say, 'My children were taken up into heaven'? So make the truth known to us." . . . And after a prayer I said to them, "Look up with your eyes to the east, and behold my children crowned with the glory of the heavenly one." And when Sitidos my wife saw them, she fell down on the ground worshipping and she said, "Now I know that the Lord has remembered me." (*T. Job* 39:11-13; 40:3-4a)

This text contains standard "taking up" language, the unsuccessful search motif (which, importantly, indicates that this is not a soul assumption), the worship of God, and, interestingly, a claim about the heavenly exaltation of the dead children. This text also shows that the influence of the Greek stories of divine removal on Jewish writers was not limited to narrative or linguistic or stylistic features, but extended even (at least in this exceptional case) to the basic question of whether assumption had to be an escape from death.[54] It also raises the possibility that Jewish followers of Jesus could have interpreted stories or rumors about his empty tomb along the lines of assumption rather than resurrection. As Arie Zwiep says, "Any serious rapture claim would need an empty tomb or at least the absence of a corpse."[55]

The early followers of Jesus were, of course, recipients of this rich religious tradition. One illustrative text is the story of Jesus' transfiguration (Mark 9:2-8 and parallels), already discussed briefly in an earlier chapter. Although this story is sometimes considered a displaced resurrection appearance,[56] it is worth considering here because of what it seems to convey theologically not about Jesus, but about Moses and Elijah. They were able to appear because they were thought to have been taken up into heaven, as discussed above.[57] Their disappearance, in addition, is narrated using standard motifs of assumption stories: the obscuring cloud (Mark 9:7 and parallels) and "not seeing" language (Mark 9:8; Matt. 17:8). In Mark they seem to appear as heavenly witnesses to the eschatological character of Jesus' earthly ministry, but in Revelation they are (evidently) the two witnesses who prophesy against the Beast and who are slain by him only to be raised from the dead and taken back into heaven (Rev. 11:3-13).[58] In *Christ's Descent into Hell*, an appendix to the *Acts of Pilate* dating probably to the fifth century, this passage from Revelation is revisited, except that here the two witnesses are not Moses and Elijah, but Enoch and Elijah.

Thus [Christ] went into Paradise holding our forefather Adam by the hand, and he handed him over and all the righteous to Michael the archangel. And as they were entering the gate of Paradise, two old men met them. The holy fathers asked them: "Who are you, who have not seen death nor gone down into Hades, but dwell in Paradise with your bodies and souls? One of them answered, "I am Enoch, who pleased God and was removed here by him; and this is Elijah the Tishbite. We shall live until the end of the world, but then we shall be sent by God to withstand the Antichrist and to be killed by him. And after three days we shall rise again and be caught up in clouds to meet the Lord." (*Acts Pil.* 25)[59]

What is remarkable about this late text is how consistent the idea of assumption has remained even to this point in the development of Christian legend: Enoch and Elijah were removed by God and preserved body and soul in Paradise for their role in the battle against Antichrist.

Other late traditions could also be mentioned,[60] but the most important assumption story in the early Christian writings is, of course, the story of Jesus' ascension, found only in Luke-Acts (Luke 24:50-53; Acts 1:6-11). As Lohfink showed, Luke's stories of Jesus' ascension into heaven were patterned after Hellenistic assumption stories, and so they contain the typical motifs and language discussed above.[61] Most scholars agree with this form-critical assessment, though some differ on the extent to which Luke was influenced by Greek stories (rather than by Jewish ones).[62] Another point on which opinions diverge is the origin of the ascension story: is it traditional or was it composed by Luke?[63] Whatever its origin, the combination of two different and distinct categories—resurrection and assumption—is evidently new (although Mark had already combined them).[64] This amalgamation indicates that the two categories were different enough from one another in Luke's view that they could be combined and still be distinct, although, obviously, the combination means Luke thought them to be compatible or at least reconcilable. This is different from the way that Mark 16 depicts the resurrection of Jesus as an assumption into the heavenly realm, an idea that is also reflected somewhat in Matthew's empty tomb story. The ascension of the risen Jesus is clearly of great importance to Luke's narrative theological framework: it is on the Gospel's narrative horizon already at Luke 9:51, it forms the Gospel's climax, and it has a prominent place at the beginning of his second volume.

What is less clear is what the ascension of Jesus signified for Luke. Perhaps it narrativizes the exaltation of Jesus to the right hand of God, as the longer ending of Mark (Ps.-Mark 16:19) suggests.[65] However, certain (admittedly difficult) texts in Luke-Acts (especially Luke 24:26; Acts 2:32-36; 5:30-31) might prohibit that reading.[66] Zwiep argues that, for Luke, the resurrection already implies Jesus' exaltation, and the addition of an assumption story expresses, quite in line with Jewish tradition, the conviction that Jesus was, like Enoch, Elijah, and Moses, being kept in heaven until the end of the age.[67] What is important to note is that Luke, whether the recipient of a tradition about Jesus' ascension or its originator, evidently thought that "resurrection" and "assumption" were sufficiently different from one another, expressing sufficiently different christological ideas, and regarded both categories as indispensable to his christological purposes. Of course, Luke did not think resurrection and assumption were at odds with each other, or else he would not have let both stand in his work; however, the assumption of Jesus in Luke-Acts is something of an anomaly in comparison with other instances in Greco-Roman or Jewish sources, for here someone is raised from the dead and then is taken up into heaven. The bodily aspect of assumption is also very important for Luke, who elsewhere stresses the straightforward corporeality of the appearances of the risen Jesus (Luke 24:12, 36-43). The ascension is one way that Luke can affirm that Jesus' ongoing existence is not in a purely "spiritual" mode and can indicate that this kind of physical postresurrection presence is only temporary.[68]

Other instances of assumption legends in early Christian writings do not add much to the picture, but two interesting examples of postmortem disappearance from extracanonical materials are worth mentioning. First, in the text known as the *Infancy Gospel of James* (late second century CE),[69] Zechariah, the father of John the Baptist (as in Luke 1), is murdered by henchmen of Herod during the violence that ensues after the departure of the wise men (as in Matt. 2:13-18). They approach him in the temple while he is performing his duties, demanding to know where he has hidden John, for Herod suspects John might be the Messiah (*Prot. Jac.* 23:1-6). When threatened by Herod's servants, Zechariah replies, "I am God's martyr. You may have my blood, but the Lord will receive my spirit, because you are shedding innocent blood in the forecourt of the sanctuary of the Lord" (23:7). When Zechariah fails to appear, one of the priests goes in to investigate, finding dried blood by the altar and hearing a voice that says that Zechariah has been murdered and will be avenged. Then the others go in to see:

> And gathering up their courage, they went in and saw what had happened. And the ornamented panel on the ceiling of the sanctuary cried out, and the priests tore [their robes] from top to bottom. And although they did not find his corpse, they did find his blood, which had been turned to stone. Greatly afraid, they went out and they told the people that Zechariah had been murdered. (24:7-10)

This story may have been generated by confusion about which Zechariah was murdered in the sanctuary. Matthew 23:34-36 and Luke 11:49-51, sayings derived from Q, refer to the murder of the prophet Zechariah in 2 Chronicles 24:20-22, and also reference innocent blood. The "not finding" language in *Infancy James* is reminiscent of 2 Kings 2 and of other assumption stories, so the disappearance of the corpse is not to be explained by supposing that the murderers had disposed of the body secretly.[70] An explanation of this disappearance is given in the *Apocalypse of Paul* (late fourth century CE). Paul meets John, Zechariah, and Abel (who is paired with Zechariah in the Q saying). Zechariah says to Paul, "I am he whom they killed while I was presenting the offering to God; and when the angels came for the offering, they carried my body up to God, and no one found where my body was taken" (*Apoc. Paul* 51).[71] In these traditions, the postmortem disappearance of the body is the divine corrective for the injustice of Zechariah's murder, particularly because Jesus himself mentions the killing as an act that represents paradigmatically the rejection of God's emissaries (Matt. 23:34-35; Luke 11:49-51).

Second, stories about the end of Mary the mother of Jesus use the standard language and motifs of assumption. The manuscript evidence for the Assumption or Dormition of Mary dates from the fifth century CE, but Stephen Shoemaker suggests that the earliest form of the story could go back to the third century.[72] It appears that the concern was not only to tell stories that legitimated the increasing veneration of Mary, but also to answer a theological problem: what fate is appropriate to the body that bore God? The physical body of the *Theotokos* could in no way suffer the dishonor of decay in the tomb, so stories were generated about her bodily assumption into heaven. In this way, the assumption of Mary is more a rescue from the after-effects of death than from death itself. In the words of Theoteknos of Livias (probably early seventh century CE):

> Even though the God-bearing body of that holy one did taste death, it was not corrupted; for it was kept incorrupt and free of decay, and it was lifted up to heaven with her pure and spotless soul by the holy archangels and powers; there it remains, exalted above Enoch and Elijah and all the prophets and apostles, above all the heavens, below God alone—who has been pleased to arrange all things for our salvation.[73]

The stories about Mary's assumption diverge greatly in the details, but typically, as in this excerpt, her death is not denied; instead, the stories sometimes combine two devices that in the earlier Jewish and Christian literary tradition were kept strictly separate. There are narratives that describe as separate events both (1) the assumption of Mary's soul, often escorted by the exalted Christ or by Michael, into heaven, and (2) the assumption of her body, which is sometimes narrated as a disappearance of her body from the tomb. The above excerpt hints at both these ideas: "It was lifted up to heaven with her pure and spotless soul." In this homily and in many other sources, the biblical characters of Enoch and Elijah are frequently mentioned as being of lesser honor than Mary; this shows that those who thought about the end of Mary in these ways did not consider their ideas about the postmortem disappearance of her body (and the assumption of her soul) to be completely in keeping with traditional ideas about assumption.[74] The combination of these two categories gave rise to another narrative development: the reunion of Mary's body and soul in heaven, which is already found in the earliest recoverable narrative about the assumption of Mary (Ethiopic *Liber Requiei* 89).[75] The assumption of the soul and the postmortem bodily disappearance in these traditions seem to carry the idea of exaltation or apotheosis, which was prevalent in older assumption stories and traditions; but the notion of rescuing a body from decay because of its dignity is something of a new development.[76]

Interpreting Empty Tombs and Missing Bodies

Most of the materials we have been considering in this chapter run against the grain of the way ancients usually thought about the afterlife: normally it was considered to have more to do with the soul than the body. As we have seen, Plutarch represents the sophisticated person who could not see how or why anyone would think that the body would have any share in the divinity. But according to popular belief, at least, there were some exceptions to the rule that when life continued after death, it continued apart from the body. One way that life could continue in the body for some individuals was assumption, an idea quite distinct from resurrection even in the early Jewish and Christian writings. Importantly, in all the Jewish and Christian texts in which a body disappears, resurrection language is never used to describe what "happened" to the person—except in the Gospel stories about the empty tomb of Jesus.

Four implications of this discussion should by now be clear. First, a missing body was far more likely to be interpreted as an instance of assumption (removal by divine agent) than an instance of resurrection or resuscitation. In general, assumption was a special divine blessing bestowed upon individuals, and resurrection in Jewish thought was normally considered to be a corporate eschatological phenomenon by which the people of God would be reconstituted. In Greek thought resurrection was not entirely unknown, although it was not expressed in the same linguistic or theological terms as in Jewish literature. The more common ideas were apotheosis (which often was associated with assumption) and *anabiōsis*, the restoration to life necessary for a hero's ongoing influence (which usually was not associated with assumption). Second, even though the tendency in the Jewish tradition was to think of assumption as an escape from death (as opposed to something that could happen after or at the point of death), certain texts display an interest in applying assumption language and associated motifs (especially divine favor and exaltation or eschatological function) to people who clearly had died. This development is evident in Jewish literature from around the turn of the era. Third, in both Greek and Jewish thought, assumption was reserved for special cases and so was associated with ideas such as divine favor and/or apotheosis (in the Greek tradition) or divine favor and/or special eschatological function (in the Jewish tradition). This also applies to the motif of the assumption of the soul, which in Jewish texts is reserved only for figures like Abraham and Moses. Fourth, as we saw in the previous chapter on Paul, the earliest resurrection tradition focused on the appearances of Jesus and did not mention at all the disappearance of Jesus' body from the tomb. If, as appears to be the case from the Jerusalem Lament saying (Q 13:34-35), some early followers of Jesus were thinking about his end in terms of assumption and eschatological function, then the focus was not on Jesus' appearances (as signifying that he was raised from the dead), but on his disappearance (as signifying that he was exalted to heaven to await his role as the Son of Man).

4. The Sayings Gospel Q:
"You Will Not See Me"

"Jerusalem, Jerusalem, who kills the prophets and stones those sent to her—how often did I desire to gather your children, like a hen gathers her nestlings under her wings, but you did not desire that. Behold, your house is forsaken. [And] I tell you, you will not see me until [the time comes when] you say, 'Blessed is the Coming One in the name of the Lord!'"

—Q 13:34-35[1]

Biblical scholars call the ancient collection of Jesus' sayings that was used by the authors of Matthew and Luke "the Sayings Source Q" (from the German word for "source," *Quelle*), or now sometimes "the Sayings *Gospel* Q." Q is part of the Two Document Hypothesis: certain features of the Synoptic Gospels (Matthew, Mark, and Luke), especially the patterns of agreement and disagreement in the wording and ordering of various episodes, have led a majority of scholars to conclude (1) that Mark wrote first and was used by Matthew and Luke as the major source for their narratives about Jesus, and (2) that the best explanation for the sayings material Matthew and Luke have in common (but did not get from Mark) is that they used a common documentary source (that is, an actual text) that is now lost.[2] Although there is still some debate on this point, in this book I take for granted that Q was an actual document, one that scholars today have "reconstructed" from Matthew and Luke and analyzed as to its contents, outlook, theology, even its compositional history.[3] As for its current designation as "gospel" among scholars of Christian origins, John Kloppenborg points out that although the word *gospel* (*euaggelion*) was not used for a literary genre in the first century, it was used to describe "a message of the decisive transformation of human life." In this sense, Q is "every bit as much a gospel" as the proclamation of Paul or the canonical Gospels.[4]

The genre of Q has proved to be an important question for understanding this text, and it is particularly significant for our study. As a collection of sayings, it has a number of analogues in ancient literature across many cultures, and these vary greatly in both form and content. But this is not to say enough about

Q, because identifying genre "is of fundamental importance in evaluating what kind of discourse Q represents."[5] Kloppenborg has argued at length that Q shares various rhetorical and generic features with both instructional collections and *chreiae* collections (a *chreia* is a short anecdote about a particular speaker, which could be rhetorically elaborated in order to develop its sense).[6] Migako Sato, on the other hand, has argued that Q is more like a book of one of the prophets, mainly because some sayings are cast as divine revelation and because Q contains different kinds of prophetic discourse (including oracles, woes, and the like).[7] The contents of Q can be rather simplistically divided into either wisdom instruction or apocalyptic/prophetic speech, but taking either as of more fundamental influence in the composition of the text does not necessarily mean that "sapiential" and "apocalyptic" materials do not *belong together.*[8] In any event, in a sayings collection such as Q, the death of the speaker is not necessarily going to be an issue, because the sayings validate themselves for the reader/hearer—they are valuable on their own terms, whether as revelatory speech, wisdom instruction, or what have you.

We would not expect Q as a "sayings collection" to include narrative material about the death and resurrection of Jesus. It does not, although some parts of Q are narrative,[9] and some of the sayings have a basic narrative framework.[10] On the other hand, the canonical Gospels contain sayings, outside of the passion narratives, about opposition to Jesus' ministry and about his death and resurrection. Three times in Mark (Mark 8:31-33; 9:31-32; 10:32-34) Jesus predicts his rejection, death, and resurrection, and the author of Mark uses these three predictions not only to foreshadow the passion narrative, but also to gather together material about how discipleship and rejection/persecution are related (see, e.g., Mark 8:31-33 and 8:34–9:1; note how prominently "leading" and "following" figure in Mark 10:32-34). The passion predictions, as they are called, are also found in Matthew and Luke, and other sayings in the Synoptics similarly look ahead to the death of Jesus and his resurrection.[11] We might expect comparable sayings in Q, since there is material in Q about opposition and faithful discipleship (e.g., Q 6:22-23), but there is no saying that makes the death and resurrection of Jesus explicit.

Instead, what we find in Q is material about how faithful prophets and emissaries of God are treated by God's people, and also about the sort of vindication they might hope for, but none of this is expressed in Q in an individualized way about Jesus, at least not overtly. So nowhere in Q is Jesus' death even mentioned, much less his resurrection; this has led some scholars to conclude that the people who composed and used Q did not consider these issues important.[12] Yet, as we will see, Q does contain material that implies not only a knowledge of Jesus' death, but even the sense that it formed a paradigmatic case of faithfulness in the face of rejection and persecution. Q also contains several sayings that speak of "the Son of Man," who in some ways is both a heavenly and an eschatological figure, and whose coming would occasion judgment. "Son of Man" is also the characteristic way Jesus refers to himself, often without any particular emphasis on any extraordinary role or status—so the reader of Q is invited to identify the

Jesus who speaks with the Son of Man who would come. This raises the question of how, in the theology of Q, the Jesus who is rejected and dies is to be identified as the Son of Man, or—in John the Baptist's terminology—the "Coming One."

Some scholars have proposed that there is a hint of an answer in Q 13:34-35, the Jerusalem Lament, which ends with a very cryptic remark: "You will not see me until you say, 'Blessed is the one who comes in the name of the Lord'" (v. 35).[13] In Luke 13:34-35, Jesus says this on his way to Jerusalem (see Luke 9:51), and this foreshadows for Luke's readers Jesus riding on the donkey's colt into Jerusalem, where the crowd acclaims Jesus with the same words from Psalm 118 (Luke 19:38). This is exactly what the author of Luke wanted to convey. When Jesus finally does arrive in Jerusalem in Luke, the reader is not misled by this "triumphal entry," for Jesus' rejection is still on the horizon: "It is unthinkable for a prophet to die outside of Jerusalem" (Luke 13:33, a saying found only in Luke). However, material from Q needs to be read in terms of its own context, at least as far as that can be reconstructed, and the entry into Jerusalem is not part of Q. Matthew places the Jerusalem Lament, in fact, after Jesus has already entered Jerusalem (Matt. 23:37-39), so that when Jesus says, "You will not see me until you say, 'Blessed is the Coming One in the name of the Lord,'" the reader has to conclude that Jesus in Matthew has the parousia in mind, not the "triumphal entry."[14]

This line looked ahead to the future "being seen" of the Coming One in its original Q context as well. As Dieter Zeller has observed, the language of "not seeing" in close connection with an eschatological prediction suggests that this cryptic remark is really a prediction of Jesus' assumption.[15] As discussed in the previous chapter, the divine removal of an individual from earth to the divine realm was often expressed using disappearance or not seeing/finding language (as, e.g., in the stories about Elijah and Xisouthros). In addition, we would expect that Jewish followers of Jesus who thought about his end in this way would more likely think of his "exaltation" in the sense of being reserved in heaven for a special eschatological role, rather than the occasion of his apotheosis, although this perhaps is not to be ruled out entirely. There is, as we will see, other evidence from Q that substantiates this reading of the Jerusalem Lament. Not only that, but the earliest version of the empty tomb story could also point to the view that Jesus had been taken away by God, rather than the view that he had been raised from the dead and was alive again on earth outside the tomb. Assumption, as the previous chapter showed, was the more common religious interpretation given to an empty tomb or a missing body. This view of removal-parousia stands in marked contrast with the resurrection-appearance schema that was foundational for Paul.

This raises a number of important questions. First, what does the disappearance of Jesus in Q 13:34-35 signify, and can it be seen as a christological answer to the problem of Jesus' death? Second, where would this idea of Jesus' assumption have come from? Was Q 13:34-35 attributed to Jesus by members of the movement who wanted to express the conviction that Jesus was exalted in heaven and would return someday? Or did some of Jesus' followers conclude for other reasons that Jesus had been taken up into heaven, and only then begin to explore the theological implications? Third, how different is the idea of "assumption" from the idea of "resurrection"? Is it possible that the people who composed and used Q thought about Jesus' vindication in both ways?

The Trouble with Q

A more fundamental question needs to be explored first, however: what use is Q in reconstructions of Christian origins? Most biblical scholars agree that the so-called Two Document Hypothesis—the theory (described above) that Matthew and Luke composed their Gospels using Mark and Q as their two source texts—is the best solution to the Synoptic Problem, but even among those scholars there is wide disagreement as to what to do with Q. How much can we infer from Q, as far as it can be reconstructed from Matthew and Luke, about its genre, composition, or social setting, given that it is a "document" reconstructed on the basis of a hypothesis? This is an important question for the present investigation, especially when it comes to two issues: the original extent of Q (what it contained versus what it did not), and the original function of Q (how it was used or regarded by the people who put it together).[16]

If we seriously consider Q as a part of a solution to the problem of the Synoptics' composition, then within the scope of the Two Document Hypothesis, the contents, history of composition, genre and function, theology, and social setting of the Q document are all fair topics for investigation. Taking this approach means that Q is not just a cipher in an equation, like x in algebra. Not all proponents of the Two Document Hypothesis agree: some are skeptical about Q altogether, while others hesitate because Q is "hypothetical."[17] Even Q scholars differ on how far to go down the road of Q.[18] Granted, caution is always required, given that the reconstructed Q is not as verifiably certain in terms of its contents as, for instance, Mark—but even Mark, because of text-critical problems, is still a reconstructed text, even if the reconstruction is not of the same order as Q.[19] It cannot be determined with certainty, for instance, whether Matthew and Luke had different versions of Q (or Mark!), or whether material unique to either Matthew or Luke could have been originally present in Q and omitted by one of the evangelists but not both. On these finer points there is room for debate, but Matthew and Luke have enough Q material in common to provide a sufficiently clear "base text." Given such a reconstructed Q—given, that is, what can be determined with a measure of certainty about the document's contents and genre—it should be fair to ask, next, the significance of both the presence of certain kinds of material and the absence of other kinds of material, as we have had to do with Paul.[20] As things stand, a reconstructed "minimal Q" should be sufficient to establish its theology both on the grounds of what it does contain and on the grounds of what it might reasonably have been expected to contain but does not.[21] Kloppenborg is right to observe that "Q does not offer a complete catalogue of the Q group's beliefs." Yet what Q does contain must be deemed significant, and what it does not contain cannot be taken for granted.[22]

More to the point is what to do with the theology of a "base text" of Q once those views have been delineated. When it comes to the Pauline letter corpus or Luke-Acts, for example, scholars suppose that they have a good idea of the authors' theological views, and tend to be skeptical of attempts to assign to those authors theological views they do not express or appear to take for granted. This is the case even though our descriptions of the theology of Paul or of Luke are necessarily limited by the kinds of literature they wrote, and by what has survived of their writings. Similarly with Q, we can reconstruct its characteristic theology by examining its contents, even if we cannot be absolutely sure that those who put Q together did not hold other views not expressed in the Q material.[23] As already noted, many Q scholars are willing to call Q a "gospel," thinking that in some way it guided or even encapsulated the theological views of those who composed and used it.[24] But we should be careful not to assume too much (one way or the other) on the basis of what is not in Q. For Q is silent on matters of great importance to how its place within the early Christian movements is to be determined. This is especially true with regard to particular interpretations of the death of Jesus or conceptions of his postmortem vindication and ongoing or future significance.[25]

The silence of Q on these matters has been viewed in several ways since Q came to be viewed as a document worthy of study in its own right.[26] A standard view for a long time was that Q was intended as a supplement to the basic kerygma about the death and resurrection of Jesus (as encapsulated, for instance, in the pre-Pauline formula used in 1 Cor. 15:3-5 + 7). On this view, Q was a collection of Jesus' ethical and missional instructions, meant for Christian groups who already "knew the story of the Cross by heart."[27] This view met with resistance after the work of Heinz Eduard Tödt, who argued that Q was not meant to supplement a kerygmatic Christianity, but originated in a "second sphere" of Christianity that did not proclaim Jesus' death and resurrection but reproclaimed his proclamation; this explains Q's silence on these topics.[28] While most advocates of Q would agree with Tödt's conclusion, many would hesitate to assume, as he did, that it was ultimately their belief in Jesus' resurrection that validated his sayings for the Q people.[29] In a slightly different take on the question, James Robinson argued that the self-evident validity of the sayings of Jesus in Q was evidence of an Easter moment, as it were.[30] To be sure, the weight of Jesus' sayings in Q—that is, they are not only instruction or ethical teaching, but words to live by in view of the coming eschatological judgment—need not presuppose any kind of elevated and/or apocalyptic Christology, just as the book of Isaiah did not need to claim any such thing for the prophet; but thinking of Jesus as apocalyptic Son of Man must, particularly if Q shows evidence that its compiler(s) knew how Jesus died.[31] As we will see, in some sayings, Q does represent such a view of Jesus, but not on the basis of a belief in his resurrection (per se).

Q and the Postmortem Vindication of Jesus

Although Q does not contain any specific references to the death of Jesus, much less a passion narrative, ignorance of his death on the part of those who wrote and used Q would be difficult to argue. It is scarcely possible to begin with that people who collected and organized sayings of Jesus into a document did not know that the Romans crucified him in Jerusalem.[32] Given this opening supposition, certain sayings included in Q must reflect knowledge of the fact and means of Jesus' death. An obvious example is Q 14:27, which connects cross and discipleship: "Whoever does not take their cross and follow me cannot be my disciple."[33] Although some prefer to see here a reference to violent opposition that need not indicate a knowledge of Jesus' death,[34] ancient conceptions of discipleship typically imply imitation, so in the Cross saying Jesus sets the pattern as one who takes up his own cross.[35] This saying also, therefore, connotes a basic martyrological interpretation of Jesus' death: the one who dies the noble death sets the pattern for those who follow. Beyond this basic view of Jesus as "martyr" (testimony or pattern), however, the Q Cross saying does not suggest a salvific or sacrificial understanding of Jesus' death, as for instance Mark 10:45 does.

Other passages in Q make a similar connection between following Jesus and rejection and violence, but with reference to the suffering of prophets. Q 6:22-23, one of the Beatitudes, is a pronouncement of blessing on those who suffer for allegiance to the Son of Man:

> Blessed are you when they insult you and [persecute] you and speak evil against you for the sake of the Son of Man. Rejoice and be glad, for your reward is great in heaven. For in this way they [persecuted] the prophets who were before you. (Q 6:22-23)

The same idea of suffering for the sake of the Son of Man is also implied in Q 12:8-9, and a little later, in Q 12:11-12, examination in a synagogue context is in view:

> Whoever confesses me before human beings the Son of Man will also confess before the angels; but whoever denies me before human beings will be denied before the angels. . . . Whenever they bring you into the synagogues, do not worry how or what you should say: for [the Holy Spirit will teach] you in that hour what you should say. (Q 12:8-9, 11-12)

Neither of these passages needs to presuppose the death of Jesus, but they do suggest that persecution is to be expected in return for allegiance to Jesus. The reference to the prophets in Q 6:23 is especially important, for it is typical of Q's approach to persecution generally.

The following sayings cluster, from the Woes in Q 11, displays a "deuteronomistic" interpretation of persecution: that is, prophets and righteous ones typically suffer at the hands of God's people to whom they are sent.

> Woe to you, because you build the tombs of the prophets, though your ancestors killed them. . . . You witness [against yourselves] that you are [children] of your ancestors.[36] Therefore also Wisdom said: I will send them prophets and

sages, and some of them they will kill and persecute, so that the blood of all the prophets that has been poured out from the foundation of the world will be required from this generation, from the blood of Abel to the blood of Zechariah who was murdered between the altar and the house. Yes, I tell you, it will be required from this generation! (Q 11:47-51)

What is important here is not so much that Q shows evidence of this view of history, for it is also found frequently in Jewish literature (see, e.g., Neh. 9:26) and appears also in the letters of Paul (see 1 Thess. 2:15-16, which may in fact be an interpolation). It was common, in fact, to predict (or rather, to see in retrospect) that this characteristic treatment of prophets would lead (had led) to the misfortunes or even downfall of God's people. This is clearest in 2 Chronicles 24, where the defeat of Joash, king of Judah, by the Aramites is interpreted as a direct result of the rejection and murder of Zechariah, son of Jehoiada the priest, who is alluded to in the saying above (Q 11:51).[37] Importantly, Q interprets "the rejection of its own messengers as in a line of continuity with the rejected prophets of the deuteronomistic tradition and with the figure of rejected Wisdom."[38]

Thus, according to Q, "this generation" will be held accountable for the blood of the rejected prophets through history; and "this generation" is also chastised for its rejection of two heroes more recent than Abel or Zechariah, namely, John and Jesus.

To what should I compare this generation, and what is it like? It is like children seated in the marketplace, who call to others and say, "We played the flute for you, and you did not dance; we wailed, but you would not weep." For John came, neither eating nor drinking, and you say, "He has a demon." The Son of Man came, eating and drinking, and you say, "Behold, a glutton and a drunk, a friend of tax-gatherers and sinners." But Wisdom has been vindicated by her children. (Q 7:31-35)

John and Jesus are depicted as "children of Wisdom," and "this generation" (also held accountable in Q 11:49-51) is berated for speaking ill of them and rejecting them. The name-calling (demoniac, glutton, and drunk) effectively places John and Jesus outside of the people of God. As Dale Allison notes, Q 7:34 recalls Deuteronomy 21:20, which stipulates that a rebellious son, a glutton and a drunk, must be taken outside the city and stoned, so that evil would be purged from the people.[39] This, as another Q saying declares, is the fate of those who in fact were sent to the people as prophets and emissaries of God (Q 13:34). These "children," most prominently John and Jesus, would vindicate Wisdom in her commissioning of them.

Q interprets not only persecution in general, but also Jesus' death in particular, within this deuteronomistic framework—although it should be noted that the Cross saying (Q 14:27) is not influenced by the deuteronomistic view.[40] The first half of the Jerusalem Lament suggests that the rejection of Jesus becomes, for Q, the pinnacle of Israel's disobedience and mistreatment of God's prophets and emissaries.[41] "Jerusalem, Jerusalem, who kills the prophets and stones those sent to her, how often did I desire to gather your children, like a hen gathers her nestlings under her wings, but you did not desire that. Behold, your house is forsaken" (Q 13:34-35a). This part of the saying is closely related to Q 11:49-51, both of which share references to the killing of prophets and an allusion to the stoning of Zechariah (2 Chron. 24:21). As a result, some Q scholars think the sayings were together in Q (following the order of Matt. 23:34-39).[42] In the Jerusalem Lament, Jesus may be speaking on behalf of Wisdom (cf. Q 11:49), as he seems to do elsewhere in Q (10:21-22). The pronouncement of abandonment on Jerusalem's house, that is, the temple (evoking Jer. 22:5), is precipitated by the rejection of the one who desired many times to collect and protect Jerusalem's inhabitants. The historical question of whether Jesus actually visited Jerusalem enough times for him to be in view as the speaker is beside the point, for this saying suggests a final and decisive rejection in Jerusalem, which leads, as is characteristic in the deuteronomistic model, to the pronouncement of abandonment. Therefore the rejection and death of Jesus in Jerusalem is, at least implicitly in Q, the paradigmatic or decisive case of the murdered prophet. (Although this may reflect a memory of the circumstances of Jesus' death, we must remember that this kind of polemic, at this stage of the Jesus movements, is entirely intramural and Jewish.)

Thus Q shows indications its compilers knew about Jesus' death and were trying to interpret it theologically. An interesting question, but a side issue here, is whether Q should be seen as evidence of a group that did not know of sacrificial, soteriological, or advanced martyrological interpretations of Jesus' death, or that knew of such interpretations but avoided them in favor of the interpretation that he died as a rejected prophet.[43] Ultimately we are thrown back on the silence of Q on the matter, and as with Paul or Luke, we cannot presume that Q would give assent to ideas for which it does not contain explicit or at least implicit evidence. Even so, Q would certainly not be alone in this regard. James is also silent, saying nothing about the death or resurrection of Jesus, yet displaying a belief in his coming as judge (James 5:7-9)— and a sense that his sayings have an ongoing validity, even though those sayings are not explicitly quoted as being from Jesus.[44] The death of Jesus, however, continues to be a problem for interpreters of Q when it comes to other sayings from Q that look ahead to a future role for Jesus, or that imply his ongoing existence in a nonearthly sense.

For the idea of a future role for Jesus, we need look no further than the sayings from Q that speak about a future or coming Son of Man. While it has sometimes been maintained that these materials originally did not refer to Jesus (but to a Son of Man figure whose appearance and eschatological role Jesus expected),[45] it is also clear that within Q, the term "Son of Man" is the characteristic title for Jesus (e.g., Q 7:34; 9:57-58). So Q 12:39-40 looks ahead to the coming of Jesus as Son of Man, even though Jesus is the speaker: "But you should know that had the householder known in which hour [of the night] the thief was going to come, he would not have let his house be broken into. You also should be prepared, because you do not know at what hour the Son of Man is coming" (Q 12:39-40).

Similarly, in Q 17:30 Jesus says, "Thus it will also be on the day in which the Son of Man is revealed," and this saying is part of a longer complex of eschatological sayings on the coming of the Son of Man and the conditions that will mark the time of his coming. The saying given above, that "the Son of Man will also confess [that person] before the angels" (Q 12:8), presumes an eschatological judgment setting. These sayings, all of which focus on the eschatological function of Jesus as the Son of Man, also imply some sort of ongoing heavenly existence for Jesus, despite his death as one of Wisdom's own. That Jesus speaks "as" Wisdom (Q 10:21-22; 13:34-35) also seems to presume some sort of exaltation. The big question is what in Q could account for this elevated view of the (post-mortem) Jesus.[46]

One possible answer is that Q presupposes the resurrection of Jesus. There is very clear evidence from Q that those who composed it (like many Jews) hoped for a future resurrection of the dead as a time of judgment and vindication. Q 11:31-32, for instance, says that the Queen of the South and the Ninevites will give eschatological testimony against "this generation"—and they will be raised (Gk., *egerthēsetai*, v. 31; *anastēsontai*, v. 32) at the judgment to do this. Both these sayings use standard biblical Greek vocabulary for the resurrection of the dead, "waking up" (*egeirō*) or "getting up" (*anistēmi*) language. Elsewhere in Q, the command "Do not be afraid of those who kill the body but who cannot kill the soul," coupled with the idea that God can destroy both soul and body in Gehenna (Q 12:4-5), might imply a belief in a bodily resurrection, as both N. T. Wright and Larry Hurtado suggest, but this is by no means certain.[47] That saying does not emphasize the eschatological survival (or reconstitution) of the body, but how the souls of the faithful live on despite death by persecution.

Wright also sees indications in Q of a belief in the resurrection of Jesus. One candidate he nominates is the notoriously difficult sign of Jonah saying. Although Matthew's version clarifies the connection between Jonah and Jesus through a reference to his death and resurrection—"The Son of Man will be in the heart of the earth for three days and three nights" (Matt. 12:40)—the original wording in Q was closer to Luke 11:29-30.[48] "But [he said], "This generation is an evil generation: it seeks a sign, and a sign will not be given to it except the sign of Jonah. For just as Jonah became a sign for the Ninevites, so [also] will the Son of Man be for this generation" (Q 11:29-30). "The sign of Jonah" probably means "the sign which was Jonah himself," rather than "the sign Jonah gave." This is clear from the assertion that "Jonah became a sign." But how exactly did Jonah become a sign for the Ninevites? One possibility, says Wright, is that this refers to "Jonah's extraordinary escape from the sea-monster," and so the correlation the saying draws between Jonah and the Son of Man must refer to Jesus' resurrection. In support of this is the following reference to resurrection: the Queen of the South and the Ninevites condemning "this generation" at the resurrection judgment (Q 11:31-32).[49]

However, according to the Hebrew Bible, Jonah's preaching to the Ninevites did not include a testimony to his rescue from the big fish: the book of Jonah reports that he said simply, "Forty more days and Nineveh will be overthrown"

(Jonah 3:4). Evoking the overthrowing of other cities, such as Sodom (e.g., Gen. 19:21), Jonah's proclamation sounds like an announcement of judgment and not an invitation to repentance; certainly the Septuagint understood the text this way (*kai Nineuē katastraphēsetai*). Yet some commentators (already *b. Sanh.* 89b) read the Hebrew as ambiguous, referring either to a catastrophic overturning or to an overturning of Nineveh's attitudes toward God.[50] Jack Sasson translates the line thus: "Forty more days, and Nineveh overturns."[51] In Q, John invites repentance, but Jesus does not, at least not directly; as with Jonah, his announcement of judgment also masks an invitation to repent. However, if this invitation is not heeded, "this generation" will be judged by the Ninevites (Q 11:32).

Here in Q, the Jonah cluster emphasizes that "they repented at the preaching of Jonah, and behold, something greater than Jonah is here!" (Q 11:32b). So the fate of "this generation" at the judgment will be worse, for they failed to repent at the preaching of Jesus the Son of Man, greater than Jonah, at whose preaching the Ninevites repented. The Son of Man becomes a sign through his preaching. This seems the most reasonable solution, though precisely how the Son of Man and Jonah are to be compared will remain a controversial question, simply because the saying is too elliptical (and the reception-history of the Jonah story too complex) to erase any doubt.[52] But even if the point of the comparison is rescue from death, there is no clear indication from Q that Jesus' resurrection from the dead is in view. Zeller, for instance, as part of his argument for assumption language in Q 13:34-35, claimed that the sign of Jonah saying alludes to Jesus' assumption and his subsequent return as judge. In his view, "just as Jonah, who was snatched away from death, came to the Ninevites authorized by God, so also Jesus, who was taken away and who in [Q 11:32] surpasses the repentance preaching of Jonah, was to become for this generation an irrefutable sign because of his return as the Son of Man."[53] In support of this, Zeller cites several Jewish texts (including Jonah 2:6) that interpret Jonah's rescue from the big fish as a kind of assumption.[54] Yet the saying itself does not suggest a judging role, which Zeller's reading requires.[55]

Nowhere in Q is resurrection language explicitly applied to Jesus, even though resurrection fits within the horizons of Q's eschatological hope. On the other hand, Q 13:34-35, the Jerusalem Lament saying, does contain standard assumption language, as already noted. There Jesus says, "You will not see me (*ou mē idēte me*) until [the time comes when] you say . . ." Similar "not seeing" language (a negated form of *horaō*) can be found in several sources, but most importantly it occurs in 2 Kings 2:12 LXX: "And Elisha was watching (*heōra*) and crying out, 'Father! Father! The chariot of Israel and its horseman!' And he saw him no longer" (*kai ouk eiden auton eti*). As Gerhard Lohfink noted, this "not seeing" language expresses, in the same way as "disappearance" language, the aftereffect of assumption: the person is not seen any longer because God has whisked him away into the divine presence.[56] These expressions all negate the Greek verb *horaō*, so that this language is the exact opposite of "appearance" language, which we have seen was also important in early Christian conceptualizations of Jesus' vindication (as in 1 Cor. 9:1; 15:5; and Luke 24:34).

Several things are noteworthy about the use of this language in Q. First, it does not describe a disappearance or an assumption, but it looks ahead to one: it is a prediction. As shown in the previous chapter, foreknowledge was a common feature in Jewish stories of assumption (as in 2 Kings 2), sometimes highlighting the importance of the instruction the sage would give in the time before God took him up (*1 Enoch* 81:6; *4 Ezra* 14:1-18; *2 Baruch* 76).[57] Second, Q 13:35 looks ahead to a future time when the inhabitants of Jerusalem would see the speaker again and acclaim him using the words of Psalm 118:26 (117:26 LXX): "Blessed is the one who comes [or: the coming one] in the name of the Lord; we have blessed you from the house of the Lord."[58] As in Matthew, this must also be in Q a reference to the parousia, a seeing-again after a period of absence. Importantly, Q refers to Jesus not only as Son of Man but also, especially in relation to John the Baptist, as "the Coming One" (Q 3:16b; 7:19). Thus Q 13:35 coordinates assumption with a special eschatological role. Zeller noted that something very similar happens when Enoch is taken up and then identified with "that Son of Man" in *1 Enoch* 70–71.[59] Interestingly, the psalm quoted here also has strong associations with the proximity of death and vindication (Ps. 117:17-18, 21-23 LXX).[60] Third, this assumption language occurs in the context of a saying that has, in my opinion, Jesus' rejection and death in Jerusalem in view. This suggests that assumption was being used as a way of affirming Jesus' vindication by God and his eschatological status in spite of his death.[61] Fourth, as seen in the previous chapter, "not seeing" language was not used to describe soul assumption scenarios, so this reference to the assumption of Jesus must connote a bodily disappearance.

Certain other features of Q make sense in light of this reference to assumption in Q 13:34-35. The first is the fact that the allusion to the story of Elijah's assumption is part of a larger rhetorical strategy in Q according to which the activities and messages of both John and Jesus are oriented to the pattern of Elijah. Most important is the way that Jesus answers John's question, "Are you the Coming One, or should we expect another?" (Q 7:19): "And he answered and said to them, 'Go tell John what you hear and see: the blind regain their sight and the lame walk, lepers are cleansed and the deaf hear, and the dead are raised and the poor have good news brought to them. And blessed are those who are not offended by me'" (Q 7:22-23).

Of particular interest in this list of Jesus' activities are the cleansing of lepers and the raising of the dead, neither of which figures in the biblical texts that seem to have influenced this saying (Psalm 146, Isaiah 61). Both of these are associated with the Elijah/Elisha cycle of stories, however (1 Kings 17:17-24; 2 Kings 4:18-37; 5:1-27). The fact that a very similar list (including the dead but not lepers) is found in a Qumran text designated by scholars the "Messianic Apocalypse" (4Q521)[62] leads John Collins to conclude that behind both texts there is the expectation of an Elijah-like figure, an anointed prophet. He notes, however, that such a figure was not as prominent either in literature or in popular belief as the Davidic messiah.[63] Kloppenborg thinks that Q splits the two roles attributed to Elijah in Malachi 3–4—inviting repentance and bringing about judgment—between John (Q 3:7-9) and Jesus (Q 3:16-17) in order to "negotiate the relationship between the two."[64] Other sayings frame the challenge to faithful discipleship in language reminiscent of the call of Elisha (1 Kings 19:19-21):

> And another said to him, "Master, first let me go off and bury my father." And he said to him, "Follow me and let the dead bury their own dead." (Q 9:59-60)

> And another said to him, "I will follow you, Master; but first let me say farewell to those at home." And Jesus said to him, "No one who puts their hand on the plow and looks back is suitable for the kingdom of God." (Q/Luke 9:61-62)

Although the second episode is not in Matthew, there are good grounds to think it was originally in Q, because it is one of three such discipleship pronouncement stories in Luke (9:57-62), and because it would have been a fitting introduction to Q's mission instructions (Q 10:2-16).[65] In 1 Kings 19:19-21, Elijah passes by Elisha, who is plowing, and he throws his mantle over him. Elisha says, "I will follow you," but then with Elijah's permission goes home to kiss his father and mother and have a last meal together: this farewell seems to have influenced the first episode, and the plowing, the second. These sayings seem to intensify the demand considerably but clearly evoke the Elisha call narrative, for "discipleship to Jesus—who must like Elijah be a prophet—takes priority over duties to parents."[66] In any case, it appears that reading Q 13:35 as a prediction of an assumption-related disappearance, evoking the language of 2 Kings 2, would be consistent with a broader pattern of depicting the activities of John, Jesus, and Jesus' followers in a manner suggestive of the Elijah/Elisha narratives.

A second feature of Q is illuminated when Q 13:35 is seen as a reference to disappearance and return: the pattern of seeing/not-seeing/seeing-again is found elsewhere in Q, coordinated with the expectation of the coming of the Son of Man and the judgment that would accompany that coming. Q contains two parables that feature absent masters returning to render judgment (Q 12:42-46; 19:12-13, 15-24, 26). This connection between absence and return for judgment implies the same connection between assumption/disappearance and eschatological function as we have noted in Q 13:34-35, but moreover in both instances the parable is preceded by material about the coming Son of Man (Q 12:39-40; 17:23-24, 37, 26-27, 30).[67] Q 12:39-40 compares the coming of the Son of Man to the arrival of a thief to break into a house: "But you should know that had the householder known at which hour [of the night] the thief was going to come, he would not have let his house be broken into. You also should be prepared, because you do not know at what hour the Son of Man is coming" (Q 12:39-40). According to Heinz Schürmann, the original metaphor about the thief (Q 12:39) was secondarily expanded with the addition of a Son of Man interpretation (Q 12:40); and the sayings complex was completed with the addition of the parable about the absent and returning master (Q 12:42-46).[68] This suggests (compositionally, at least) that belief in Jesus as the eschatological Son of Man was expressed as requiring his absence before his presence and revelation.

The eschatological material in Q 17 also places an emphasis on the absence of the Son of Man, and then his sudden presence: "If they should say to you, 'Look, he is in the desert,' do not go out; or 'Look, he is inside,' do not follow. For just as the lightning goes out from the east and flashes over to the west, so also will the Son of Man be [on his day]" (Q 17:23-24).[69] Immediately following this is the Q parable of the entrusted money, in which a master leaves and then returns to render judgment on his slaves (Q 19). Regardless of how the composition of Q is understood, or how in particular these parabolic materials came together redactionally with the more explicit warnings about the coming Son of Man, these materials confirm the importance of the absence-return scenario for Q. Instead of thinking about Jesus' postmortem vindication as a resurrection that results in his renewed presence, the framers of Q stressed instead his removal by God and installation as the Son of Man despite his crucifixion. This emphasis on disappearance and absence is in stark contrast to Paul's emphasis on the risen Christ's presence in the appearances.

An important question, if we are correct in seeing a reference to Jesus' assumption in the Q material, is how those who composed and used Q arrived at this notion. There are two different options. One is that the Jerusalem Lament saying was attributed to Jesus in order to give a (traditionally Jewish) account for the belief that Jesus was returning in a special eschatological capacity, to execute judgment as the Coming One, the Son of Man. As noted above, Zeller pointed to *1 Enoch* 70–71 as a parallel to Q on this point. Thus, in this scenario, Jesus' end was described as an assumption as a way to explain, or theologize, how he could be the Son of Man. This would have involved understanding assumption realistically as a miraculous intervention by God on behalf of someone divinely favored, but not necessarily as an escape from death. As we have seen, the proximity of the prediction of his disappearance and return in Q 13:34-35 to the deuterono-mistic interpretation of Jesus' death suggests that assumption is the means of his postmortem vindication. As seen in the previous chapter, there are instances in Jewish literature of assumption language being used, whether euphemistically or in a realistic sense, for those who had died.

It is possible, especially when comparable instances in ancient literature are taken into account, that assumption language was used in Q as a secondary ratio-nalization of Jesus' eschatological role. For example, as noted in the previous chapter, it appears that assumption and apotheosis were secondarily credited to Herakles and Arsinoë II Philadelphos in order to explain why their veneration as gods, already ongoing, was justified. A similar development took place in Jewish apocalyptic literature with respect to other figures. There are no traditions in the Hebrew Bible to the effect that Ezra or Baruch was taken up into heaven, but their assumptions are mentioned in *4 Ezra* and *2 Baruch*.[70] The motif of foreknowl-edge allowing for a period of special eschatological instruction to the community of the elect seems to be the deciding factor: assumption is credited to Ezra and Baruch in order to legitimate their instruction, and this may have been necessary because of the stature accorded Enoch in the Enochic literature as a rival seer and sage. In the end the assumptions of Ezra and Baruch originate in imitation of an

Enochic precedent: according to the "Book of Luminaries," Enoch was allowed one year in which to instruct his sons before he would be taken away from them (1 Enoch 81:6). So Ezra is included among those who "from their birth have not tasted death" and whose role in the eschatological drama was thus guaranteed (4 Ezra 6:26; also 14:9); in the meantime he was to write down his special revelation for the elect (4 Ezra 14:22-48; see also 2 Bar. 76:1-5).[71] Thus Q 13:35 could have been a redactional creation used to explain why Jesus was viewed as a figure of future apocalyptic significance.

On the other hand, if assumption was used in Q as a way of explaining how Jesus could be the coming Son of Man, then we are still in need of an explanation of why the Jesus movement behind Q thought that in the first place. One standard approach is to say that resurrection faith was the origin of this expectation in Q.[72] But, as Kloppenborg points out, Q shows no evidence of either resurrection language applied individually to Jesus or the sort of exaltation-to-heaven exegesis (as in the application of Psalm 110 to Jesus in Acts 2:34-35 or in 1 Cor. 15:25) that was common in some circles in early Christianity.[73] We are left with the possibility that the Q people thought Jesus would return as the Son of Man because they thought he had been taken up into heaven—and here we could speculate that this view arose as a natural conclusion drawn from rumors or traditions about Jesus' empty tomb. In this connection, it is important that Q 13:35b suggests a bodily disappearance ("You will not see me until . . .") and uses neither the euphemistic language sometimes found in epitaphs ("he was taken away from us") nor the conception of assumption applied to the soul (as in, for instance, the Testament of Abraham).[74] Though assumption may have been a conclusion to draw from talk about Jesus' empty tomb, it would be unfounded to speculate further that the assumption/disappearance model of vindication was more "primitive" than the resurrection/appearance model.[75] One reason that certainty is impossible is because of questions about the origins of the empty tomb tradition.

To the Origins of the Empty Tomb Tradition

In addition to Q, another early source described what happened to Jesus following his death in terms of disappearance, rather than appearance, and that is the narrative source behind Mark 16:1-8. There is considerable disagreement whether the author of Mark composed the end of his Gospel or used as source material a narrative or tradition that had come to him.[76] But there are good grounds for thinking that Mark used a story that described the discovery of the empty tomb but invited the conclusion that Jesus had been taken up into heaven, and a rough idea of the shape of this story can be seen once elements characteristic of Markan redaction are removed. This view—that Mark used a story that was originally a disappearance story—was first proposed by Elias Bickermann in 1924.[77] Mark 16:7, which is a redactional doublet of Mark 14:28, brings a reference to the appearance traditions into a story that originally did not have the appearances of the risen Jesus on its narrative horizon: the young man tells the women, "But go, tell his disciples and Peter that he is going ahead of you into Galilee: you will see him there, just as he told you." This is probably an interpolation into an earlier version of the story.[78] As we saw in the appearance tradition cited by Paul, it is said here in Mark that Jesus was raised from the dead and was to appear to Peter (1 Cor. 15:4-5; see also Luke 24:34). Aside from this prediction of an appearance to Peter and the disciples, and the word *ēgerthē* ("he was raised") in verse 6, there is nothing in Mark 16:1-8 that needs to suggest the kind of resurrection-plus-appearances scenario found in the other Gospels, which tend to display the risen Jesus as a risen-out-of-the-tomb Jesus. Instead, in the Markan story the emphasis is on Jesus' absence: this is a disappearance story. "You are looking for Jesus of Nazareth, who was crucified," the young man in white says to the women. "He was raised, he is not here. Look, here is the place where they put him" (Mark 16:6). As it stands, Mark affirms, as the other Gospels do, that Jesus' tomb is empty because he was raised from the dead; yet otherwise the young man describes an unsuccessful search for the body, such as would be found in an assumption-disappearance story.[79] Because of the nature of the literary evidence, it is impossible to say whether the Q saying and the pre-Markan empty tomb story are related: we cannot know if the narrative developed out of the saying or the saying out of the narrative (or even a rumor about an empty tomb), or if they are unrelated deployments of the same basic concept.

In any event, these observations about the role of the disappearance tradition in Q and Mark raise some questions about a common understanding of the origin of the empty tomb story. Rudolf Bultmann proposed that "the purpose of the story is without doubt to prove the reality of the resurrection of Jesus by the empty tomb."[80] More recently, Gerd Lüdemann has argued, as noted in an earlier chapter, that "those who handed down these traditions 'concluded' from the message that the crucified one had risen that the tomb of Jesus was empty. The present story is as it were the product of a conclusion or a postulate."[81] On this view, the pre-Pauline kerygmatic formula (1 Cor. 15:3b-5) represents the original view, that Jesus was raised by God and appeared, that is, was present, to his followers. If Jesus had been raised and was appearing, as the early proclamation held, the natural conclusion would be that his tomb was empty. Lüdemann's proposal is aided by his view of Paul's understanding of resurrection. "On the one hand, Paul knows no witnesses to the empty tomb, but on the other hand, he imagines the resurrection of Jesus in bodily form, which seems to require the emergence of the body of Jesus from the empty tomb."[82] Paul, on Lüdemann's view, would be congenial to the idea of an empty tomb, and thus he certainly would have mentioned such a tradition had he known of one. (We have, however, already seen the difficulties with that line of thinking.) Thus, Lüdemann concludes, the empty tomb stories cannot predate Paul, but make better sense as a conclusion "inferred from the dogma" on the basis of a flesh-and-bones understanding of resurrection.[83] In keeping with this view, others suggest that the Markan conclusion to the story ("And they told nothing to anyone, for they were afraid," Mark 16:8) is a thinly veiled explanation for the late origin of the tradition.[84]

However, since an empty tomb story need not presuppose resurrection, one could also argue that the empty tomb story arose in relation to the view that Jesus had been taken immediately into heaven and was waiting there until his eschatological time should come. As with Lüdemann's proposal, this would require a bodily interpretation of assumption (rather than an assumption of the soul or a euphemistic use of removal language). But Q poses another difficulty for Lüdemann's scenario: if the empty tomb with its emphasis on the disappearance of Jesus arose as a conclusion from the resurrection kerygma, how can the disappearance language in Q be explained, given that Q shows no evidence of the kind of passion-resurrection kerygma necessary to draw the conclusion that the tomb was empty? As suggested above, the assumption-return model of postmortem vindication may have developed as a result of followers of Jesus hearing about an empty tomb tradition and drawing a conclusion other than resurrection. But neither is it impossible that the Q people were reacting to a secondary empty tomb story, that is, one that arose in response to traditions about resurrection. Ultimately, given the nature of our evidence, it is impossible to say with certainty which came first: the resurrection kerygma or the empty tomb; assumption belief or the empty tomb; or the resurrection kerygma or assumption belief.[85] What is important is that we have evidence of two apparently divergent expressions of Jesus' postmortem vindication by God, expressions that the narratives of the Gospels gradually bring into harmony with one another.

How Different Is Assumption? How Different Is Q?

To describe resurrection and assumption as "apparently divergent expressions of Jesus' postmortem vindication" might seem to be "making difference"[86]—that is, finding diverse or divergent viewpoints where the ancient participants may not have understood things in those terms. After all, early Christian texts and traditions seem to equate or connect resurrection with exaltation without much trouble; why should they not use assumption language to express the same basic idea? Or, as Hurtado has recently written, "several christological schemas are reflected in various New Testament writings, and they all seem to have emerged and circulated alongside one another in Christian circles."[87] The pre-Pauline hymn in Philippians 2:6-11, for instance, does not explicitly refer to resurrection, but only to death and exaltation—without expressly stating the means by which God exalted Jesus—and it has a decidedly eschatological conclusion (cf. Phil. 2:10-11 with 1 Cor. 15:24-28). Similarly, the author of Hebrews conceives of Jesus' ongoing existence and exaltation in heaven in connection with a priestly role but refers to the resurrection only in a closing doxology (Heb. 13:20) and does not emphasize the parousia.[88] Yet one would scarcely doubt that the author of Hebrews believed that Jesus was raised from the dead. Could it be that the assumption language in Q 13:35 merely expresses something similar to resurrection-exaltation or expresses it in slightly different language?

In one sense, this is unlikely, because originally assumption and resurrection used different language (being taken up versus being woken up) in order to express different things and to raise different connotations. The concepts did not overlap, either: one would not claim that someone like Elijah who had been taken up by God had "risen from the dead." As Arie Zwiep contends, "From the perspective of [a history-of-religions approach], strictly speaking, resurrection and ascension (in the sense of a bodily [assumption]) are competitive (not to say mutually exclusive) conceptualisations."[89] Zwiep thinks the difference is that resurrection happens to people who have died, and assumption happens to people who do not die (which is, as we have seen, not strictly adhered to in either Greek or Jewish sources). The associated theological concepts were different as well. On the one hand, resurrection implies divine favor and vindication, since it involves the reversal of wrongful death; so does assumption, even if it suggests an escape from death. In some cases, the vindication of resurrection is expressed specifically in relation to elevation or dominance over the oppressors of those expecting God to raise them up, usually because the wicked cannot hope to share in the resurrection (see 2 Macc. 7:14), but sometimes because the resurrection of all the dead was a precursor to universal judgment. When resurrection language was used as the category for explaining what God had done for Jesus after his death, this does not necessarily lead directly to the claim that he would return as the eschatological judge, even though the resurrection was thought of as a future eschatological event. For Paul the intermediate step had to do with God granting the risen Christ universal authority (as in Daniel 7, although Paul does not use "Son of Man" language). Luke, in contrast, recognizing assumption as the means whereby a person is taken away to await his or her eschatological role, found that assumption (ascension) following resurrection made better sense of the belief in Jesus' return than did resurrection alone. So the angels tell the disciples, "Men of Galilee, why do you stand looking up into heaven? This Jesus, who has been taken up (*ho analēmphtheis*) from you into heaven, will likewise come in the same way that you saw him going up into heaven" (Acts 1:11). This explains why Luke combined resurrection and assumption in his christological schema.[90] Mark combined these two categories as well, but unlike Luke he did not take a consecutive approach, but a coincident one, narrating the resurrection of Jesus using the disappearance narrative he had received. This will be discussed in the following chapter.

If assumption cannot simply be equated with resurrection, is there a sense in which assumption language in Q could express exaltation alongside other ideas? Looking at Philippians 2:6-11, we cannot say much for certain about the hymn's original logic of vindication: the bare affirmation that God "highly exalted" Jesus (v. 9) could equally presume resurrection or assumption.[91] Both positions have been taken by scholars,[92] although the hymn simply does not display an interest in how Jesus was exalted by God: it only asserts the divine favor extended to Jesus because of the manner of his death and the universal acclaim or submission that has become his right as a result of that divine favor. Divine favor is the explicit basis of Jesus' vindication here, not resurrection or assumption. As many scholars have argued, the exaltation of Jesus here is best understood over against imperial claims about the universal authority, or even the apotheosis, of the Roman emperor.[93]

Yet, as Hurtado correctly notes, "Paul clearly did not find the passage deficient for shaping the attitudes of the Philippian believers."[94] He means that had Paul perceived any christological deficiencies in the hymn, those did not prevent him from using it to hortatory ends. Paul may not have known (or cared?) about the theology of exaltation the hymn presupposed in its original setting. But when he used it, he intended it to be read in the context of his own thought, as outlined in the letter and in his previous contact with the Philippians, in which resurrection was obviously the means of Christ's postmortem vindication (as in Phil. 3:10-11). The hymn would then be read or interpreted within that theological framework. The point is that when we come to Q, there is nothing else besides the assumption-return scenario to provide an interpretive context for various statements about Jesus' ongoing significance or future eschatological role. The christological schema that makes use of assumption language, then, could possibly be an addendum to (or even a stand-in for) some other christological schema—but we just do not have evidence for any other schema in Q. This is remarkable, since Q seems to know and approve of the idea of resurrection, but only as a corporate event of the eschatological future and not as a mode of Jesus' individual vindication or exaltation.[95]

These are important points, for they have to do with the "difference" of Q's Christology. On the one hand, we cannot simply presume that the interpretation of Jesus' death as "for sins" and belief in his resurrection were universal among the early Christian movements, despite their importance to prominent canonical authors like Paul. It is unlikely that all early Christians would have known the language and ideas of the pre-Pauline kerygmatic formulation; and some, apparently, had they known such language and ideas, preferred to express their convictions about the significance of Jesus in other, sometimes starkly different terms.[96] This applies equally to canonical and noncanonical early Christian writings. The author of James, for instance, shows an awareness of Paul's writings, or at least of Pauline thought (James 2:21-24), but does not have much to say about the death and resurrection of Jesus. In addition, some scholars think that Luke avoids a "sacrificial" understanding of Jesus' death and thinks instead along other lines (cf. Mark 10:42-45 with Luke 22:25-27).[97] From what we can tell from Q, the Q people either did not know of such sacrificial interpretations or knew of them but preferred to interpret Jesus' death along deuteronomistic or mimetic/martyrological lines. In other words, Jesus' death was viewed either as symptomatic of the rejection of prophets (as in Q 13:34) or as setting the pattern for followers to imitate (as in Q 14:27), but not as an atoning sacrifice or price of release in relation to sin (as in Rom. 3:24-25 and Mark 10:45 respectively). Similarly, it appears that some of Jesus' followers after his death thought about his vindication by God in terms not of resurrection but of assumption. Others besides the Q people were thinking along such lines, as the tradition behind Mark 16:1-8 appears to suggest. What this indicates is that there was some diversity in how the earliest Christian movements understood the significance of Jesus' death and in how they viewed his vindication, and not all would have expressed their convictions along the lines of 1 Corinthians 15:3b-7.

On the other hand, those who composed and used Q were apparently not apathetic about the kinds of concerns that other circles in early Christianity were struggling with: how to make sense of Jesus' death, and how to express the convictions that God had vindicated him and that his role in God's future plans was assured. For Q, in its final form at least, the salvific importance of following Jesus' teachings (e.g., Q 6:47-49) has been augmented with reflections on the (coming?) salvific importance of his person—that is to say, Q has a "Christology."[98]

For our purposes, the most significant observation to draw from Q is that some of Jesus' followers were talking about the end of Jesus in terms quite different from those familiar to the Pauline congregations. While some of the chronological questions are impossible to answer, the evidence from Q suggests that at the beginning of the trajectory of the empty tomb stories lie two different convictions about the fate of Jesus. I use the word "convictions" purposefully, because behind what seem to be different linguistic options lie beliefs about the significance of Jesus and about the nature of his ongoing life in and on behalf of these communities of faith. As we will see, the process of bringing these two different convictions into harmony with one another is begun by the author of Mark.

5. Mark: When the Bridegroom Is Taken Away

"The members of the wedding party cannot fast while the bridegroom is with them, can they? As long as the bridegroom is with them, they cannot fast. But days will come when the bridegroom will be taken away from them, and then they will fast, on that day."

—Mark 2:19-20

And after they went into the tomb, they saw a young man sitting on the right side, dressed in a white robe, and they were alarmed. But he said to them, "Do not be alarmed. You are seeking Jesus the Nazarene, who was crucified. He has been raised, he is not here; see the place where they laid him. But leave now, and tell his disciples and Peter that he is going ahead of you into Galilee, and you will see him there, just as he told you." And they got out and fled from the tomb, for trembling and perplexity had seized them; and they did not tell anyone anything, for they were afraid.

—Mark 16:5-8

Early in Mark's Gospel, it comes to the notice of the Pharisees that Jesus and his disciples are not engaging in the customary religious practice of fasting. When asked why, Jesus replies with an analogy about a wedding party: guests at a wedding do not fast, but they feast as long as the festivities continue. Jesus says, however, that a time is coming for his followers "when the bridegroom will be taken away from them, and then they will fast, on that day" (Mark 2:20).[1] The imagery recalls Isaiah 62:5, in which God is compared to a bridegroom rejoicing over his bride; the metaphor here suggests "the joy of the dominion of God."[2] The saying implies that the ministry of Jesus is a time for celebration, as long as he is present announcing God's kingdom, healing the sick, casting out demons, and speaking with authority. The beginnings of this have been narrated up to this point in Mark.

The saying's evocative conclusion shifts the focus away from all this, how-ever. It invites the hearer to imagine a scene in which a wedding cannot proceed because the groom has been "taken away" by some violent force, whether death, enslavement, or conscription, leaving behind a shocked and grieving bride with shattered hopes. Is this how Jesus will leave his followers? This suggests that when Jesus' bereft disciples fast, it will be a sign of mourning (as in 2 Sam. 1:11-12), but another possibility is that Jesus in Mark foresees their fasting to be necessary as part of petitioning God for deliverance from eschatological troubles (see Mark 13:5-27). Fasting in early Judaism was commonly connected with corporate petitions to avert disaster (Joel 1:14-15), as well as with corporate or individual penitence and mourning.[3] The contrast between the saying's beginning and its conclusion is very stark, and as Joel Marcus points out, this is because "Jesus' death . . . has created a new situation in which the original tradition can be pre-served only by altering it radically."[4]

This saying is the first hint in Mark's narrative that Jesus will come to a violent end. It also foreshadows the shock and grief that Mark conveys in his story about the discovery of the empty tomb: there the story ends as the female disciples flee in fear, finding comfort neither in the restored presence of the risen Jesus nor in commiseration with any of his other followers. It is tempting to see in the bridegroom saying a reference to Jesus' removal by assumption, the aftereffect of which Mark narrates in the empty tomb story: "He is not here" (Mark 16:6). The passive verb in Mark 2:20 ("the bridegroom will be taken away") might suggest this; similar language is found in Wisdom 4:10-11, although with different verbs.[5] Yet in Mark 2 the reader finds none of the associated motifs of assumption: there is no sense of divine favor or vindication, nor of any future eschatological role, nor the idea that the time between prediction and removal should be used for the instruction of the faithful. The focus of Mark 2:20 is entirely on the experience of those left behind by the violent removal of Jesus, which is the note on which Mark's Gospel concludes (16:8). Additional endings (including "canonical" Ps.-Mark 16:9-20) are best understood as attempts by early Christian scribes and copyists to alleviate the difficulties of the original ending.[6] Mark's other early readers—the authors of Matthew and Luke—did the same, just as many read-ers today fill in the blanks with pieces from the other canonical accounts.[7] Once secondary additions to Mark 16 and hypotheses about lost original endings[8] have been eliminated, however, readers must confront the problems posed by the text, which ends at verse 8. This chapter offers a reading of Mark 16:1-8 that attempts to resolve some of the narrative problems of the story, but also to describe how (and explain why) the author of Mark has combined the disappearance tradition with the appearance tradition in telling the story of the empty tomb as a "resur-rection" story.

As already seen, there are several reasons for concluding that Mark 16:1-8 was based on a traditional story about the disappearance of Jesus. First, it is consistent with the genre: the body has disappeared, there is an unsuccessful search for the body, witnesses are overcome with fear and amazement, and someone offers a theological interpretation of the event.[9] Second, there are indications that the author has edited source material. One such indication is verse 7, which repeats almost verbatim what Jesus tells the Twelve in Mark 14:28: "But after I have been raised, I will go ahead of you into Galilee." Both verses are Mark's own composition, and 16:7 in particular—which stresses the prominence of Peter as a resurrection witness—seems to have been influenced by an appearance tradition similar to that preserved by Paul in 1 Corinthians 15:5.[10] Without verse 7, the response of the women makes sense as a reaction to their meeting with the young man dressed in white.[11] The description of this figure as a "young man" is also Markan, for the women's reaction seems more appropriate to the appearance of an angel, which Mark's source may have narrated; a similarly mysterious "young man" appears in Mark 14:51-52. Pheme Perkins and Gerd Lüdemann also note several other reasons for considering that there was originally a pre-Markan version of the story.[12] However, in the end, whatever the source narrative was like, the ending of Mark's Gospel is thoroughly Markan, full of Markan vocabulary and echoes of themes found earlier in the Gospel. It must be understood by seeing it in context of the Gospel's narrative shape.

The Revelation of the Son of God

"Seeing" is very important to the narrative and theological shape of Mark's Gospel. Scholars have long recognized, for instance, that the two stories in which Jesus restores sight to blind men (8:22-26; 10:46-52) serve as a narrative frame (or "inclusio") for the material in between.[13] In the first of these stories, Jesus must adjust the cure of the blind man at Bethsaida, whose sight is faulty after his vision is initially restored: "I see people walking around, but they look like trees" (Mark 8:24). It is important to see that "blindness" is Markan code for failure to understand Jesus' teaching, identity, and purposes: having eyes but not being able to see puts the disciples at risk of being outsiders in relation to Jesus and the kingdom message (8:14-21; cf. 4:11-12), at risk of being grouped with Jesus' opponents.[14] These two healings enclose a long section in which, following an initial insight into Jesus' messianic identity (Mark 8:27-30), the disciples hear from Jesus three predictions that as the Son of Man he must be rejected, suffer, be put to death, and rise again (8:31-33; 9:30-32; 10:32-34). The disciples persist in misunderstanding, and they fail to accept this; Jesus attempts to correct them by explaining how following him requires risk and radical self-denial (8:34–9:1; 9:33-37; 10:35-45) in what are essentially renewals of their initial call.[15] Thus the initial insight is not sufficient. Jesus' followers require an additional touch from him in order for their perception of his mission to be complete, although, as Eugene Boring observes, the story of the blind man at Bethsaida "is full of promise."[16]

In the middle of this section of Mark 8:22–10:52 is the transfiguration, a scene that provides for the reader another clue as to how to see Mark's narrative shape. The transfiguration (Mark 9:2-10) is one of three epiphany scenes found at the beginning, middle, and end of the Gospel. Boring describes these epiphany scenes as divine interventions of apocalyptic history into the "story time" of the Gospel.[17] In all of these scenes, the identity of Jesus as God's Son[18] is disclosed, and in each scene, seeing is crucial.[19] These scenes are therefore "epiphanies" in the technical sense of the word, since they involve the "sudden and unexpected manifestation of a divine or heavenly being experienced by certain selected persons as an event independent of their seeing, in which the divine being reveals a divine attribute, action, or message."[20] The first is the baptism of Jesus (Mark 1:9-11).[21] In this very brief story, Jesus is the recipient of the epiphany. Just as he is coming up out of the water, the narrator says, he sees the heavens being torn apart and the Spirit descending like a dove to him (v. 10). The "tearing" of the heavens (evoking Isa. 64:1) is an "irreversible cosmic change" that marks the beginning of God's re-creative activity through the Spirit.[22] The way Mark tells the story, Jesus is the one who "sees" the heavens torn asunder, and the voice from heaven addresses him directly, saying, "You are my beloved Son; I am very pleased with you" (v. 11). The narrator does not make it clear whether anyone apart from Jesus sees and hears this, so although the reader is drawn into the epiphany, this is meant primarily for Jesus himself. The precise significance of this divine anointing and approval of Jesus is not initially clear, but his endurance of demonic testing, his authoritative teaching, his control over malevolent spiritual forces and illness, his mastery of the Scriptures, and his knowledge of the divine will all indicate that the descent of the Spirit has imbued him with divine authority and power as the initiator and herald of the reign of God (1:14-15; see also Isa. 42:1; 61:1-3, other texts to which Mark probably is alluding).[23] Thus Jesus is God's Son, in the first place, because he is acting on God's behalf, as the (Spirit-)anointed one— and in Mark's story this knowledge is confirmed (or possibly given) to him at his baptism, for he is the one who sees the heavens opened and the Spirit descending.[24]

At the transfiguration, the central epiphany scene, Peter, James, and John are witness to a metamorphosis of Jesus (Gk., *kai metemorphōthē emprosthen autōn*).[25] Although some scholars have thought that Mark 9:2-8 was originally a resurrection appearance story,[26] in Mark's presentation it is another *apokalypsis* (revelation) of the divine realm, which once more breaks into normal time and space. In this instance, those who "see" are the three disciples (vv. 2, 4, 8). The narrator focuses on the clothing of the transfigured Jesus, which became "brilliantly shining, white like no fuller on earth is able to whiten" (Mark 9:3). In both Jewish and Greco-Roman literature, denizens of the divine realm, or humans who have come into contact with that realm (e.g., Moses in Exodus 34, or Elijah in *Lives of the Prophets* 21), are sometimes described in such glowing terms.[27] However, John Paul Heil thinks that Jesus' appearance most closely reflects "the heavenly glory promised to the righteous in general after their death" in certain early Jewish texts; this means that "the temporary transfiguration of Jesus into a heavenly figure enables the heavenly figures of Moses and Elijah to appear and speak with him."[28] Elijah and Moses are able to appear alive from heaven because they were both taken alive into heaven (according to early Jewish tradition, as seen in an earlier chapter). Somehow, one assumes, the heavens have been opened again to allow Elijah and Moses to return temporarily to earth, although this is not made explicit in the narrative either. Jesus is "transfigured" but does not "appear" in the sense that Elijah and Moses do, because "he has been with them all the time."[29]

The transfiguration of Jesus is an act of God because, in Mark's language, "he was transformed," and the passive verb suggests God as the agent. At the same time, it also illustrates that Jesus can converse with Elijah and Moses and share in the glory of their exalted heavenly state because he belongs with them in some sense, and this adds a new dimension of meaning to the title "Son of God."[30] After a brief interchange with Peter (who, according to the narrator, characteristically misunderstands the situation), they return to heaven under the cover of an overshadowing cloud, from which is heard a voice that says, "This is my beloved Son; listen to him" (v. 7). Then "suddenly, when they looked around, they saw no one any longer, except Jesus alone with them" (v. 8). Elijah (and Moses with him) disappeared just as he did in the first place, as Mark tells it; once again, the language here is very close to 2 Kings 2:12 LXX, where it says that after Elijah's assumption Elisha "did not see him any longer."[31] In contrast, Jesus himself remains behind. Peter Bolt suggests that at the transfiguration the narrative conditions are all present for Jesus to be translated into the divine realm, as Elijah and Moses had been, but this does not happen. In Bolt's view, this is because Jesus "rejected the opportunity to avoid death through apotheosis and embraced his future suffering for the sake of the divine plan."[32] To consider this a "rejected opportunity" strains the logic of the story—could Jesus be offered an escape from the divine plan after the first passion prediction (Mark 8:31-33)? But Bolt is correct that the narrator's observation that the disciples see "Jesus alone with them" emphasizes a difference between the story of Jesus and stories told about the ends of Elijah and Moses. The way of Jesus must lead through suffering *and death* to vindication (Mark 10:32-34). With this story coming right in the middle of Mark's central section, the command "Listen to him!" (v. 7) is best taken as a directive to heed Jesus' predictions of his suffering and death (Mark 8:31-33; 9:30-32; 10:32-34) as events that disclose his identity as Son of God.[33] When Jesus' removal into the divine realm does take place, however, it is to be interpreted as "the Son of Man rising from the dead" (9:9). Thus "an important purpose of the transfiguration account is to foreshadow the transformation of Jesus' body and its translation into heaven."[34] The disciples see that Jesus is Son of God in such a way that he is at home with the heavenly visitors Elijah and Moses, but the fact that they see him left behind when the visitors depart indicates that there is still more to be accomplished before he himself is "taken away."

The death of Jesus in Mark, another apocalyptic event, is the third epiphany scene (Mark 15:33-39). Darkness covers the land "from the sixth till the ninth hour" (v. 33), and this is just the kind of heavenly portent that would have been expected at the death of a great ruler.[35] At the same time, this motif also alludes to the book of Amos:

And it will happen on that day, says the Lord God, that the sun will set at noon, and the light will grow dark upon the earth on [that] day; and I will change your feasts into mourning, and all your songs into a dirge; and I will put sackcloth on every lap and baldness upon every head; and I will make him as the mourning of a beloved one, and those with him as a day of distress. (Amos 8:9-10 LXX)

The voice from heaven declares Jesus to be "my beloved Son" at the baptism and at the transfiguration, but the voice is distinctly silent in this passage; God's absence is acutely felt by Jesus, and this is expressed in his cry, which echoes Psalm 22: "My God, my God, why have you abandoned me?" (Mark 15:34).[36] Only the intertext from Amos declares Jesus still to be beloved of God; therefore the darkness is probably best interpreted as a sign that the heavenly realm is in mourning at the passing of the beloved (Amos 8:10).[37] The tearing of the temple veil is a second portent at the death of Jesus, and it mirrors the tearing of the heavens at the baptism (cf. Mark 1:10 with 15:38: both use the passive of the verb *schizō*). Some have thought the tearing of the temple veil signified for Mark the destruction of the temple. Although Mark has an interest in this (see 11:12-25; 13:1-2; 14:57-58), the similarity to 1:10 suggests that in these events "the divine presence is not localized, either in an earthly holy place or in the heavens."[38]

This process begins with Jesus' baptism and comes to a climax at his death. The result is almost immediate: "Now when the centurion who had been standing opposite him saw that he breathed his last in this way, he said, "Truly this man was God's son" (Mark 15:39). Scholars have long debated how such a declaration can make sense. The key has seemed, to some, to lie in the word translated above as "in this way" (Gk., *houtōs*). Some have concluded that this refers to the divine portents—at least the darkening of the skies, if not the tearing of the temple veil (which it is not clear the centurion is positioned to see).[39] This at least is how the author of Matthew read the scene, although in his presentation there are other portents in view (see Matt. 27:51-54). Others have concluded that this is a sarcastic remark, one that continues the mockery at the cross (Mark 15:29-32): just as Jewish wags call him "the Messiah, the King of Israel" (vv. 31-32), a Roman wag addresses him with the title reserved for the emperor, "God's son" (v. 39). Moreover, the Greek itself for "God's son" is ambiguous, for the definite article ("the") is lacking. In Greek, *huios theou* could mean either "a son of a god" of "the Son of [the] God"—either is possible, grammatically speaking.[40] Importantly, however, "son of god" without the definite article is part of the title Augustus used in correspondence in the Greek-speaking parts of his empire: *Autokratōr Kaisar theou huios Sebastos*, that is, "Emperor Caesar Augustus son of god."[41]

Ultimately, it is ambiguous whether this character is making a sincere confession or not, but given the prominence of irony in Mark's passion narrative, it matters little, as Clifton Black recently has observed.[42] For the author of Mark and for his sympathetic readers, however, the remark of the centurion prefigures the confession of the crucified Jesus as Son of God among Gentiles; and it signifies that Jesus' identity as Son of God is only fully disclosed when one sees him fulfill his Father's will on the cross (see 14:35-36). This identity, narrated through these three epiphany scenes, is disclosed only gradually and under the control of Mark's secrecy motif: announcement of it comes first at the baptism (as it were) to Jesus himself, then at the transfiguration to the disciples (who are commanded to secrecy), and finally at Jesus' death to the whole world (the Roman *oikoumenē*), with the centurion as its spokesman. In uttering this remark, the centurion acclaims Jesus, victim of the Roman imperial might, with a title reserved for the ruler of the world.[43] As Boring observes, the one who "sees only the crucified Jesus *sees* who he really is (*alēthōs*, 'truly'). This seeing is not a human attainment, but the gift of God, and in this respect the centurion is the model for all later believers."[44] In these three pivotal scenes, then, Jesus is declared Son of God, twice by a voice from heaven, and once—when that voice is silent—by a Roman centurion.

Seeing Mark 16:1-8 as the Conclusion of the Gospel

These three scenes form the narrative spine of Mark's Gospel, and their centrality indicates that the career, origin, and death (and resurrection) of Jesus are decisive for the unfolding of God's will for human history. A fourth such interruption occurs at the conclusion of the Gospel, but it is unlike the others. In Mark 16:1-8 there are three visual indications that the divine realm has broken through again: first, a massive stone removed from the mouth of the tomb; second, a character designated as simply "a young man in dressed in a white robe"; and third, a missing body. Here, in contrast with the other three scenes, revelation comes primarily through "not seeing." Granted, the female disciples are also told that they will see Jesus in Galilee (v. 7), but this seeing lies outside the story and beyond the scope of the Gospel. The other difference between this story and the other epiphanies is that in this scene there is no declaration of Jesus as Son of God. When the young man in white speaks to the alarmed women, he says, "You are seeking Jesus the Nazarene, the one who was crucified. He was raised; he is not here" (Mark 16:6). Jesus is identified by his place of origin and by the means of his death—but this latter description, the "Crucified One," names him as the rejected and suffering Son of Man as well as the subject of early Christian proclamation (as Paul says in 1 Cor. 1:23 and elsewhere).[45]

This final scene, then, is the inverse of the three earlier epiphany scenes, and it is exactly the opposite of what the reader should be expecting. After all, Jesus by now in Mark's Gospel has predicted four times that he would rise from the dead; a reader familiar with early Christian traditions about the appearances of Jesus after his death would probably expect a scene at the tomb to conclude the Gospel with the risen Jesus appearing to his followers and commissioning them to carry forth the kerygma of his death and resurrection. Not only that, but a reader familiar with early Christian understandings of the meaning of Jesus' resurrection might expect something along the lines of what Paul writes, quoting an early creedal formula in the salutation of his letter to Rome: "He was designated 'Son of God' in power according to the spirit of holiness by the resurrection of the dead" (Rom. 1:4). Perhaps such a reader would have been expecting an announcement that Jesus' resurrection has confirmed that he is the Messiah, the Christ, as Peter says in Acts: "God has made this Jesus whom you crucified both Lord and Christ" (Acts 2:36, following a lengthy exegetical piece on Jesus' resurrection, vv. 24-35). A reader familiar with Greco-Roman myths about apotheosis might have expected a story with an empty tomb and a missing body to include some kind of acclamation of Jesus as a god, as the exalted Romulus declared in Plutarch's *Life of Romulus*, or some kind of affirmation that he had been divine all along, similar to the conclusion Chaereas made when confronted with Callirhoe's empty tomb.[46]

Why does Mark's concluding story not include an affirmation that Jesus is the Messiah or Son of God? Boring suggests this is because Mark wanted to emphasize the ongoing importance of the career and death of Jesus: "The Risen One, the Christ and Son of God, the Son of Man who is to come on the clouds, is not to be separated from the career of the crucified man of Nazareth."[47] The genre of Mark's concluding story may also offer a clue, however. Mark used a disappearance story, following the narrative pattern of assumption, and according to Adela Yarbro Collins, this is because it was "a culturally defined way for an author living in the first century to narrate the resurrection of Jesus."[48] Given the expectation that the resurrection would involve all of God's people, Collins says, the affirmation that Jesus "had been raised from the dead as an individual . . . seemed quite similar to the claims that Enoch, Elijah, Moses, Romulus, and others had been taken, including their earthly bodies, to heaven."[49] In other words, to explain how claims about Jesus' individual resurrection could be reconciled with the basic idea that resurrection was a *corporate* eschatological hope, Mark narrated Jesus' resurrection as an assumption. His story emphasizes the aftereffects of Jesus' resurrection using the elements of a disappearance story.[50] In the tradition, after all, assumption is something that happens to an individual, while resurrection was typically understood as corporate and eschatological (that is, it would only happen at the end of the age). In my opinion, Mark did this because he had inherited a traditional story about the discovery of the empty tomb by female disciples; however, as noted above, such disappearance stories often included some kind of theological interpretation.

The closest thing to such an interpretation here is the single word *ēgerthē*, "he was raised" (16:6), which explains why "he is not here." In Mark's original Greek, there is no connecting conjunction (such as "therefore") that might explain how to understand the connection between the two statements. Importantly, however, the announcement precedes its implication: as we will see in other deployments of the story, the empty tomb is displayed as a result of God raising Jesus (rather than as a fact that led to the conclusion that he had been raised). The proclamation of the resurrection precedes the observation of the empty tomb. As in the transfiguration, the passive verb here suggests that this was done by God, but the text offers no explicit interpretation as to what this could mean *for Jesus*. Did his removal into the divine realm signify that he was really God's Son? Did his resurrection from the dead mean that God had confirmed him as the Messiah or exalted him as Lord? By failing to provide an explicit answer to these questions, Mark in effect decenters both the early resurrection proclamation, which identified the risen Jesus as Christ/Messiah, Lord, Son of God; and the Greco-Roman apotheosis myth, which connected disappearance with apotheosis and with the veneration as hero or god of the one taken away, or (in the case of Roman emperors such as Julius and Augustus) of their successors as *divi filius*. In other words, he uses the language of resurrection and the narrative motifs of assumption but reconfigures certain aspects of the theological significance of each.

The Resurrection of the Son of Man

Why has Mark decentered these theological paradigms, and where does he direct the reader's focus instead? One answer has already been seen: Mark preferred to use the title "Son of God" for Jesus in relation to his Spirit-filled career (Mark 1:9-11; see also 3:11), his status or origin (9:2-8; see also, again, 3:11), and his obedient death (15:34-39; see also 14:35-36). Mark's early readers could have taken "Son of God" as a multivalent term, which could have messianic or anti-imperial connotations, or which could imply Jesus' divine origin. Regardless, the narration directs readers to understand the title mainly in terms of Jesus' activity. This can be seen in the way "Son of God" figures prominently in the three epiphany scenes described above, but it can also be seen in the way the evangelist used what Jesus has to say about his mission, present and future, as the "Son of Man" to adjust or correct the disciples' (and the readers') expectations as to what "Messiah" or "Son of God" should be and do.[51] This happens several times in Mark's presentation of the story of Jesus.

First, after Peter acclaims Jesus as Messiah (8:27-30), the narrator says that "he began to teach them that the Son of Man must suffer many things, and be rejected by the elders and the chief priests and the scribes, and be killed, and after three days rise again" (8:31). The other passion predictions also use the title Son of Man for Jesus as rejected, suffering, executed, and rising (9:31; 10:33-34; see also 9:12). Second, when confronted with the question of whether he was claiming to be "the Messiah, the Son of the Blessed One" (Mark 14:61), Jesus responds to the chief priest with a saying that conflates Psalm 110 with Daniel 7: "I am; and you will see the Son of Man seated at the right hand of the Power, and coming with the clouds of heaven" (v. 62). This focuses on the future career of Jesus the Son of Man, when he would come as judge, imbued with divine authority. Importantly, the saying is presented, as are two related sayings in Mark (13:26; 16:7), using the not-seeing/seeing dynamic found also in Q 13:34-35: after a period of absence, the Son of Man[52] (in Q 13:35, the Coming One; but see also Q 12:39-40; 17:23-24) will suddenly appear. These sayings will be discussed further below. Third, all three of the Son of God epiphanies described above are redefined contextually in relation to Jesus' self-presentation as Son of Man. After his baptism, Jesus the Son of God announces the kingdom of God, calls disciples, teaches, casts out demons, heals the sick (the blind, the lame, the skin-diseased), forgives sins, feeds the hungry, raises the dead, and rules on questions of Torah observance—as "one having authority" (1:22, 27; 2:10).[53] However, when Jesus heals a paralytic in Mark 2:1-12, he does so saying that it is "in order that [his critics] may know that the Son of Man has author-ity (Gk., *exousia*) on earth to forgive sins" (2:10). This remark uses language from Daniel 7, in which the "one like a human being" receives authority from the Ancient of Days (Dan. 7:12, 14 LXX). This authority Jesus delegates to his followers, both during his ministry (Mark 3:15; 6:7) and in the time before his return as Son of Man (13:34). After Jesus is declared at the transfiguration for the second time to be the "beloved Son [of God]," he warns the three disciples not to tell anyone what they had seen "until the Son of Man had risen from the dead" (9:9). Thus Jesus' rightful status as Son of God, and the revelation of this glorious status to the disciples, is to remain hidden until after both his suffering (as an indispensable part of his mission, 8:31; 9:12; 9:31; 10:33-34; and espe-cially 10:45) and his resurrection (the vindication of that suffering, 8:31; 9:9; 9:31; 10:33-34) provide the correct interpretive lenses. As to the final epiphany of Jesus as Son of God, at his death, there is no explicit Son of Man statement to clarify its correct interpretation.

However, there are some significant indications that the reader is to interpret the empty tomb story as the (partial) vindication of Jesus the Son of Man. First and foremost, Son of Man is the typical self-designation of the Markan Jesus in his predictions of his resurrection (8:31; 9:9; 9:31; 10:33-34).[54] Second, as Simon Gathercole has recently observed, the multivalence of the term "Son of Man" in Mark—given that it is used in different contexts for Jesus as having authority, Jesus as suffering and rejected, Jesus as vindicated through the resurrection, and Jesus as coming again at the end of the age—is held together by Mark's narrative arc. "The narrative pattern which holds the Son of Man sayings together is: *the authoritative Son of Man revealed—the authority of the Son of Man rejected—the authority of the Son of Man vindicated.*"[55] Yet the resurrection of the Son of Man (predicted in Mark 9:9) is only his partial vindication, since it remains for him to come, to be seen, and to receive his full "power and glory" (see 13:26). This can happen because, in his "resurrection," as Mark tells it, Jesus the suffering and rising Son of Man has been removed into the divine realm in order to await his revelation as the coming Son of Man at "the end" (13:7, 13). This revelation would comprise both his gathering of the elect (13:27; presumably this means their cor-porate resurrection) and his vindication before his oppressors, when they will see him (13:26; 14:62). Until then, Jesus will be absent, and his followers are not to be misled by false reports of his presence (13:21-23).Thus, third, the empty tomb story itself, as a disappearance story that emphasizes the absence of Jesus, invokes the assumption-return scenario we observed in the Sayings Gospel Q.

The women arrive at the tomb expecting to find a dead but present Jesus, for they bring spices to anoint the body—possibly to complete what was impossible to finish at the onset of the Sabbath (15:46; 16:1-3). They seem not to know that Jesus has already been anointed for burial by an unnamed woman (14:3-9), but their desire to care for him after his death, which should be interpreted as a con-tinuation of their discipleship and service (15:40-41; 16:1) and their observance of the Sabbath have brought them to the tomb at just the right time.[56] After find-ing the stone already rolled away, the women are alarmed to see a young man in white sitting inside the tomb. His explanations are strikingly reminiscent of the not-seeing/seeing and absent/present dynamic found also in Q 13:34-35 and in related sayings such as Q 12:39-40:

> "You are seeking Jesus the Nazarene, who was crucified. He has been raised, he is not here; see the place where they laid him. But leave now, and tell his disciples and Peter that he is going ahead of you into Galilee, and you will see him there, just as he told you." (Mark 16:6-7)

> "[And] I tell you, you will not see me until [the time comes when] you say, 'Blessed is the Coming One in the name of the Lord!'" (Q 13:35)

> "But you should know that had the householder known in which hour [of the night] the thief was going to come, he would not have let his house be broken into. You also should be prepared, because you do not know at what hour the Son of Man is coming." (Q 12:39-40)

What all these sayings share in common is the idea of an extended absence and then a restored presence. In Mark, the invitation to inspect is the concrete demonstration that "he is not here," but the reference to the encounter in Galilee is the outcome of Jesus' removal by God.[57] The Q sayings about the coming of the Son of Man (see also Q 17:23-24, 26-30) talk about a period of absence followed by an unmistakable visible presence, and they hint at the restored presence as a time of separation and judgment. This is confirmed by the parables in Q that describe an absent master returning from a journey and evaluating his slaves' conduct, as in Q 12:43: "Blessed is that slave whose master, when he comes, will find him so doing" (that is, doing what he had directed).[58]

Mark 16:7 refers obliquely to resurrection appearances in Galilee, although this reference is subsumed narratively to the theme of absence. There are three indications that Mark 16:7 is referencing an appearance tradition, such as the one preserved by Paul in 1 Corinthians 15:3-5 + 7: (1) the use of the passive of the verb egeirō for "he was raised," where elsewhere Mark uses anistēmi; (2) the priority of Peter; and (3) the use of the verb horaō for seeing the risen Jesus, a detail not found in Mark 14:28, the sister saying to 16:7.[59] The language of a future "seeing," however, in the context of Mark is strongly reminiscent of sayings about the coming of the Son of Man: both Mark 13:21-27 and 14:62 use the future "you/they will see the Son of Man . . . coming" (again, the verb is horaō). Does this mean that Mark 16:7 refers not to a resurrection appearance, but to the coming of Jesus the Son of Man—that is, the parousia?[60] The strong connection made in some Jewish texts and traditions between assumption and special eschatological function, seen for example in traditions about Elijah and in the Jerusalem saying in Q 13:34-35, would support this conclusion. Mark uses a traditional disappearance story as a way of focusing the reader's attention on the future role of Jesus, rather than on his temporary risen presence, which, according to the appearance tradition, gave special authority and insight to those who claimed such experiences (see, e.g., 1 Cor. 9:1; 15:8-11; Luke 24:44-49). Thus Mark is suppressing the appearance tradition in general. In doing so, Mark also suppresses a tradition about an appearance of the risen Jesus to the women; whether such a tradition was originally situated *at the tomb* will be explored in chapter 7 below.

The words of the young man are ambiguous and should probably be taken in two ways. First, just beyond the timeline of the narrative, the women and the other disciples should expect to see the risen Jesus in Galilee, although—as with the bridegroom saying in Mark 2:20—the focus of the story is on the absence of Jesus. For the women in the story, alarm, fear, trembling, and perplexity (*ekstasis*) are appropriate responses to a confrontation with the in-breaking divine realm; the three disciples react similarly at the transfiguration (9:6).[61] The sights they see—the stone rolled away and the young man in white sitting inside the tomb— are themselves signs of the nearness of the divine. This young man wears the white garments of the divine realm, and he knows the meaning of Jesus' disappearance and the details of his future contact with the disciples. The women react in fear as if they had seen an angel.[62] It is possible that Mark's source story narrated the appearance of an angel, and that in his effort to downplay the epiphanic qualities of the story, the author has demoted the angel to a symbolic figure, a "young man" (*neaniskos*); this recalls the odd incident at Jesus' arrest where a "young man" wearing only a linen garment runs away naked when seized by those who arrest Jesus (14:51-52).[63] In any event, within the constraints of the narrative, the reader must assume that this figure has removed the stone so that the women can enter the tomb and see that Jesus is gone.[64]

Thus, more importantly, what the women do not see—the body of Jesus— also points to God's decisive act. It signifies that God has taken the dead Jesus away in order to await his return as the Son of Man, and this means rescue from death, restoration to life, and exaltation in heaven.[65] This is very much along the lines of what the Wisdom of Solomon says of "the Righteous One" (Wisdom 2–5), except that in Mark's story of Jesus there is a physical "taking away," whereas in Wisdom the removal language is euphemistic for untimely death.[66] Mark interprets the disappearance of Jesus' body as (bodily) "resurrection," at least partly because his christological sensibilities lie close to the kerygma that Paul transmitted: "Christ died for our sins according to the Scriptures, was buried, was raised from the dead according to the Scriptures" (see 1 Cor. 15:3-4 with Mark 8:31; 9:31; 10:33-34; 10:45; 14:24). However, Mark does not narrate the appearances (1 Cor. 15:5-8) but only suggests them indirectly. Second—and "let the reader understand" (Mark 13:14)—this story also recalls Jesus' warning to flee from Judea in the time of great oppression that would precede the coming of the Son of Man (13:14-20); this warning applies above all to Mark's audiences. The time before the Son of Man's coming would be defined not only by great oppression but also by the absence of the Messiah and by "false messiahs and false prophets" declaring his presence (vv. 21-22); these conditions are also predicted in Q (Q 17:23-24). The elect must not be deceived, but must "watch" (Mark 13:23), for they will see signs in the heavens before they will see "the Son of Man coming in the clouds with much power and glory" (vv. 24-26). When the women flee from the tomb, so also Mark's original reader must flee from Judea into Galilee while enduring the oppression that marks the days of the absence of the Son of Man.[67] As in other texts from this era, the Son of Man is a representative figure (although he never loses particularity as Jesus of Nazareth).[68] Just as he endured suffering and rejection and self-giving before vindication, so also must the community of the Son of Man, whose vindication will come when they finally "see" him, particularly because the Son of Man will finally be seen in all his power and glory by all—including those who rejected him. So, in a final ellipsis, the author of Mark invites his readers to correct the acclamation of Jesus as universally authoritative Son of God (15:39) with ideas about Jesus' future revelation and vindication as the Son of Man (16:7), and has them look not to the legitimating presence of the risen Christ but to the absence and future return of the risen Son of Man.

We are now able to speak with more clarity as to how and why Mark has ended his Gospel as he has, decentering both the Greco-Roman disappearance-apotheosis myth and the early Christian resurrection-appearance traditions. In both instances, the clue is found in Mark's deployment of the character Jesus the Son of Man. First, Mark subverts Roman imperial theology, which combined the apotheosis of the dead emperor (by both funeral rite and legal decree) with the acclamation of his successor as *divi filius*. As already seen, the Roman centurion—because the death of Jesus precipitates a divine revelation that he as a character in the narrative is prepared to accept, or at least to symbolize—acclaims Jesus with the same title when he sees him die both as victim of imperial violence and as one obedient to his Father's will. There is a deep irony that runs all the way through Mark's passion narrative: those who mock and torture Jesus and call him "Messiah" and "King of Israel" (15:32) do not know that this is what he is, although the narrator and the reader do.[69] In a similar vein, the centurion's acclamation, coming from a Roman, gives Jesus the title reserved for the ruler of the inhabited world, though his installation as King of Israel and Ruler of all awaits his coming as the Son of Man, when his "glory and power" will be seen and acknowledged by all. A similar association of resurrection, parousia, and universal authority is seen in 1 Corinthians 15:23-28.

Mark's closing story decenters imperial theology by using the narrative foundation of apotheosis—the assumption or disappearance story—to express a vindication that is at least partly deferred. The centurion's remark "Truly this was God's son" is proleptic and still awaits fulfillment. In place of an acclamation of Jesus as Son of God at the tomb he left empty, there is only "You are seeking Jesus the Nazarene, who was crucified. He has been raised, he is not here; see the place where they laid him" (16:6). This "place" that the young man indicates is the niche inside the tomb where the body had been put but that is now empty.[70] "He is not here" must be interpreted not in terms of the Greco-Roman paradigm, which understood assumption as the occasion of deification, but in terms of the Jewish idea that the one taken away was being reserved in heaven for his role at the end of the age. According to Mark, Jesus is already God's Son, particularly because of his obedience to the Father's will. The full postmortem vindication of

Jesus, for now postponed, is nearly at hand in Mark's view, but the interim is a dangerous time for Mark's readers, for they, like the women at the tomb, are at serious risk of becoming victims of Rome as Jesus had.

Second, the closing remark that "they told nothing to anyone, for they were afraid," requires the reader to imagine that eventually they did tell the story, for otherwise Mark's transmission of the story has no explanation.[71] This sense that the women's flight is a narrative suspension of the true end of the story also illuminates how and why Mark has ended his story without an appearance of the risen Jesus.[72] In the other resurrection narratives, and in the letters of Paul, the appearances of Jesus serve to reconfirm and to commission his followers, to legitimate their interpretation of the Scriptures, and to validate their authority as they evangelized and oversaw new movements.[73] Mark, because of the historical circumstances of his own circle, does not leave his reader with the validating presence of Jesus, probably because he is not interested in the transfer of authority from Jesus to his designees in the interim. As Donald Juel perceptively remarked, there is in this story a "critical tension . . . between blindness and insight, concealment and openness, silence and proclamation," and this tension is not resolved.[74] This means that Mark's narrative focus is on the behavior of the disciple in the intervening time between the resurrection of Jesus and his coming as the Son of Man. This same theme of faithfulness in the interim is also found in Q material about slaves whose master is absent (e.g., Q 12:42-46). In this sense, the future is "open," as is the ending of Mark.[75] For in some ways, the reaction of the women and the open ending of Mark present a challenge to the readers and their present conduct as disciples of Jesus.[76]

It is a topic of long debate how best to understand the behavior of the women in this story. They are highlighted as followers who do not desert Jesus even in death (15:40-41), but in fleeing from the tomb they fail to follow the risen Jesus who was already going ahead to Galilee (16:8). They are the first recipients of the announcement of Jesus' resurrection (v. 6), but in remaining silent they fail to tell the other disciples the message that Jesus has been raised from the dead (v. 8). Victoria Phillips points out that because the narrator provides "an inside view" of the women's thoughts and feelings, "Mark induces the reader to identify with the women."[77] Thus Mark presents a characterization in which "their emotions are understandable; [but] their actions—flight and the decision to be silent—are wrong."[78] Mark's readers are challenged to consider how they will respond to the call to follow and to proclaim, and his description of the women's response echoes earlier episodes in the Gospel. Their alarm and fear recall those followers of Jesus who were "alarmed" and "afraid" as Jesus "was going ahead of them" on his way to Jerusalem and to rejection, suffering, and death (10:32-34). These followed initially but deserted Jesus in the end (14:50-52); Jesus himself was "alarmed" (or "terrified") as he confronted the Father's will in Gethsemane (14:33), but he went to the cross.[79] Their silence recalls the story of the leper who, once healed by Jesus, disregards the command to "tell nothing to anyone," but instead goes out and begins "to proclaim it freely and to spread the word widely" (1:44-45). Therefore, in order to emphasize following Jesus and proclaiming the good news of his resurrection as necessary aspects of the disciple's behavior while the Master is still absent, Mark chooses not to narrate an appearance of the risen Jesus. He does retain the basic components of the resurrection kerygma, that is, "he was raised" and "he appeared," but opts out of the legitimating implications of the appearance traditions.[80]

Assumption as Resurrection, and Resurrection as Assumption

Mark's great contribution to the development of the Easter story is the fact that he combined the disappearance (assumption) tradition with the resurrection (appearance) tradition. There are good grounds for thinking that he did this in the first place because he had inherited a story about the discovery of the empty tomb, but even if arguments in favor of a traditional basis for Mark 16:1-8 do not convince, the story as it stands still has much more in common generically with assumption narratives than it does with appearance reports or narratives. The prominence of the assumption paradigm in Mark's narrative ending shifts the focus from the temporary presence of the risen Jesus to his absence before his return as the Son of Man. Yet Mark, of course, was evidently also aware of the resurrection appearances and of their importance in some circles; he was also heir to the passion-resurrection kerygma, which was fundamental to the proclamation and theological work of Paul. This is evident in the way he integrates into his narrative structure predictions of both Jesus' passion and resurrection, as well as theological claims that Jesus' death was "on behalf of many" (10:45; 14:24; see also "on behalf of our sins" in 1 Cor. 15:3). Yet in telling an assumption story, he omits any acclamation of Jesus as "Son of God" and thus decenters the Greco-Roman apotheosis myth in favor of the Jewish idea that those taken away by God are reserved in heaven for their role at the end of the age. And in telling a resurrection story, he omits any appearance of the risen Jesus that could authorize the mission of leaders in the Jesus movements in favor of a focus on the risk of discipleship and proclamation in the interim period of Jesus' absence. This means that the appearance of Jesus to his followers in Galilee (Mark 16:7) must be understood by Mark as an appearance of the (risen but) taken-away Jesus from heaven (and not from out of the tomb).[81] This is an epiphany along the same lines as the appearance of the deified Romulus to Julius Proculus, but of course the closer analogy within Mark is the appearance of Elijah and Moses from the heavenly realm in the transfiguration.

Mark has exploited the theological ideas normally associated with both assumption and resurrection and has combined them in such a way that the foundation for the Easter story as it will be developed by Luke, Matthew, and John has been laid. For in relying on both the "disappearance" characteristic of the assumption paradigm and the kerygmatic announcement that "he was raised from the dead," Mark has told a story in which Jesus "was raised" in such a way that there is no question that the body is absent from the tomb: Jesus is dead and gone but also has been raised by God. According to Mark, then, the Crucified One has been taken away into heaven and raised by God, and now is there in a bodily way (just as Elijah and Moses and one supposes Enoch as well), waiting to appear as the Son of Man. This ultimate revelation is just around the corner (Mark 13:24-27). In some ways, this removes the ambiguity present in the Pauline material about the "bodily" nature of Jesus' resurrection (although, of course, Paul insisted on the resurrection "body" even though he conceived of it as "spiritual"). As we will see, at least Matthew (as far as we can tell) follows Mark in conceiving of the resurrection of Jesus as a bodily translation into the divine realm. For the other evangelists, as they received and redeployed the story, Jesus' tomb is empty because he was raised out of it—absent from the tomb, but present outside of it—and they narrate his removal into the divine realm as a subsequent (not identical) event. As we will see in the following chapters, Luke, Matthew, and John each have unique contributions to make to the development of the Easter story, and all of these contributions can be best understood as narrative "improvements" that reconcile the disappearance tradition more fully with the appearance tradition.

6. Luke: "Why Do Doubts Arise in Your Hearts?"

And they found the stone had been moved away from the tomb, but when they entered, they did not find the body of the Lord Jesus. And as they were puzzling about this, behold! two men dressed in clothing as bright as lightning stood near to them. And they became terrified and bowed their faces to the ground; and the men said to the women, "Why do you seek one who is living among the dead? He is not here, but has been raised. Remember how he told you, while he was still in Galilee, that the Son of Man must be handed over into the hands of sinful men and be crucified and on the third day rise." And they recalled his words . . . .

But Peter got up and ran to the tomb, and peering in he saw only the linen cloths; and he went home marveling at what had happened.

—Luke 24:2-8, 12

And he said to them, "Why are you so disturbed, and why do doubts arise in your hearts? See my hands and my feet, that it is I myself; handle me and see, for a spirit does not have flesh and bones as I have."

—Luke 24:38-39

Luke's version of the empty tomb story is quite different from its Markan source, and it includes some important narrative developments. As shown above, Paul talks about visionary appearances of the risen Christ without mentioning an empty tomb, and Mark's narrative suggests a tangible disappearance without an appearance, tangible or otherwise. Despite this, Paul and Mark both use the category of resurrection to express Jesus' vindication and ongoing existence—as does Luke. Mark began the process of bringing the empty tomb together with the appearance traditions by narrating Jesus' resurrection as a disappearance story, and by referring to (though not narrating) a Galilean appearance of the resurrected Jesus, in which Peter would figure strongly. Mark therefore shows knowledge and acceptance of the appearance traditions but avoids a narrative situation in which the risen Jesus is present, even temporarily, to validate the movements associated with Peter and the others. Luke, on the other hand, makes the next logical step in bringing the empty tomb narrative in line with the appearance traditions: in Luke's version, Peter—first on Paul's list and singled out by the author of Mark—visits the empty tomb to see for himself (Luke 24:12).[1] This is probably the most important change Luke introduces, and it illustrates that Luke was acutely aware of the problems the empty tomb story posed. There are other significant adaptations as well, the most obvious being that Luke, in contrast to Mark, does describe appearances of the risen Jesus: one involving two unnamed disciples on the road to Emmaus (Luke 24:13-35), and one involving "the Eleven and those with them" that extends to the end of the Gospel (24:36-53). Luke also refers to an appearance to Simon (Peter), though it is not narrated directly: it is what "the Eleven," which of course would include Peter, are proclaiming (24:34). According to Luke, these appearances of the risen Jesus all occur in or around Jerusalem, and they conclude with Jesus being taken up into heaven from Bethany (24:50-53),[2] apparently on the same day, the first day of the week (as noted in Luke 24:1). Unlike Mark, whose disappearance story together with a predicted reappearance at a distance (eschatological and geographical) evoked assumption stories in both the Greek and Jewish milieus (Romulus, Elijah), Luke's stories about tangible appearances of Jesus in the vicinity of Jerusalem seem more to imply a getting up or rising (Gk., *egeirō*) out of the tomb, which the women discover already open.

In comparison with Mark's account, there are "two men" at the tomb in Luke, and they are more clearly angels than was Mark's "young man" (Luke 24:4; Mark 16:5). This alteration is minor in relation to how Luke changes what the women are told at the tomb. The directive the women receive in Mark, to "go and tell his disciples and Peter that he is going ahead of you to Galilee" (Mark 16:7), is now in Luke a reminder of the passion predictions: "Remember how he told you, while he was still in Galilee . . ." (Luke 24:6). Luke preserves Mark's reference to Galilee, but only as the location of earlier discipleship and instruction; Luke avoids referring to the appearance in Galilee at least partly because of his preference for Jerusalem as the site of the resurrection appearances. Another motivation for this change appears to be to restrict the role of the women as bearers of the Easter proclamation. The women in Luke no longer receive a commissioning to tell the Easter message to the other disciples, although they do tell the others (Luke 24:9-10) as they did not in Mark (16:8). Some scholars see this change as an attempt by Luke to decrease the status or role of the women at the tomb, or even to decrease the status of Mary Magdalene in particular as a primary Easter witness.[3] In this view, the changes Luke makes to Mark's empty tomb story are symptomatic of an interest among some early Christians to limit carefully the roles women could play in leadership. This will be discussed in detail below.

As to Peter's visit to the empty tomb (Luke 24:12), some commentators see this addition as arising from the need to have the women's testimony about the empty tomb verified by a competent male witness, for women were not acceptable as witnesses in Jewish antiquity.[4] Recent study has shown, however, that this was not always or necessarily the case.[5] A negative view of women's testimony could be implicit in verse 11: the apostles think the women's report about the empty tomb is "nonsense" (*lēros*), and so they do not believe it. Luke's choice of word for their view of the report, however, is probably due more to its content (an empty tomb and a vision of angels) than to its source (the women); the reader, after all, knows that the women's report is true, and this does not present the apostles in a positive light. As we will see, questions about the empty tomb story, or more specifically about the nature of the resurrection, and not questions about the reliability of the women, lie at the root of this. In Luke 24:12 we find two important apologetic additions, both of which are attempts to defend the empty tomb story Luke has received in his source text, Mark. First, Luke adds an apostolic verification of the report. Peter, whose status is elevated by Luke elsewhere in the Gospel (see, e.g., Luke 22:31-32), thus becomes, of the disbelieving apostles, the first to make steps toward belief in Jesus' resurrection by running to the tomb and marveling at what he saw.[6] The second apologetic addition is the description of the grave clothes, which were not mentioned in Mark. When Peter looks into the tomb, he sees *only* the linens, which not only means that he does not see the body, but also suggests that the body was not stolen, for someone moving or hiding the body would have taken the grave clothes with it. Thus Luke 24:12 provides apostolic testimony that Jesus left the tomb on his own.

How Luke Adapts the Empty Tomb Story

A close look at the particular changes Luke makes to Mark 16:1-8 helps put the addition of Peter's visit into its proper context. Luke omits the women's odd question: "Who will roll the stone away for us?" (Mark 16:3), because in Mark it only drew attention to the narrative problem of how the women thought they would be able to anoint the body, with no real plan for removing the stone. The problem of how the women expected to gain access to the body still remains in Luke, but the action moves so quickly to the discovery of the open tomb (24:2) that the reader is scarcely aware of it. Luke 24:2-3 contrasts the women's two discoveries: they found (*heuron*) the stone moved away, but they did not find (*ouch heuron*) the body. By telling the story this way, Luke avoids a delay in Mark's narrative. In Mark the reader does not know whether the body is there until the young man points out its absence to the women, who were apparently distracted by his presence in the tomb (Mark 16:6b). Luke makes this clear immediately, using language that was common in Hellenistic assumption stories. As we saw in the story about Chaereas and Callirhoe, witnesses would typically seek but not find the body (*Chaer.* 3.3; Luke 24:2-3, 5), and that was considered sufficient proof of a divine removal. It is perhaps inevitable that a narrative feature associated with assumption would have crept back into Luke's resurrection story, because, after all, Jesus' body has disappeared. In contrast with Mark, in Luke this language indicates that Jesus' body was removed by resurrection, not assumption. The assumption (ascension) of Jesus comes later in Luke 24:50-53 (also Acts 1:9-11). This contrast between the discovery of the open tomb and the nondiscovery of the body of Jesus is paralleled in Luke 24:12, where Peter sees the linens but not the body. When the women and then Peter view the inside of the tomb, they are puzzled (24:4a, 12b): this illustrates that the empty tomb never leads to resurrection faith, but only to wonder and amazement, possibly because there are so many ways to explain a missing body.

Following Mark, Luke resists calling these men "angels," at least here in the tomb narrative (24:4), even though they appear suddenly, are brightly arrayed, and are later described as angels by the disciples journeying to Emmaus (24:23). In redacting Mark, Luke avoids, as he does elsewhere, the characteristically Markan words often translated as "alarm" or "dismay" or "amaze" (*ekthambeō*, *thambeō*).[7] In Luke 24:5 the women are simply frightened and bow their faces to the ground.[8] When the men speak, they draw attention to the women's search for Jesus, just as the young man did in Mark. Their question, "Why do you seek the living one among the dead?" (Luke 24:5), notes the fruitlessness of their search and communicates that Jesus is alive. Luke eliminates the designation "who was crucified" from Mark as well. It is questionable whether the words "He is not here, but was raised" were originally in Luke, but if they were, they reflect the same connection between absence and resurrection made by Mark (Mark 16:6).[9]

The men in the tomb tell the women to remember what Jesus had said while he was still in Galilee. These women, not named in this context until verse 11, had been with Jesus in Galilee (see 8:1-3, where they are named, and 23:55-56, where they are not). The reminder of the three passion predictions (Luke 9:22; 9:44-45; 18:31-34) is meant not only for the women but also for the reader. By doing this, Luke is able to retain the reference to Galilee in Mark (Mark 16:7; Luke 24:6) but can avoid referring to a resurrection appearance there, for (as noted above) Luke situates all the appearances in the vicinity of Jerusalem. During Jesus' ministry, his disciples did not understand what he meant by predicting his suffering, death, and resurrection. This idea is present in Mark (e.g., Mark 9:32), but Luke deepens it through the narrator's remark that Jesus' meaning was concealed or hidden from the disciples (Luke 9:45; 18:34). Likely, this was meant to indicate that God prevented them from understanding. But now, at the empty tomb, everything becomes plain, or at least it should begin to become plain. At least the women remember what he said, but this is the beginning of a process that must also involve an encounter with the risen Jesus in which he would "open their minds to understand the Scriptures" (24:45).

For Luke, the death and resurrection of Jesus are to be interpreted as the fulfillment of the divine plan, and therefore as the fulfillment of the Scriptures and of Jesus' own teachings about himself. This emphasis, not present in the resurrection narratives of the other Gospels, occurs elsewhere in Luke 24 and also in Acts (see Luke 24:25-27, 44-47; Acts 2:22-36; 4:24-28; 13:26-39). Given the apparent importance of this theme to the author, it may be simply a side effect of the characteristically Lukan emphasis that the women are told to remember and not to go and announce (as they are in Mark and the other Gospels). Some scholars see their response—of remembering and then telling without being told to—as a confirmation of their true discipleship.[10] However, as noted above, others see this change as part of Luke's effort to diminish the role of the women who find the empty tomb. As Ann Graham Brock argues, this is consistent with the writings of Luke, who "never provides divine justification for women to preach."[11]

It is difficult to avoid this interpretation, especially given the reference to "the apostles," by whom Luke means "the Eleven" (24:9-10; see also Luke 6:13; Acts 1:26). Luke restricts the designation "apostle" to this authoritative group of male disciples[12] who, in this context, stand in sharp contrast to the women. In narrating the search for an apostolic replacement for Judas, Luke clearly has only male candidates in mind (Acts 1:21-22). Luke would have an interest in downplaying the role given to the women at the tomb, whether this would consist in simply adjusting the words of the figures at the tomb so that they are not commissioned with the resurrection proclamation, or suppressing a resurrection appearance to a figure like Mary Magdalene (which could have provided legitimation for women in leadership roles).[13] As already seen, Paul is sometimes thought to have taken a similar approach to appearances to women.[14] By way of contrast, in the Fourth Gospel Mary is sent by the risen Jesus and leaves the tomb uttering a very apostolic proclamation: "I have seen the Lord" (John 20:18; cf. 1 Cor. 9:1). In some circles in the early Jesus movements, Mary was singled out as the recipient of special revelation,[15] and later Christian tradition hailed her as "the apostle to the apostles."[16] Although it is certain that Luke avoided the Markan commissioning of the women by the young man, it is not certain that he avoided describing an appearance of the risen Jesus to the women, especially Mary Magdalene, as Brock has recently suggested.[17] It is impossible to say whether Luke knew of such a tradition, and indeed whether such a tradition was always linked with the empty tomb story (as it is in Matthew and John). So Luke omits the Markan commissioning of the women, not only because he is interested in reminding the reader of the passion predictions, but probably also because he wished to limit the role given to the women. Nevertheless, in Luke's story of the empty tomb, it is still the women and not "the apostles" who initially have the story right.

The Appearance to Simon (Peter) and His Visit to the Tomb

As suggested above, Mark 16:7 (a doublet of Mark 14:28) betrays Mark's awareness of traditions that the risen Jesus appeared to Peter and others. The author of Luke is more clearly aware of these traditions. As many scholars have recognized, the secondhand statement about an appearance of the risen Jesus to Simon (Peter) at the conclusion of the Emmaus encounter (Luke 24:34) provides evidence that Luke knew, if not 1 Corinthians, at least the tradition Paul was quoting in 1 Corinthians 15:3-5 + 7.[18] When the two formulations are compared, the distinctively Lukan features can be seen as consistent with the author's work elsewhere.

Luke 24:34   . . . that "the Lord indeed was raised, and he appeared to Simon."

1 Cor. 15:5   . . . and that he has been raised on the third day according to the Scriptures and that he appeared to Cephas . . .

Both statements connect resurrection and appearance. Both are introduced with "that," which often indicates the presence of a fragment of tradition. Both have a passive form of the verb "to raise" (*egeirō*), and both have "and he appeared" (*kai ōphthē*), although the names for Peter differ. This last detail is not insignificant, for there has been some question whether the Cephas of Paul's letters is the (Simon) Peter of the Gospels and Acts.[19] However, the names Cephas and Peter are virtually synonymous nicknames, Aramaic and Greek respectively, and John 1:42 indicates that the two names were remembered as referring to the same person.[20] In Luke 24:34, the pre-Pauline appearance tradition is adapted to Luke's preferred name, Simon. Luke 24:34 also uses the title "the Lord," which is Luke's preferred title for the risen Jesus.[21] "The third day" would be an obvious piece to omit, because within the narrative "today" would be more suitable. Luke also adds the adverb "indeed" (or "really"), which seems—coming from the Eleven as this does—appropriate after their reaction to news of the empty tomb (Luke 24:9-11).[22] Luke also does not have the formulaic "according to the Scriptures," because, in Luke's narration, the disciples do not yet understand that Jesus' death and resurrection were foretold by Scripture. Luke 24:44-47 makes this clear, for the risen Jesus needs to "open their minds to understand the Scriptures" (v. 45) and to make explicit the connection between the testimony of Scripture and his own predictions (vv. 46-47). Jesus rebukes the two disciples on the way to Emmaus for their foolishness and slowness of heart, and explains things from Scriptures there as well (24:25-27). Verse 34, therefore, is quite clearly the creation of Luke on the basis of either 1 Corinthians 15 or the pre-Pauline appearance tradition.[23] An apparent awareness of other features in Paul's argument for the resurrection of the dead, as we will see below, also suggests that Luke adapted Paul's version of the tradition.

The verse also gives the sense that it was placed where it is quite deliberately. It intrudes awkwardly into the narrative; the story would conclude much more neatly without it, and so it could be a Lukan insertion of traditional material.[24] Occurring where it does, it also overshadows the news of the two disciples who have hurried back to Jerusalem to announce their encounter with Jesus (24:33, 35)—in fact, the announcement the reader expects them to make is completely displaced by the kerygmatic announcement associated with Peter. Thus, it must be important that this reference to the appearance to Peter occurs precisely here. Narrative time seems generally to be compressed in Luke 24: the journey to Emmaus occurred "on the same day" as the discovery of the empty tomb (24:13). But at the end of the journey, although it was late enough to propose that the stranger stay over, the disciples still return to Jerusalem "at the same hour" and meet up with the Eleven and the others (24:33); then, while they were discussing these things, Jesus himself stood among them (24:36). There is no narrative clue that the remainder of Luke describes separate appearances, but only one, which concluded when Jesus led them out to Bethany and was carried up into heaven (24:50-53). The tendency, especially when reading Luke 24 in a synopsis, which breaks the narrative into successive pericopae, or when trying to harmonize Luke 24 with the "forty days" of Acts 1:3, is to miss this narrative compression.

Luke 24:34 cannot refer to Peter's visit to the tomb, for it was there that Peter determined Jesus' absence, and Peter had not yet experienced Jesus' presence. The way the disciples on the road describe Peter's visit, a verbal link with the initial discovery of the empty tomb is created: "They found (*heuron*) it just as the women said, but they did not see him" (24:24; cf. *heuron* in 24:2-3).[25] Again, the emphasis is on "not seeing," but not "seeing," which is the emphasis in verse 34. The reader could conclude that this appearance to Peter took place before the encounter on the Emmaus road, since the two disciples hurry back to Jerusalem and find the rest gathered there and already proclaiming the news. In any case, even though the chronological order of the appearances is not entirely clear, the appearance to Peter still has priority, for this appearance (and not the appearance to the disciples at table) is the one that generates the kerygmatic announcement, "The Lord has been raised and has appeared." This is consistent with Jesus' saying to Peter at the Last Supper: "But I have prayed on your behalf, that your faith might not fail; and you, once you have turned back, strengthen your brothers" (22:32).

If the appearance to Peter is given this precedence in Luke 24, this may have been an inference Luke drew from the placement of Cephas (Peter) in Paul's list. Originally, of course, this placement might not have signified chronological priority, but priority of some other kind; given the nature of the sources, however, a certain judgment is nearly impossible. It is interesting that both Mark and Luke single out Peter when adapting their empty tomb stories to bring them in line with the appearance traditions, and these three (1 Cor. 15:5; Mark 16:7; Luke 24:34) are the only references that might suggest the kind of priority we are discussing here.[26] The scarcity of such references might indicate, as Lüdemann has suggested, something of a suppression of the tradition that Peter was the primary resurrection witness, but of course certainty is impossible.[27] Probably Luke did not know a traditional narrative about an appearance to Peter; otherwise he would have used it. So he had to opt for this redactional placement of the (Petrine) kerygmatic statement he adapted from 1 Corinthians 15 (Luke 24:34).[28]

Taken together, Luke 24:12 and 24:34 mean that for Luke the primary witness of the risen Jesus, and the originator of the resurrection proclamation, authenticates the empty tomb, and so appearance and disappearance converge on the character of Peter. But why? It may be that Luke was using Peter's visit to the tomb as a response to charges from outsiders that the story of the empty tomb was "nonsense" (*lēros*, 24:11), although it would be odd for Luke to attribute an outsiders' criticism to the primary insiders, "the Eleven." Is Luke only trying to give some credibility to a story that, according to Mark, has only female witnesses to support it? This too is possible, although as noted above the testimony of women was not always or necessarily considered suspect or inferior. Another possibility has been suggested by Lüdemann, who thinks that in the pre-Lukan tradition the women's visit was combined with the appearance to Peter according to the following logic: "If the tomb was empty and Jesus appeared to Cephas, then the latter must have inspected it before he could accept the reality of the appearance."[29] Given Luke's very materialistic, flesh-and-bones narration of the resurrection appearances (see Luke 24:36-43, discussed below), this makes sense, although the narrative order in Luke 24—inspection before appearance—is exactly the opposite of what Lüdemann suggests. In any event, the author himself seems to be responsible for this combination.[30] For Luke 24:34 is deliberately placed so as to preempt the two disciples' announcement, which signifies that the resurrection proclamation, in Luke's view, originated with the appearance to Peter. The other piece of the puzzle is the evidence that shows that Luke 24:12 is the author's own creation, not an earlier tradition (as shown for Luke 24:34).[31] There is more to be said, however: Luke wants the reader to conclude something *substantial* about what the empty tomb means for the appearances.

Are We Seeing a *Pneuma*?

Having Peter, the primary witness of the appearance traditions, verify the empty tomb is a significant development, since it narrowly limits how the appearances can be interpreted. It requires complete bodily continuity between the dead Jesus in the tomb and the risen Jesus who appears—which is very different from the complete transformation Paul envisioned. Of all the Gospels, Luke is the most explicit about the mode of Jesus' postresurrection bodily existence. When he appears suddenly among the Eleven and the rest (24:36), Jesus himself explains that he is not a spirit (Gk., *pneuma*), for he has flesh and bones as a spirit cannot.

> Now, while they were speaking, he stood in the midst of them and said to them, "Peace to you." But they were startled, and became frightened, thinking they were seeing a spirit. And he said to them, "Why are you troubled, and why do doubts arise in your hearts? See my hands and my feet, that it is I myself; handle me, and see, because a spirit does not have flesh and bones as you see that I have." And after he had said this, he showed them his hands and his feet. And while they were still in disbelief on account of joy and marveling, he said to them, "Do you have anything to eat in here?" So they gave him a piece of grilled fish; and he took it and ate it in front of them. (Luke 24:36-43)[32]

In Greco-Roman antiquity, it would not be out of the question to see someone who was dead, and as seen earlier in chapter 1, such experiences would be open to a variety of interpretations. Although such an apparition could be interpreted as the aftereffect of assumption-apotheosis (as in the case of Romulus), typically it would be interpreted as some aspect of the dead person—that is, the soul, shadow, or daimon—becoming visible to living persons. We would call this a ghost—as ancient Greek and Latin speakers would as well, with varying terminology—or possibly, a "postmortem apparition."[33] In fact, most current translations render *pneuma* here in Luke 24:37, 39 not as "spirit" but as "ghost."[34]

According to ancient thinking, certain types of people were more likely to appear after their death in ghostly manifestations. As noted above, the typical view was that those who had died young (or before marriage), those who had died violently, and those whose bodies were not given proper burial or cremation were more likely to have a restless postmortem existence and to cause trouble for the living.[35] Jesus, executed as a criminal, would of course fall into the category of those dead by violence. Virgil (70–19 BCE) held that among those doomed to a restless afterlife, excluded for a time from rest in Hades, were people unjustly executed or who took their own lives.[36] Lucian (c. 125–80 CE) has one of his characters number the crucified (or impaled) among those especially given to appearing in ghostly manifestations: "such as, if a person hanged himself, or had his head cut off, or was impaled on a stake, or departed life in some other way such as these" (Lucian, *Philops.* 29).[37] Sarah Iles Johnston shows, in addition, that the violent means of death is not as critical in such cases as the dishonor associated with it.[38] This consideration is especially important given Luke's emphasis on Jesus' innocence (see Luke 23:4, 13-16, 20-22, 47; Acts 7:52; 13:28).[39]

An outsider could have concluded that followers of Jesus who were talking about his postmortem appearances had simply seen his ghost. As it seems, this would not have been considered unusual or extraordinary. But Luke makes it clear to his readers that however the appearances of Jesus could have been interpreted, they were epiphanies of someone who had been raised from the dead—with an empty tomb. As already seen, this is confirmed by Peter himself when he finds the tomb empty except for the grave clothes. The fact that Luke does not narrate an appearance of the risen Jesus at the tomb (as Matthew and John do) may be explained, as seen above, through either Luke's ignorance of such a tradition or his desire to restrict the role of the women to attesting the empty tomb—not announcing the resurrection. Another potential concern arises, however, in view of the interpretation of the resurrection appearances as ghostly apparitions: Kathleen Corley explains that tomb visitation and lamentation by women came to be associated in ancient Mediterranean culture with necromantic practices of conjuring the dead.[40] The corpus of spells and incantations called the Greek magical papyri attests to this, in particular to the ways that body parts could be used to control the ghosts of the dead—and the shade or spirit (often called a *daimōn*) of a person who died by violence would be particularly powerful if controlled. Hans Dieter Betz writes that given this background one is "justifiably astonished" that any of the evangelists chose to narrate resurrection appearances at the tomb.[41]

Further confirmation that the followers of Jesus had not seen (or conjured) his ghost is sometimes found in the demonstrations and explanations the risen Jesus makes in Luke 24:36-43. This passage in Luke 24 reads like an apologetic response to the view that the disciples of Jesus had really only seen his ghost (see Origen, *Cels.* 3.22; 7.35). If the risen Jesus were a ghost, he would not be as tangible as Luke's story depicts him, since for the most part in antiquity ghosts were thought of as intangible and were depicted using "all the obvious metaphors of insubstantialness: shadows, breaths of air, smoke, and dreams."[42] A classic example of this is when, in his visit to the underworld, Odysseus attempts three times to embrace his dead mother, Anticleia, and three times she slips through his arms (Homer, *Od.* 11.204–8).[43] On the other hand, in some ancient literary sources, ghosts take on a variety of embodied states, maintaining in some instances the physical state or attire of the individual at death or afterward, or even eating with the living (as Jesus does according to Luke-Acts) or physically affecting them otherwise.[44] As seen in chapter 1, some of the more substantial ghosts were not exactly ghosts but reanimated persons ("revenants") who would leave their graves to visit or torment the living, eventually to die again and leave their corpses behind.[45] In Luke-Acts, however, Jesus does not leave his corpse behind but is taken bodily into heaven (Luke 24:51; Acts 1:9-11) and remains there in that state (as suggested by Acts 7:56).

There is, however, something striking about Luke's use of "spirit" (*pneuma*) in this context. Eduard Schweizer thought that the "shadowy, non-corporeal existence" that *pneuma* denotes in Luke 24:37, 39 is quite different from the typical meaning of *pneuma* in Hellenism.[46] In fact, *pneuma* is not among the words typically used for the apparition of a human person who had died. The typical Greek terms include *phasma* and *phantasma* (phantom), *eidōlon* (apparition), *daimōn* (roughly, spirit of a dead person), and, less frequently, *skia* (shadow) and *psychē* (soul). These words were often used synonymously and connoted apparitions with varying degrees of "corporeality."[47] *Pneuma*, on the other hand, came to be used, but almost exclusively in Jewish Greek, for that part of the human person that survives death (e.g., *1 Enoch* 103:4; Luke 23:46; Acts 7:59; Heb. 12:23; 1 Peter 3:19); and according to Terence Paige, "not a single Gentile, non-Christian writer prior to the late second century ever used *pneuma* to signify a 'demon,' 'ghost,' or 'spirit' of any sort. When Plutarch or Lucian (or Theophrastus before them) refer to such things, the terms used are always *daimones, daimonia*, or *phasmata*—never *pneumata*."[48] Moreover, no other source in Jewish or Christian Greek before Luke uses *pneuma* for "ghost," that is, for the apparition of a dead person's spirit.[49] It would be unusual, then, for Luke to use *pneuma* to refer to a "ghostly" interpretation of the appearances of the risen Jesus—it is simply the wrong word. If that is what was intended, any of those words listed above would have been more appropriate. To understand *pneuma* as "ghost" here also makes little narrative sense: would Jesus' followers, while they were talking about his resurrection and recent appearances (Luke 24:34-36), be surprised by his reappearance and interpret it as a ghostly apparition?

This suggests that Luke had some apologetic motivation for describing a resurrection appearance in precisely these terms (not *pneuma*, "spirit," but having *sarx kai ostea*, "flesh and bones"), but probably the idea that Jesus' followers had only seen his ghost is not a view he was particularly concerned about. Sometimes it is proposed that Luke was attempting to respond to either docetic or Marcionite views about the body of Jesus. Although there are problems with both these views, here at least we are closer to the answer, since Luke's narration situates this alternative understanding of Jesus' risen body within the circle of the Eleven, so that insider views (characterized as doubts or disputations, 24:38) about the risen Jesus are being challenged (contrast Matt. 27:62-66; 28:11-15).

So why does Luke use *pneuma* here? The surprise and misunderstanding of the disciples in Luke 24:37 allows Jesus to correct their understanding in a very explicit way, using both physical demonstration and verbal explanation, in the verses that follow (Luke 24:37-43). This strategy, including the unusual use of *pneuma*, is a clue that Luke is not responding to the outsiders' view that the disciples had seen Jesus' ghost, but rather to "pneumatic" interpretations of the appearances that may have been current in some circles of the early Christian movement. After all, those who are entertaining the view that the risen Jesus was "spirit" (v. 37) are the apostles! As already seen, exactly what Paul meant by a "spiritual" (*pneumatikos*) body in his explanation of resurrection in 1 Corinthians 15 is a debated point. This is important, for if commentators today disagree about Paul's meaning, we may well expect that ancient readers also had their share of difficulty. In other words, Paul's own views aside, he could have been understood as talking about a "resurrection" that was "spiritual" and that could occur without any revivification or transformation of the natural body (1 Cor. 15:50). Also, the pre-Pauline tradition about the appearances of the risen Christ could have been understood as referring to visionary (that is, merely visionary) experiences that did not require anything special to happen to Jesus' corpse. First Peter 3:18 ("put to death in the flesh, made alive in the spirit") is also open to a similar interpretation, one that would have been obvious to many in the various contexts of early Christianity.

For Luke, this kind of "pneumatic" or "spiritual" understanding of Jesus' ongoing existence after the resurrection is simply not possible. This is why the risen Jesus himself, in Luke, states explicitly that he is not a *pneuma*, but "I myself," and has flesh and bones and a working digestive system, such as *pneumata* cannot have. He also offers his hands and feet for inspection, presumably to demonstrate his crucifixion wounds. The nonpneumatic nature of the risen Jesus is clear as well in Acts 10:41, which describes how the chief witnesses of the resurrection ate and drank with Jesus (see also Acts 1:4). The significance of the terminology cannot be overstressed: Paul says that resurrection bodies are pneumatic, and that "the last Adam became a life-giving spirit" (1 Cor. 15:44-49), and here Jesus says he is not a *pneuma* (Luke 24:39); Paul says flesh and blood cannot inherit the kingdom of God (1 Cor. 15:50), and here Jesus says that he has flesh and bones. What is more, when Jesus dies in Luke 23:46, he says, "Father, I commit my spirit into your hands," which quite obviously suggests a separation of spirit from body.[50] In Luke 24 Jesus is not a spirit without a body. Again, as argued above in the discussion of 1 Corinthians 15, we must be cautious not to impose an anachronistic dichotomy of "spiritual" versus "material" onto ancient thinking about such things. But for Luke the risen Jesus is anything but pneumatic, and in fact, Jesus himself describes such a view as allowing doubts to arise in their hearts (Luke 24:38).

Having the chief witness of the appearances of Jesus validate the empty tomb—and thus the flesh-and-bones corporeality of both the resurrection and the subsequent appearances—goes a long way for Luke in his apologetic for the nonpneumatic resurrection of Jesus. As James Robinson wrote:

> This reduction of resurrection appearances to religious experience . . . is the foil against which the non-luminous resurrection appearances at the ends of the gospels . . . are composed. . . . This apologetic against a ghostlike experience has pushed Luke to emphasize the "flesh and bones" of the resurrection, which is clearly one step nearer "orthodoxy" than was Paul (1 Cor. 15:50).[51]

In Robinson's view, Luke is reacting against the gnosticizing possibilities that a pneumatic view might represent—including the Pauline identification of Christ with the Spirit (2 Cor. 3:17-18), which Luke avoids by separating the resurrection appearances so carefully from the gift of the Holy Spirit at Pentecost.[52] As we will see, it is more likely that Luke was concerned about the "reduction of resurrection appearances to religious experience" than about Gnostic or docetic interpretations of the resurrection appearances. It is probably more appropriate, if Luke was written in the first century, to look elsewhere to map out his apologetic concerns—although it is true that his narration would be very conducive to anti-Gnostic and anti-docetic readings in the second century and beyond.[53]

Strictly speaking, docetism denies the reality or physicality of Jesus' body, not just in the postresurrection appearances, but during his life and career as well. When Ignatius of Antioch (d. c. 107 CE) wrote, "I know and believe that he was in the flesh also after the resurrection" (*Smyrn.* 3:1), he meant, "after the resurrection as well as before the resurrection" (see, for context, *Smyrnaeans* 2). He then went on to describe a resurrection appearance and to repeat a post-Easter saying much like Luke 24:39:

> And when he came to those of Peter's circle, he said to them: "Take, handle me and see that I am not a bodiless daimon." And immediately they touched him and believed, being united to him in flesh and spirit. . . . And after his resurrection, he ate and drank with them as a fleshly person, even though he was spiritually united to the Father. (Ignatius, *Smyrn.* 3:2-3)[54]

The exact parallel "handle me and see that I . . . not . . ." (*psēlaphēsate me kai idete hoti . . . ouk . . .*, Luke 24:39b; *Smyrn.* 3:2a) suggests Ignatius's direct knowledge of Luke.[55] The expression "those with Peter" could have been inferred by Ignatius from the immediate context (Luke 24:33-34). Either way, the physicality of Jesus' existence both before and after his death and resurrection inheres in the immediate context of Ignatius's *Letter to the Smyrnaeans* as the major issue at stake, and his polemic is directed against those who thought Christ suffered in appearance only (*to dokein, Smyrnaeans* 2). Nowhere in Luke is an interest in proving the physicality of Jesus' body during his lifetime, or in showing that he really suffered in the body, made this explicit. So, because Ignatius refutes those who thought Christ suffered in appearance, and does not deny the pneumatic quality of the postresurrection appearances; and because Luke is not interested in demonstrating the physicality of Jesus' body before the resurrection, we are justified in distinguishing Luke's "anti-pneumatic" apologetic from Ignatius's "anti-docetic" apologetic.

Yet even if "nonpneumatic" is an appropriate term for Luke's understanding of the risen Jesus, it is still clear in Luke 24, from Jesus' sudden appearances and disappearances, and his ability to go unrecognized, that there is something different—unearthly, perhaps, is the best word—about his ongoing existence. Most commentators recognize the parallels with descriptions of disappearing gods in Greco-Roman antiquity: we should conclude that for Luke the risen Jesus simply does what is appropriate to his risen status.[56] Given the flesh-and-bones "reality" of Jesus' body in Luke 24 and the fact that the ascension for Luke signifies the end of the resurrection appearances (Acts 1:2-3), a case can be made for the view that Jesus is in an intermediate but entirely bodily state in Luke 24—he is risen but not exalted.[57] But this is not to say that Jesus in Luke has a "spiritual" body such as Paul was describing simply because it is capable of unusual behavior.[58] Luke is intent on claiming the exact opposite, as we have seen, and to try to suggest otherwise is to read 1 Corinthians 15 forcibly into Luke 24.[59] What is more, Luke has the risen Jesus describe such a view of his postresurrection existence as the "questionings" or "doubts" (*dialogismoi*) that may arise in the hearts of the faithful (24:38), rather than the views of skeptical outsiders.

While it seems probable that this is simply Luke's way of describing what (in his view) is a deficient understanding of the resurrection of Jesus and his ongoing existence, the theme of doubt and/or hesitant faith is common throughout the Easter stories. As Christopher Evans noted, the theme "needs careful handling, for it is not undifferentiated."[60] As a literary device, doubt is present (even if only by implication) in scenes in which the risen Jesus goes unrecognized; but when doubt is introduced explicitly, it is almost always doubt about the resurrection itself. The theme is not inherent in the resurrection traditions, but is something added later, at a time long after the appearances of the risen Jesus had ceased and believers had to reckon with the problem of the resurrection. This is clearest in John 20:24-29, in which Jesus says to the disbelieving Thomas, "Blessed are those who do not see and yet believe" (20:29). In Luke as in John, doubt is dispelled when the risen Jesus reveals himself: the disciples' original disbelief of the women's report (Luke 24:11) becomes disbelief on account of joy (24:41); and Peter's wondering about the empty tomb (24:12) becomes the wonderment of the believers at the resurrection (24:41). However, the characterization of a pneumatic view of Jesus' postmortem existence as "doubts" (*dialogismoi*)[61] means that Luke 24:36-43 is quite pointedly not about failing to believe in the resurrection of Jesus, but about failing to believe that Jesus was raised not as *pneuma* but in a revivified flesh-and-bones body, as "I myself" (24:39).

Luke's Apostolic Control of the Empty Tomb Story

There is another way to come at Luke's response to Paul on this question, and that is to examine the different ways that Paul and Luke describe Paul's experience of the risen Christ. Luke tends to make supernatural experiences material, as many scholars have noted. A striking example is found in Luke's redaction of the baptism of Jesus: the Holy Spirit descended "in bodily form" like a dove (Luke 3:22; cf. Mark 1:10). This is, as we have been arguing, also the case in the way that the risen Jesus is depicted in Luke 24. By contextual association, Luke makes the appearance language of 1 Corinthians 15:5-8 concrete as well. The Lord appeared (*ōphthē*) to Simon (24:34), and although Luke cannot make the nature of that experience explicit by narrative means, evidently because he has no narrative source for the appearance to Peter, the reader naturally assumes that the risen Jesus appeared to Peter materially (and not merely in a vision or dream). Peter inspects the tomb, whose emptiness indicates that the body is missing as a result of the resurrection, as the presence of the grave clothes shows. This alone would suggest a flesh-and-bones appearance to Peter, but the appearances of the risen Jesus to the two on the road (24:13-33, 35) and to the Eleven and the others (24:36-43, 44-49) are quite obviously concrete experiences as well. The connection of Luke 24:34 with these narratives requires the reader to conclude that Peter's experience—despite the "visionary" language required by the kerygmatic formulation in Luke 24:34—was exactly the same.

Luke hesitates, however, to make Paul's experience of the risen Jesus tangible in precisely the same way. Here an examination of the different Greek expressions Luke uses to describe visionary phenomena clarifies the matter. The most significant terms are the nouns *optasia* and *horama*, and the aorist passive of *horaō*. Luke uses *optasia* only three times, twice when there is some suspicion about the reality of what has been seen by others (Luke 1:22; 24:23), and once when Paul himself refers to his Damascus road experience as a heavenly *optasia* (Acts 26:19).[62] *Horama* is used eleven times in Acts: for instance, in Ananias's vision about Saul (Acts 9:10) or Peter's vision about the net (10:17, 19; 11:5), both of which seem to be ecstatic visions (Acts 10:10; 11:5). One particularly important usage is in Acts 12:9, when Peter thinks his release from prison is a vision, a *horama* (that is, not really happening). So *horama* is Luke's typical expression for a personal visionary experience, a hallucination, even if given by God. Luke's use of the aorist passive of *horaō* is not entirely unambiguous, either. He uses it for various appearances: God (Acts 7:2); angels (Luke 1:11; Acts 7:30, 35); Moses and Elijah at the transfiguration (Luke 9:31); the risen Jesus (Luke 24:34; Acts 13:31); even the tongues of fire at Pentecost (Acts 2:3).[63] Luke seems to understand these occurrences as tangible rather than merely visionary, because in some instances other more concrete expressions (for standing, sitting, resting, and so forth) make clear the tangibility of the occurrence. This seems consistent with Luke's tendency to make it clear whether such events are tangible or not.

When Luke describes Paul's Damascus road experience, it is as a private visionary experience rather than a tangible encounter with the risen Jesus like the disciples had before Jesus' ascension (Acts 9:3-9; 22:6-11; 26:12-18). Interestingly,

Paul's experience is both luminous and auditory: it consists of a light from heaven and a voice. Of course, it is a "real" event from the perspective of Luke, and not a (merely ecstatic) vision as others clearly were, since it was audible and/or visible to the others with Paul—even if Luke evidently is not compelled to keep the story's details straight on subsequent retellings. Luke twice uses the aorist passive of *horaō*—as in the appearance traditions—to describe what happened to Paul (Acts 9:17; 26:16). Paul, as we have already seen, includes himself on the list of those to whom the risen Christ appeared: "Last of all," he writes, alluding to the chronological gap between his experience and the others, "he appeared also to me" (*ōphthē kamoi*, 1 Cor. 15:8). The fact that he uses the same language to describe his experience suggests that he thinks that all the appearances mentioned were the same not only in significance and result (the legitimation of authority) but also in character, as Wilhelm Michaelis suggested.[64] When Luke, on the other hand, describes manifestations of the risen and exalted Jesus, such as those experienced by Paul and by Stephen (Acts 7:55-56), they are different from the appearances in Luke 24 both chronologically and substantially: chronologically, of course, because they occur after the ascension, but also substantially, because the ascension indicates that Jesus will no longer appear in his physical body on earth. When Luke does use *ōphthē* to describe what happened to Paul (Acts 9:17; 26:16), it perhaps is a concession to Paul's own use in 1 Corinthians 15:8. Despite the similarity in language, reading Luke and Acts together makes it clear that Luke did not view the appearances to Peter and to Paul as the same in character, or in implication.

Luke's most important adaptation of the Markan empty tomb story is his addition of Peter's visit to the tomb (Luke 24:12). In Luke, the story about the disappearance of Jesus' body from the tomb is thus brought another step closer to traditions about the appearances of the risen Jesus, when Peter—the primary appearance witness—confirms that the tomb is empty. This not only takes the authoritative word on the empty tomb away from the women who discover it and transfers it to the leader of Luke's twelve apostles; it also restricts the authorizing appearances of the risen Jesus to those tangible, flesh-and-bones appearances experienced by the Eleven (later the Twelve). Luke evidently was acutely aware of the problems the empty tomb story posed, and so made some apologetic additions: (1) the apostolic verification, which functions both to validate the story itself (not its original witnesses) and to consolidate the narration of the resurrection appearances; and (2) the reference to the grave clothes, which indicates that the women and Peter were at the right tomb (not some other empty tomb) and that the body had not been moved or stolen.

In the end, Peter's visit to the tomb in Luke 24:12 probably has less to do with corroborating the (supposedly) inferior testimony of the women than it has to do with how Luke thinks the appearances are to be understood. Peter's visit restricts the interpretation that can be given to the appearances, and this redactional addition is consistent with Luke's emphasis that Jesus was raised in a flesh-and-bones body. Luke was not exactly combating a docetic view, for typically such views disputed the reality of Jesus' body entirely, or the reality of his suffering, and not simply the tangibility of his resurrected state. According to his later detractors, Marcion (d. c. 160 CE) also had similar "pneumatic" ideas about what Jesus' body was like—both before and after the resurrection.[65] Yet in Luke the risen Jesus insists that he is not a *pneuma*; and given that the primary apostolic witness of the resurrection validates that the risen Jesus is not "pneumatic," the empty tomb story in Luke becomes an important part of the validation of the Twelve, which Luke identifies as the core of the Jerusalem group.

In this way, at least as the book of Acts represents Christian origins, all subsequent offshoots of the Christian movement must trace their origins and legitimacy back to the Jerusalem group and the twelve apostles, whose authority is based on a (bodily) continuity with the mission of Jesus, mediated through the tangible resurrection appearances. Luke concludes, and Acts begins, by connecting the authority of the Twelve with the ministry of the earthly Jesus and the tangible appearances of the risen Jesus.

> Then he said to them: "These are my words, which I spoke to you while I was still with you, that everything written about me in the Law of Moses and in the Prophets and in the Psalms must be fulfilled." Then he opened their minds to understand the Scriptures; and he said to them, "Thus it has been written that the Messiah must suffer, and rise from the dead on the third day, and that repentance for the forgiveness of sins must be preached in his name among all the Gentiles, beginning from Jerusalem: you are witnesses of these things." (Luke 24:44-48)

This closing saying works on a number of levels: the risen Jesus validates the authority of the Twelve as (the primary) resurrection witnesses, their mission "beginning from Jerusalem" and including the Gentiles, and he also validates the new post-Easter hermeneutic, which finds Christ in the Scriptures (see, e.g., the application of Psalm 16 and Psalm 110 to Jesus in Acts 2:24-36). Even Paul, who considered himself an apostle "not from human beings nor from a human source, but through Jesus Christ and God the Father who raised him from the dead" (Gal. 1:1), according to Luke-Acts has his authority as a missionary (not apostle) given to him not by the risen Jesus directly, but through the mediation of the Twelve. In using the primary resurrection witness to authenticate the nature of the appearances as body-out-of-the-tomb, flesh-and-bones occurrences, Luke is defining what "resurrection" is like and confirming its "reality," its verifiability through the established witnesses. For the language of Luke 24:36-43 leads us to conclude that in Luke 24 the author is combating the understanding of resurrection Paul presents in 1 Corinthians 15 (or perhaps an interpretation of it). But not only that: Luke is also restricting whose authority in the Christian movement finds authentication through direct connection with the risen Jesus. Although Luke probably wrote after Matthew, the Lukan development of the empty tomb story is not as dramatic as in Matthew, where disappearance and appearance come even closer together: Jesus appears to the women as they are leaving the tomb. Jesus is not in the tomb because he is present, risen, outside it.[66]

There are some serious problems in establishing the original text of Luke 24. In the late nineteenth century, the textual critics B. F. Westcott and F. J. A. Hort identified nine places in which witnesses belonging to the normally expansive "Western" text-type preserved shorter (and more original) readings than their otherwise favored "neutral" text (exemplified by the codices Sinaiticus and Alexandrinus).[67] Westcott and Hort called these "Western non-interpolations" because they believed that the Western text had preserved the original, and because they did not want to call them "neutral interpolations."[68] Seven of these shorter readings are found in Luke 24. In the table that follows, the bracketed words are omitted in the Greek uncial Codex Bezae Cantabrigiensis (D) and several recensions of the Old Latin version (it), and, in some cases, also by a few other witnesses:

Luke 24:3	. . . but they did not find the body [of the Lord Jesus].
Luke 24:6	"[He is not here, but was raised.] Remember how he told you . . ."
Luke 24:12	[But Peter got up and ran to the tomb, and peering in he saw only the linen cloths; and he went home wondering at what had happened.]
Luke 24:36	[and he said to them, "Peace to you."]
Luke 24:40	[And after he said this, he showed them his hands and his feet.]
Luke 24:51	. . . he went away from them [and was carried up into heaven].
Luke 24:52	And [worshipping him] they returned to Jerusalem with great joy . . . .[69]

To these seven identified by Westcott and Hort as interpolations should also be added Luke 24:9, which also has a shorter reading in the same Western witnesses:

Luke 24:9	. . . and returning [from the tomb] they announced all these things to the Eleven . . . .[70]

In each of these instances, virtually all other textual witnesses testify to the longer reading. There has been an increasing tendency among scholars to evaluate the longer readings as original to Luke,[71] owing mainly to a reassessment of their external attestation, in particular the third-century papyrus manuscript P[75], which includes the longer readings.[72]

However, Bart Ehrman has argued that the longer readings are interpolations: he thinks they are anti-docetic corruptions of the original, which the Western witnesses preserve. Ehrman states that he evaluates each of the seven (among others) individually but finds a common tendency uniting all the longer non-Western readings. He writes:

The non-Western *interpolations* evidence [a theological] *Tendenz*; for in these cases, the "Western" text evidences no scribal tendency at all, but simply attests the original text that came to be corrupted in another stream of the tradition early on in the history of its transmission. Moreover, these secondary corruptions of which the Western tradition is innocent all work in the same direction: each functions to counter the docetic Christologies that can be dated to the time of their creation, the early to mid-second century.[73]

Other scholars have tried to establish a single origin or tendency for the longer readings, which they think are non-Western interpolations.[74] Although some argue that it is better methodologically to treat each of the textual problems individually, and weigh each on its own merits,[75] Mikeal Parsons and Michael Wade Martin are probably justified in suspecting (at least) that the variant readings noted above are related. Martin's probability study shows how unlikely it is that this collection of textual problems—whether we consider them to be omissions or interpolations—are seven (or eight) completely unrelated instances of scribal interference or error.[76] We will return to this question below.

Ehrman thinks that Luke 24:12 was added in order to emphasize "that the Christ who died in the body was also raised in the body."[77] According to our study above, this is certainly what the verse emphasizes, but in dispute is whether its presence in Luke 24 is the work of an orthodox corruptor or the author of Luke. The question is complicated and has generated much scholarly discussion. In his many publications on this verse, Frans Neirynck has argued that evidence of Lukan composition weighs heavily against arguments of later insertion.[78] Neirynck highlights the following three Lukanisms: the pleonastic use of the participle "having got up" (Gk., *anastas*), the verb "to wonder" (*thaumazein*), and the participle "that which has happened" (*to gegonos*). In particular he is impressed by "wondering at what had happened" (*thaumazōn to gegonos*): "The joining [of the two] in one expression creates a valid example of Lukan style."[79] On the other hand, the historical present "he sees" (*blepei*) has been characterized as non-Lukan, for Luke tends to "correct" this use of the present tense when working with Mark; but the historical present does occur in material unique to Luke.[80] The participle "stooping down," or better, "peering in" (*parakupsas*), and the word used for the linens (*ta othonia*) are also described as non-Lukan by Ehrman; Neirynck takes *parakupsas blepei* as a double verb of seeing developed by Luke from Mark's similar formulation "looking up they see" (*anablepsasai theōrousin*, Mark 16:4), which also has an aorist participle used pleonastically with a historical present.[81] Complicating matters further, exactly the same words ("and peering in he sees . . . the linens") are found in John 20:5, which must mean either that a later interpolator added Luke 24:12 using the Fourth Gospel as source material, or that the author (or redactor) of the Fourth Gospel used Luke. Neirynck thinks the Fourth Gospel shows evidence here of Luke's influence.[82] This seems probable because elsewhere there are other verbal parallels between Luke 24 and John 20 at points where the text of Luke is not uncertain (so those parallels cannot be secondary scribal assimilations of Luke to John).[83]

Neirynck complains that "it is inherent in the interpolation theory that no effort is made to understand Lk 24:12 in the context of Lk."[84] Luke 24:12 makes excellent sense in its immediate context. First of all, it makes good narrative sense as a rejoinder to the originally negative appraisal of the women's report by the Eleven (v. 11). It also fits in connection with verses 2-3: the women did not find the body, and Peter sees only the linens (and not the body).[85] Luke 24:12 is also consistent with the recollection later in the chapter, in which the two disciples on the way to Emmaus say, "And some of us went to the tomb and found things just as the women had said, but they did not see him" (Luke 24:24).[86] Without verse 12, verse 24 would make little sense. "Some of us," of course, suggests more than Peter, although as John Muddiman has pointed out, "Cleopas and his companion have to minimise the importance of the visits to the tomb, which are not grounds for hope"; they do this by using a "vague plural" for the visitors ("some women of our group," v. 22; "some of those with us," v. 24, though Peter went alone).[87] In addition, as Jacob Kremer argues, each resurrection story in Luke 24 ends with something of a correction or counterbalancing of an initial response of disbelief or lack of recognition, and the opening scene is more consistent with this pattern if verse 12 is original.[88] Were it not for the omission of Luke 24:12 from the Western witnesses, its originality would scarcely be questioned.

We have not yet asked *why* Luke 24:12 is missing from the Western witnesses that lack it. Here there are two pertinent issues. First, there is the transcriptional problem of whether it is more likely that Luke 24:12 was added to or omitted from Luke. The unlikelihood of any scribe omitting material that would be congenial to proto-orthodox Christology is the cornerstone of the case against the originality of verse 12 (and the other longer readings as well). Second, there is the question, raised earlier, whether the shorter readings in Codex Bezae and others (or the longer readings in all other witnesses) should be seen as part of a larger single phenomenon or scribal tendency, one way or the other.[89] These two issues are not necessarily related. For even if the omissions (or interpolations) all come from the same hand, this does not necessarily mean that hand had the same purpose in making all the changes that resulted in the phenomena we now have to deal with. Not all the changes may have been motivated by the same concern (whether anti-docetism or something else).[90] Thus, whereas proponents of the originality of Luke 24:12 need to find transcriptional reasons for the Western omission of all the longer readings, a single purpose does not need to be sought. Yet on either side of the question, such solutions have been proposed.[91]

In the particular case of Luke 24:12, then, it seems justifiable to ask about the scribal rationale behind its absence without inquiring (at least at this point) whether the same rationale led to the other six shorter readings in the Western text—even if we agree tentatively that all seven instances are related through their origin at the hand of a single scribe or in a single manuscript. It is possible that an early scribe omitted Luke 24:12 because of a perceived inconsistency in the number of people visiting the tomb (as noted above, see vv. 12 and 24), although some other reason may have been the impetus.[92] The parallels with the Fourth Gospel cannot be dismissed on the grounds of scribal harmonizing, as seen above. Other considerations—matters of Lukan style, consistency with the context, and external attestation—must be weighted more heavily than transcriptional probabilities, so the view that Luke 24:12 was original to Luke 24 and is the work of the author of Luke is well supported.

For the other longer readings, the likelihood that they all arose from a single source means that they should similarly be taken as original and not as secondary expansions, but they all must be accounted for on both contextual and transcriptional grounds. Since my argument in this chapter does not rest on the originality of any of the other longer readings in Luke 24, my discussion can be brief. First, Luke 24:3 and the longer reading, "the body [of the Lord Jesus]." The title "Lord Jesus" is a Lukan title for the risen Jesus, as discussed above. Ehrman is concerned that the usage does not fit here, since as yet the women do not believe that Jesus was raised, but this is unfounded: the term is not being used by the women, but by the narrator.[93] Bruce Metzger and others think the words were omitted under the influence of Luke 24:23, which reads simply "his body."[94]

Next, in Luke 24:6, the longer reading is not an exact harmonization to the other Synoptics: the longer reading "he is not here, but was raised" can be explained as a Lukan adaptation of the Markan source.[95] It could have been omitted as redundant after the question, "Why do you seek the living one among the dead?" (24:5). "From the tomb" (Luke 24:9) does not make sense as an orthodox interpolation, despite Martin's recent attempt to explain it as such; Metzger puts down the omission to a transcriptional error.[96] Next, in Luke 24:36, the peace greeting seems to have no effect on the frightened disciples, and this may have been grounds enough for its omission.[97] Luke 24:40 probably was omitted, as numerous scholars have noted, because it seemed redundant after verse 39; it makes little sense as an "anti-docetic interpolation."[98] The reference to the ascension could have been omitted as contradicting the chronology of Acts 1:3-11, which describes a forty-day interval in which the appearances took place; as already noted, the narrative of Luke 24 implies that all the events took place on the first day of the week. Acts 1:2 nevertheless presumes that Luke's first volume concluded with some reference to the ascension.[99] Without a reference to the ascension, the motif of worship (Luke 24:52) would also have made little sense.[100]

The complexities of these problems, as well as the methodological concerns that attend them, make certainty impossible. On the whole, however, if it is correct to treat these textual problems as related, three considerations tip the scale in favor of the originality of the longer readings: (1) none of the longer readings can seriously be considered non-Lukan; (2) their omission in the Western witnesses can be explained plausibly; (3) the age and character of the non-Western witnesses that attest to longer readings in Luke 24 must be taken seriously.

7. Matthew: "And Behold, Jesus Met Them"

"All authority in heaven and on earth has been given to me."
—Matthew 28:18

And behold, Jesus met them, saying, "Greetings!" And they came up and took hold of his feet and worshipped him. Then Jesus said to them, "Do not be afraid: go and tell my brothers that they should go into Galilee, and they will see me there."
—Matthew 28:9-10

"Say that his disciples came by night and stole him while you were sleeping." . . . And this story has been disseminated among Jews to this very day.
—Matthew 28:13, 15

Ulrich Luz has remarked that "the narrative fictions in Matthew's Gospel . . . contrast strangely with his overall marked loyalty to tradition."[1] By "narrative fictions" Luz means newly created stories that Matthew did not receive from either textual or oral sources or, on a larger scale, the rearrangement of episodes creating a new chronological order of the Jesus story. (We have already seen an example of this phenomenon in the previous chapter: the Lukan addition of Peter's inspection of the empty tomb.) Luz argues that the purpose of Matthew's fictions "is to identify his Jesus story with the present situation of the community . . . to serve the 'collective memory.'"[2] Matthew's "Jesus story" is not simply an archive of Jesus' activities and teachings, but a vehicle through which he continues to speak to the community. This is because "Jesus has to give answers to the questions of Matthew's present time and cannot simply remain in the past as a figure of the past."[3] The contrast to which Luz refers, between Matthew's loyalty to his traditions and sources and his ability to make bold innovations in service of the message to his community, is illustrated perfectly in his deployment of the empty tomb story.

In some ways, Matthew's use of the Markan empty tomb story is fairly conservative, for the author takes both the text and theology of Mark 16 quite seriously. When Matthew has Markan material to work with, he makes relatively minor adjustments to smooth out the story—changing the motivation for the women to come to the tomb, or modifying what the angel says to them, or fixing the end of the pericope so that the women do in fact go to tell the disciples. He is especially conservative where sayings material is transmitted (in Matt. 28:5-7), and less so when adapting Mark's narrative structure to his own way of telling the story. Matthew also seems, as we will see, to retain Mark's conceptualization of Jesus' resurrection as an assumption into the heavenly realm (although this is not explicit) as that which installs Jesus as the exalted Son of Man, with "all authority given" to him. On the other hand, Matthew makes some dramatic and innovative additions to the story. In particular, we will see (1) a guard placed at the tomb at the request of the Jewish authorities, (2) an angel descending from heaven to roll the stone away from the mouth of the tomb, (3) an appearance of the risen Jesus as the women leave the tomb, and (4) an appearance of the risen Jesus to the Eleven in Galilee. The two appearances may be based on older traditions (cf. Matt. 28:9-10 with John 20:14-18; and Matt. 28:16-20 with 1 Cor. 15:5), but they are situated and told in ways that are distinctly Matthean. The appearance to the women at the tomb is curiously very similar to the appearance of the angel, something we will have to consider. The other two additions are fictional, that is, Matthean creations, in one way or another. Our challenge will be to discern how they serve the collective memory of Matthew's community and early audiences.

These two particular innovations illuminate how Matthew understood the resurrection of Jesus. The guard at the tomb makes sense as Matthew's apologetic response to the charge that the disciples had stolen the body of Jesus in order to fabricate a resurrection. As seen in an earlier chapter, there were many such stories in Mediterranean antiquity about people contriving to hide their bodily remains so that it would be concluded that the gods had taken them away and that they should be properly venerated.[4] Consistent throughout these stories is the idea that hiding bodily remains was meant to lead to the conclusion not that the person was alive again on earth, but that he or she had been transported into the divine realm. Obviously the best way to prove that someone had risen from the dead would be not to empty their tomb but to produce them living—but by Matthew's time it was deeply ingrained in the traditions that Jesus appeared only to his followers, and even then, as we have seen, these appearances did not always erase doubt about his rising. Although Matthew was trying to explain the genesis of the body-theft rumor—and not to prove that Jesus had been raised from the dead—early Christian readers of Matthew almost immediately seized on the Matthean depiction of the chief priests as knowing "everything that had happened" at the tomb (Matt. 28:11) and put these characters to use as hostile witnesses to the truth of the resurrection. Justin Martyr (*Dial.* 108) provides an early example of this use of Matthew.[5] What is interesting is that already in Matthew's community, the resurrection of Jesus was conceived of in terms of an empty tomb; the two went together. This must be at least partly due to how Mark told the story, but neither can we exclude the possibility that the disappearance tradition was being interpreted in Matthew's setting in light of the resurrection kerygma. Another Matthean innovation, the raising of the holy ones at the crucifixion of Jesus (Matt. 27:52-53), should probably be understood in relation to this resurrection debate.

The addition of the angel's descent to the tomb also illustrates how Matthew understood the resurrection. Having the women discover the tomb open, as they do in the other Gospels, would pose a problem given that Matthew has already situated a guard at the tomb. This would require some explanation: if the guards were watching, who opened the tomb, and what happened? In the other Gospels, of course, it is not explained, because the narratives do not provide any characters to watch; but one could suppose either that Jesus, having risen, pushed the stone away himself and got out of the tomb, or that the angel or angels had done it, whether to let Jesus out or to show that he was gone. The kind of physical presence of the risen Jesus Luke adopts might be in keeping with the former idea, but Luke simply does not make this clear. Because Mark's narration of the resurrection used the narrative elements of a disappearance/assumption story, as argued above, Mark's readers could conclude that if Jesus was taken up into heaven, the tomb probably was opened by the young man. Yet this is not clarified by Mark either. In Matthew, on the other hand, the reader knows that the angel rolls the stone away to show the women that it is empty. Thus Matthew comes close to the idea that the empty tomb can serve as a demonstration of the resurrection. And yet Matthew has also taken seriously the Markan connection between Jesus' disappearance from the tomb and his exaltation as the Son of Man. The risen Jesus clearly speaks already as the exalted Son of Man in Matthew 28:18, echoing Daniel 7:13-14: "All authority has been given to me in heaven and on earth."[6]

Despite all this, probably the most important change Matthew introduces into the empty tomb story is the appearance of Jesus as the women are leaving the tomb. Although the narrator does not say where this happens—only that Jesus suddenly appears (v. 9) to the women after they left the tomb quickly and were running to tell the disciples (v. 8)—there is a strong narrative connection with the tomb. This signifies a greater narrative development in the empty tomb story than anything we saw in Luke, because it provides a stronger validation of the empty tomb's meaning than any testimony that could be offered by either an angel or an apostle. The interpretive key to the empty tomb is the depiction of the risen Jesus alive outside it.

How Matthew Adapts the Empty Tomb Story

In the introduction to the story, Matthew has tidied up and significantly abbreviated his Markan source text (Matt. 28:1; Mark 16:1-4).[7] Of the "many women" disciples who according to Matthew followed Jesus from Galilee and witnessed his death (Matt. 27:55-56), only two, Mary Magdalene and Mary the mother of James and Joseph, see the tomb and sit there awhile after the burial (27:61), and only these two return on the first day of the week (28:1). It is not entirely clear why Matthew would have omitted Salome from his Markan source, but he has evidently assimilated the witnesses of the empty tomb to the witnesses of the place "where he was laid" (Matt. 27:61; Mark 15:47). Here in Matthew they come only "to see the tomb" (Matt. 28:1), and not "so they might anoint him" (Mark 16:1). For Matthew, the anointing of Jesus' body in preparation for its burial has already taken place in Matthew 26:6-13 (so also in Mark 14:3-9, although the women come to anoint the body in Mark 16 nonetheless). Narratively, coming "to see" the tomb makes better sense given the addition to the story of the guard and the seal on the tomb, for these would have prevented the women from accessing and attending to the body. In doing this, Matthew has created a more realistic situation, since any public mourning of an executed criminal would be out of the question.[8] Yet narrative congruity rather than verisimilitude must have been the motivation here, since enclosing this story is another (in two parts, Matt. 27:62-64 and 28:11-15), which is, it must be admitted, manifestly implausible (as will be seen below).

By changing the motivation for the women coming to the tomb, Matthew has also eliminated the need for the odd (but dramatic) discussion the women have on the way to the tomb in Mark: "Who will roll the stone away for us?" (Mark 16:3). Some scholars have sought to explain "seeing the tomb" as a reference to the Jewish custom of visiting tombs until the third day in order to prevent premature burial.[9] "The women who come (surely with sadness) to confirm Jesus' death become (with great joy) the first witnesses of the resurrection."[10] Another compelling reading is offered by Warren Carter, who notes (as we have above in relation to Mark) the importance of "seeing" in the Gospel of Matthew. "Seeing the light" has to do with perceiving God's saving activities on behalf of humankind (Matt. 4:16; Isa. 9:2), and in Matthew "to 'see' this light involves more than witnessing it, but encountering God's salvific action in the midst of darkness."[11] Carter thinks on this basis that the women, in seeing the death of Jesus and in coming to see the tomb, "unlike the male disciples have comprehended and acted on Jesus's teaching about his death and resurrection."[12] Like the Jewish opponents of Jesus, the women have heard and understood his predictions that he would die and be raised after three days (Matt. 12:38-40). This is part of a well-developed contrast in Matthew 27:57—28:15 between the activities of the opponents and the guards, who wish to subvert the proclamation of the resurrection, and those of the women, who carry it as they have been commissioned. We will return to this contrast below.

Instead of telling how the women discover the open tomb, Matthew narrates its opening directly. As explained above, this is required by the stationing of the guard. In keeping with the apocalyptic (that is, revelatory) nature of this scene, the angel descends from heaven in the middle of an earthquake; earlier, at the crucifixion of Jesus, an earthquake is connected with the splitting of rocks, the opening of tombs, and the raising of the saints (Matt. 27:51-53, discussed below). The reader knows that again "God is beginning to act; now he is demonstrating his power."[13] More than that, by narrating the appearance of the angel, Matthew makes the women's encounter with the young man (Mark 16:5-8) conform more closely to the narrative pattern such stories normally take. W. D. Davies and Dale

Allison show that other similar stories follow a fixed pattern: (1) the introduction of the human character(s); (2) the appearance of the angel; (3) the reaction of fear; (4) the word of consolation; (5) the giving of revelation; (6) the command; and (7) the obedient response.[14] The angel does not descend here only in order to convey God's message to the women, as in other angelophany stories; here the angel's initial action is to roll the stone away from the tomb so that the women can see that it is empty, and to frustrate those who planned to prevent the resurrection proclamation by keeping the tomb sealed.[15] The demonstration of the empty tomb, together with its interpretation (Matt. 28:5-7), is the revelation the angel gives.

The narration of the angel's descent in Matthew 28:2 has led some commentators to think that Matthew has abbreviated a tradition that lies behind *Gospel of Peter* 9.35—10.42.[16] This text describes the descent of angels, but the stone rolls away by itself, and the angels escort the risen (actually, *rising*) Jesus out of the tomb and then accompany him on his ascent into heaven (this is not described explicitly, but see also *Gos. Pet.* 13.56). There is no need to suppose that Matthew is suppressing a description of the resurrection in a tradition he has received; there is sufficient evidence of Matthean composition here to suppose Matthew has created this part of the story.[17] In any case, Luz is correct that "Matthew obviously thinks, as do all authors of the New Testament, that although the resurrection of Jesus is an event that takes place in time . . . it is not visible and describable."[18] The resurrection must take place behind closed doors, as it were. There is also a traditional reason for this, in that Matthew has received a text (the Gospel of Mark) that explains the resurrection not as a resuscitation—as in the highly symbolic Ezekiel 37:1-14, or his own account of the raising of the holy ones (Matt. 27:52-53) who get up out of their tombs and walk into Jerusalem— but as an assumption into heaven. If this happens to someone dead in a tomb, it cannot be narrated from the perspective of any witnesses (especially unfriendly ones).[19]

The angel is described using language similar to Matthew's account of the transfiguration (Matt. 17:2) and to theophanies and angelophanies in Daniel (Dan. 7:9; 10:6).[20] As in Daniel 10, bystanders who are not meant to be involved in the epiphany do not see what happens (Dan. 10:7; similarly Acts 9:7; 22:9). Here the guards at the tomb quake with fear (Gk., *eseisthēsan*) and become "like corpses" out of their fear of the angel (Matt. 28:4). Beyond the clear irony that those guarding Jesus' corpse have become like dead men themselves, this description also prevents the guards from hearing the content of the angel's message. Evidently they have seen the angel and the empty tomb; the reader assumes this is part of the report they give to their superiors of "everything that happened" (28:11), because they are instructed to provide an explanation for the missing body (v. 13).

"Do not be afraid," the angel says to the women: although the narrator has not described them as afraid, the characteristic beginning of an angelophany (Dan. 10:12, 19) is the granting of divine calm to those who rightly fear a manifestation of God's agents.[21] John Nolland suggests that the command comes in response to the women witnessing the reaction of the guards: since the Greek includes the emphatic subject pronoun *humeis*, Nolland suggests that the meaning is something like "The guards were right to fear, but you do not need to be afraid."[22] Jesus himself speaks the same words of comfort when he appears to the women (Matt. 28:9-10; see also 14:27; 17:7). The angel, of course, knows why the women have come to the tomb, and the characteristic assumption motif of search for a body is invoked: "I know that you are seeking Jesus who was crucified." Here, however— just as in Mark—this is subjugated to the resurrection proclamation.[23] This part of the angel's speech forms a tidy little chiastic structure, as follows:

a He is not here,
b for he has been raised,
b' just as he said;
a' come behold the place where he used to lay. (Matt. 28:6)

This is a careful elaboration of the form of the saying in Mark: "He has been raised, he is not here, behold the place where they put him" (Mark 16:6).[24] Mark's Greek does not offer any help to clarify the logical connection between the statements—no conjunctions join these clauses—but they seem to move in a linear way from the resurrection proclamation to its result and then to the demonstration of the result. Here, by contrast, the demonstration of the empty tomb (a, a'), which focuses on the absence of Jesus, encloses a two-part announcement of his resurrection (b, b', only four words in Greek): the disappearance tradition is invoked in support of the resurrection. The first two words, translated "for he has been raised," both clarify that Jesus' tomb is empty because he was raised, and that this raising is God's act of vindication (signified by the passive voice) in light of the crucifixion (see v. 5). The second two, translated "just as he said," recall Jesus' predictions that he would rise from the dead, many of which use the title Son of Man (Matt. 12:40; 17:9; 17:22-23; 20:18-19).[25] Thus a proclamation of God's act on Jesus' behalf and a reminder of his foreknowledge of this part of the divine plan form the nucleus of this important part of the angel's message. As in Mark, the connection the author creates here with earlier Son of Man material invokes Jesus in that designation in the empty tomb scene. As we will see, this is an important theme in Matthew 28: one the author found already in Mark, but one that is heightened by the way the risen Jesus speaks in the closing pericope.

The demonstration of the empty tomb, thus subordinated to the proclamation of the resurrection, raises another question about Matthew's presentation: if the tomb was already empty, how did the risen Jesus get out? Early Christian interpreters explained this by reading Matthew's sealed and guarded tomb as equivalent to the locked houses inside which Jesus could suddenly appear in Luke and John (Luke 24:31, 36; John 20:19, 26).[26] But Matthew, as a reader of Mark, may have found helpful Mark's depiction of the resurrection as an assumption out of the tomb, presuming that if an angel were to roll the stone away, what one would find would be an empty tomb (this after all is what the tradition says), not a risen Jesus waiting to come out and show himself. This is because there is a fundamental reluctance in the earliest traditions to narrate the resurrection itself—at least, not until the *Gospel of Peter*. This reluctance arises because the two core traditions of appearance and disappearance did not supply the raw materials for narrating the resurrection *itself*. Whether because of his loyalty to the tradition (which had only delivered to him appearance stories and a disappearance story), or because of his theological conviction that the resurrection of Jesus "is not visible and describable," evidently a story that described Jesus rising from the dead was a fiction Matthew was not willing to create. What he does recount, however, is an appearance of Jesus at the tomb, an episode that brings together both disappearance/assumption (from the tomb) and resurrection/appearance (at the tomb) as a narrative expression of the announcement at the tomb: "He is not here, for he has been raised, just as he said; come see the place" (v. 6). When the women see (for one must assume they heed the angel's instruction to come and see) the empty place where Jesus' body used to be, they must interpret this in light of the announcement the angel brings: "He has been raised, just as he said." But does this prepare them to see Jesus himself when they later hurry from the tomb to tell the disciples?

The angel commissions the women in much the same way as the young man did in Mark 16:7, but here in Matthew 28:7, the author introduces a few important changes. First, the angel commands them to "go quickly and tell," rather than "leave and tell" (as in Mark). The difference seems minimal, but the verb for "go" (*poreuthe-isai*, v. 7) here creates a link with the commissioning of the Eleven (*poreuthentes*, v. 19).[27] Thus the women are instructed to go to the disciples with the message of the resurrection of Jesus, just as the disciples themselves will be instructed by the risen Jesus to go in order to make disciples, baptize, and teach. The message "that he has been raised from the dead" is phrased to echo confessional formulae.[28] Yet is it correct that this commissioning is limited strictly to their announcement to the disciples, as Luz suggests?[29] If so, this is consistent with a similar emphasis we noted in Luke, although here in Matthew the women are not called upon only to remember (see Luke 24:6-8). If Matthew intended to limit the role of the women as Luz suggests, perhaps this is because the author must have the Eleven as the nucleus of the discipling, baptizing, and teaching mission of the new movement (Matt. 28:16-20). On the other hand, as we will see below, it is the women who are given the commissioning with the true story of the empty tomb, in contrast with the guards, whose story closely parallels this one.

Second, in contrast with Mark, here the angel instructs the women specifically to give the resurrection proclamation, "He has been raised from the dead," along with the reminder (see 26:32) that Jesus would go ahead of them into Galilee. As we will see below, Galilee is important to Matthew not only as the origin of Jesus' mission, but also as the origin of his own circle in the Jesus movements.[30]

Third, Peter is no longer mentioned, as in Mark 16:7. This is a bit of a puzzle in light of the prominent position given to Peter in Matthew (Matt. 16:17-19), but some have suggested that this is because of Peter's denial of Jesus (26:69-75).[31] The last the reader hears of Peter in Matthew, he leaves the high priest's courtyard weeping bitterly. More probably, however, the author simply wants to leave him as one of the group (the Eleven, v. 17) because he had not received an appearance tradition in which Peter was singled out.[32]

Fourth, the angel's message concludes with the solemn statement "Look, I have told you." This marks the message of the angel as "the most important thing in the text," for its contents are things "that human beings can neither discover nor rationally infer."[33] It also creates a sense of urgency that is carried into the next verse.

Finally, Matthew corrects Mark's final verse by having the women leave the tomb quickly, as instructed, with fear and great joy, running to tell the disciples. But Matthew does not only make this change to correct Mark; he wishes to depict the women as obedient and joyful, although still afraid because of their encounter with the divine realm; this is so that the risen Jesus may meet them on good terms.

"And Behold, Jesus Met Them": The Risen Jesus at the Tomb

Mary Magdalene and the other Mary, and the readers of Matthew, are completely unprepared for the encounter with the risen Jesus as they leave the tomb (Matt. 28:9-10). The angel, after all, has just said that the disciples would see Jesus in Galilee, and now here he is; verses 9-10 seem to be an insertion by the author rather than an intrinsic part of the empty tomb story. But has Matthew inserted a traditional story or his own creation? Scholarship has generally been divided on this question. John 20:14-18 also describes an appearance of Jesus to Mary at the tomb, and the parallels between Matthew and John suggest to some scholars that there is an early tradition underlying Matthew 28:9-10.[34] Here they rely on arguments from either similar structure or similar vocabulary. Gerd Lüdemann, following up on a suggestion first made by C. H. Dodd, points to the common formal framework of Matthew 28:9-10; 28:16-20; and John 20:19-21.[35] The fivefold pattern Dodd perceived was as follows: (1) the situation—Christ's followers bereft of their Lord, (2) the appearance of the Lord, (3) the greeting, (4) the recognition, and (5) the word of command.[36] In Lüdemann's view, this common structure is sufficient grounds to posit an early appearance tradition behind Matthew 28:9-10, though he proposes that it originally narrated an appearance not to the women at the tomb but to some other group of disciples elsewhere.[37] Of course, the similarity in structure does not mean Matthew could not have composed this: the command "fear not" (28:10), which seems entirely unnecessary, seems to be a concession to how epiphany stories are typically told. Luz suggests that there is a "christological dimension" here, for the command not to be afraid indicates that "the meeting with the Risen One is not a meeting with just another human being but a meeting with a divine being."[38]

As for vocabulary, similarities between Matthew and John include the historical present "he says" with "to them/her" (feminine), the instruction to "go and tell" (not precisely parallel in Greek), and "my brothers" as a designation for the disciples. Both Frans Neirynck and Robert Gundry have detailed how much of this, and most of the rest of 28:9-10, is consistent with the Matthean mode of expression.[39] The strong evidence of Matthean style suggests that Matthew wrote this himself. The reputation of Mary Magdalene in certain circles of the Jesus movements as a visionary, however, probably does not ultimately originate in this small piece of Matthean redaction; rather, Matthew has some basic knowledge of an appearance to Mary and has narrated it in the context of his empty tomb story in this way. This would explain why the story offers so little in terms of new content (cf. John 20:14-18).

On a cursory reading of Matthew 28:1-10, the unexpected ("and behold," v. 9) appearance of Jesus as the women are leaving the tomb seems almost redundant. What Jesus tells the women does not seem to impart anything substantial when compared with what they were already told by the angel (vv. 5-7); contrary to Luz's opinion, it is not clear here that the women are excluded from seeing Jesus in Galilee (although 28:16 makes it clear the Eleven are the only ones present).[40] The redundancy of the Christophany beside the angelophany so impressed some early critical scholars that they suggested that 28:9-10 was a later gloss added to the text of Matthew, but there is no text-critical evidence in support of this.[41] The evidence of Matthean composition here, noted above, makes scribal interpolation unlikely. Despite this evidence, Gundry still suggests that Matthew was dependent here upon the lost ending of Mark (which in his view must have included an appearance to the women and to the disciples in Galilee, as here in Matthew), where the women needed a second command, this time from Jesus himself, to carry forward the good news of the resurrection.[42] On this view the redundancy is created by Matthew's redactional improvement of the women's response in verse 8. This is altogether improbable, but it does illustrate the problem of reading verses 9-10 with the previous section.

In any case, Matthew 28:9-10 actually does advance the story, even if only slightly: the angel's command to tell the disciples that Jesus was going ahead to Galilee is now a command from the risen Jesus, who calls the disciples "brothers," that they should go there. It is important here that the risen Jesus commissions these women first, who are also the first to see and to respond to him as the Risen One. After Jesus meets and greets them, with a rather everyday greeting (*chairete*, which can mean anything between "Good morning" and "Rejoice"),[43] immediately the women "draw near and worship" him, taking hold of his feet.[44] Clearly this for Matthew is the appropriate response to such an encounter (see also 28:17), and there is no hint here that it is unwelcome in any way (see, in contrast, John 20:17). The grasping of the feet has been explained in various ways, whether as a customary part of the act of veneration[45] or as an emphasis that the risen Jesus had a tangible physical body.[46] Allison notes that folklore across cultures reflects the idea that "the feet of otherworldly beings" can be of a dubious nature.[47] Likewise, in the second-century writing called *The Epistle of the Apostles*, the risen Jesus reassures his disciples by having them examine his footprints: "For it is written in the prophet, 'But a ghost, a demon, leaves no print on the ground'" (*Ep. Apos.* 11).[48] We have seen that concerns about tangibility are sometimes thought to reflect a response to the view that the disciples had only seen Jesus' ghost, or some kind of vision, but this is not always certain because of the inconsistent insubstantiality of ancient ghosts; in any event, this does not seem to be a concern for Matthew.

The appearance in Galilee, in which Jesus uses exalted language suggestive of Daniel 7, could be considered an apocalyptic vision, but Matthew gives no indication that he needs to control how the appearance of Jesus is narrated; he is more concerned about the standard themes, such as commissioning and doubt, than about what Jesus' body is like after the resurrection. So when Jesus appears outside the tomb and the women hold his feet, the reader knows this cannot be a vision, but why does Matthew introduce this appearance here and describe the encounter in this way? The appearance to the women is told like this because Matthew wants Jesus to be seen at the tomb in order to respond to how the empty tomb is being interpreted. To do this, Matthew brings the appearance tradition into the disappearance story directly (as Luke did indirectly by bringing Peter, a resurrection witness, to the tomb).[49]

Matthew's work in this pericope is connected with a larger redactional schema related to his apologetic for the empty tomb. Interestingly, whereas Luke's work in the empty tomb story is aimed at correcting what, in his view, was a deficient understanding of the resurrection within the early Christian movements, Matthew is trying to address the implications of outsiders' reactions to his community's stories and proclamation of the empty tomb of Jesus. This can be seen in his additional material about the guard at the tomb, material that first appears in Matthew (Matt. 27:62-66; 28:11-15). For Matthew, the guard at the tomb both guarantees narratively that the disciples had not stolen Jesus' body and accounts polemically for the origin of the story as a purposeful deception on the part of the Jewish authorities (the chief priests and the Pharisees). Simply put, the story itself is improbable and unhistorical.[50] The other Gospels know nothing of a guard at the tomb, and it seems questionable that the Romans would guard a tomb or grave in which an executed criminal was interred (if burial had happened). Besides, prohibitions against tampering with or breaking into tombs were evidently taken seriously.[51] Luz thinks these two episodes are Matthean fiction, especially the role played by the Jewish authorities, which he calls "historically grotesque," although he does allow that there may have been an earlier tradition that the tomb was watched.[52]

Matthew has woven his material about the guard at the tomb in and around the stories about the empty tomb and the appearances of Jesus. Scenes focusing on Jesus and the disciples are broken up by scenes focusing on the guard and the authorities, and Matthew has created some interesting parallels between these scenes.[53] Of particular note is how both the women and the members of the guard are given a commission to tell something (*eipate* + *hoti* + direct speech: Matt. 28:7; 28:13), and they both go to announce their news (*apaggellō*: Matt. 28:8, 10; 28:11).[54] Matthew's story also displays little interest in clarifying what the members of the guard saw and heard at the tomb. Matthew is ultimately more interested in presenting the two proclamations as parallels, which shows that his apologetic intends not to prove the resurrection, but to disprove a "rival interpretation" of the empty tomb.[55] Two details help us determine Matthew's view of the contrary story as he was aware of it. First, the initial concern is that the disciples of Jesus, after removing the body, could announce that he had been raised from the dead. This indicates that the rumor originally arose in response to resurrection proclamation, which probably included an empty tomb story or report. Second, the narrator states that "this story has been disseminated among Jews until this very day" (Matt. 28:15), indicating that the rival interpretation was current in Matthew's time and place.

Not mentioned at all in Matthew since the conclusion of the "woes" (Matt. 23:39), "the Pharisees" approach Pilate together with the chief priests to propose placing a guard at Jesus' tomb (Matt. 27:62). Matthew consistently depicts the Pharisees as hostile to Jesus but not directly involved in his death.[56] However, they are needed here as witnesses to Jesus' prediction of resurrection: as seen earlier, the sign of Jonah saying is given in reply to "some scribes and Pharisees" (Matt. 12:38-40), and their concern that the "last deception will be worse than the first" (27:64) echoes Jesus' words about the exorcised man whose demons return (12:45, which correlates this to "this generation"). Another possibility is that Matthew considers "the Pharisees" to be the origin or perpetuators of the rival interpretation of the empty tomb. Anthony Saldarini suggests that "for Matthew the Pharisees are rival teachers, with an understanding and practice of Judaism distinct from and hostile to Jesus'. They symbolize the leaders of the postdestruction Jewish community of which Matthew is a dissident member."[57] Unlike *Pharisaioi*, the expression *Ioudaioi* (Judeans, Jews) is rare in Matthew.[58] In Saldarini's opinion, Matthew uses it here polemically, attempting to delegitimize the traditional Jewish leaders (as with the Pharisees), but it does not mean that Matthew has become "totally separate from his ethnic group or religion."[59] On this view, Matthew uses *Ioudaioi* in 28:15 to polemicize against part of the Jewish people, so that "not all those in Israel, but only some, those who have rejected Jesus' resurrection, are included in this designation."[60] Saldarini is thinking here of the leadership primarily. Luz sees the context for the composition of this Matthean story as one of a more decisive break: "Matthew employs fictional devices to present his readers with the definitive separation of the community from the Jews."[61] In any case, this background to the story of the guard at the tomb sheds some light on why Matthew would want to depict the risen Jesus at the tomb: it is part of his counternarrative response to the rumor that the disciples had stolen the body. The disciples could not have stolen the body, according to Matthew's narration, for the following reasons: (1) the tomb was sealed and guarded so neither they nor the women had access to it; (2) the guards saw the angel (not the disciples) open the tomb and display it empty; (3) the rumor originated as an "official" response to the news (kept secret by the guard and the authorities) of the events at the tomb; and (4) Jesus was seen outside the empty tomb, and he spoke to the women, gave them a message to tell the disciples, and was able to be touched by them.

The significance Matthew attaches to the appearance to the women is clarified in a different way by another piece of Matthean redaction, the raising of the holy ones at the death of Jesus (Matt. 27:52-53). This is situated by Matthew among the apocalyptic "acts of God" that mark the death of Jesus as an eschato-logical event: the temple veil is torn, the earth is shaken, the rocks are split, the tombs are opened, and many bodies of saints who had fallen asleep are raised. These things provoke the centurion's confession, for he and others see "the earth-quake and the things that happened" (Matt. 27:53).[62] There are numerous prob-lems here for the interpreter, including the source of this material, the timing of the raising and the subsequent appearance of the holy ones, whether the raising was among the things seen by the centurion and the others—but above all why this was included, particularly here at the death of Jesus.

Davies and Allison have noted a number of parallels between this scene and the empty tomb scene in Matthew 28:1-8: both are introduced with Matthew's characteristic "and behold" (*kai idou*); both have an earthquake; both include the opening of tombs and a resurrection (described with the aorist passive of *egeirō*); the guards (*hoi tērountes*) in both scenes are stricken with fear; participants in both scenes enter Jerusalem; and female witnesses, including Mary Magdalene and the other Mary, are present at both scenes.[63] The connection between this event and the resurrection of Jesus is further strengthened for the reader by the phrase "after his resurrection" (*meta tēn egersin autou*, Matt. 27:54), if it was original to Matthew.[64] But even apart from this phrase, the parallels noted above suggest that the reader is invited to interpret the raising of the holy ones together with the resurrection of Jesus.

This gives further insight into the questions about Jesus' resurrection being confronted by the Matthean community. The raising of the saints in Matthew 27:52-53 is a corporate event, since it involves "many," and it is also apocalyptic (at least proleptically) because it occurs along with other apocalyptic signs at the crucifixion, the tearing of the veil and the earthquake.[65] The apocalyptic weight of this scene is evident in its verbal affinities with prophecies of resurrection from the Hebrew Bible (Ezek. 37:12-13; Zech. 14:4-5).[66] It is probably safe to assume that these two would have been standard texts in discussions about resurrection in the Jewish community of which the Matthean group was a part. This raising is temporary and only a foreshadowing of their vindication; but the fact that the raised saints go into the city and show themselves is important. Some scholars have seen here a foreshadowing of the final judgment: the verb used for their appearance has some juridical connotations, as if the raised saints were going in to hold the city (and the generation) responsible for their blood.[67] This would be clearer, admittedly, if the holy ones were described as persecuted or killed (see Matt. 23:29-39) rather than having "fallen asleep."

It has already been shown that claims about an empty tomb were part of the wider conversation between Matthew's community and members of other Jewish groups. Matthew's unique material about the guard displays, as we have seen, an interest in refuting a charge current "among Jews" that the disciples had manufactured a "resurrection" by stealing the body. Matthew's unique material about the raising of the holy ones, understood against this polemical setting, may have an interest in showing that Jesus' resurrection was not in contradiction to standard views about resurrection being both corporate and apocalyptic. As we have already seen, resurrection belief in Second Temple Judaism was normally corporate and apocalyptic in orientation, and it was never a mode of individual vindication, although individuals could hope for their own vindication in the coming resurrection (2 Maccabees 7). Thus an obvious question to a first-century Jew (whether or not a member of a Jesus group) would be how the resurrection of Jesus should be connected theologically with the hoped-for eschatological resurrection. Paul dealt with this problem by claiming that Jesus was raised as the "first fruits," whose resurrection not only precedes but also determines and guarantees the resurrection of the rest (1 Cor. 15:20-24). Later Christians thought in terms of descent of Christ into Hades to rescue the patriarchs (later called the "Harrowing of Hell").[68] In Matthew's situation, the question may have been, "If Jesus has been raised, then where are the others, and where is the end?" Matthew replies (narratively) by showing that others were raised and that the end had, in a way, been foreshadowed by God at the death of Jesus. There are other questions raised by this passage, but for our purposes, it illustrates how Matthew's redactional work in these last chapters was informed by questions about the resurrection of Jesus that outsiders were asking.

Matthew's appearance of the risen Jesus at (or near) the empty tomb is really a concrete narrativization of the claim, found already in Mark, that the tomb is empty because Jesus was raised out of it: "He is raised, he is not here" (Mark 16:6; cf. Matt. 28:6). It is one of three parts of a concerted response to outside challenges to the community's belief in and proclamation of the resurrection of Jesus. First, in response to charges that the resurrection of Jesus could not have happened since it was not corporate and did not signal the end (since no corporate eschatological raising of the dead had yet occurred), Matthew added the raising of the saints and other apocalyptic elements to the Markan story of the death of Jesus. Second, in response to a rival interpretation of the empty tomb that had the disciples stealing the body, Matthew has the women at the tomb receive from the angel the commission to tell the right version of the story ("he has been raised just as he said," 28:6), in contrast with the version of the chief priests and Pharisees ("that deceiver said," 27:63). It is interesting, incidentally, that the empty tomb does not seem to be in dispute here, whether because in Matthew's Jewish circles resurrection would be unthinkable without an emptied tomb, or because it was simply granted (given the difficulty of proving or disproving in which empty tomb Jesus was originally interred). Matthew also attributes the motivation for the guard at the tomb, and the propagation of the subsequent deception, to the chief priests and the Pharisees, the representatives of the formative Judaism Matthew's community found itself at odds with. Finally, Matthew has Jesus appear to the women as they are leaving the tomb (1) to demonstrate that the tomb is empty because Jesus is up and around outside it, and not for any other reason, and (2) to reinforce the basis of the proclamation of the resurrection and empty tomb as the authenticated view.

"All Authority Is Given to Me": The Risen Jesus as the Exalted Son of Man

Matthew 28:16-20, the appearance to the Eleven on a mountain in Galilee, is by all accounts a dense and carefully constructed story. Although there has been considerable disagreement among scholars about how to classify the appearance and commissioning,[69] and (as one would expect by now) about the nature of the original tradition behind the story,[70] most agree that the vision of the "one like a son of humankind" in Daniel 7:13-14 LXX has exercised significant influence on the language attributed to the risen Jesus in this final appearance. This is seen in expressions such as "all authority has been given" and "all nations," but also in the "heavenly triad" (in Daniel, the Ancient of Days, the son of humankind, the angels, but in Matthew, Father, Son, and Holy Spirit), in the transfer of power from God to a designated human being, and in the worship of God's designate.[71] There are other intertextual allusions here, for instance, to commissionings involving Moses,[72] but our interest here is in how the risen Jesus speaks as the exalted Son of Man and what that means in Matthew's view both for Jesus as the Risen One and for the community that owes its foundation and allegiance to him.

Wendy Cotter has pointed out the similarities between the scene in Matthew 28:16-20 and apotheosis scenes in Greek literature: this is "the appearance of [a] hero whose body has been transformed so that it is fitting for paradise. . . . The divinized Jesus first announces his cosmic authorization to his followers (v. 18) and then exercises that authority in a mandate to them."[73] What distinguishes the claims of the exalted Jesus, however, is that he claims a cosmic authority through the appeal to the vision of the one like a son of humankind in Daniel 7.[74] The allusions to Daniel 7 here would evoke for any reader familiar with the Scrip-tures the term "Son of Man," which to this point in Matthew has occurred some thirty times. As in Mark, the term is broadly used in Matthew, but it is always Jesus' characteristic self-designation, whether in relation simply to his individual humanity; or to his authority while on earth; or to his rejection, suffering, death, and resurrection; or to his future career as eschatological savior and judge. (In Q, the term has a considerably narrower range of application.) In Daniel 7:13, the one like a son of humankind came to the Ancient of Days on the clouds, "and authority was given to him, and all the nations of the earth forever, and all glory was serving him; and his authority was an everlasting authority which will never be taken away, and his kingdom [an everlasting kingdom] which will never be destroyed" (7:14 LXX).[75] This figure comes to his authority after the destruction of the fourth and most terrifying, most destructive beast (Dan. 7:1-8, 11-12). The one like a son of humankind also clearly represents "the holy ones," for as the angel tells Daniel, "these great beasts are four kingdoms which shall perish from the earth; and the holy ones of the most high will receive the kingdom, and they will possess the kingdom forever and ever" (Dan. 7:17-18; also v. 27).[76] This is the basis of the delegation of authority in the mission oracle in Matthew 28:18-20: "The backdrop of Daniel thus points to the Jewish Deity as the One who autho-rizes Jesus, and who thus authorizes the community."[77]

For Matthew, Jesus is already the exalted Son of Man and has already received "all authority," even though his full revelation awaits his coming on the clouds, his gathering of the elect, and the final overthrow of Rome (see Matt. 24:27-31).[78] Other Son of Man sayings in Matthew similarly emphasize Jesus' *future* authority as judge (Matt. 19:28-30; 25:31-46; 26:64), rather than his postresurrection authority. On what basis then can he claim this authority? Here a comparison with Q and with Mark could be illuminating. First, as seen in Mark, "the resurrection of the Son of Man" is depicted as an assumption by means of which Jesus is (raised and) preserved so that he may return as the Son of Man; this return was expected sooner for Mark's readers than for the women who flee from the tomb. In Matthew, I would argue, this understanding of the resurrection as an assumption that installs Jesus in the presence of God is still present; a hint of it was seen in the fact that when the angel rolled the stone away from the tomb, Jesus was already gone—removed, one should perhaps infer, into the divine realm from where he appears. Unlike the Apocalyptic Discourse, which predicts much turmoil and suffering before the coming of the Son of Man (Matt. 24:3-31), in this closing passage, the "end of the age" is only a distant prospect (28:20); the focus instead is on the mission of the disciples and the founding of a movement rather than on the Son of Man exerting his claim on the world directly.

In this sense, the authority of Jesus the exalted Son of Man is delegated to his followers, who will (in keeping with the imperial imagery) "conquer" the nations by making disciples who follow all that Jesus commanded (vv. 19-20). This mandate explains the delay, in contrast with Mark. Another saying from Q is equally illuminating: "All things have been handed over to me by my Father, and no one knows the son except the Father, nor [does anyone know] the Father except the son and the one to whom the son decides to reveal him" (Q 10:22). In Q, this saying occurs in the context of mission instructions (10:2-16), just as the saying we are considering in Matthew 28. It provides justification for the mission in Q as a saying that not only pronounces a blessing on those who receive the message (see also 10:21) but also authorizes the messengers because the one who delegates them has received all things from the Father.[79] This saying thus situates Jesus uniquely as one who mediates revelation. But why is Jesus able to speak this way in Q? Paul Hoffmann thought this saying makes the best sense in the light of what he called the Q people's "apokalypsis of the Son," a revelation connected with Easter faith,[80] and John Kloppenborg explained it in light of an implied "functional identification of Jesus and Sophia," so that no special moment of authorization needs to be narrated in Q—Sophia/Wisdom is always "vindicated by her children" (Q 7:35).[81] Given its Danielic tone, the saying could also be explained in relation to the apocalypticism of the death-assumption paradigm. Christopher Tuckett has pointed out that the saying might reflect equally "Son of Man" ideas as well as "the sonship language of Wisd 2–5 . . . where it is the righteous sufferer, and perhaps the *follower* of Wisdom, who is the 'son' of God."[82] As seen in an earlier chapter, this "Righteous One" in Wisdom 2–5 is removed by God through an early death (using language drawn from Genesis 5 LXX on the assumption of Enoch) and exalted in front of his onetime oppressors.[83] Regardless of whether those who compiled and redacted Q knew of this material in the Book of Wisdom, the point is that we have here in Q an elevated, even Danielic, self-description of Jesus, and that this oracle delegates authority to the Q mission. Even in Q, the interim time between the disappearance of Jesus and his return as the Son of Man is to be used in faithful service (see Q 12:39-40, 42-46), which involves mission in his name.[84] In its Matthean deployment (11:27), Q 10:22 still justifies the mission of the disciples, but it does so (in light of Matt. 28:18) by projecting the Easter authority of the Son back into his life, something Matthew also does elsewhere (e.g., Matt. 18:20). Here, however, "all things" refers to revelation rather than authority and rule.[85] Matthew also perceives the Wisdom Christology of the Q saying and appends to it another saying Jesus uttered as the exalted Wisdom: "Come to me, all of you who labor and are burdened down . . . . Take up my yoke upon you and learn from me" (Matt. 11:28-30).[86]

Matthew, of course, is heir both to Mark and to Q, and to their ideas about Jesus, his end, and his future role. Yet in view of the delay of the Son of Man's coming, Matthew has had to revise significantly the eschatological framework and the eschatological sayings of both Mark and Q. This reshaping accounts for his composition of the apocalyptic discourse in Matthew 24–25.[87] His concern there, as I argue elsewhere, is mainly to salvage the dominical material and to reconfigure it in an eschatological scenario that suits his own context.[88] In other words, what Jesus said about the end is still valid, even if the way he said it in Mark and Q needs adjusting to suit Matthew's perspective on God's activities in history. The same applies to Matthew's perspective on the postmortem exaltation of Jesus. Clearly Matthew still expects the Son of Man to come, but in the meantime he is exalted with all authority already given to him by the Father and can delegate that authority to his own emissaries. In terms of the means of that exaltation, there are reasons to think Matthew is heir to the "resurrection as assumption" pattern established by Mark. But in terms of the reception and the exercise of that authority, Matthew sees that beginning now, as also in Q 10:22.

Finally, it is worth observing that this resurrection appearance occurs in Galilee. Of course, this is exactly what the angel (Matt. 28:7) and Jesus himself (26:32; 28:10) have predicted, but there is no reason to suppose that the core tradition on which Matthew relies had transmitted its location. As already noted, both Ulrich Luz and James Robinson have argued that Matthew shows evidence of both literary and sociohistorical descent from Q and its community. Their reasons for this, besides the obvious literary connections, are similar. Luz argues mainly that "church offices" (prophets, sages, scribes) that Q refers to are still important in Matthew, so that "the Q traditions reflect for the [Matthean] church experiences from its own history."[89] Robinson thinks that Matthew's compositional patterns in chapters 3–11 can be explained as an attempt to "archive" Q, in particular its mission instructions, as a relic of the Matthean community's past, even though its future lies in the mission "to all nations" (28:19).[90] If Q can be situated in Galilee, as some suggest,[91] then Galilee is important to Matthew not only as the place where Jesus' kingdom proclamation began, but also as the origin of his own community (which by the time of the writing of the Gospel was situated in Syria, possibly Antioch). Admittedly, this is somewhat speculative, but it illustrates helpfully that Luke's pattern of a singular beginning of the Jesus movement in Jerusalem can be disputed (one does not assume that had the story in Matthew continued the Eleven would go back to Jerusalem to regroup). It also illustrates that the appearance to the women at the tomb, which in Matthew's story is the first appearance of the risen Jesus, has its main function in demonstrating the reality of the resurrection of Jesus in front of the contested empty tomb. Again we see another author who thinks the empty tomb story needs help in order to speak coherently to his situation.

8. John: "Where I Am Going, You Cannot Come"

"Little children, I am only with you a little while longer; you will look for me, and just as I said to the Jews—'where I am going, you cannot come'—I now say to you as well."
—John 13:33

Thinking he was the gardener, she said to him, "Sir, if you have moved him, tell me where you have put him, and I will get him." Jesus said to her, "Mary." And she turned around and said to him in Hebrew, "Rabbouni!" (which means Teacher). Jesus said to her, "Do not touch me, for I have not yet ascended to the Father; but go to my brothers and tell them that I am going up to my Father and your Father, to my God and your God." So Mary Magdalene went and announced to the disciples: "I have seen the Lord," and [she reported] these things that he had said to her.
—John 20:15-18

Then the Jews answered and said to him, "What sign will you show us [to authorize] you to do these things?" Jesus answered and said to them, "Unmake this temple and in three days I will raise it up." So the Jews said, "Forty-six years this temple has been under construction, and in three days you will raise it up?" But he was speaking about the temple of his body.
—John 2:18-21

In the Fourth Gospel, the accommodation of the disappearance tradition to the appearance tradition continues: one finds here both Luke's addition of Peter as the primary resurrection witness who validates the story of the empty tomb, and Matthew's inclusion of an appearance of Jesus at the tomb, witnessed by the women who discover the empty tomb and encounter the angel. The question that immediately arises is how best to explain these parallels. Was the author of the Fourth Gospel a recipient of the same basic traditions that lie behind Matthew 28:9-10 and Luke 24:12? Did the author use Matthew and Luke as source texts? Or was he somehow the recipient of secondary oral traditions, that is, stories circulating through different communities in the Jesus movement, but ultimately originating from the oral performance of the other Gospels?[1] Although such questions are important, they are ultimately not really consequential to our study, because there are other questions to ask about the meaning of the text. The narrative developments of the apostolic witness to the empty tomb and of the appearance to the women at the tomb are deployed, characteristically, within the literary, theological, and mythic framework of John.

Two illustrations of this can be seen in John 20:1-18. First, beside Peter at the tomb, in fact running alongside and then ahead of him to the tomb, is the Beloved Disciple (John 20:3-10); thus the fact that the tomb was discovered empty is corroborated also by the witness whose testimony is, according to the evangelist, the core of the Fourth Gospel (21:24).[2] Similarly, in John there is not a crowd of women at the tomb, but only Mary Magdalene (20:1-2, 11-18), and it is Mary alone to whom Jesus appears at the tomb, and she whom he commissions with the message, "I am going up to my Father and your Father, to my God and your God" (20:17-18). This at least partly is a factor in the importance of Mary Magdalene as a character in John, for even though she is only mentioned once elsewhere in John (19:25), she is placed both at the crucifixion and at the tomb alongside the Beloved Disciple, and of course she is the first to see the risen Jesus in John. In addition, the extended scene—interrupted by the inspection of the tomb by the two disciples—of Mary alone at the tomb is also in keeping with the evangelist's preference to narrate recognition scenes in which individuals are challenged, often at considerable length and with deeply revealing dialogue, to perceive who Jesus is and how to accept his cosmic significance.[3] However, there is more going on in John's empty tomb story than these two characteristically Johannine turns on the narrative, as we will see.

One of the distinctive features of John is the importance it gives to "signs." Craig Koester defines a sign in John as "an action that brings the power of God into the realm of the senses," normally an extraordinary action but one whose correct interpretation depends on whether the one interpreting the sign already has a relationship with Jesus that can provide context.[4] In John, the empty tomb is one aspect of the sign of Jesus' resurrection (the body of Jesus is the other). As in the other Gospels, the empty tomb in John signifies that God has raised Jesus (where proclamation of the resurrection is theologically prior, as in Mark 16:6), but this is not all that the empty tomb signifies. It also is related to the idea of Jesus' departure, which according to the Fourth Gospel is the final leg of Jesus the Son's cosmic journey.[5] The Son (the Word) comes from and is sent by the Father; he reveals the Father and fulfills his will during his time on earth; and he departs from his beloved on earth in order to return to the Father and resume his place of prominence in the glory of the Father.[6] The theme of Jesus' departure is especially important to his last discourse (John 13:31–17:26), an extended section in which Jesus, just before his arrest, speaks privately to the disciples about what his departure will mean for them. Interestingly, in a few places, departure language (Gk., *hupagō* and other verbs) is used together with language typically associated with assumption. "Seeking without finding" language is common (John 7:33-36; 8:21-24; 13:33), as in the line given at the beginning of this chapter: "I am going away, and you will search for me; where I am going, you cannot come" (13:33; also 7:33-34; 8:21). "Not seeing" language also is found connected with this theme in a saying remarkably similar to Q 13:35, which (as seen above in chapter 4) is one of the pivotal pieces of evidence for the early emergence of the disappearance tradition:

> "A little while and you see me no longer, and again a little while and you will see me." (John 16:16)

> "[And] I tell you, you will not see me until [the time comes when] you say, 'Blessed is the Coming One in the name of the Lord!'" (Q 13:35b)

The Q saying suggests that Jesus' disappearance is connected with his future role as the Coming One; whether he comes in judgment upon those who acclaim him (too late) is a disputed question.[7] On a surface reading, John 16:16 could refer to the brief hiatus between Jesus' death and resurrection—after all, the disciples did not see him, and then they saw him again.[8]

Taking the full scope of the Johannine descent-ascent paradigm into account, however, this text has a deeper meaning, for it points to the prolonged physical absence of Jesus from his followers—he came from the Father and must return to the Father (John 16:28). This begins with the resurrection but is not complete until the Son finally ascends to the Father. As Jesus says to Mary when he is with her at the tomb: "Go to my brothers and tell them that I am going up to my Father and your Father, to my God and your God" (20:17). Martinus de Boer observes that "the grammar of these two statements [I am ascending to my Father/my God; I am going away to the Father/God] is identical," so that "the conclusion seems inescapable that the theme of Jesus' departure as enunciated in the Last Discourse (and in some earlier passages) looks forward *not* to the event of Jesus' death by crucifixion as recounted in ch. 18–19, but to his *ascension* as announced in his resurrection appearance to Mary Magdalene."[9] The ascension is the departure to the Father, and the resurrection itself points ahead to it and the appearances point back to it, as will be argued below. Jesus' followers may mourn at his becoming absent, but they have both a mission to carry out and empowerment for that mission in their reception of the Holy Spirit (20:21-23). In John this "not seeing" amounts to a crisis of faith for the reader—how can they believe in him whom they have not seen?[10] Yet "blessed are those who believe without seeing," the risen Jesus tells Thomas (John 20:29). The period of Jesus' absence in Q and Mark, however, presents a crisis of discipleship. In Q 13:35, the absence of Jesus signified his future apocalyptic role, and in the Q parables about returning masters, the theme was used to encourage faithful discipleship in the time before his coming. Similarly, in Mark, the absence of Jesus was used to spur the reader on to endure the dangers of discipleship before the coming of the Son of Man, which evidently was expected soon. Here in John, however, the time of the absence of Jesus, though still characterized by the risk of persecution from the Jews and hatred by the world, is the long-term prospect for the Johannine community. As Jesus explains in John 13–17, his followers cannot prevent him from leaving them, but he does not leave them alone (he sends the Advocate), and they will see him soon (not only in the revelation of the Advocate, but also when they join him in the mansions of the Father).

How John Adapts the Empty Tomb Story

Normally there are reservations about supposing John's direct literary dependence on one or more of the Synoptics, because the Fourth Gospel is so different—in its framework, in the individual episodes it relates, and particularly in the way it represents the voice of Jesus. As seen in the previous chapters, however, in some of John's resurrection stories (John 20), and in the passion narrative as well (John 18–19), it is justified to suppose that the evangelist not only was well acquainted with the other Gospels, but in some places used one or another as literary source material. On the other hand, the story as told here is thoroughly Johannine. In John's empty tomb story, all of the basic elements of the story as it already appeared in Mark are present: a visit by female disciples (though in John only Mary Magdalene is mentioned) to the tomb early in the morning on the first day of the week (John 20:1), the discovery that the stone has been rolled away and the tomb is empty (vv. 1-2), an encounter with angels in the tomb (vv. 11-12), and a flight from the tomb (v. 2). John's focus on Mary might be a factor, as suggested above, of the intention to narrate an individual encounter with the risen Jesus; but John 20:2 suggests knowledge of other forms of the story that feature a group of women, since Mary says, "We do not know where they have put him."[11] The first-person plural also "marks the problem as not merely personal but communal."[12]

The report to the two disciples and their inspection of the tomb have precursors in Luke 24:9-12, as already noted; here the evangelist appears to have relied closely on the text of Luke, at least in his description of the inspection of the tomb (20:3-10). In particular, Luke and John agree in five consecutive words in Greek: *kai parakupsas blepei ta othonia*, "and having stooped/peered he sees the grave clothes" (Luke 24:12; John 20:5). Frans Neirynck, taking *parakupsas* as a verb of seeing, explains the phrase "having peered he sees" as Luke's adaptation of Mark 16:3 (*anablepsasai theōrousin*, "and having looked up they see"); this together with other evidence of Lukan style (especially "having got up he ran," and "marveling at what had happened") makes Luke 24:12 the work of Luke himself. This means that the verbatim agreements here must be evidence that the author of the Fourth Gospel used Luke 24:12 as the source text for John 20:3-10.[13] There is also some close agreement between John and Matthew in what Jesus says to Mary (and in Matthew, to the others) at the tomb. The combination of (1) the unusual designation of the disciples as "brothers" and (2) the command to go tell them about the risen Jesus' itinerary (3) in a saying to women (or a woman) at the tomb makes it very probable that the author of John was influenced by Matthew 28:9-10 in telling this appearance story.[14]

It is difficult to say precisely how John 20:1-18 came together into a single narrative, but a few things seem clear.[15] Working from the basic story of the discovery of the empty tomb, the evangelist has inserted the piece about Mary's report to the two disciples, which, as just noted, he seems to have derived from Luke 24:9-11.[16] Mary does not seem even to look into the tomb until verse 11, after she has returned from telling the two disciples that "they have taken the Lord out of the tomb" (v. 2). Without verses 2-10, we would have a story of Mary arriving at the tomb and seeing it already open (v. 1), then standing outside the tomb weeping before stooping (or peering) into the tomb and interacting with the angels (vv. 11-13). This insertion creates a bustle of trips back (into the city, one assumes) and forth to the tomb—and this provides the author an opportunity to stress the rivalry between Peter and the Beloved Disciple. Mary's guess that "they have taken the Lord" is also repeated (vv. 2, 13, 15). The text does not explain who Mary thinks may have done this, whether enemies preventing even the most basic burial for Jesus, or tomb robbers, or Joseph and Nicodemus, or "the gardener" (v. 15). As Koester notes, "Theologically, this is important for the evangelist. It makes clear that resurrection is not the obvious answer to an open tomb. Therefore, any belief that Jesus has risen and is alive must overcome this alternative explanation."[17]

As to the angelophany, we find it in a substantially muted form. The angels themselves are only incidentally present: one sits at the head, and the other at the feet, of the place where the body of Jesus had been, but they offer no interpretation of the meaning of the empty tomb—there is no proclamation of the resurrection (cf. Mark 16:6; Matt. 28:6; Luke 24:5-6), nor is there a directive to go and tell the news to the other disciples (Mark 16:7; Matt. 28:7), but only the question, "Woman, why do you weep?" (John 20:12-13). This is the question Jesus also asks further along in the story (v. 15), after Mary mistakes him for the gardener (vv. 14-15). Thus John reproduces, but in a different register, the Matthean coordination of Jesus' saying with that of the angel (Matt. 28:7, 10). The typical reaction of fear is also absent, as it was in Matthew; in fact, the narrator here gives Mary no reaction at all to the presence of the angels except her response to their question. One almost thinks that the evangelist included the angels as a concession to the earlier deployments of the story but significantly diminished their importance to the story.[18] In any event, as Raymond Brown notes, it is the following Christophany that interprets the empty tomb, and not the angel: "John [thus] begins a process that culminates in the second-century *Epistula Apostolorum*, 10, where the angelophany in the tomb is replaced entirely by a christophany [outside the tomb]."[19]

The inspection of the empty tomb by Peter and the Beloved Disciple, which (as suggested above) probably was written into the core story of Mary at the tomb, appears in a considerably expanded form in comparison with the brief note in Luke 24:12. In Luke, Peter gets up and runs to the tomb to see for himself, evidently because the Eleven (himself included) initially did not believe the women's report, dismissing it as nonsense or worse. After seeing the tomb empty except for the linen grave clothes, he returns home "marveling at what had happened." As shown in chapter 6 above, this was Luke's own contribution to the story, the intention evidently being to have the primary resurrection witness (a primacy Peter is given in Luke 24:34) validate the women's story that the tomb was empty. Although the empty tomb does not lead to Easter faith, only to wonder or amazement, Peter's inspection controls the way that the appearances can be narrated: Jesus must appear in such a way as to leave an empty tomb, that is, in a flesh-and-bones body, not in a visionary experience (Luke 24:39). In some ways, the intention appears to be the same in the Fourth Gospel, since questions about the body of Jesus after the resurrection are entertained here, as the encounter between Thomas and the risen Jesus seems to show. However, as will be seen below, the bodily continuity of Jesus before and after the resurrection is not conceived in the same way as in Luke.

Because the Fourth Gospel (and probably the community behind the Gospel)[20] traces its origins to the testimony of "the disciple Jesus loved" (John 21:24), whoever that may have been, this disciple is included as a corroborating witness to the empty tomb alongside Peter. Possibly, the Beloved Disciple does not replace Peter as the apostolic witness because Peter's importance to the origin of the resurrection proclamation cannot at this point be denied. In any case, Peter's solitary run to the tomb in Luke 24:12 becomes a footrace with the Beloved Disciple in John 20:3-4. Although the Beloved Disciple outruns Peter and arrives at the tomb first, the narrative still gives precedence to Peter, for he (once he arrives) enters the tomb where the other disciple only stooped and peered in to see the grave clothes (vv. 5-7). Only after Peter has noticed the placement of the grave clothes does the Beloved Disciple enter and see for himself. What Peter sees is explained in great detail: "Then, following him, Peter also came, and he went into the tomb; and he saw the linen cloths lying there, and the face-cloth, which had been on his head, lying not with the other cloths, but off on one side, all folded up" (John 20:6-7). As in Luke, the point seems to be that the body was not simply moved or stolen—otherwise, whoever did this would have taken the body in the grave clothes.[21] Andrew Lincoln also notes that there is a contrast intended with the raising of Lazarus, who needed help to get out of his grave clothes (John 11:44).[22] The point of the separation of the grave clothes, which is described very deliberately, is less clear, at least until the reader comes to the observation that the two angels (who apparently are not yet in the tomb when Peter and the other disciple enter) were sitting in the tomb, "one at the head and one at the feet, where the body of Jesus had been lying" (v. 12). This would indicate that the author is envisioning the *arcosolium* type of tomb, which had wide but shallow shelves or troughs on which to place a body (rather than a narrow but deep *loculus* niche, into which one would place a body head-first, with only the feet showing).[23] In any case, Mary scarcely notices the angels or their placement, but the fact that their location is (again) so deliberately described has led some commentators to conclude that the two angels were meant to represent the two cherubim on either side of the Ark of the Covenant (Exod. 25:17-22). This would be to situate the divine presence in between, where the resurrected body of Jesus had been lying.[24]

Like the other canonical Gospels, John displays a certain ambivalence toward the empty tomb itself. In Mark, as seen above in chapter 5, when the women see the tomb, they flee in fear (probably fear of the divine), even though they have had the empty tomb's significance explained to them by the young man: "He was raised, he is not here" (Mark 16:6). In Luke the women do not flee in fear, but leave the tomb musing on Jesus' predictions of his death and resurrection (Luke 24:6-8), but not on the meaning of the empty tomb; and Peter, having seen the tomb and the grave clothes, leaves "marveling" but not believing (24:12). Here in John the narrator presents a puzzling sequence of actions and reactions: first the Beloved Disciple sees but does not enter (John 20:5); then Peter comes and goes in and sees (vv. 6-7); next the Beloved Disciple enters, sees the grave clothes, and believes (v. 8); then the narrator says, "For they did not as yet know the Scripture, that he must rise from the dead" (v. 9); and finally they go home (v. 10). What did the Beloved Disciple "believe" if he and Peter did not yet understand from the Scriptures that Jesus must rise again? One possibility is that the Beloved Disciple believed only after seeing the sign of the empty tomb and grave clothes that Jesus had risen from the dead; verse 9 then explains that he was able to believe without the additional insight into the Scriptures that a postresurrection experience of Jesus would have given. Another possibility is suggested by Sandra Schneiders: "The beloved disciple believed that on the cross, though he truly died, Jesus was exalted into the presence of God. The face cloth of his flesh (i.e., his mortality in which his glory had been veiled during his pre-Easter career) is now definitively laid aside."[25]

In any event, the Beloved Disciple is the first to believe (notice, however, that the text does not claim belief for Peter). The Beloved Disciple's coming to belief would be exemplary for the reader of John, for he is able to believe without an understanding of the Scriptures and even without an encounter with the risen Jesus (see 20:29).[26] This character is introduced in the story of the tomb inspection because his already close relationship with Jesus enables him to interpret the sign of the empty tomb (including the folded grave clothes) in a way even Peter is not yet prepared to do.[27] The Beloved Disciple, after all, reclined against Jesus' side (Gk., *kolpos*) at the supper (John 13:23), language that recalls how the unique God (the Word) who resides in the Father's bosom (*kolpos*) was able to make him known (1:18).

Another possibility is that the Beloved Disciple "saw and believed" only the report of Mary, that the body of Jesus was no longer in the tomb; only later would he believe that Jesus had been raised from the dead.[28] The idea of progressive belief can also be found in John 4:46-53, where the nobleman first believes Jesus' word that his son will live and then later believes together with his whole house (absolute, with no object stated). There, however, the beginning of trust has an object, the word of Jesus; here in John 20:8 "he saw and believed" (absolute, with no object stated). As for Peter, by now he must have believed Mary's report, but this is not made explicit. He is not yet ready to understand the full significance of the sign of the empty tomb, for his insight into the Scriptures had not been kindled by a direct experience of the risen Jesus.[29] Koester correctly notes that "the subdued conclusion to this scene works against the idea that seeing the empty tomb is a sure way to believe and comprehend the resurrection."[30] In John's narration, this personal encounter was still to come for Peter and the other disciples (John 20:19-23), but it is near at hand for Mary (20:11-18), who meanwhile has returned to the tomb.

"I Have Seen the Lord": Mary Magdalene's Encounter with the Risen Jesus

The appearance of Jesus to Mary is similar to recognition scenes found elsewhere in John, although this one is significantly shorter than the others. Here she does not misunderstand the role or significance of Jesus, as others do in other recognition scenes (see, e.g., John 4:7-42); rather, she mistakes him for the gardener, a mistake most commentators put down to the theological idea that the risen Jesus must reveal himself. As Lincoln says, "There is still the need for the giving of recognition."[31] Luke also stresses the idea that the risen Jesus must make himself known through some demonstration of his identity (Luke 24:30-31, breaking bread; 24:39, revealing his pierced hands and feet).[32] However, Mary's encounter with Jesus also has some similarities to scenes in Hellenistic novels in which long-parted lovers are slow to recognize each other, just as Callirhoe recognizes Chaereas by the sound of his voice (*Chaer.* 8.1.7).[33] Likewise here, Jesus initiates Mary's recognition through greeting her by name (John 20:16; cf. Matt. 28:9) and commissions her directly with a message having real content: "I am ascending to my Father . . ." (cf. John 20:17 with Luke 24:5-9; Matt. 28:7, 10). Mary's message to the others is reported in almost exactly the same language Paul used for his own experience of the risen Christ: "I have seen the Lord" (John 20:18; 1 Cor. 9:1). Thus Mary here is the *apostolorum apostola*, the "apostle to the apostles." This designation is of course secondary to John—something along these lines first appears in a commentary on the Song of Songs attributed to Hippolytus of Rome (d. c. 236 CE)[34]—but it may accurately reflect Mary's status as a visionary and leading figure in some circles of early Christianity.

The appearance to the women in Matthew 28:9-10, as argued in the previous chapter, is a Matthean composition, but it may have been based on an earlier tradition of a resurrection appearance to women. If Mark had been aware of such a tradition, he apparently suppressed it to emphasize the absence of Jesus and the demands this poses for the disciples, and to deemphasize the legitimation of leaders in the movement. Matthew and John both tell a story about an appearance to Mary Magdalene, but she is only singled out in John (she is not mentioned by name in the appearance story itself in Matt. 28:9-10). In other texts, including the *Gospel of Mary*, the *Dialogue of the Savior*, and the *Gospel of Philip*, Mary is presented as a visionary and mediator of revelation, sometimes superior to other followers, including Peter.[35] This figure emerges once the Mary of the texts is distinguished from the composite "Mary Magdalene" of early Christian interpretation, which tended to conflate various women, named and unnamed, in the canonical Gospels into the portrait of a former prostitute.[36]

Many scholars proceed from the assumption that both Matthew 28:9-10 and John 20:14-18 reflect an earlier tradition.[37] The question is complex, however, because aside from later extracanonical sources, which themselves may be dependent upon the canonical texts for Mary's reputation as a visionary, Matthew and John are the only sources for an appearance to Mary (and they might not be independent sources). In other words, if the commonalities between Matthew and John in this episode are to be put down to John's (even secondarily oral) knowledge of Matthew,[38] then direct evidence for a common tradition underlying both stories diminishes. Pseudo-Mark 16:9-10, part of the secondary longer ending of Mark, should be counted as neither early nor independent evidence. On what basis, then, can it be claimed that there was a tradition, predating both Matthew and John, of an appearance to Mary?

One consideration is the possibility, mentioned above in chapter 2, that Paul's list does not name Mary Magdalene not because the tradition of her experience of the risen Jesus is late or secondary, but because he (or his material) has suppressed her as a resurrection witness.[39] This silence on its own says little, but such a suppression would be consistent with the development noted in Luke, where the women are not even commissioned by the angels, and it could explain the rather diffuse picture one gets of Mary in the different early texts. As Claudia Setzer remarks in relation to female witness to the resurrection in general, "The evangelists seem to erase partially the women's role from the narrative. Their discomfort hints at how firmly entrenched the tradition of women's involvement must have been, since the authors do not feel free to eliminate it."[40] In John, as well as in Matthew, the prominent role given to Mary might be seen as a relic of this remembered "involvement," just as the retention of Peter in the inspection of the tomb could signal his prominence in the pre-Johannine tradition (a prominence seen in Paul and Luke). One wonders how John 20:14-18 would have been received had there not been already a reminiscence of Mary as a visionary in some circles, particularly given that she receives a special and apostolic announcement. Jane Schaberg suggests that "it is more probable that the tradition of a protophany [first appearance of the risen Jesus] to Mary Magdalene has been suppressed, than that it came into being later." Her argument rests mainly on the "intricate fit" she sees between the appearance to Mary and the empty tomb tradition. She lists eighteen correspondences between Matthew and John that indicate to her a core tradition of an appearance to Mary at the tomb.[41]

Along different lines, Mary Rose D'Angelo has discerned a common structure in both the appearance to Mary in John 20:14-18 and the vision of the exalted Son of Man in Revelation 1:10-19. Both visions begin with (1) an orientation of the seer, symbolized by a physical turning toward the vision, and include then (2) an admonition, (3) a commission, and (4) a first-person oracle. Despite the different genres of the texts in which they are recounted, these two visions clearly share, according to D'Angelo, the same context—early Christian prophecy.[42]

Two things distinguish D'Angelo's form-critical evaluation from C. H. Dodd's view of the formal structure of the resurrection appearance reports.[43] First, the orientation to the vision indicates something of the preparatory practices that could initiate or invite a visionary experience, although these practices "are not fully recoverable."[44] According to Dodd, in the resurrection appearance reports, Jesus simply appears. Second, D'Angelo is correct that in these two examples the admonition, commissioning, and oracle are all clearly distinct from one another (Dodd had the more general "word of command" as the final element in the structure of the appearance reports). In particular, the isolation of the saying of the risen Jesus as an oracle indicates that the author of John understood and depicted Mary's experience as one that issued in a prophetic utterance.[45] "One might imagine her proclaiming it among the assembled companions of Jesus, beginning with the oracle formula: 'thus says the Lord.'"[46]

Mary thus is commissioned to carry an oracle that, as we will see below, communicates the correct interpretation of the sign of the resurrection of Jesus. One wonders, therefore, how some commentators somehow were able to relegate this appearance to Mary to a lower status, of a personal but unofficial nature, than the others.[47] The appendix to the Fourth Gospel does not even seem to count it (John 21:14).[48] In part this diminution of the appearance to Mary is related to a feature of the story that does not seem consistent with this weighty commissioning: the apparent reserve of the risen Jesus in this encounter. After Mary recognizes Jesus, he says to her, "*Mē mou haptou*, for I have not yet ascended to the Father." It is difficult to know precisely how to translate the Greek, because the verb *haptomai* can mean touch or hold,[49] and because the grammar of the clause can indicate either a prohibition of an intended or attempted action (as in "Do not touch/hold me") or a command to stop an action already in progress (as in "Stop touching/holding me"). The present tense of the verb suggests that the latter is more probably correct, although such distinctions were not always observed as scrupulously by ancient authors as they are by modern grammarians.[50] Harold Attridge suggests the vivid "Don't be touching me," which conveys both the ingressive aspect of the present tense and the possibility that the action has at least been attempted.[51] This translation must also be reconciled somehow with the invitation to touch that the risen Jesus gives to Thomas (John 20:27, which uses *pherō* and *ballō* with finger/hand instead of *haptomai*).

Of the many possible solutions to this interpretive question, two in particular commend themselves. The first is the reading that takes Jesus' command as prohibiting any attempt to situate the community's experience of (the risen) Jesus in his bodily presence after the resurrection.[52] Schneiders, for instance, says that this indicates that their time of relating to one another as mortal human beings is at an end, and that "the place where Mary will now encounter Jesus as he really is, glorified and risen, is the community; Mary must pass over from the pre-Easter to the Easter dispensation."[53] Thus Jesus does not reject Mary's attempt to be physically close to him, but the attempt to keep him with his followers rather than have him return to the Father. De Boer sees this as an answer to an early problem within the Johannine community. In John 12:34 the crowd has this criticism for Jesus: "We have heard from the Law that the Messiah is to remain forever. How can you say that the Son of Man is to be lifted up?" Originally, de Boer argues, this was a criticism against those who believed in Jesus as the Messiah—why did he leave if he had come to save the world? Christologically, however, in the Fourth Gospel the negative side of Jesus' departure (his absence from human history, although this is mitigated by the presence of the risen Jesus in the Comforter) is far outweighed by its positive side (his return to the Father and to his original state of glory).[54]

The second option, seen already in the writings of Origen, is that the encounter between Mary and the risen (or arising) Jesus takes place at a moment when Jesus' resurrection/exaltation is not complete. D'Angelo notes that *mē mou haptou*—if taken as a command not to touch—has an interesting parallel in the *Life of Adam and Eve*, in which Adam tells Eve not to let anyone touch his body after he dies: "But when I die, you should leave me alone, and let no one touch me (*mēdeis mou hapsētai*) until the angel of the Lord says something about me; for God will not overlook me, but will seek his own vessel which he has formed" (31:3). Later in the story it comes about that the dead Adam is taken up in a chariot of light, seen in a vision by Eve and Seth; Adam thereafter is installed in the third heaven until the judgment, while his body is buried in the paradise on earth (*L.A.E.* 33–41). D'Angelo suggests that in between Adam's death and the assumption of his body, contact with his body is forbidden because it can cause ritual impurity. She does not suggest the same concern is in view in John, but notes instead the liminality of these embodied states: "Adam describes what is necessary for the time when he is dead but not yet buried; Jesus is raised but describes himself as not yet ascended to God."[55] D'Angelo also refers to Origen's reading of John 20:17, according to which "the state of Jesus is different when he encounters Mary from when he meets the disciples."[56] Thus Mary encounters Jesus just after he has risen but before he ascends to the Father, which is the culmination of the process of departure.[57] Thomas and the others encounter him after his ascension is complete, and he appears from the heavenly realm. D'Angelo suggests that "the uniqueness of the appearance may award Mary a special status"; indeed, it confers on her "a unique privilege,"[58] as shown not only in the oracle she carries but also in the fact that in John she is the first to proclaim the resurrection. "I have seen the Lord," she says (20:18), and the other disciples echo her announcement (20:25) after their own encounter with Jesus. In contrast with the other versions of the empty tomb story, proclamation of the resurrection is first credited to a leading figure in the post-Easter community, rather than to a representative of the divine realm (as in Mark 16:6; Matt. 28:6; Luke 24:5).

Both these readings make sense within the broader context of the Fourth Gospel, and both readings, interestingly, play on different aspects of the assumption paradigm. In the first reading, there is an emphasis on the difference between how Jesus is present with his followers before Easter and how he is present with them afterward. Thus Jesus can say to Mary, "Do not prevent me from returning to the Father," as it were, but he can still invite Thomas to touch him, since the two encounters are oriented toward different questions in the community.[59] The

Thomas episode shares some parallels with the resurrection appearance of Luke 24:36-43—the greeting of peace, the invitation to touch, the theme of doubt—and yet in John the issue is (contrary to a surface reading) less the physicality or tangibility of the body of the risen Jesus, and more the *need for* physical demonstration (which in Luke the risen Jesus is only too happy to give). In John 20:27 Jesus invites Thomas to "bring your finger . . . and *see*," and "bring and put your hand . . . and become not unbelieving but believing," that is, to accept the revelation of Jesus' post-Easter identity as mediated by the community's proclamation that "we have seen the Lord" (20:25). As already noted, in both Q and Mark the absence of Jesus is interpreted in relation to his preservation for his eschatological role, and the time of his absence posed serious demands for disciples awaiting the return of their Master/Judge. In the Fourth Gospel, however—in keeping with John's characteristic muting or reshaping of eschatological themes current in other circles in early Christianity—this absence is at the same time the interim before his return (14:1-4) as well as the time of life in the community under the care and direction of the Comforter, the Holy Spirit, his surrogate presence (14:16-19; 16:7-16).

The Spirit cannot come until after Jesus is glorified (John 7:37-39), but Jesus breathes the Spirit on the disciples in his first encounter with them as a group (20:22). One assumes that this has happened because the Son's glorification is complete. So the second reading of John 20:17 stresses how the departure of Jesus from earth and his return to the Father is not only the culmination of his cosmic journey, but also a process in itself, encompassing his glorification through his death, his return to life out of the grave, and his ascent to the Father. Therefore, in the Fourth Gospel, the resurrection, the assumption/ascension, and the giving of the Spirit are all related, as they are in Luke-Acts, but without the Lukan stress on the physical resurrection appearances as occurring in an extended interim period of forty days between resurrection and ascension. Rather, they are all part of one continuous process.[60] Yet maybe the idea that Mary somehow interrupted Jesus in the middle of this process—just after rising and just before ascending—seems to attribute to the Fourth Gospel a crude, even naive attempt to explain what in the other Gospels happens behind closed doors (of tombs).[61] Perhaps it does, but D'Angelo thinks it is more an attempt to express "the holy and awesome process" Jesus undergoes.[62] Yet one does not need to look too far into the second century to find the same process narrated in a much more explicit way, in the *Gospel of Peter*. There the resurrection of Jesus is depicted as both resuscitation and transfiguration, with Jesus being helped out of the tomb by two angels (*Gos. Pet.* 10.39-42); later the women at the tomb are told that "he has gone away to the place from which he was sent" (13.56), but him they do not see (for he has departed). The text seems to go on to describe an appearance by the lake, although the manuscript breaks off before the story is told (14.60).

Recently, Schaberg has attempted to account for the special status of Mary as resurrection witness and apostle in a reading of John 20:14-18 that focuses on intertextual allusions to 2 Kings 2, the story of Elijah's assumption and Elisha's succession. In part Schaberg depends on the view that John 20:14-18 narrates

Mary catching Jesus *as he is ascending*, for he says to tell the others, "I am ascending."[63] In 2 Kings 2, witnessing Elijah's ascent allows Elisha to receive what he asked of his master, a double portion of his spirit (the eldest son's share), which, along with his reception of the prophet's mantle, marked him off as his successor.[64] This reading is part of a larger and much more complex reconstruction of the *basileia* (kingdom) movement of Jesus, which Schaberg thinks drew on apocalyptic and prophetic texts, such as Daniel 7, about the "Human One" (as a symbolic embodiment of corporate suffering and vindication).[65] Here in John 20, Schaberg finds only "shards" of a succession tradition that is erased in other texts dealing with Mary (such as Matt. 28:9-10 and Ps.-Mark 16:9-10).[66] Mary does not witness Jesus' ascension in John, and beyond the announcement she makes in 20:18, one does not learn to what extent she has taken up Jesus' mantle, so that Schaberg's reading is enticing but not entirely convincing. On the other hand, situating the empty tomb (disappearance) tradition at its emergence within an apocalyptic context that provided the framework for its interpretation and elaboration does, in my opinion, make good sense of the relevant data. What I argued above concerning Mark, Schaberg argues for the emergence of the core conviction of Jesus' postmortem vindication: "Not finding the body is the catalyst for a radical modification of the Danielic tradition, with resurrection understood as translation, and vice versa."[67] In Q, as we have seen, the succession of Jesus by his followers is likened to Elisha's succession of Elijah (Q 9:61-62), and Jesus' own vindication is expressed along the lines of Elijah's assumption into the divine realm to await his role in the eschatological drama (Q 13:35), in keeping with traditions in Jewish apocalypticism about other figures.

Here in John, as in Mark, resurrection and assumption are found together. In Mark's conception the association is oriented to the apocalyptic paradigm, and the "resurrection of the Son of Man" is signified by the empty tomb and the expectation of his imminent return (Mark 13:24-27; 14:62). In the Fourth Gospel, in contrast, this apocalyptic idiom has been muted: the term "Son of Man" expresses the identity of Jesus the Word made flesh as the one who descends from heaven and ascends back into heaven (John 3:13; 6:62), and his disappearance and absence signify his return to the glory of the Father (17:4-5). "Now has the Son of Man been glorified, and God has been glorified in him. . . . Little children, I am only with you for a little while longer; you will search for me, and just as I told the Jews that 'where I am going you cannot come,' I now say to you as well" (John 13:31, 33). The resurrection of Jesus, in relation to both appearance and disappearance, thus functions as a sign of this return to the Father to account for Jesus' post-Easter absence and presence.

Seeing Is Believing? The Resurrection of Jesus as the Eighth Sign

As in Matthew, it is important that here in John the risen Jesus appears outside the tomb. In John, however, the effect is not only to stress the continuity between the body buried and the body raised, as an answer to questions about the empty tomb—although this is clearer here than in Matthew because of the empty grave clothes and the inspection of the tomb by the apostolic witnesses. Here it also signals that the empty tomb and grave clothes (on the one hand) and the body of Jesus, now present with Mary (on the other), are two aspects of the same sign—the resurrection of Jesus.

Throughout the first half of the Fourth Gospel, "signs . . . play a positive theological role in calling attention to Jesus' origin, power, and purpose,"[68] and yet the Gospel itself shows a considerable degree of ambivalence about them. At the beginning of the Gospel, the signs seem to be numbered (John 2:11; 4:54), and the first sign, the turning of the water into wine (2:1-11), inspires Jesus' followers to "believe in him" (v. 11). In Jerusalem at Passover, the narrator says that "many believed in his name when they saw his signs, which he was performing" (2:23), although these are not explained (the only activity mentioned in the context is the temple incident, which led to opposition, 2:13-22). Once again the signs are linked with belief in Jesus. Jesus evidently despairs of this in John 4:48, when he tells a nobleman seeking healing for his son, "Unless you [plural] see signs and marvels, you will never believe." Yet the nobleman does believe, eventually and in stages, as noted above (4:50, 53). In some cases, the sign leads to an extended discourse about its revelatory meaning in relation to the person of the Son (John 5, 6); in others, the revelation comes not through Jesus' proclamation but through engagement with questions about his identity (John 9, 11). That signs can lead to a positive response that still misunderstands Jesus and his purposes can be seen after the feeding of the multitude, where the crowd that had been fed wishes to seize Jesus and make him king (John 6:14-15).

Three incidents invite the reader to consider how the resurrection of Jesus functions as a sign. First, when Peter and the Beloved Disciple inspect the empty tomb, as discussed above, what they see (the empty tomb, the grave clothes separated and folded) leads the Beloved Disciple to belief, but not Peter. Second, in the incident with Thomas (John 20:24-29), belief/doubt is a prominent issue, just as in other resurrection stories (Matt. 28:16-20; Luke 24:36-43). Again, what Thomas sees leads him to believe, but Jesus is not impressed. Thomas says, "Unless I see . . . and put my finger . . . and my hand . . . I will never believe," and Jesus says, "Have you come to believe because you have seen me? Blessed are those who believe without seeing" (20:25, 29). Third, and probably most important, is the conversation between Jesus and the Jews in the temple incident.

> Then the Jews answered and said to him, "What sign will you show us [to authorize] you to do these things?"[69] Jesus answered and said to them, "Unmake this temple and in three days I will raise it up." So the Jews said, "Forty-six years this temple has been under construction, and in three days you will raise it up?" But he was speaking about the temple of his body. (John 2:18-21)

The straightforward sense of Jesus' answer is that it is a threat against the temple, and this is how the saying is understood in the other Gospels (Mark 14:57-58; Matt. 26:60-61; with Mark at least presenting it as falsely attributed to Jesus). The Fourth Evangelist, however, remembers this as a veiled saying about the resurrection, at least partly because the "body" of Jesus becomes the new locus of the divine presence for God's people.[70] Schneiders sees the fulfillment of the saying when he stands up, risen, *into* the midst of the disciples, that is, within the community of faith (John 20:19-23).[71] But this saying is uttered in response to a demand for a sign to authorize Jesus' activities in the temple. As in Matthew 28:18, authorization by God is here connected with resurrection, even though in the Fourth Gospel Jesus has no real need of a postmortem authorization, because he has been sent from the Father with full knowledge of the Father's will and full authority to carry it out. This authority extends to his death and resurrection: "No one takes my life away from me, but I lay it down of my own accord. I have authority to lay it down, and I have authority to take it back again. I received this command from my Father" (John 10:18).

As with the extended discourses that follow the signs in chapters 5 and 6, there is also an extended discourse connected with the sign of the resurrection, but here it precedes the sign. Once Judas leaves the scene at the supper (13:21-30), Jesus says that he is leaving to return to the Father, and he explains in advance what his departure will mean for them in the Farewell Discourses (13:31–17:26). Here "Jesus speaks in such a way as if he were already risen or glorified. There is a remarkable melting of the horizons of time within these chapters."[72] Of chief concern in these chapters is what the absence of Jesus will mean for the disciples (and what it means for the Johannine community). Jesus says many times in these chapters that he is going to the Father (14:12, 28; 16:10, 28; also 13:1), and that where he is going the disciples cannot come (13:33); he also speaks at length of the grief that his followers will face when he leaves them (16:20-24). Both de Boer and Jörg Frey think that the absence of Jesus was a problem for the author and his community.[73] De Boer suggests that in response to questions from outsiders about why the Son had left (without saving the world, as claimed by the Johannine community), the answer would be that his resurrection needed to be understood correctly as his ascension—that is, as his return to the Father, to the glory that was rightly his in the Father's presence (16:25-30; 17:1-5). The sign of this is the empty tomb, with the grave clothes folded—the absence of Jesus. The resurrection must be understood as Jesus' return to the Father. Interestingly, as noted above, the evangelist uses "not seeing" language to express this idea of Jesus' return to the Father as a journey that results in absence: "A little while, and you will no longer see me" (John 16:16a).

But Jesus goes on to say, "And again a little while, and you will see me" (v. 16b). As noted above, this kind of language in Q 13:35 and Mark 13:24-27 (see also Q 17:23-24; Mark 14:62) refers to the sudden appearing, after a period of extended absence, of Jesus as the Coming One/Son of Man. Here, however, it seems to suggest a brief hiatus between Jesus' death and resurrection: the disciples will see him again on the first day of the week.[74] Yet if the absence of Jesus in the first part of the saying refers to the departure of the Son from this world, are we to understand this part of the saying as another reference to the return of Jesus in his eschatological role? This idea is not absent from John, but it is typically muted under the dominant paradigm of realized eschatology. As Frey puts it, "Johannine eschatology emphasizes the present gift of life and the decision or judgment happening in the present."[75] The return of Jesus to judge and to grant life to his followers is far less prominent in John. Far more prominent in John 13–17 than the return of Jesus is the idea that he will send another, the Advocate (or Comforter or Helper), as his surrogate presence (14:16-17, 25-31; 15:26-27; 16:7-15). He will not leave the disciples alone but will send the Holy Spirit, whom the community will experience as the restored presence of Jesus (now risen and returned to the Father). This is how the disciples will see him after "again a little while."[76] This reading of John 16:16b is confirmed by a similar passage correlating the gift of the Spirit to the presence of Jesus: "And I will ask the Father, and he will give you another Advocate to be with you forever, the Spirit of truth, which the world cannot receive, because it neither sees nor knows it; you know it, because it remains with you, and it will be among you. I will not leave you as orphans, I am coming to you" (John 14:16-18).[77] This is not a prediction of the second coming, but that the risen and glorified Jesus will come to his followers as the "Spirit of truth."[78] The sign of this is the renewed (but temporary) bodily presence of the glorified Son. The resurrection must be understood as that which restores Jesus to his followers, but in the Spirit, which he breathes on them (John 20:22-23).

John's narration of the sign has fully eclipsed the angel's pronouncements seen in the other Gospels. Recall that in Mark the observation of the empty tomb was subordinated to the announcement of the resurrection: "He has been raised, he is not here" (Mark 16:6). In Matthew the same subordination is expressed in slightly different terms: "He is not here, for he has been raised, just as he said; come behold the place where he used to lay" (Matt. 28:6). Here in John the angels have nothing to say but to ask Mary why she weeps; they do not announce the resurrection or interpret the empty tomb (John 20:12-13). Even the risen Jesus, when he meets Mary, commissions her with a message not about his resurrection but about his return to the Father (20:17). The two traditions we have been examining in this book, the disappearance tradition and the appearance tradition, in their earliest recoverable expressions, were pronouncements: on the one hand, "You will not see me" (Q 13:35), and on the other, "He has been raised and has appeared to Cephas" (1 Cor. 15:5). Thereafter, those telling the *story* of Jesus sought in different ways to reconcile them narratively to one another, and while it did not entirely prove impossible, neither were the tradents and authors able to efface the distinctives of either tradition entirely. Here in John, narration of the resurrection as sign overshadows the proclamation altogether in the empty tomb story. Just as the angels' words in Mark and Matthew tended to control the disappearance tradition by means of the resurrection proclamation, so also here: although in the special case of the Beloved Disciple, seeing (one half of) the sign led to his belief (John 20:8-9), it was not so with Mary or with Peter. For Mary, the full meaning of the empty tomb could only be perceived once the Rabbouni spoke her name and she encountered him.

9. Rewriting the Empty Tomb: Early Christian Deployments and Developments

So when they saw [the angels descend and remove the stone], those soldiers woke up the centurion and the elders—for they also were present keeping watch. And as they were reporting what they had seen, again they saw three men coming out of the tomb, two of whom were supporting the other, and a cross was following them. And the heads of the two reached as far as heaven, but [the head] of the one they were leading by the hand reached beyond the heavens. And they heard a voice from the heavens saying, "Did you proclaim to those who sleep?" And an answer was heard from the cross, "Yes."

—Gospel of Peter 10.38-42

The womb and Sheol shouted with joy and cried out about your resurrection. The womb that was sealed, conceived you; Sheol that was secured, brought you forth. Against nature the womb conceived and Sheol yielded. Sealed was the grave which they entrusted with keeping the dead man. Virginal was the womb that no man knew.

—Ephrem the Syrian, *Hymns on the Nativity* 10.6-7[1]

The first thing to be observed about the early Christian reception of the empty tomb story is that in some ways it was not well received at all. Later canonical writings and early extracanonical texts all but ignore it, and when it does surface again in the second century and later, most of the theological interests of its canonical deployments are lost or ignored. It is never taken on its own as proof of the resurrection, probably because the hiding of remains was a well-known ruse in staging a disappearance and apotheosis (Origen, *Cels.* 2.55-56), and not because there was a widely known rumor that the disciples had stolen the body. Early Christian interpreters follow the canonical Gospels in insisting that those who witnessed the empty tomb were never convinced that Jesus had risen from the dead, but were left afraid, alarmed, or puzzled by what they saw (Mark 16:8; Matt. 28:8; John 20:9-10). For the most part, early Christian authors seem uninterested in the theological concerns the canonical evangelists display in their retellings of the story; but the conviction expressed in Mark, that the story of Jesus' resurrection is best told along the lines of a postmortem assumption out of the tomb and into the divine realm, does appear to surface in some later texts.[2] According to Maurice Goguel, this idea crops up from time to time even into the fourth century but sometimes is awkwardly combined with descriptions of the reanimation of Jesus' corpse.[3] On the other hand, the interest of Luke in using the empty tomb to control the manner in which the resurrection appearances are conceptualized is not discerned by early authors who share Luke's interest in stressing the tangibility or physicality of the appearances; they tend to fall back on the depictions of the appearances.

For example, when Ignatius (d. c. 107 CE)[4] explains why he "know[s] and believe[s] that he was in the flesh also after the resurrection," he passes over the empty tomb in silence but relies on an appearance story similar to the one told in Luke 24:36-43 (Ignatius, *Smyrn.* 3:1-2). Likewise, in order to counter Marcion's apparitionistic Christology, Tertullian (d. c. 225) refers to the empty tomb only to highlight the disbelief of the apostles, which is dispelled by the flesh-and-bones appearances of the risen Jesus (*Marc.* 4.43).[5] In another context, Tertullian affirms that Christ was raised in the same flesh in which he was buried, but still displays an ambivalence about the empty tomb.

> But in what manner has Christ risen again, in the flesh or not? Without a doubt, if (as you hear) he died and was buried according to the Scriptures in none other than the flesh, you must concede that he was raised in the flesh. For that which fell in death and which was laid in the tomb, this also rose again, not as much Christ in the flesh as the flesh in Christ. (*Res. Mort.* 48.7)

Notice here, however, that in stressing the fleshly continuity between the crucified Jesus and the risen Christ, Tertullian is interpreting 1 Corinthians 15:3-4, not the empty tomb story, and he invokes none of its narrative features (disciples as witnesses, angels as witnesses, grave clothes) to show that the same flesh that was buried also rose.

One hesitates to try to account for this, but it may simply be that in its ancient contexts, the empty tomb signifies much but proves nothing—even when it comes to the physicality of the resurrection appearances. As the authors of Matthew and John clearly knew, a missing body could be explained in any number of ways (Matt. 27:64; 28:13; John 20:2, 13-15).[6] More importantly, however, even those willing to credit the crucified Jesus with an apotheosis along the lines of others whose bodies had disappeared could explain Jesus' disappearance in sensible Platonic terms. As seen above, Greek and Roman authors could explain the disappearance and apotheosis of figures like Romulus as the translation of the individual's soul/daimon or virtues out of the body, which then dissolved (Ovid, *Metam.* 14.816-28), because, after all, bodies are in no way fit for the divine realm. Thus in affirming the empty tomb to those Christians who questioned the bodily nature of the resurrection appearances or of Jesus' premortem existence, the heresiologists may have been aware that they were still open to the claim by outsiders that the resurrection of Jesus was an apotheosis. That is, his disappearance could still be interpreted as a private spiritualized vindication that had nothing to do with the physical aspects of the human person, whether for Jesus or for those who (to use Pauline language) had been incorporated into Christ.[7] This would be a problem, for the place of the body (or flesh) in salvation was a disputed issue in the first several Christian centuries.

The empty tomb story would eventually figure in certain kinds of apologetic arguments, especially in readings that sought to emphasize the guilt and obduracy of the Jews as part of the early Christian rhetoric of supersessionism, but also in readings that sought to explain the prominent role given to women in the story, or to defend early Christian teachings such as the perpetual virginity of Mary. In addition, just as the later canonical evangelists sought in different ways to correct the perceived deficiencies of the Markan version of the story, so also did early Christian interpreters and retellers of the story. This can be seen in both the scribal additions to the Gospel of Mark and in certain narrative expansions of the story, such as those found in the *Gospel of Peter* and in the *Epistle of the Apostles*, both of which probably were composed in the second century CE.[8] Other significant developments in the use of the empty tomb story in early Christianity include the reuse of certain narrative motifs from the story in tales about the deaths of Christian apostles, martyrs, and other saints, the rediscovery and memorialization of the tomb of Jesus (in the time of Constantine), and the continuing effort to conflate details from the four canonical Gospels into one (more or less) coherent Easter story.

The Additions to Mark 16

Although according to scholarly consensus the various additions to Mark 16—including the so-called shorter ending, the longer ending (Ps.-Mark 16:9-20), and others—were not part of the original composition, they are important for understanding how early Christians were reading the story. By the middle of the second century, when the longer ending probably was written,[9] the endings of Matthew, Luke, and John were sufficiently well known that anyone could see that it would be a mistake to let Mark be read without a proper ending, one in which the risen Jesus appears to his followers. As James Kelhoffer notes, "The decision by the [longer ending's] author that the end of Mark was deficient [was] only possible at a time when the four Gospels had been *collected and compared with one another.*"[10] This argument is strengthened by the fact that there is substantial evidence supporting the literary dependence of the longer ending of Mark on the other three Gospels.[11] There could have been another motivation for these scribal additions, however. By the second century there were in existence other texts that also claimed to transmit "new" revelation in the name of the risen Jesus, sometimes in the form of a resurrection dialogue (e.g., *The Book of Thomas the Contender*). Rather than leave Mark's ending open, vaguely predicting an appearance in Galilee (Mark 16:7), some readers perhaps would have wanted to tie up its loose ends by retelling the "authentic" resurrection appearances found in the other three Gospels, for this would restrict resurrection-oriented revelations and commissionings to the time during which the risen Jesus was physically present, and to the "apostolic" witnesses privileged by the canonical writings.

The longer ending describes three resurrection appearances, all of which are found in the other canonical Gospels: an appearance to Mary Magdalene (16:9-11, also found in Matthew and John); an appearance to two disciples as they were walking in the country (vv. 12-13, also in Luke); and finally a commissioning of the Eleven (vv. 14-18, also in Matthew, Luke, and John) and the ascension (vv. 19-20, also in Luke and Acts). Kelhoffer argues that the addition should be understood as a forgery, that is, as a text whose author intended it to be understood as an original part of another writing. Like the *Epistle to the Laodiceans*, which was not written by Paul but which was viewed by many ancient Christians as authentic, the longer ending was viewed as part of Mark even though its contents add to it a number of significantly non-Markan ideas.[12] What Kelhoffer does not consider, however, is how the longer ending might be understood as an example of epitome, since in its condensed reports of incidents narrated in Matthew, Luke, and John, it is stylistically reminiscent of the short summaries of major works that were common in Hellenistic Greek and Latin literature.[13] The analogy is not precise, however, since longer Mark presents epitomes of resurrection appearances from other Gospels—and not of Mark itself.

The first two parts of the longer ending note that the risen Jesus appeared first to Mary Magdalene (Ps.-Mark 16:9-11; see Matt. 28:9-10 and John 20:11-18)—although this appearance is not situated at the tomb—and then to two unnamed disciples on the road (16:12-13; Luke 24:13-35). Neither of these appearances is given any content, as to the way in which Jesus appeared, or the reaction of the percipients, or any dialogue exchanged—only that when the appearances were reported to the others, they did not believe (Ps.-Mark 16:10-11, 13).[14] These two incidents are clearly ordered (16:9, 12), which indicates that the author was attempting to harmonize the resurrection appearances in their correct order and to do so was comparing the chronologies of the endings of the other Gospels. The idea of disbelief comes from Luke 24:11 and is found elsewhere in early Christian texts about Jesus' resurrection, but it is not entirely clear why the longer ending stresses this theme through repetition. One possibility is that the author had understood the idea that we have seen to this point in our study of the empty tomb and appearance narratives: namely, neither the empty tomb nor a report of the resurrection leads to Easter faith, but only a direct encounter with the risen Jesus (as in John 20:14-16).[15] Even the kerygmatic announcement that "the Lord has indeed risen, and has appeared to Simon" (Luke 24:34) does not convince those who were already confessing it, for according to Luke they were entirely unprepared for his next appearance (24:37), and their disbelief continues even after his insistence, "It is I myself," and not a *pneuma* (24:39-41; see also Matt. 28:17).

On the other hand, despite the straightforward reporting of the longer ending that "he appeared" (Gk., *ephanē*, v. 9; *ephanerōthē*, v. 12), and despite the fact that Jesus upbraids the Eleven for their unbelief and hardness of heart (v. 14),[16] it is the appearance to the Eleven that is given the most narrative weight and the most content, and not these first two appearances (cf. also Matt. 28:16-20 with 28:9-10). In the longer ending, Mary is not commissioned by the risen Jesus (contrast John 20:17), and the two whom Jesus met on the road unawares are not instructed in the interpretation of the Scriptures (contrast Luke 24:25-27, 35). The focus is entirely on the Eleven, their commissioning to proclaim the gospel and to baptize, and the signs that were to accompany the belief of their hearers. Thus, the appearance to the Eleven controls and validates the other two appearances, and any commissioning or signs must be relegated to the authority of the apostolic group. As Kelhoffer has shown, the signs that accompany those who believe—exorcism, glossolalia, immunity to snakebite and poison, and healings (vv. 17-18)—are consistent with descriptions of early Christian miracle-working in the canonical and apocryphal Acts, where typically such deeds are done by recognized leaders rather than by "those who believe" (v. 17).[17] Yet their activities are implicitly validated through their connection with the apostolic group, the epicenter of proclamation, belief, and baptism (vv. 15-16).

One other question about the longer ending is the kind of resurrection appearances it presumes, for in verse 12 it says that "he was made manifest *in a different form* to two of them while they were walking along, going into the country." Since verses 12-14 clearly summarize the Emmaus Road story from Luke 24:13-35, the idea that the risen Jesus appeared "in a different form" could be a succinct way of saying that these two did not recognize Jesus until he broke bread with them (Luke 24:30-31, which the longer ending does not summarize). Luke's own explanation is that "their eyes were prevented from recognizing him" (24:16). The longer ending offers no such explanation but uses "different" to describe "the phenomenon of bodily transformation" (see also Luke 9:29).[18] Yet, as Paul Foster explains, this description is consistent with the tendency in the second century to reflect on Jesus' postresurrection state using language of polymorphism, that is, describing him as appearing in different forms. Polymorphic language for the body of Jesus is not limited to descriptions of his postresurrection state—it was also useful to "those with docetic proclivities," since it could "highlight a transcendence of the physical by the purer spiritual manifestation of Christ."[19] However, it also was found particularly suitable to descriptions of Jesus' postresurrection body, since as Foster argues, "Changed physical state demonstrates both lack of constraint by the mortal body and transcendence over the earthly realm."[20] In this regard, polymorphic language—like the language Marcion evidently used for the body of Jesus—could possibly trace its origins to ideas such as the transformation of the "natural body" into the "spiritual body" in 1 Corinthians 15.[21]

Like the longer ending, the shorter ending also addresses the perceived deficiencies of Mark's earliest recoverable ending, but much more concisely: "And they reported promptly to those of Peter's group everything they were commanded. After this Jesus himself also sent forth through them from east to west the sacred and incorruptible proclamation of eternal salvation. Amen." Since the shorter ending continues directly the line of narrative thought left off abruptly in Mark 16:8—even though the statement that "they did not tell anyone anything" is immediately contradicted—it actually is a more economical solution to the problem of Mark's ending than the longer ending. "Those of Peter's group" occurs also in Ignatius, *Smyrnaeans* 3:2, but probably the author of this ending was simply explaining that the women eventually obeyed the instruction of the young man, who singled out Peter (Mark 16:7). This ending also, in decidedly non-Markan vocabulary, summarizes the basic theological idea that an appearance of the risen Jesus should culminate in a commissioning for proclamation (here, *kērugma*).[22] This message is emphasized as being of universal and eternal significance.

Also worth noting here is the addition found at the beginning of Mark 16:4 in the Old Latin Codex Bobbiensis (it^k), a manuscript produced probably around 400 CE, but which preserves a considerably earlier form of the text.[23] Incidentally, Bobbiensis is the only manuscript that includes only the shorter ending of Mark without the longer ending. Its scribal insertion in Mark 16:4 describes angels descending and then ascending with Jesus, possibly "as he [was] rising in the glory of the living God," although the correct wording of this insertion is difficult to determine.[24] Placed where it is, it seems to describe more or less what the author of Mark had in mind (minus the angels, however): a direct assumption of Jesus out of the tomb and into the presence of God. It thus should be considered as part of an increasing interest in the second century and later to show how Jesus rose from the dead and came out of the tomb.

Narrative Expansions of the Empty Tomb Story

The most important narrative expansions of the empty tomb story are found in the second-century writings the *Epistle of the Apostles* and the *Gospel of Peter*. The former text dispenses with the angelophanies of the canonical versions of the story and has the risen Jesus comforting and commissioning the women himself:

> They [Sarah, Martha, and Mary Magdalene] carried ointment to pour out upon his body, weeping and mourning over what had happened. And they approached the tomb and found the stone where it had been rolled away from the tomb, and they opened the door and did not find his body. And as they were mourning and weeping, the Lord appeared to them and said to them, "Do not weep; I am he whom you seek. But let one of you go to our brothers and say, 'Come, our Master has risen from the dead.'" (*Ep. Apos.* 9–10)[25]

Interestingly, this version of the story fails to mention the time and day of the discovery, possibly assuming such details were widely known. Sarah and Martha are newcomers to the tomb story. The elimination of the angel should also be understood as the natural result of the literary process begun in Matthew and John, where the appearance of the risen Jesus at the tomb first stood awkwardly beside (Matt. 28:2-7, 9-10) and then made entirely redundant (John 20:11-13, 14-18) the appearance of the angel(s).[26] Thus the appearance tradition, in *Epistle of the Apostles*, has completely overshadowed the epiphany of the earliest literary version of the disappearance story (Mark 16:1-8). After the women make two trips to the apostles, who do not believe that Jesus has risen from the dead, Jesus himself accompanies the women (*Ep. Apos.* 9–11). The encounter that ensues (chaps. 11–12) has the same apologetic features as Luke 24:36-43 and Ignatius, *Smyrnaeans* 3:1-2:

> "Why do you doubt and why are you not believing? I am he who spoke to you concerning my flesh, my death, and my resurrection. And that you may know that it is I, lay your hand, Peter, (and your finger) in the nailprint of my hands; and you, Thomas, in my side; and also you, Andrew, see whether my foot steps on the ground and leaves a footprint. For it is written in the prophet, 'But a ghost, a demon, leaves no print on the ground.'" (*Ep. Apos.* 11)

The apostles then handle Jesus and repent of their unbelief, but Jesus does not eat anything in front of them (cf. Luke 24:41-43; Ignatius, *Smyrn.* 3:3). Thereafter, in a very long discussion, Jesus instructs the apostles concerning their missionary activities, the time of the end, and other matters (*Ep. Apos.* 13–50) before he ascends into heaven (chap. 51).

Thus the bulk of the work takes the form of a revelatory discourse set in the context of a single resurrection appearance and probably represents a proto-orthodox response to Gnostic revelatory discourses.[27] In contrast with Gnostic ideas about the body, the *Epistle of the Apostles* affirms the resurrection of the flesh (*Ep. Apos.* 21–26), and indeed the fleshly character of Jesus' earthly existence; therefore it is not surprising that the writing takes the same approach as Ignatius and Tertullian took against their opponents' apparitionistic Christologies. As with those authors, the *Epistle to the Apostles* does not display an interest in the tomb story as "proof" of the resurrection of the flesh. In fact, the believer's resurrection of the flesh is connected equally with the incarnation as with the resurrection of Christ. For the risen Jesus says, "As the Father awakened me from the dead, in the same manner you also will arise in the flesh"; but he also says, "Without having flesh I put on flesh and grew up, that [I might regenerate] you who were begotten in the flesh, and in [this] regeneration you obtain the resurrection of the flesh" (*Ep. Apos.* 21). Like the longer ending of Mark, the *Epistle of the Apostles* also takes as foundational the Lukan chronology of interim flesh-and-blood resurrection appearances before Jesus' bodily ascension into heaven; as noted above, this effectively restricts revelation in the name of the risen Jesus. The empty tomb story here is only minimally expanded by the addition of another report to the apostles and a duplication of the theme of disbelief (see Luke 24:11; Ps.-Mark 16:11, 13-14). The empty tomb itself seems only to be an expected part of the scenery in the story, which is the opposite of what we find in the so-called *Gospel of Peter*, in which the tomb is a very busy place indeed.

The identification of the fragmentary gospel text of the Akhmîm codex (P.Cair. 10759, a manuscript dated from the seventh to the ninth century CE) with the second-century *Gospel of Peter* has become somewhat traditional, although Paul Foster has recently called into question early support for that identification.[28] According to the church historian Eusebius, Serapion (bishop of Antioch 199–211 CE) knew of and condemned a writing known as the *Gospel of Peter* whose contents apparently were open to docetic interpretation.[29] Because the text identifies the narrator's voice as that of Simon Peter, the Akhmîm gospel was immediately identified as the *Gospel of Peter* at its publication in 1892.[30] However, Foster points out that ancient papyrus fragments (particularly P.Oxy. 2949 and 4009, both c. 200 CE) that some scholars have more recently proposed as early witnesses to the Akhmîm gospel text cannot be identified with certainty and so should be excluded as support for the late-second-century circulation of the text.[31] This means that early evidence for the Akhmîm gospel is lacking; but in any event, if its identification with the "Gospel of Peter" known to Serapion is taken tentatively as correct, the gospel itself must have been in circulation by the end of the second century. As to the text's purported docetism, more recent analysis of the text has corrected that early assessment: as Foster observes, "The text does not present a radically unorthodox form of Christianity; rather it seeks to make canonical traditions more lively and engaging."[32]

As seen in the citation at the beginning of this chapter, the empty tomb story in this text includes significantly more legendary accretions than its counterpart in the *Epistle of the Apostles*. The most prominent of these is the description of the emptying of the tomb: two angelic figures descend from heaven, the stone rolls away by itself, and the figures enter the tomb and escort out the weakened but rising Jesus, followed by the cross (*Gos. Pet.* 10.39-42). All three figures are described in mythic proportions. Foster is correct that the *Gospel of Peter* "provides minimal reflection on the heightened miraculous depictions it narrates." But it seems here, as with the longer ending of Mark, in this "resurrection or post-resurrection context, bodily metamorphosis is used to stress that the raised figure no longer belongs exclusively to the earthly realm."[33] As seen in the previous chapter, this emphasis on the liminality of Jesus' just-raised or still-rising body is also found in John 20:17, where Jesus instructs Mary not to touch him. The size of the rising Jesus in the *Gospel of Peter* is unique, however. If this description was meant to emphasize the power and grandeur of the risen Jesus and his angelic companions, this is at odds with the idea that he needed their help to exit the tomb. This is more consistent with the death cry of Jesus earlier in the narrative: "My power, my power, you have abandoned me" (*Gos. Pet.* 5.19).[34] In any event, once the rising Jesus and his angelic escorts and the cross exit the tomb, the narrative shifts to the next scene, and the reader does not learn where they go (at least not yet).

Gospel of Peter 8–13 includes several features found in the Matthean story—the consultation with Pilate, the sealing and guarding of the tomb, and the depiction of the opening of the tomb—but it also includes additional novelistic and legendary accretions to the story. Although some scholars (most notably John Dominic Crossan) have argued that the *Gospel of Peter* was based on a core document that actually predates the Synoptics, their theories also allow that the *Gospel of Peter* at points is dependent on one or more of the Synoptics.[35] Other scholars conclude that the text is entirely dependent on the Synoptics.[36] As to the empty tomb story, the guard at the tomb has a parallel in Matthew, although there are narrative features drawn from the other Gospels as well—for instance, the women meet a "young man dressed in a [brightly shining] robe" (*Gos. Pet.* 13.55; Mark 16:5). Many of the features not found in the other Gospels betray a pronounced anti-Judaism: the resurrection occurs in full sight of the guards and the elders of the Jews, who are also gathered at the tomb (*Gos. Pet.* 8–10); and Pilate, when he learns of the resurrection, advises the centurion and the soldiers to say nothing rather than be stoned by the Jews for publishing news of the resurrection (11.47-49). This is consistent with the general depiction of the Jews in the *Gospel of Peter* as more involved with the sentencing and killing of Jesus: Herod gives the order for Jesus' execution (1.2) and delivers him to "the people" (2.5), who apparently abuse and crucify him (3.6–4.11) and take the body down from the cross and hand it over to Joseph (6.21-23).[37] Early in the second century, Christian literature continues to attribute greater involvement and animosity to "the Jews" in texts about the death and resurrection of Jesus.[38] Consistent with this emphasis are depictions of Pilate that increasingly present him as less culpable and more pious, so that his character serves as a foil against which to emphasize the guilt and stubbornness of the Jews (see *Gos. Pet.* 1.1; 11.46). This tactic can be seen developing in the canonical Gospels as well.[39]

Other expansive features in the *Gospel of Peter* are more benign: for example, Joseph buries Jesus in his own family tomb, in "the Garden of Joseph" (6.24), and Mary Magdalene and the other women are described as coming to the tomb in order to mourn for Jesus, to do "what women are accustomed to do for their dead loved ones" (12.50-54). "Weeping and mourning" were also seen in the longer ending of Mark (16:10) and in the *Epistle of the Apostles* 9–10. As already noted, Byron McCane argues that the earlier canonical texts do not portray Jesus as either buried in a family tomb or publicly mourned, even while they display an interest in depicting the burial of Jesus with increasing dignity.[40] A shameful burial, whether by others (such as Acts 13:29 suggests) or by someone friendly to Jesus' movement, may be a distant historical reminiscence; in any event, it is simply a more plausible story given the restrictions on the burial and mourning of convicted criminals. The *Gospel of Peter* thus continues the trend of dignifying the burial of Jesus already found in the canonical Gospels, but—interestingly—the text still describes the open mourning of the women as a potentially dangerous activity, not because of the Roman authorities, but because the Jews "were inflamed with anger" (12.50).

The scene of the women at the tomb is also expanded considerably, with extra dialogue that continues to emphasize the risk they were taking (12.52, 54). The text corrects the problem found in Mark, where the women arrive at the tomb to anoint the body with no clear plan of how they will remove the stone (Mark 16:1, 3). In *Gospel of Peter* 12.53-54 the women discuss this and say in the end that even if they cannot get into the tomb to sit beside the body and complete the necessary tasks, "let us place the things we have brought by the door [of the tomb] as a memorial, and we will weep and mourn until we have to go home" (v. 54). When they arrive, of course, they find the tomb already open and a young man, very handsome and dressed in a brightly shining robe, sitting in the middle of the tomb. While he does not commission them to take the message of the resurrection to the other disciples, what he does say to them gives the reader an indication of where the risen Jesus has gone: "Why have you come? Whom do you seek? Surely not him who was crucified? He has risen and has gone. And if you do not believe, stoop down and see the place where he used to be lying—he is not [there]. For he has risen and has gone away to the place from which he was sent" (*Gos. Pet.* 13.56). Noteworthy here is the combination of details from different canonical Gospels: a young man dressed in a robe (from Mark 16:5) asks why they have come (cf. Luke 24:5); he says that if they do not believe (cf. John 20:8), they should stoop down and look (see Luke 24:12; John 20:5, 11); he signals that the place where Jesus used to lie is now empty (Mark 16:6; Matt. 28:6); and he says that Jesus has gone to the place from which he was sent, which is a distinctly Johannine concept (see John 20:17). This last detail is important, for it indicates that the *Gospel of Peter* conceived of the resurrection as an event in two stages: first a resurrection (conceived as a resuscitation) and then an assumption into the heavenly realm. This pattern, as argued above, can also be seen in Luke and John.

The depiction of Jesus exiting the tomb is remarkable but not unique. Similar descriptions may be found in other sources, including *Martyrdom of Isaiah* 3, which is part of a short interpolation perhaps predating the *Gospel of Peter*.[41] In this Christian pseudepigraphical text, Isaiah learns that "the Beloved" will be "crucified together with criminals . . . and buried in a grave," after which "the angel of the Holy Spirit and Michael, the chief of the holy angels, would open his grave on the third day," and that "the Beloved, sitting on their shoulders, will come forth" (*Mart. Isa.* 3:13-17).[42] Despite the physical language, it is unclear whether this was meant to describe a bodily/fleshly resurrection, since later in the book the saints are described as being clothed in saintly garments but leaving their bodies in the world (4:16-17). This text shows an awareness of the Matthean motif of guards at the tomb (3:14) and also gives a greater role to angels in the resurrection, as in the *Gospel of Peter* and the Codex Bobbiensis addition to Mark 16:4. The role of angels in the resurrection itself, rather than only in the display or interpretation of the empty tomb, may signal that early Christians were attempting to give a more concrete explanation of how it "happened." This stands in marked contrast with the earliest texts about Jesus' resurrection, which offer only the barest explanations, whether more or less theological—for example, "Christ was raised from the dead by the glory of the Father" (Rom. 6:4) or "He truly raised himself" (Ignatius, *Smyrnaeans* 2). More often, the earliest affirmations of the resurrection of Jesus simply fall back on the divine passive, and as seen in the previous chapters, the earliest resurrection narratives are best explained as attempts to reconcile the appearance tradition and the disappearance tradition—rather than as accounts of how the resurrection happened. The original absence from the traditions of an account of Jesus exiting the tomb, as Goguel explained, evidently "was, beginning from the second century, considered to be a lacuna which some tried valiantly to fill, albeit quite timidly."[43]

A fragment of the *Gospel of the Hebrews* (c. 150?) cited by Jerome suggests a straightforward exit from the tomb: "And after the Lord had given the linen cloth to the slave of the priest, he went to James and appeared to him" (*Gos. Heb.* frag. 7; Jerome, *Vir. ill.* 2).[44] Some later Christian authors also describe Jesus exiting the tomb. In his *Divine Institutes* (written 305–11), Lactantius wrote: "But on the third day, before light, there was an earthquake and suddenly the tomb was opened; and the guards, being stunned and stupefied with fear, did not see a thing—but he came out of the tomb living and uninjured, and set off for Galilee, but in the tomb nothing was found but the clothing which had confined his body" (*Inst.* 4.19). In his focus on the guards, Lactantius completely bypasses the women as witnesses and the angels as interpreters; this heightens the culpability of the other witnesses. Lactantius also says that the risen Jesus preferred to go straight to Galilee rather than risk appearing to the Jews, lest they repent (4.20). Other authors also interpret the prediction of Galilean appearances in this way (Tertullian, *Apol.* 21.21). It explains why Jesus did not simply appear to everyone to disprove the allegation that the disciples had faked a disappearance by stealing the body.

Goguel also noted that some of these texts make a striking correlation between the exit of the risen Jesus from the tomb and the harrowing of hell.[45] This makes sense, particularly since the tendency was to see Christ's proclamation "to the spirits in prison" (1 Peter 3:19) as a trip to the underworld while Jesus was dead in the tomb. If early Christians understood the resurrection of Jesus as the beginning of the general resurrection of the dead, there needed to be some way to account for what happened to Jesus as "an inclusively communal event" rather than "an exclusively individual" one; otherwise, the corporate logic of early Jewish resurrection theology is strained.[46] Attempts to address this problem can be seen in both Paul's use of the "firstfruits" analogy (1 Cor. 15:20-24) and Matthew's strange piece about the raising of the bodies of the holy ones (Matt. 27:52-53)—but certainly by the second century there was also a well-developed idea that Christ had descended to the abode of the dead to liberate the righteous dead, or at least to proclaim liberation to them (1 Peter 3:19-20; 4:6).[47]

This correlation between the descent to the dead and the exit of Jesus from the tomb is found in the *Gospel of Peter*, where, as Jesus comes out of the tomb, a voice from heaven asks, "Did you proclaim to those who sleep?" and the cross, in reply, says, "Yes" (*Gos. Pet.* 10.41-42). Lactantius, writing considerably later, also makes this connection, although he was relying on a skewed reading of the Lukan exegesis of Psalm 15:10 LXX (Acts 2:25-27), according to which Jesus' soul would not be abandoned in Hades (*Inst.* 4.19).[48] Rufinus (d. 411) is among the Christian commentators who depicted the descent into hell in narrative form; he wrote that after Christ was victorious in Hades and had brought the spoils (the patriarchs and others) to heaven, he returned and reanimated his dead body in the tomb because he had already been victorious over death (Rufinus, *Symb.* 29). One can see how incompatible this is with the Markan depiction of the resurrection as a postmortem assumption or removal into the divine realm. Others resisted this narrative development of the emptying of the tomb: for instance, John Chrysostom (c. 349–407) states that it would be superfluous to see the beginning of the resurrection of Jesus when the disciples have seen its results— an emptied tomb and a present Jesus (*Hom. Acts* 2).

The Empty Tomb Story and Early Christian Apologetic

One of the issues the empty tomb story posed for its earliest interpreters was the prominent role given to the women in the story, in particular, Mary Magdalene. As argued above, this role is deeply embedded in the tradition, and this was an aspect of the story of Jesus' resurrection that evidently needed some defense. According to Origen (c. 185–254), Celsus thought Mary's reputation as a resurrection witness added to the dubious quality of the claim that Jesus had risen from the dead. "So who saw this? A frenzied woman, you say, and possibly some other one [convinced by] the same witchcraft" (Origen, *Cels.* 2.55).[49] Many early Christian writers therefore sought to give a positive interpretation to the women at the tomb. John Chrysostom, for example, praised their bravery in coming to the tomb given the animosity of the Jews; their generosity in spending their money on the spices to anoint the body; and their devotion to Jesus in wanting to embrace the body (*Hom. Matt.* 88.2). More than that, because the risen Jesus commissioned the women with the news of his resurrection, he brought honor and healing to the female sex (*Hom. Matt.* 89.3). Probably here Chrysostom reflects the traditional reading that the women, by their obedience and devotion, and through Christ's commission to them, rectify the sin of Eve. As Katherine Jansen notes, the interpretive themes of "woman as redeemer of Eve's sin, as first witness of the Resurrection, and as the bride/church/synagogue . . . became familiar motifs in Western exegetical tradition."[50] Other symbolic readings are also found: in his comment on Jesus' command to Mary not to touch him (John 20:17), Augustine says that Mary symbolizes the Gentiles who do not touch Christ (spiritually, by their belief) until after his ascension (*Tract. Joh.* 121.3). As allegorical interpretation flourished in early Christian hermeneutic, such deeper readings became more common. Ulrich Luz notes that such interpretations tended to focus on the hearing of the word, with the women representing souls seeking new life, the shining angel being the illuminating word of truth, the stone representing the hindrance of unbelief, and so forth.[51]

The question of how the risen Jesus got out of the tomb, which evidently was a concern to the author of the *Gospel of Peter*, is one that arises in apologetic

---

uses of the empty tomb story, mainly in situations where the Matthean narrative has been read closely. The combination of the Matthean motifs of sealed tomb and guards with the apparent ability of the risen Jesus, depicted in Luke and John, to appear and disappear suddenly, even behind locked doors (Luke 24:31, 36; John 20:19, 26), meant that for early readers the risen body was a "spiritual" body, to use Paul's language if not quite his conception, which Jesus was able to make materialize and dematerialize at will. Thus the risen Jesus found the stone and the seal to be no barriers to his exit from the tomb, just as the locked doors where the disciples were gathered were no barrier. One prominent apologetic use for this line of thinking is the defense of the perpetual virginity of Mary: just as the risen Jesus was able to rise and to exit the tomb without breaking the seals or disturbing the guard, so also the infant Christ was able to be born without violating Mary's virginity.[52] Such a line of thinking seems to require that Christ's body have the same kind of miraculous properties in the process of birth as well as in the postresurrection state; it is not clear whether these interpreters gave any thought to this problem. This reading simply drew a conclusion from one mystery (the resurrection) and applied it to another (the virgin birth). An early correlation between tomb and womb is found in the writings of Origen:

> For it was necessary for one who was unlike the rest of the dead—having already in his death manifested living signs, in the water and the blood— even being, so to speak, a new dead person, to be put in a new and clean tomb; so that just as his birth was purer than any other (since he was born not by sexual union but from a virgin), so also his burial should be purer, as shown through the symbolism of his body being placed in a new tomb built not from various stones having no inherent unity, but quarried and hewn from a single and entirely unified rock. (*Cels.* 2.69)

Later authors, such as Jerome (c. 345–420), Ephrem of Syria (c. 306–373), and Augustine (354–430), are fond of this line of argument, emphasizing that Jesus was put in a brand-new tomb in which no one had ever been laid (Matt. 27:60; John 19:41).[53] Although these authors may have been defending the doctrine of Mary's perpetual virginity (against, for instance, Jovinian, who was condemned in 393 for denying it), they seem also to have had devotional or catechetical purposes.

When it came to defending the resurrection, most early Christian authors, as noted above, evidently did not find the empty tomb story useful. Other arguments proved more popular and durable, such as the fearlessness of the resurrection witnesses, who knew they would share in the same kind of vindication as Jesus. This argument is found already in 1 Corinthians 15:30-32 (see also Ignatius, *Smyrn.* 3:2; Origen, *Cels.* 2.56). The empty tomb story could be used as a "proof" of the resurrection, however, when the Matthean additions to the story were stressed: the seal and the guards, and the complicity of the Jews in spreading abroad the counternarrative that the disciples had stolen the body (Matt. 28:15). As Justin (c. 100–165) accuses Trypho:

And not only did you not believe when you learned that he had risen from the dead, but, as I said earlier, you sent chosen and appointed men into all the world proclaiming, "A certain atheistic sect has arisen from a certain Galilean deceiver [named] Jesus, whom we crucified, but his disciples stole him by night from the tomb . . . and now they are deceiving people, saying that he has been raised from the dead, and been taken up into heaven." (*Dial.* 108)

Here Justin repeats Matthew's assertion that the story that the disciples had stolen the body originated among "the Jews" (Matt. 28:13-15), although there is a chance he knew of such a rumor himself. In Matthew, this rumor arose not as a response to claims about the resurrection of Jesus, but as a response to the events of the resurrection themselves: "Some members of the guard went into the city and told the chief priests everything that had happened" (28:11). In saying that the Jews "did not believe when [they] learned that he had risen from the dead," Justin implies what later authors make much more explicit. Because Matthew 28:11-15 depicts the chief priests and the Pharisees (who need to be present as witnesses to Jesus' Jonah saying, Matt. 12:38-42) as fully aware of the events the guards have seen at the tomb, they could be claimed as hostile witnesses to the resurrection:

> For indeed this even proves the resurrection, that is, that they said that the disciples had stolen [the body]. It is practically a confession that the body was not there. And therefore when they confess that the body was not there, their custody of the tomb, and the seals, and the cowardice of the disciples all show that the theft [of the body] must be false and unbelievable; and on this basis the demonstration of the resurrection is shown to be irrefutable. (John Chrysostom, *Hom. Matt.* 89.2)

Chrysostom therefore can ask, "Have you seen how they labor involuntarily on behalf of the truth?" (*Hom. Matt.* 89.1). An additional ingredient often found in this line of interpretation is the idea drawn from the second-century apologists that the testimony of the Scriptures to the resurrection of Jesus makes the Jews even more culpable for their disbelief (as in, e.g., Lactantius, *Inst.* 4.19; Cyril of Jerusalem, *Cat.* 14.14-15), while in contrast the risen Jesus opens the minds of the apostles to understand the Scriptures (Luke 24:45-48; Lactantius, *Inst.* 4.20).

Empty Tomb Motifs in Early Christian Hagiography

Scholars have long noted the similarities between the ancient Greek hero cults and the early Christian cults of saints.[54] These include (1) an interest in narratives concerning the life and death of venerated figures, (2) the commemoration of such figures on special days, (3) and a particular interest in their burial sites (whether or not they were thought empty or known to have rivals).[55] Helmut Koester gives a particularly vivid example of how these similarities could lead to interesting crossovers: a vaulted hero tomb in Philippi, whose original dedication to Epiphanes Exikestou had long been forgotten, came to be identified centuries later as the tomb of St. Paul and became an important site for pilgrims to commemorate the apostle on their way to the Holy Land.[56] Koester also suggests that hero worship did not really enter popular Christianity until the discovery and memorialization of Jesus' tomb by Constantine (discussed below), since the veneration of that site legitimized a similar fascination with the grave sites of the saints. "As worship at the tomb of the founding hero Jesus became the primary object of pilgrimages to Jerusalem, also the tombs of the apostles and martyrs were now discovered and monuments built to honor their memory."[57] However, the apocryphal acts and stories about martyrs demonstrate that there was already an interest in the death of these figures by the second century. The prevalence of the hero cult in the late Hellenistic age may have been an influence in how Christians thought about their heroes long before the discovery of Jesus' tomb. In the Hellenistic period, there was considerable openness to counting benefactors and prominent individuals of the recent past—not only of the epic past—worthy of receiving heroic honors.[58]

James Skedros observes significant parallels in religious outlook between the kind of hero veneration promoted in Philostratus's *Heroikos* (written c. 225–235?)[59] and the early Christian martyr/saint cults.[60] First, they shared a concept of "sacred space" according to which burial sites or locales in which the figure was known to appear had sacred or even magical or miraculous properties (*Her.* 3.6). Second, there was a shared belief that physical objects could convey "divine or supernatural power," so that great respect was shown for the physical remains or relics of those so venerated (*Her.* 8.1). Third, the stories about martyrs have pronounced didactic or moralistic tendencies, which Skedros suggests in the *Heroikos* are supplanted by a concern to demonstrate the existence of heroes, and the reasons for venerating them, by telling their stories. Two more details are also significant: first, both heroes and saints were thought to have an ongoing influence for those who venerated them; and second, both heroes such as Protesilaos (*Her.* 10.1–11.6) and saints such as Paul (*Mart. Paul* 11.6-7) were sometimes depicted as appearing after their death.

Although typically Greek heroes and Christian saints were venerated at their burial sites, some particularly illustrious Christian saints, like a few Greek heroes, were thought to have been taken away into the divine realm at the end of their lives. Certain narrative elements from the canonical empty tomb stories reappear in stories about the deaths of certain apostles and saints, beginning from the late second century. These narrative elements and the stories in which they appear are catalogued in the following table.

Early Christian Tomb-Visit Stories[61]

Canonical Gospels: narrative features	Gospel of Peter	Epistula Apostolorum	Martyrdom of Paul	Acts of John	Acts of Peter	Acts of Thomas	Ethiopic Liber Requiei	(Acts of Pilate)	Life of Symeon	Chariton, Chaereas and Callirhoe
significant interval after burial (Matt., Mark, Luke, John)	√					√	√			√
early morning visit (Matt., Mark, Luke, John)	√		√	√				√		√
fear/grief/alarm (Matt., Mark, Luke, John)	√		√					√		
mysteriously opened tomb (Matt., Mark, Luke, John)	√	√								√
miraculous portents (Matt.)	√						√		√	
clothing remains (Luke, John)				√						
empty tomb/missing body (Matt., Mark, Luke, John)	√	√		√		√	√	(√)	√	√
distinguished/apostolic witness at tomb (Luke, John)			√				√	(√)		√
angelic witness (Matt., Mark?, Luke, John)	√						√			
hostile witness (Matt.)	√						√	√		
guard/seal (Matt.)	√						√	√		
apparition at/near tomb (Matt., John)	(√)	√	√			√	√			
apparition at a distance (Matt., Mark, Luke, John)	√?	√	√		√	√	(√)	√		
interpretation of divine activity (Matt., Mark, Luke, John)	√			√			√	√	√	√
rationalizing explanation of disappearance (Matt., John)	√					√				
flight/hurried return from tomb (Matt., Mark, Luke, John)	√	√								
other narrative features										
magical/miraculous properties of tomb				√	√					
veneration at/of tomb							√			

For the sake of comparison, details from Chariton, *Chaereas and Callirhoe*, are also included. Also included on the table are details from the remarkable tale from the *Acts of Pilate* (fifth to sixth century?)[62] of the disappearance of Joseph of Arimathea from a locked, sealed, and windowless house (*Acts Pil.* 12.1–16.1); this tale has some important narrative similarities with the empty tomb story. In this story, the Jews lock Joseph up for burying Jesus, intending to kill him and feed his body to the birds once the Sabbath has passed; but Jesus rescues Joseph, spiriting him away and showing him the empty tomb and the grave clothes before dawn on the first day of the week (12.1-2).[63] This rescue appears to be in response to Joseph's piety and bravery in attending to the burial.

In most of these tomb stories, some but not all of the narrative motifs found in the canonical stories recur. The reason for this should be obvious: the authors and tradents of these acts were reluctant, of course, to attribute both a bodily disappearance (such as with John or Symeon of Neapolis) and an appearance at the tomb (such as with Paul), for to do so would be to claim the same post-mortem elevation for these saints as for Jesus. That is, it would be to claim that Jesus' resurrection was not unique, that God could raise certain other special individuals before the general resurrection of the dead. This reserve is cast aside in the stories about the end of Mary, however. Manuscript evidence shows that by the fifth century, stories about the end of Mary—often called her "dormition" (falling asleep) or her "assumption"—were circulating in numerous languages and locales and showing great diffusion in narrative traits. Broadly speaking, these stories narrate the death of Mary as a soul assumption or a bodily assumption, or both.

Recently, Stephen Shoemaker has argued that the Ethiopic *Book of Mary's Repose* is one of the earliest forms of the very diffuse dormition tradition.[64] In this version of the tale, the apostles—who have all been miraculously gathered from the corners of the earth to witness Mary's end—are taken on a long tour of heaven and hell, and so the work devolves into an apocalypse. But the *Book of Mary's Repose* narrates first the assumption of Mary's soul into heaven, received into a pure garment by Christ and Michael, and escorted thus into Paradise:

> And then the Lord took her soul and placed it in Michael's hands, and they wrapped it in a fine garment, so splendid that one could not keep silent. And the apostles saw Mary's spirit as it was given into Michael's hands: a perfect form, but its body was both male and female, and nevertheless one, being similar to every body and seven times white. (Ethiopic *Liber Requiei* 67–68)[65]

Then the Savior instructs Peter to place Mary's body in a new tomb and to guard it (chap. 70), for the chief priests wish to burn Mary's body; when they try to seize the body, the funeral procession is miraculously protected (chaps. 72–73), and when one of the Jews attempts to overthrow the bier, his arms are cut off; he later repents and is healed when he kisses Mary's body (chaps. 73-76). Even the high priest repents and blesses Mary (chap. 76).[66] The apostles sit and discuss various issues while they attend the tomb; then, after three days, Christ and Michael return with ten thousand angels and they all ascend with Mary's body into the clouds, and her soul and body are reunited at the Tree of Life in Paradise:

> And while Paul was sitting at the entrance [of the tomb] and speaking with them, behold, the Lord Jesus came from heaven with Michael. . . . And [angels] descended on three clouds, and the number of angels on a cloud appeared to be ten thousand angels in the presence of the Savior. And our Lord said to them, "Let them bring the body of Mary into the clouds." And when her body had been brought, our Lord said to the apostles that they should come to him. And they ascended into the cloud, and they were singing with the voice of angels. And our Lord told the clouds to go to the East, to the area of Paradise. And when they arrived together in Paradise, they placed Mary's body beside the Tree of Life. And they brought her soul and placed it in her body. And our Lord sent his angels to their places. (Ethiopic *Liber Requiei* 88–89, excerpted)

This part of the story has many of the narrative motifs typically found in assumption stories: clouds, angels, "going up" language. One thing it lacks, however, is the earth-bound perspective of the witnesses (see, e.g., 2 Kings 2:11-12; Acts 1:9-11), because the narrative follows the apostles on their tour of the heavenly realm (and elsewhere).[67]

In this version of the story, the empty tomb of Mary is not a topic of interest, but in others, it is.[68] Certainly by the fifth century there existed not only narratives about the assumption of Mary, but also liturgies and sacred sites in Palestine associated with various significant points in her life, including her dormition.[69] The stories themselves were immensely popular and influential in late antique Western Christianity, but since they bordered on apocryphal, they show evidence of idiosyncratic and localized narrative and symbolic developments.[70] It should come as no surprise that a story that originally had significant similarities with Greek and Roman stories about the disappearance and apotheosis of various heroes and other illustrious figures should have certain of its narrative elements applied equally to early Christian saints and martyrs who were thought deserving of an elevated postmortem status.

Visiting the Empty Tomb at the Church of the Holy Sepulchre

Not long after the emperor Constantine gained control of the Eastern Empire by defeating Licinius in 324 CE, excavations began in Jerusalem (Aelia) at the site that was to become the location of the Church of the Holy Sepulchre. Nearly two centuries earlier, the emperor Hadrian refounded Jerusalem as the Roman city Aelia Capitolina, and made the Temple Mount the site of a temple of Jupiter (Dio Cassio, *Hist. Rom.* 69.12-14). It seems that this was the cause of the Second Jewish War (the Bar Kokhba Revolt), which ended in 135, rather than a response to it—but details are sketchy.[71] As part of Hadrian's rebuilding program, along the new colonnaded Cardo Maximus (the main north-south street) there was built a forum and, according to Eusebius of Caesarea (c. 260–c. 340), a cultic site consecrated to Aphrodite or Venus.[72] Eusebius implies that there was a long-standing memory that Jesus' tomb was under this temple, and that the ungodly conspired to hide it (*Vit. Const.* 3.25–26). When Sozomen wrote his *Church History* in the early fifth century, he suggested on the other hand that "the pagans" purpose-fully built the temple there in order to desecrate a site at which Christians were known to worship, and that the true site of the tomb was subsequently forgotten and had to be revealed (*Hist. Eccl.* 2.1). In reality, however, the main street was the obvious place to situate a temple. According to Eusebius, Constantine ordered the temple demolished (though it may already have been in ruins) and the impure soil excavated and carted away, and underneath was discovered the tomb of Christ.

> And finally that venerable and most holy testimony to the Savior's resurrection appeared; and that most holy cave, by coming to light again after going down into the darkness, presented a symbol of the Savior's own coming to life, for it came into the light again after going down into the darkness; and it allowed those who had come to the place to see manifest the history of the wonders that had been accomplished there. (Eusebius, *Vit. Const.* 3.28)

The tomb itself, as Eusebius describes it, rises from the dead; he already understands the place itself to evoke the story of Jesus' resurrection, just as other visitors to the site would similarly find it a place for reliving the "memory" of the resurrection.

This was the site of Constantine's Church of the Resurrection, the construction and features of which are described at great length by Eusebius (*Vit. Const.* 3.30-39). The tomb itself, once excavated, was covered by a small building (the aedicule). Presumably because of John 19:41, which situates the burial of Jesus in a garden near the crucifixion place, the discovery of the tomb also occasioned the discoveries of Calvary and the true cross (including the nails and the notice written by Pilate). In the writings of fifth-century church historians such as Sozomen, the legendary accounts of these discoveries are associated with Helena, Constantine's mother, and not the emperor himself (Sozomen, *Hist. Eccl.* 2.1), and the order of things has changed: first Helena discovers the cross; and then she clears the site and builds the church. The veracity of the cross was tested, according to Rufinus (d. 411), by curing a dying woman (*Hist. Eccl.* 10.7-8), but according to Paulinus of Nola (d. 431), by resurrecting a dead man (*Epis.* 31.4-5). As Jonathan Z. Smith comments, "It is the presence of the Cross and its power to resurrect, rather than the resurrection of the tomb itself, that guarantees the authenticity of the site in these later traditions."[73] Jerome indicates that by 393 the Church of the Resurrection was at least in the vicinity of "the Cross" (*Jo. Hier.* 11); but even earlier, Cyril of Jerusalem mentioned relics of the true cross in his catechetical lectures, which were delivered in the Church of the Resurrection around 380 (*Cat.* 4.10).[74]

Recent excavations at the site have revealed that the area was from around the seventh century BCE a limestone quarry, and that there are at least four tombs dating to the first century BCE at the site. A layer of arable soil from the first century BCE would make the site consistent with John's description of it as "a garden" (John 19:41).[75]Additionally, at the time of Jesus the location would have been outside the city wall—where of course crucifixion and burial sites would need to be located—although a newer wall built by Herod Agrippa in 41–44 CE would have placed it within the walls of the city thereafter, and in the time of Constantine.[76] In addition, ashlars (large hewn stone blocks) used in a retaining wall from the time of Hadrian have been found at the site.[77] Eusebius implies that Constantine or his advisers may have been aware of an old tradition that associated the site with the crucifixion and burial of Jesus; or it may have been "revealed" to them as Sozomen suggests. Jerome Murphy-O'Connor's argument that early Christians knew where Jesus had been buried because "the Jerusalem community . . . held liturgical celebrations at the site until AD 66" has absolutely no supporting evidence prior to the fourth century.[78] As Hans Dieter Betz remarks, "The tomb was only 'rediscovered' when it was needed. It can scarcely be misunderstood in the politics of religion that the 'cave of salvation' was discovered under a Temple of Venus in 326 CE."[79]

Regardless, the church soon became a destination for pilgrimages, and depictions of the Holy Sepulchre began to appear in Christian art by the fifth century; considerably later, churches and cemetery structures and small-scale models used in liturgy all commemorated the tomb aedicule (monument) at the Church of the Resurrection.[80] By the sixth century, and possibly earlier, pilgrims could get souvenirs—small clay bottles (ampullae) and clay tablets depicting the Holy Sepulchre—which they may have used as apotropaics, that is, as warding charms.[81] Gregory of Tours (d. 594) indicates they kept snakes away and could cure diseases (de Glor. Mart. 6).[82] No wonder, since the tomb itself was such a sacred place: according to Jerome, demons would flee the bodies they possessed when in the presence of the tomb (Jerome, Epis. 46.8).

The legendary accounts of the discoveries of the tomb and the cross confirmed that this was the place: "Its locative specificity and thick associative content, rather than its arbitrariness . . . guarantees the site's power and religious function."[83] One aspect of that religious function was demonstration: Cyril of Jerusalem claimed that together with the angels, and the apostles who ran to the tomb and saw the grave clothes, and the women who took hold of Jesus' feet, the tomb itself was among the "many witnesses to the Savior's resurrection." "Even this stone, which at that time was rolled away, and which lies here to this day, bears witness to the resurrection. . . . And [so also does] this house of the Holy Church, which was built and adorned (as you see) by the Emperor Constantine of blessed memory, because of his great love of Christ" (Cyril of Jerusalem, Cat. 14.22). Interestingly, in this context Cyril has no longer any need to appeal to the Jews as hostile witnesses; but standing next to the tomb aedicule, one finally could simply recite the narrative elements of the empty tomb story as proofs of the resurrection. How could anyone doubt here, where (in Smith's words) "story, ritual, and place could be one"?[84] Yet the certain proof of the resurrection that the Holy Sepulchre now afforded meant that those who persisted in disbelief and denial would have a great array of witnesses against them, including not only the original participants in the drama of the crucifixion and resurrection, but also the hill of Golgotha and the tomb with its stone that were *here* "to this day" (Cyril, *Cat.* 13.39).

It was therefore now possible for the believer not only to be present at the location of Jesus' death and resurrection, but also, through contemplation and veneration, to be spiritually present at the events themselves—because "place" in the narratives finally coincided with "space" in the real world.[85] This could be brought about through participation in ritual, as Cyril's assimilation of the act of baptism (in the Church of the Holy Sepulchre) to the interment and resurrection of Christ shows (*Cat. Myst.* 2.4).[86] But Jerome provides some striking examples of how piety shown at the Holy Sepulchre could be the occasion of reflection, which could lead to imaginative reenactment and participation:

> In former times the Jews used to reverence the Holy of Holies, because the cherubim, the mercy seat, the ark of the covenant, the manna, Aaron's rod, and the golden altar were inside. Does not the sepulchre of the Lord seem to you more worthy of reverence? However often we go inside, each time we perceive there the Savior in the linen grave clothes, and lingering a little we see the angel sitting at his feet, and the face-cloth folded at his head. (*Epis.* 46.5)[87]

This letter displays the rhetoric that by now was common—that the Holy Sepulchre was the temple of the new Christian Jerusalem.[88] Through the Scriptures the events of the passion and resurrection became the communal memory of Christianity, but these could be evoked and even participated in through the ritualized visitation of sacred sites in the vicinity of Jerusalem. According to Smith, the late fourth-century *Pilgrimage of Egeria* reveals that this involved "commemoratization, memorialization, and recollection" at prescribed sites that were visited in a prescribed order and at which prescribed readings would be heard.[89] Much of this activity converged at the Church of the Holy Sepulchre. Thus sacred space and ritual meet the story-order of the founding narratives and the history of God's saving acts. Smith explains that this convergence resulted in the development of the Christian year and the adoption of an eclogadic lectionary (liturgical readings taken not in continuous order but in order appropriate to Christian time).[90]

Uneasy Easter Stories

In some ways, the development of the Easter story reaches its conclusion—logically, at least—with the composition of full-scale conflations of the Gospel narratives. The beginning of this process can be seen in Mark, which began the process of reconciling the appearance and the disappearance traditions; the Fourth Gospel is the intracanonical climax of this endeavor, since there we find not only the combination of the apostolic inspection of the tomb with the appearance of the risen Jesus at the tomb, but resurrection combined with assumption in a two-stage scenario (similar to what is found in Luke). Postcanonical texts carried on the effort of telling the resurrection stories as the story of Easter. The *Gospel of Peter*, as shown above, combines various narrative traits from Mark, Matthew, and John with its own legendary additions, in keeping with the interests of whoever produced that text. Given this compositional tendency to conflate, it is almost natural that later authors would continue in this mode in their own retelling of the story. Thus already Justin could refer to both the guard at the tomb and the ascension into heaven (*1 Apol.* 21), and much later John Chrysostom could import Peter's inspection of the tomb into his homily on Matthew 28:11-14 (*Hom. Matt.* 90.2). This is possible because of a hermeneutic that straightforwardly identifies the narrative with the events it represents.

The Diatessaron composed by Tatian sometime around 170 CE is the earliest known Gospel harmony and was immensely influential in Eastern Christianity.[91] Unfortunately, it does not survive, owing to its replacement in fifth-century Syrian Christianity by the four canonical Gospels.[92] Scholars disagree as to its original language and form. A Syriac form evidently was in liturgical use in Edessa by the end of the second century, but an early Greek fragment, the Dura Europas parchment, might be a scrap of a Greek Diatessaron.[93] This fragment reproduces only the description of Joseph of Arimathea from Matthew 27:56-57 (with additional information from the other Gospels).[94] Ancient and medieval translations of the Diatessaron differ considerably from one another and at times seem to testify more to its influence than to its actual text, although a commentary on the text by Ephrem gives a better idea in some instances. Ephrem's commentary, however, provides little insight into how the Diatessaron treats the empty tomb story: he comments only on Joseph's request for the body and the burial (*Comm. Diat.* 21.20-21) and at greater length on the encounter between Jesus and Mary Magdalene (21.22-29).

According to Foster, Tatian's approach was to work from Matthew first, adding unique material from the other Gospels into Matthew's sequence, and harmonizing diverging accounts of the same episode or saying.[95] If the Arabic harmony (twelfth or thirteenth century CE) gives any indication of Tatian's original work,[96] it was a clever, painstaking, and often convoluted harmonization of the many divergent details in the story. For example, after the women ask, "Who will remove the stone for us?" (only in Mark 16:3), there is an earthquake and the angel descends to the tomb (Matt. 28:2) as if in answer to their request (Arabic *Diat.* 52.47-48). The angels provide a little more of a challenge: after Matthew's tomb-opening angel leaves, the women enter the tomb and encounter Mark's young man, and then Luke's two men in shining garb (52.52—53.1). These two both remind the women of what Jesus taught while in Galilee and instruct them to tell the disciples that Jesus would go ahead of them into Galilee (Luke 24:6-7; Mark 16:7; Arabic *Diat.* 53.3-7). The various trips from and back to the tomb are rather elaborately combined, as may be expected. First, the women leave and tell no one (Mark 16:8), but Mary goes to Peter and the Beloved Disciple, who return to inspect the tomb (Luke 24:12; John 20:2-10); back at the tomb, Mary encounters the risen Jesus (John 20:14-18) and then somehow arrives back in town telling the disciples, "I have seen the Lord." Even though Mary has been back and forth from the tomb by this time twice, the other women have not yet arrived in town with their news; on their way to tell the disciples, Jesus appears to them (Matt. 28:9-10), but only long after he met up with Mary Magdalene at the tomb (Arabic *Diat.* 53.7-25, 31-36). The others do not believe them (53.37-38).

Other early Christian commentators were similarly anxious to show that the Gospel stories did not necessarily conflict with one another, while at the same time acknowledging that a surface reading might lead one to believe that they did. This is clear in Augustine's work *On the Consensus of the Evangelists*, which is not exactly a Gospel harmony, but a serial discussion on different points of discord. Like the Arabic Diatessaron, Augustine is concerned to reconcile the obvious differences in the texts (such as whether the women came while it was dark or as it was dawning, or how many angels were at the tomb, or whether the women were inside the tomb or not). In fact, he claims that this task of arranging all the details into a single coherent narrative must be undertaken "so that it may be known that they said everything correctly, without any contradictions" (3.25.70).[97] Augustine is able to solve many problems through imaginative set design and stage direction, always assuming a direct correspondence between the narratives and the facts they purportedly relate; it helps that he identifies the Beloved Disciple as the author of the Fourth Gospel (Lat., *ipse* [the one who reports the inspection of the tomb] *est enim discipulus, quem amabat Iesus*, 3.24.69). He proposes, for instance, that the sighting of two angels by the women was divided into two reports of one on the stone, as in Matthew, and one inside the tomb, as in Mark (3.24.63). Or he suggests (3.24.67) that there was a small enclosure outside the door of the tomb, so that someone could possibly be "in" the tomb before "entering" it. One wonders whether this proposal was based on his knowledge of the structures at the Church of the Holy Sepulchre.

More serious problems are solved in other ways. The prediction that the disciples would see the risen Jesus in Galilee (Mark 16:7; Matt. 28:7) suggests an almost immediate appearance there, but Augustine acknowledges that according to Luke and John, several appearances in the Jerusalem vicinity took place before any in Galilee (Luke 24:13-53; John 20:19-29; *de Cons. Ev.* 3.25.79-80). How can this be resolved? First, Augustine states that neither in Mark nor in Matthew is it said that Jesus would appear soon, or right away, in Galilee, or in Galilee but nowhere else (3.25.80). Second, he says that the appearance in Galilee (Matt. 28:16-20) must have taken place outside of the eight days between the first appearances and the appearance to Thomas (John 20:19-29) unless the appearance in Galilee was to some other eleven disciples and not "the Eleven" (3.25.81). Finally, he suggests that since the prediction was the utterance of an angel, it must be a prophetic saying, one that is open to alternative interpretations (3.25.86). Galilee, he says, can mean either "transmigration" or "revelation." "Transmigration" signifies that the grace of God has passed from Israel to the Gentiles, and "revelation" signifies that whereas in his earthly career Jesus took the form of a servant, now as the risen Christ he reveals himself as one with the Father, "in accordance with that ineffable light which illuminates every person coming into the world" (3.25.86; see John 1:9).

These conflations are part of a larger hermeneutical program in early Christianity, in which the four Gospels must be seen to offer a single, undivided testimony to the life, death, and resurrection of Christ. Even within the canon, only a very narrow range of diversity (narrative, chronological, theological) was acceptable; otherwise the truth of the Gospel witness to Christ would be in jeopardy. These large-scale conflations of the Gospel tomb stories should be understood as part of the larger project—undertaken by many interpreters for many reasons and in many contexts and with many different results—to address the perceived shortcomings of the empty tomb story. When the empty tomb was not considered sufficient proof for the resurrection, the "testimony" of the chief priests and the guards in Matthew was brought to bear on the problem, so that the empty tomb could not be interpreted in any other way than that the risen Jesus left it empty. (Eventually the Church of the Holy Sepulchre would also provide supporting testimony.) When individual versions of the story were considered deficient—Mark 16:1-8 in particular—they were augmented by scribes, harmonized by interpreters, or rewritten by imaginative retellers. This tendency was already seen in Matthew and Luke, both of which correct the Markan ending (so that the women tell the other disciples, whether they were instructed to do so or not). But because Matthew and Luke sought to correct the Markan version in different ways in their own retellings of the story, they added to the story's diffuse character. The retellings and rewritings, as we have seen in this chapter, did not end with the Fourth Gospel but continued as scribes and interpreters and theologians grappled with the meaning of the empty tomb. And just as with the canonical Gospels, these new retellings and rewritings sought to address current questions—not only about the resurrection of Jesus, but also about the scope of God's saving plan, about the nature of apostolic/ecclesial or biblical authority, about the role and status of the heroes of the faith, and about many other matters—in ways that made sense to the current Christian imagination.

10. Revisiting the Empty Tomb: Why Beginnings Matter

So let us carefully consider, brothers and sisters, out of what sort of material we have been fashioned, and who [we are] and as what sort of people we have come into the world, and out of what sort of tomb and darkness the one who formed and created us has led us into the world, having prepared in advance his benefactions before we were born.

　　—*1 Clement* 38:3

Sometime near the end of the first century, these words were written to the Christian community in Corinth. I refer to them here for two reasons, the first of which is that it is a very early Christian text that uses the image of people being led out of a darkened tomb as a metaphor for coming into community together under the benefaction of God. Like Paul before him, this author is able to use this image without any sense that it should reflect the narratives of the discovery of the empty tomb of Jesus. Paul, in Romans 6, says similarly that whoever has been baptized into Christ has also been crucified and buried with him, so that "just as Christ was raised from the dead through the Father's glory, so also we should walk in newness of life" (Rom. 6:4). As in 1 Corinthians 15, resurrection is understood here as a transformation that leads to life on a new plane of existence. Perhaps Paul thought that his argument in Romans 6 was perfect as it was, and that it was better not to overburden it with related images such as stones or grave clothes. (He would have been right, of course.) Or perhaps he thought the idea of disappearance would run counter to his emphasis on "newness of life." The author of *1 Clement*, on the other hand, uses this image without even connecting it (explicitly or implicitly) with the resurrection of Christ. This is the inverse of a pattern we have observed in early Christian literature, that is, that those writing about the resurrection of Christ in the first few Christian centuries tend not to refer to the empty tomb stories as support for their theological considerations about how Christ was raised and what it all meant.

　　Why was this? I have suggested it is related to an ambivalence about these narratives, an ambivalence that arose early and quickly became the dominant mode of reflection on the story of the women discovering the open and empty tomb of Jesus. In its earliest recoverable deployment, the disappearance tradition was simply an oracle of Jesus that spoke of his rejection by "Jerusalem" as the reason for both the withdrawal of divine protection ("Your house is left forsaken") and his disappearance ("You will not see me any longer") until the time should come for him to return as "the Coming One" (Q 13:34-35). As argued earlier, we have no way of knowing whether this oracle was the basis for the origin of the disappearance story, or whether it is the result of scribal reflection on the Scriptures that took an empty tomb report or rumor as its starting point. In any case, as soon as Mark used the traditional disappearance story for the narrative conclusion to his Gospel, it was subordinated to the resurrection proclamation: "He has been raised, he is not here" (Mark 16:6). This resurrection proclamation took the appearances of the risen Christ, not the empty tomb, as the core experiences accounting for the theological conviction that God had vindicated Jesus after his death. We have seen how Luke, Matthew, and John all had different ways of narrating this subordination, by increasingly bringing the appearance tradition to bear upon the disappearance story. The empty tomb story, practically from the very beginning, was thought to be in need of apologetic help and theological support from the appearance tradition.

So when I began to write this book, I was convinced that the resurrection paradigm quickly overshadowed the assumption paradigm, particularly (but not only) in the developing corpus of narratives about the end of Jesus. I am still convinced of this, for it is seen everywhere in the texts, gradually reinforcing itself in various ways. The Easter window I referred to in the introduction of the book illustrates this dominance pointedly. The image of the risen and present Jesus meeting Mary completely dominates the presentation: one only catches a glimpse of the edge of the tomb at the margin of the window, and the saying announcing Jesus' absence from the tomb is relegated to a narrow script at the bottom, where (given the context of the image) it is almost completely overshadowed by "But is Risen." It also became clear that whenever the story was adjusted or adapted in a particular text, the additions or alterations could always be explained in relation to the broader literary and theological shape of that particular writing. What surprised me as I studied these narratives and their interpretive history more closely, however, is how resilient and how influential the disappearance/assumption paradigm appears to have been. From Mark's narration of the resurrection of Jesus using the motifs of a disappearance story, to the insistence in John that the risen Jesus had yet to "ascend to the Father" (John 20:17), to the *Gospel of Peter* and beyond, assumption remained an important way of expressing the postmortem exaltation of Jesus.

The second reason I refer to the exhortation from *1 Clement* 38 is that it counsels the hearers, in the interest of promoting due humility, to consider the "stuff" (Gk., *hulē*) from which God fashioned them. In the context, Clement is writing about the formation of the community, using language that suggests the creation story in which God formed Adam, the dusty person, by hand and breathed life into him (Gen. 2:7; evoked in 1 Cor. 15:42-49). The development of the Easter story (!) may have been that deliberate in its individual stages, but overall it was an organic process of successive literary productions composed and received in different contexts. Considering the raw materials from which the stories have been formed has, I hope, afforded greater insight into the stories themselves, and also into the contexts and concerns of those who first found them valuable for formulating and expressing their views about the significance of Jesus after his crucifixion. The raw materials themselves, however, also explain a great deal. In early Jewish sources, resurrection is often connected with the vindication of martyrs and other faithful ones at the end of the age, and we have seen that some of Jesus' followers interpreted his postmortem appearances as signs both of God's vindication of his message and of the beginning (postponed in part) of God's new age. The disappearance tradition explains how and why early Christians conceived of the postmortem Jesus as exalted to heaven and returning as the Coming One, and how they accounted for the hiatus between his two careers as the earthly and heavenly Son of Man. This kind of validation is different from that provided by the idea of resurrection, and yet there are points where convergence and mutual influence were possible.

At the end of this study, what is sometimes called the Easter story might now seem a little like a patchwork quilt—made of various unrelated pieces, each with a history of its own, and sometimes conflicting with its neighbors—and to some extent, that is not an inappropriate image. After all, the stories as they stand really read better individually; reading them together, one becomes distracted too easily by the details to really appreciate the bigger picture each one creates on its own. On the other hand, as we will see here, the story is in some respects remarkably coherent, despite the fact that it originated from two traditions and developed in a variety of successive deployments.

Beginnings That Converge Narratively

Beginnings matter not because they provide the earliest, most primitive, most authentic understanding or account; they matter because they are part (only part) of the stuff of which endings are fashioned (to continue with Clement's turn of phrase). At the beginning of the Easter story lie two different expressions, one about the postmortem appearances of Jesus to his followers and another about his disappearance, which was a culturally conditioned way of talking about his absence (whether conceived of as his "being taken away" by God as a preservation for a future role, as in Q and Mark, or as the "return to the Father" of the preexistent Son of God, as in John). We have observed how these two ideas originally, as far as we can tell, had separate tradition histories. Their earliest expressions did not really overlap at all, at least linguistically. Paul talked about resurrection and appearances, but not about the empty tomb; and in Q, which does not express Jesus' individual postmortem vindication using the idiom of a resurrection from the dead, there is a deep sense that it is the absence of Jesus the Son of Man that is important, but this is an absence before the renewed presence (parousia) of the Coming One. So these two ideas traveled separately and used different language, but there is more to say here than simply to affirm that early

Christians thought about Jesus being alive after his death in different ways and with different implications.

We have also observed how these two traditions converged in the narration of the Easter experiences. Although there is good reason to suppose that both narrative as well as kerygmatic traditions circulated before Mark was written, this Gospel provides the earliest surviving resurrection story. Mark 16:1-8 is a story that does not, however, describe the aftereffects of resurrection (which would require a risen Jesus!), but the aftereffects of assumption. This means that resurrection for Mark is a strictly bodily affair, but not exactly in the sense that Jesus got up in a revivified body and left the tomb—rather, God took him bodily into heaven. In using the narrative motifs of a disappearance story to narrate the claim that "he has been raised," the author of Mark took the first recoverable step in bringing the disappearance tradition in line with the appearance tradition— and he did this without describing an appearance of the risen Jesus, but alluding to one that would happen, as it were, off-screen (Mark 16:7). This had two results. The first is that the appearance predicted in Mark's ending must be understood as an appearance in Galilee but from the divine realm, just like the appearance of Romulus to Julius Proculus and that of Elijah and Moses to Jesus and the three disciples in the transfiguration story. This retains the visionary qualities of the appearance tradition as Paul understood it, but it also (and this is the second result) created a narrative scenario in which empty tomb and resurrection must go together, at least partly because of the importance of Mark as a source for the later Gospels.

Matthew's story of the resurrection also seems to presume the same understanding of resurrection as assumption, since when the tomb is opened Jesus is already gone, and one figures he has been taken bodily into heaven (although it must be noted that the narrator does not draw attention to this in the typical way). The way Matthew tells it, Jesus' opponents wanted to prevent his disciples from announcing his resurrection by ensuring that they could not steal the body. This tells us infinitely more about Matthew's setting than about the events after the crucifixion: it indicates that the empty tomb and resurrection proclamation were understood as going together, a combination that probably had been made in some circles already before Matthew read Mark. Part of Matthew's strategy to answer questions about his community's resurrection proclamation was to attribute the origin of the body-theft rumor to Jesus' opponents as a lie they told despite their knowledge to the contrary. Depicting Jesus appearing to the women as they leave the tomb is another part of Matthew's apologetic strategy, although here he probably was relying on an earlier appearance story (which might not have been situated at or outside the tomb).

Luke evidently was more concerned with how the resurrection appearances were being interpreted by early Christians than with how the resurrection proclamation was being viewed by outsiders. In order to answer a "visionary" interpretation of the experiences of those who saw Jesus after his death, he situated Peter, one of the primary resurrection witnesses, at the tomb to verify the report of the women. By doing this Luke excluded the interpretation that Jesus' followers had only experienced him "spiritually." This may have been directed at Paul's argument in 1 Corinthians 15, or at those who after Paul were interpreting his language about "spiritual bodies" in a purely visionary way. It was Luke's unmistakable concern to defend the resurrection appearances as tangible, flesh-and-bones events—in contrast with "pneumatic" understandings—that led us to discern the motivation for having Peter inspect the tomb. Luke thus gives the impression that Jesus rose from the dead out of the tomb (that is, and not into heaven) in a way that Matthew and Mark do not, but the assumption paradigm has still left its mark. For Luke still uses the disappearance tradition: the ascension of the risen Jesus into heaven is his way of shutting the door on the resurrection appearances and looking ahead to the return of Jesus (Acts 1:11).

At the canonical end of the narrative trajectory of Easter, the Fourth Gospel combines the innovation of Matthew (Jesus at the tomb) with that of Luke (the apostles at the tomb) in a way that still takes seriously Mark's depiction of the resurrection as an assumption into the divine realm. Although Jesus' request that Mary not touch him (John 20:17) has proven to be notoriously difficult to interpret, Mary Rose D'Angelo's recent reappraisal of a reading first seen in Origen seems to make good sense of the unusual request: in John's view, there is something transcendent or liminal about the risen Jesus' bodily presence, and he had best not be touched until his return to the Father is complete.[1] This means that (as also in the off-screen appearance mentioned in Mark 16:7 and in Matthew 28:16-20, and also in the view of Paul) when Jesus appears to his followers later in the Gospel (John 20:19-23, 26-29; 21:4-23), he appears in a glorified state from heaven. In the Fourth Gospel the return of the Son to the Father is understood as encompassing Jesus' death, resurrection, and ascension in such a way that it is difficult to understand sometimes at what point the "glorification" of the Son comes to its conclusion. At the same time, the core idea of the Q saying was expanded into a major trope in the Farewell Discourses of John 13–17: where he was going, they could not come; a little while, and they would see him no more, but then see him again.

These narrative adjustments to the empty tomb story all show that the story itself was something of a problem, something that needed further explanation and elaboration and defense, rather than simply stimulating theological reflection on its own. We have also seen the way that the not-finding of Jesus' body was consistently, in the message of the angelic interpreters, subordinated to the proclamation that "he has been raised." Almost from the start, the disappearance tradition was viewed as one that needed to be controlled, whether through kerygmatic subordination or through deliberate retelling. It is clearest in Luke (but also in the other canonical Gospels) that narration is control—that how one tells the story of the empty tomb controls or limits the interpretive options presented by the claim "Christ has been raised from the dead." So the two traditions converge narratively. At the end of this trajectory, everything is narrated and nothing is left untold—even the emergence of Jesus from the tomb, whether fresh from his descent to the dead, resuscitated, and ready to ascend (in the *Gospel of Peter*), or just up and handing his grave clothes over to the guard (in the

Gospel of the Hebrews). Thus the appearance tradition finally enters—*literally*—the empty and enticingly suggestive space of the disappearance tradition when the rising Jesus appeared in the tomb and on his way out. This indicates that the evangelists (canonical and noncanonical) continued to see the disappearance tradition as secondary to the appearance tradition, and yet it left marks on their stories that are still evident, if one knows where to look. This paradoxical pattern of attempted subordination and persisting influence is seen in the narrative, apologetic, and hagiographical deployments of the empty tomb story well beyond the second century.

Beginnings That Converge Theologically

Having traced the two traditions from their emergence in the theology of Paul and in the sayings of Q, what we have not observed to this point is how the beginnings of Easter are similar. One point of similarity is that both originate (as far as we can tell) in visionary experience. The Q saying about the disappearance of Jesus the Coming One (Q 13:34-35) is an oracle, and by this I mean it is a "saying of the Lord" in the sense that it originated in the context of prophetic, spirited speech. It involves Jesus speaking in the voice of the Wisdom of God who sends the prophets but who is rejected and is then removed by God. The idea of Wisdom sent by God but rejected by humankind is found in *1 Enoch* 42:1-3, but here on the lips of Jesus, the removal by God that follows this rejection by Jerusalem is a theological explanation for how Jesus, rejected and killed, can still be the Coming One, the returning Son of Man. Wisdom does not return, but someone taken up by God and preserved for a special role in the eschaton could. This saying, therefore, makes the best sense if we understand it as a prophetic (or even scribal) expression of a theological conviction held by Jesus' followers. Paul, as we have seen, thought of his own visionary experience(s) of the risen Lord as an instance (or instances) of Christ appearing to him in the same mode that he appeared to the others, and to the same effect. Here his language about resurrection as a "spiritual" thing makes good sense. This is not to say, on the one hand, that there may not have been an early tradition about women discovering Jesus' tomb open and empty, that the prophetic utterance necessarily gave rise to the narrative tradition. It is the case, however, that the earliest expression of the disappearance tradition is a piece of prophetic speech. It is also important that Mark understood and deployed his traditional narrative source in a way that suggests he was (or would have been) in agreement with the theological convictions expressed by Q 13:34-35—that Jesus was rejected in Jerusalem and now was no longer here, but was coming again as the Son of Man (see Mark 14:62). On the other hand, it is quite probable that in other circles contemporary with (or earlier than) Paul's mission, the resurrection appearances were being understood in very tangible terms. The Jewish texts about resurrection show diversity on how resurrection was conceived, but in many (or even most) of them, the physical body is somehow reconstituted and revivified by God's re-creative power. This is the idea we get especially from the Gospel of Luke. For Paul the visionary, however, the emphasis was more on resurrection as a transformation that would change what was mortal and corruptible into something immortal and incorruptible.

A second point of similarity is that both these expressions have significantly corporate implications. In the contemporary analogues to the two traditions, however, this was not necessarily the case. Assumption, whether it led to a special eschatological function or to apotheosis, was always an individual affair: Romulus, Herakles, Aristeas, Xisouthros, Enoch, Elijah, Moses, Ezra, Baruch, and the others were all taken up individually and thus were set apart from the rest of humanity by being exalted (or at least removed) to the divine realm in this way. How, then, does the exaltation of Jesus through his assumption make any real difference to his followers? Paul had the opposite problem with the resurrection model—if resurrection was expected to be corporate, why had it only happened to one person? And if it was supposed to be the great remaking of God's people at the end of the age, where was the end? Paul's answer was that the resurrection of Jesus had made him the New Adam, and that all those incorporated (I use that word deliberately) into him would eventually be raised, but only after he puts all his enemies under his feet (1 Cor. 15:23-28). Just as one naturally (Gk., *psychikon*) bears the image of the dusty person, Adam, so also one can bear the image of the New Adam spiritually (*pneumatikon*), if united to him in his death and resurrection through baptism (Rom. 6:1-11); and the resurrection of Christ takes root in the believer as "newness of life," as being "dead to sin but alive to God in Christ Jesus" (vv. 4, 11). At the same time, Paul affirms that those who are "of Christ" will be raised with him "at his coming" (1 Cor. 15:23). Thus resurrection retains its corporate and eschatological character but is applied in the first place to the first fruits, Christ. But what about the assumption of Jesus?

In its earliest deployment in Q, the disappearance tradition provides, in my opinion, an answer to the death of Jesus—but Q consistently reflects on persecution and trials in a corporate way, so that John and Jesus, and their predecessors the prophets, and their followers, are viewed together as suffering the typical fate of emissaries sent to God's people. At the same time, Jesus is understood as the climactic or paradigmatic example of the rejected prophet. Q also pronounces blessing and predicts heavenly reward for those who suffer revilement and persecution "because of the Son of Man" (Q 6:22-23). Even though Q 13:34-35 (about the disappearance of the Coming One) and other sayings such as Q (about the heavenly or returning Son of Man) clearly distinguish Jesus the speaker from the community, there seems to be a representative connection between "the Son of Man" and those who maintain allegiance to him. In some ways, this conclusion depends on seeing in the "Son of Man" language in Q the same kind of representative function of "the Human One" that one also finds in Daniel 7 and the Similitudes of Enoch (*1 Enoch* 37–71), and of the "Righteous One" in Wisdom 2–5.[2] In those texts, the transcendent figure embodies the community of the faithful, and one way this is expressed is through language that connects the figure with the community: for instance, in Wisdom 2–5, the Righteous One stands for "the righteous," or the one like a son of humankind receives authority as the "holy ones" will in Daniel 7. This representative function of the exalted figure encompasses not only the hoped-for vindication of the community (understood as occurring in the context of an eschatological judgment on their oppressors), but also the persecution of the community in the meantime. This background helpfully illuminates how the Son of Man figure functions in Q, particularly in relation to corporate expressions of persecution.[3] Importantly, the "Son of Man" figure in *1 Enoch* 37–71 turns out (in an ending that may not have been original to the work) to be Enoch the seer, who has been taken up into the heavenly realm. An angel discloses to Enoch, "You are that son of man who was born for righteousness," and he is told, "All will walk on your path since righteousness will never forsake you; with you will be their dwelling, and with you, their lot, and from you they will not be separated forever and forever and ever" (*1 Enoch* 71:16).[4] Here the community identifies with "that Son of Man" by following his pattern of justice. In Q the emphasis is on faithfulness under threat of persecution, but the reward is heavenly blessing (Q 6:22-23) or vindication before angels (Q 12:8-9) or even sharing with Jesus in his role as judge (Q 22:28-30). It may be that thinking about Jesus' vindication in terms of disappearance or assumption had considerable formative impact on how some circles in the early Jesus movements thought scripturally about the future of Jesus and what it meant for them.

Thus, although both the disappearance tradition and the appearance tradition are about Jesus in the sense that they convey ideas about his postmortem vindication by God, in their earliest expressions, as well as in the narratives that arose (textually at least) afterward, these ideas were never only about Jesus. They never conveyed ideas about a private vindication that had no meaning beyond what it meant for Jesus—they had a community focus, and they arose and found narrative expression, elaboration, and deployment in communities that sought to describe how life should be in light of God's vindication of Jesus.

Notes

Introduction

1. See, e.g., Ulrich Wilckens, "The Tradition-History of the Resurrection of Jesus," in *The Significance of the Message of the Resurrection for Faith in Jesus Christ*, ed. C. F. D. Moule (London: SCM, 1968), 51–76, esp. 71; and, recently, James D. G. Dunn, *Jesus Remembered* (Christology in the Making 1; Grand Rapids: Eerdmans, 2003), 840, 864.

2. Willi Marxsen, *The Resurrection of Jesus of Nazareth* (London: SCM; Philadelphia: Fortress Press, 1970), 71. See also John Dominic Crossan, "Empty Tomb and Absent Lord (Mark 16:1-8)," in *The Passion in Mark: Studies on Mark 14–16*, ed. W. Kelber (Philadelphia: Fortress Press, 1976), 135–52, who calls Mark's empty tomb story an "anti-tradition" in contrast to the appearance traditions Paul describes (152).

3. Dunn, *Jesus Remembered*, 840, citing Wilckens, "Tradition-History," 71–72; John E. Alsup, *The Post-Resurrection Appearance Stories of the Gospel Tradition* (Calwer Theologische Monographien 5; Stuttgart: Calwer; London: SPCK, 1975), 85–116; and several others.

4. See Elisabeth Schüssler Fiorenza, *Jesus, Miriam's Child, Sophia's Prophet: Critical Issues in Feminist Christology* (New York: Continuum, 1995), 124; for critique, see Mary Rose D'Angelo, "'I Have Seen the Lord': Mary Magdalen as Visionary, Early Christian Prophecy, and the Context of John 20:14-18," in *Mariam, the Magdalen, and the Mother*, ed. Deirdre Good (Bloomington: Indiana University Press, 2005), 95–122, esp. 104–5.

5. E.g., Rudolf Bultmann, *The History of the Synoptic Tradition*, trans. John Marsh (rev. ed.; Oxford: Blackwell, 1963), 287; Gerd Lüdemann, *The Resurrection of Jesus: History, Experience, Theology* (London: SCM; Minneapolis: Fortress Press, 1994), 121. Where possible, I will also refer to the more recent edition of Lüdemann's work on the resurrection: *The Resurrection of Christ: A Historical Inquiry* (2nd ed.; Amherst, N.Y.: Prometheus, 2004). Although the 1994 edition remains the fuller and more comprehensive discussion, the 2004 edition shows some important changes in Lüdemann's views.

6. See Wilhelm Michaelis, "ὁράω, εἶδον, κτλ," in *TDNT* 5.315–82, esp. 358–59; Lüdemann, *Resurrection of Jesus*, 48.

7. Dunn, *Jesus Remembered*, 840.

8. For the argument that Paul (or the tradition he cites in 1 Cor. 15:3-7) straightforwardly assumes the empty tomb, see N. T. Wright, *The Resurrection of the Son of God* (Christian Origins and the Question of God 3; London: SPCK; Minneapolis: Fortress Press, 2003), 321.

9. The arguments in this book presume the Two Document Hypothesis, which proposes that Mark was the earliest Gospel written, that Matthew and Luke (independently of one another) used Mark as a textual source for their new compositions, and that the agreements between Matthew and Luke in non-Markan sayings material is to be explained through their use of a written sayings collection or sayings source designated by scholars as Q. For a fuller discussion of the Synoptic Problem, see Christopher M. Tuckett, "Synoptic Problem," *ABD* 6:263–70; and for a fuller discussion of the evidence requiring a theory

of literary interdependence and supporting the Two Document Hypothesis, see Robert H. Stein, *Studying the Synoptic Gospels: Origin and Interpretation* (2nd ed.; Grand Rapids: Baker, 2001), 29–152.

10. I argue this case at some length in Daniel A. Smith, *The Post-Mortem Vindication of Jesus in the Sayings Gospel Q* (LNTS 338; London and New York: T. & T. Clark International, 2006).

11. Gerhard Lohfink, "Der Ablauf der Osterereignisse und die Anfänge der Urgemeinde," *TQ* 160 (1980): 162–76 (here, 168–69); see similarly (though not citing Lohfink) Dunn, *Jesus Remembered*, 866–70.

12. D'Angelo, "I Have Seen the Lord," 102.

13. Pseudo-Mark 16:9-20, the so-called longer ending of Mark, has the resurrection stories of the other Gospels in view; it is comprised mainly of short summaries of narratives told more fully in Matthew, Luke, and John. It should probably be called the "longest ending," for in the manuscript tradition there are three: (1) Mark 16:8; (2) Mark 16:20; and (3) the so-called shorter ending of Mark, which follows Mark 16:8 in the manuscripts that contain it. Sometimes printed in footnotes of modern-language editions of the New Testament, the shorter ending reads as follows: "And they reported promptly to those of Peter's group everything they were commanded. After this Jesus himself also sent forth through them from east to west the sacred and incorruptible proclamation of eternal salvation. Amen." For further discussion of these alternative endings, see pp. 133-35 below.

14. John Dominic Crossan, *The Cross That Spoke: The Origins of the Passion Narrative* (San Francisco: Harper & Row, 1988), 282–83.

15. Pheme Perkins, *Resurrection: New Testament Witness and Contemporary Reflection* (Garden City, N.Y.: Doubleday, 1984), 91, 93.

16. Jane Schaberg, *The Resurrection of Mary Magdalene: Legends, Apocrypha, and the Christian Testament* (New York and London: Continuum, 2002), 212–13 and n. 44 (reacting to Perkins).

17. Wright, *Resurrection*, 611.

18. Wolfgang Fritz Volbach, *Elfenbeinarbeiten der Spätantike und des fruhen Mittelalters* (3rd ed.; Mainz: Von Zabern, 1976), 79–80.

19. Ernst Kitzinger, *Byzantine Art in the Making: Main Lines of Stylistic Development in Mediterranean Art, 3rd–7th Century* (Cambridge: Harvard University Press, 1995), 39–40.

20. Kurt Weitzmann, *Age of Spirituality: Late Antique and Early Christian Art, Third to Seventh Century* (New York: Metropolitan Museum of Art, 1979), 454; following Weitzmann in this are David R. Cartlidge and J. Keith Elliott, *Art and the Christian Apocrypha* (London and New York: Routledge, 2001), 222.

21. This interpretation draws more (as the reader may suspect) from the argument of this book than from the history of Christian art, for "the resurrection of Jesus itself is never portrayed as an event; that is characteristic of the entire first millennium," as noted by Ulrich Luz, *Matthew: A Commentary* (3 vols.; Hermeneia; Minneapolis: Fortress Press, 2001–07), 3:600.

22. Maurice Goguel, *La foi à la Résurrection de Jésus dans le christianisme primitif* (Paris: Leroux, 1933), 213–33.

23. See famously John Dominic Crossan, *Who Killed Jesus? Exposing the Roots of Anti-Semitism in the Gospel Story of the Death of Jesus* (San Francisco: HarperSanFrancisco, 1995), 160–88.

24. See Byron McCane, *Roll Back the Stone: Death and Burial in the World of Jesus* (Harrisburg, Pa.: Trinity Press International, 2003), 92–93 and 107n6, citing N. Haas, "Anthropological Observations on the Skeletal Remains from Giv'at ha-Mivtar," *IEJ* 20 (1970): 38–59; and J. Zias and E. Sekeles, "The Crucified Man from Giv'at ha-Mivtar: A Reappraisal," *IEJ* 35 (1985): 22–27.

25. Translations of biblical and other ancient texts are the author's own unless otherwise noted. The bibliography lists the various original language sources on which these translations are based.

26. McCane, *Roll Back the Stone*, 89. See similarly Raymond E. Brown, "The Burial of Jesus (Mark 15:42-47)," *CBQ* 50 (1988): 233–45.

27. McCane, *Roll Back the Stone*, 102.

28. For the former view, see above, p. 175 n. 5; for the latter view, see, e.g., Crossan, "Empty Tomb and Absent Lord," 152.

29. See below, p. 132.

30. See below, pp. 66-67, 72-73.

31. Dunn also draws attention to the "tension between appearances on earth and appearances from heaven," but this is a tension that only arises when the appearances are narrated in relation to the empty tomb, as in Matthew, Luke, or John (*Jesus Remembered*, 858).

32. See below, pp. 109-10.

33. See the discussion below, pp. 123-24; see also, e.g., Raymond E. Brown, *The Gospel according to John: Introduction, Translation, and Notes* (2 vols.; AB 29–29A; Garden City, N.Y.: Doubleday, 1966–70), 2:1003.

34. For discussion, see D'Angelo, "I Have Seen the Lord," 100–102.

Chapter 1

1. The Greek word for "proclamation" is *kērygma* (e.g., 1 Cor. 15:14).

2. So, e.g., Rudolf Bultmann, *The History of the Synoptic Tradition*, trans. John Marsh (rev. ed.; Oxford: Basil Blackwell, 1963), 290; Gerd Lüdemann, *The Resurrection of Jesus: History, Experience, Theology* (London: SCM; Minneapolis: Fortress Press, 1994), 121.

3. See Luke 24:31, 36; John 20:19, 26 (disappearance and appearance); Luke 24:16, 31; John 20:14-16; 21:4, 12 (unrecognized identity); Matt. 28:17; Luke 24:37-38, 41; John 20:25, 27 (questions and doubts).

4. For Paul's "Damascus Road" experience, see Acts 9:1-19; 22:4-16; 26:9-18; see also Acts 13:30-31, where Paul says that the risen Jesus appeared to others (not including himself).

5. The passive of *horaō* is used, e.g., for a king being seen together with his army (Plutarch, *Them.* 12.2), for souls of the dead flitting around tombs (Plato, *Phaed.* 81d), and for a torch appearing in the heavens (Diodorus Siculus, *Bibl.* 15.50).

6. Cf., e.g., Gen. 1:9 LXX ("and the dry land appeared") with Exod. 16:10 LXX ("the glory of the LORD appeared").

7. It should be noted, however, that the Septuagint also uses the same expression for someone "appearing" before an elder or superior (as Joseph before his father in Gen. 46:29 LXX, or Moses before Pharaoh in Exod. 10:28 LXX).

8. See H. J. de Jonge, "Visionary Experience and the Historical Origins of Christianity," in *Resurrection in the New Testament: Festschrift J. Lambrecht*, ed. R. Bieringer et al. (BETL 165; Leuven: Peeters, 2002), 35–53, who notes (44–45) six different senses in which *ōphthē* is used for theophanies in the LXX.

9. Luke 24:34; Acts 9:17; 13:31; 26:16; 1 Cor. 15:5-8; 1 Tim. 3:16 (?); and Heb. 9:28 (which refers to the parousia).

10. Reginald H. Fuller, *The Formation of the Resurrection Narratives* (New York: Macmillan, 1971), 30.

11. "Some scholars have emptied the *ōphthē* . . . of 1 Cor. 15 of its normal visual associations, claiming that as a formula of legitimation it need not advert to real or imagined visions": so Dale C. Allison, *Resurrecting Jesus: The Earliest Christian Tradition and Its Interpreters* (New York and London: T. & T. Clark, 2005), 237, citing W. Michaelis, "ὁράω, εἶδον, κτλ," *TDNT* 5:358. Allison himself thinks "this is wholly unlikely." Dieter Zeller, "Erscheinungen Verstorbener im griechisch-römischen Bereich," in Bieringer, *Resurrection in the New Testament*, 1–19, takes a similar position (ibid., 3–4), against Anton

Vögtle, "Wie kam es zum Osterglauben?" in Rudolf Pesch and Anton Vögtle, *Wie kam es zum Osterglauben?* (Düsseldorf: Patmos-Verlag, 1975), 9–131 (esp. 58); see also Rudolf Pesch, "Zur Entstehung des Glaubens an die Auferstehung Jesu," *TQ* 153 (1973): 201–28 (esp. 214–15). Pesch later modified his view: "Zur Entstehung des Glaubens an die Auferstehung Jesu: Ein neuer Versuch," *Freiburger Zeitschrift für Philosophie und Theologie* 30 (1983): 73–98.

12. Ulrich Wilckens, "The Tradition-History of the Resurrection of Jesus," in *The Significance of the Message of the Resurrection for Faith in Jesus Christ*, ed. C. F. D. Moule (London: SCM, 1968), 51–76; here, 59.

13. E.g., according to Plato, souls not set free from the body in purity retain something of the visible corporeal nature, and thus they "appear" (*ōphthē*) "wandering around the tombs and monuments" (*Phaed.* 81d). Of course, the religious associations of *ophthēnai* in the biblical tradition (divine presence, commissioning, etc.) are absent in instances such as this.

14. See Jack Winkler, "Lollianos and the Desperadoes," *JHS* 100 (1980): 155–81, esp. 160–65 on "narrative expectations" concerning descriptions of ghosts; Gregory J. Riley, *Resurrection Reconsidered: Thomas and John in Controversy* (Minneapolis: Fortress Press, 1995), 48–51; D. Felton, *Haunted Greece and Rome: Ghost Stories from Classical Antiquity* (Austin: University of Texas Press, 1999), 1–37; Daniel Ogden, *Greek and Roman Necromancy* (Princeton, N.J.: Princeton University Press, 2001), 219–30; Deborah Thompson Prince, "The 'Ghost' of Jesus: Luke 24 in Light of Ancient Narratives of Post-Mortem Apparitions," *JSNT* 29 (2007): 287–301.

15. See Zeller, "Erscheinungen Verstorbener," 4–12, for examples and discussion; see also Sarah Iles Johnston, *Restless Dead: Encounters between the Living and the Dead in Ancient Greece* (Berkeley: University of California Press, 1999), 127–99.

16. See Ogden, *Greek and Roman Necromancy*, 163–90; Daniel Ogden, *Magic, Witchcraft, and Ghosts in the Greek and Roman Worlds: A Sourcebook* (Oxford: Oxford University Press, 2002), 179–205; Hans Dieter Betz, "Zum Problem der Auferstehung Jesu im Lichte der griechischen magischen Papyri," in Betz, *Gesammelte Aufsätze I: Hellenismus und Urchristentum* (Tübingen: Mohr Siebeck, 1990), 230–61; Leda Jean Ciraolo, "Supernatural Assistants in the Greek Magical Papyri," in *Ancient Magic and Ritual Power*, ed. M. Meyer and P. Mirecki (RGRW 129; Leiden: Brill, 1995), 279–95.

17. This terminology avoids the pejorative connotations of "superstition" or "paranormal" normally associated with "ghost."

18. See John Dominic Crossan, "The Resurrection of Jesus in Its Jewish Context," *Neot* 37 (2003): 29–58 (esp. 46–47), who says that postmortem apparition is not resurrection. See also the excellent and candid discussion in Allison, *Resurrecting Jesus*, 269–99.

19. Allison, *Resurrecting Jesus*, 278–82, with extensive documentation.

20. This is the sense in which Luke 24:37-39 is normally understood. For further discussion, see pp. 91-93 below.

21. For a translation of the story, see Ogden, *Magic, Witchcraft, and Ghosts*, 159–61. Ogden explains (161) that this should be considered an instance of a "revenant," i.e., the manifestation of a ghost that makes use of its former body. For a more detailed discussion of revenants in Greco-Roman literature, see Felton, *Haunted Greece and Rome*, 25–29.

22. Hans Dieter Betz, "Hero Worship and Christian Beliefs: Observations from the History of Religion on Philostratus's *Heroikos*," in *Philostratus's "Heroikos": Religion and Cultural Identity in the Third Century C.E.*, ed. E. B. Aitken and J. K. Berenson MacLean (SBLWGRW 6; Leiden: Brill, 2004), 25–47 (esp. 24–25).

23. Walter Burkert, *Greek Religion: Archaic and Classical*, trans. J. Raffan (Oxford: Basil Blackwell; Cambridge: Harvard University Press, 1985), 190–208.

24. W. K. C. Guthrie, *The Greeks and Their Gods* (Boston: Beacon, 1985), 220–21; Charles H. Talbert, "The Concept of Immortals in Mediterranean Antiquity," *JBL* 94 (1975): 419–36 (esp. 420–29).

25. Burkert, *Greek Religion*, 203.

26. The older consensus that the hero cult differed substantially from the cult of the gods in ancient Greece has undergone recent revision: see Gunnel Ekroth, *The Sacrificial Rituals of Greek Hero-Cults in the Archaic to the Early Hellenistic Periods* (Kernos Supplement 12; Liège: Centre international d'étude de la religion grecque antique, 2002); Ekroth, "Heroes and Hero-Cults," in *A Companion to Greek Religion*, ed. Daniel Ogden (Oxford: Blackwell, 2007), 100–114, esp. 106–8: "Rituals considered as typical for heroes, and as distinguishing them from the gods in general, must be considered as marginal features in hero-cults" (107). The failure of ancients to observe the distinction was already noted by A. D. Nock, "The Cult of Heroes," *HTR* 37 (1944): 141–74 (esp. 143–47).

27. Burkert, *Greek Religion*, 204–5.

28. For the authorship and date of this work, see *Flavius Philostratus: Heroikos*, ed. and trans. J. Berenson MacLean and E. Bradshaw Aitken (SBLWGRW 1; Atlanta: SBL, 2001), xlii–xlv.

29. Protesilaos can be hugged and kissed, tend the vines, exercise, etc. (*Her.* 11.2; 2.8; 11.4; 13.1-4); although he still shows a scar of his fatal wound, the wound itself was washed away together with his body (12.4). Betz thinks that "Philostratus apparently presupposes here a difference between a corporeal and incorporeal body" ("Hero Worship," 35n42). Philostratus prefers the verb *phainomai* for these appearances (e.g., *Her.* 2.11; 7.11; et al.), or the present passive of *horaō* (*Her.* 18.2), which parallels the aorist passive *ōphthē* (1 Cor. 15:5-8; Luke 24:34) except that the appearances of Protesilaos and the others are still continuing; for Paul the resurrection appearances are at an end (see 1 Cor. 15:8).

30. Jackson P. Hershbell, "Philostratus's *Heroikos* and Early Christianity: Heroes, Saints, and Martyrs," in Aitken and MacLean, *Philostratus's "Heroikos": Religion and Cultural Identity*, 169–79 (here, 174), citing Samson Eitrem, "Zu Philostrats *Heroikos*," *Symbolae Osloenses* 8 (1929): 1–56 (esp. 28–29). It should be noted that the terms *anabioō* and *anabiōsis* do not occur in the New Testament writings, for which *egeirō* and *anistēmi* (and their cognates) are the standard terms for "resurrection."

31. Betz, "Hero Worship," 44.

32. Howard C. Kee, *Miracle in the Early Christian World: A Study in Sociohistorical Method* (New Haven, Conn.: Yale University Press, 1983), 78 (for citation) and 78–83 (for the origins of Asklepios); see also Emma J. Edelstein and Ludwig Edelstein, *Asclepius: A Collection and Interpretation of the Testimonies* (Baltimore: Johns Hopkins University Press, 1945), 2:1–138.

33. Nancy Bookidis, "Religion in Corinth: 146 BCE to 100 CE," in *Urban Religion in Roman Corinth: Interdisciplinary Approaches*, ed. D. Schowalter and S. Friesen (HTS 53; Cambridge: Harvard University Press, 2005), 141–64 (here, 163); see also Mabel Lang, *Cure and Cult in Ancient Corinth: A Guide to the Asklepieion* (Princeton, N.J.: American School of Classical Studies at Athens, 1977).

34. *IG* 4.1, 121–22; Greek and English translation in Edelstein and Edelstein, *Asclepius*, 1.221–37, dated c. 4 BCE. No such table of cures was found in the Corinthian Asklepieion. Some of the Epidauros cures involved minor surgical procedures, and it appears from poppy decorations on an artifact from the Epidauros Asklepieion that *enkoimēsis* could have been induced narcotically: see Helen Askitopoulou et al., "Surgical Cures under Sleep Induction in the Asclepieion of Epidauros," *International Congress Series* 1242 (2002): 11–17.

35. One thing we cannot assume is that they thought the appearances Paul describes were like the appearances narrated in the conclusions of the canonical Gospels, which were not written yet.

36. Contrast Rev. 1:9-20, describing an apocalyptic vision that occurred after the seer "became in the spirit on the Lord's day" (v. 10).

37. Betz, "Hero Worship," 45; David Aune, "Heracles and Christ: Heracles Imagery in the Christology of the New Testament," in *Greeks, Romans, and Christians: Essays in Honor of Abraham J. Malherbe*, ed. D. Balch et al. (Minneapolis: Fortress Press, 1990), 3–19; Adela Yarbro Collins, *The Beginning of the Gospel: Probings of Mark in Context* (Minneapolis: Fortress Press, 1992), 138–48; Lawrence M. Wills, *The Quest of the Historical Gospel: Mark, John, and the Origins of the Gospel Genre* (London: Routledge, 1997), 23–50.

38. Aune, "Heracles and Christ," 19; see also Charles H. Talbert, *What Is a Gospel? The Genre of the Canonical Gospels* (Philadelphia: Fortress Press, 1977; repr., Macon, Ga: Mercer University Press, 1985).

39. Betz, "Hero Worship," 45.

40. Ibid., 46.

41. Ibid., 46–47; Zeller, "Erscheinungen Verstorbener," 14.

42. However, if we take the "revelation" mentioned in Gal. 1:16 as the same experience as that mentioned in 1 Cor. 15:8, then we would be justified in adding the Damascus area to the list (since Paul said that he "returned" there after going off to Arabia, Gal. 1:17).

43. Betz, "Hero Worship," 46; Helmut Koester, "On Heroes, Tombs, and Early Christianity: An Epilogue," in *Flavius Philostratus: Heroikos*, 257–64 (esp. 259–61). Koester notes, however, that once the tomb of Jesus was "discovered" in the fourth century, "fullfledged hero worship of Jesus" was possible (ibid., 263), but at the same time the hero cult was morphing into the cult of saints.

44. Zeller, "Erscheinungen Verstorbener," 14–15.

45. Ibid. On the divinity of such figures, see Talbert, "Concept of Immortals," 419–20; cf. David Aune, "The Problem of the Genre of the Gospels: A Critique of C. H. Talbert's *What Is a Gospel?*" in *Gospel Perspectives: Studies of History and Tradition in the Four Gospels*, ed. R. T. France and David Wenham (Sheffield: JSOT Press, 1980–86), 2:9–60 (esp. 12–13); Wills, *Quest of the Historical Gospel*, 227n35.

46. These similarities are discussed in detail in chapter 3 below.

47. Zeller, "Erscheinungen Verstorbener," 14–18.

48. See Gerhard Lohfink, *Die Himmelfahrt Jesu: Untersuchungen zu den Himmelfahrtsund Erhohungstexten bei Lukas* (SANT 26; Munich: Kösel, 1971), 32–34; John E. Alsup, *The Post-Resurrection Appearance Stories of the Gospel Tradition* (Calwer Theologische Monographien 5; Stuttgart: Calwer; London: SPCK, 1975), 224–26; Talbert, "Concept of Immortals," 423, 433–34; Wendy Cotter, "Greco-Roman Apotheosis Traditions and the Resurrection Appearances in Matthew," in *The Gospel of Matthew in Current Study: Studies in Memory of William G. Thompson, S.J.*, ed. David E. Aune (Grand Rapids: Eerdmans, 2001), 127–53, esp. 132–38.

49. Plutarch, *Rom.* 27.5; Dionysius of Halicarnassus considered the rumor that Romulus was murdered and his body parts scattered to be the more plausible version of the story (*Antiq. Rom.* 2.56.3).

50. As, e.g., in Acts 2:32-33; 5:30-31; Phil. 2:9.

51. Zeller, "Erscheinungen Verstorbener," 3.

52. On this point see Origen, *Cels.* 3.22ff.: to Celsus's claim that the appearances of the risen Jesus amount to nothing more than ghost stories, Origen counters with examples concerning heroes in the Greco-Roman tradition. It is uncertain, however, that we can conclude from this, as Dieter Zeller does, that epiphanies of heroes "had according to the people of antiquity a higher level of reality than the apparitions of ghosts of the dead" (Zeller, "Erscheinungen Verstorbener," 13).

53. Some texts, e.g., *3 (Hebrew) Enoch*, describe the (postmortem) transformation of human beings into angels. See the discussion in Kevin P. Sullivan, *Wrestling with Angels: A Study of the Relationship between Angels and Humans in Ancient Jewish Literature and the New Testament* (AGJU 55; Leiden: Brill, 2004), 85–141.

54. Cf. Michael E. Stone, "A Reconsideration of Apocalyptic Visions," *HTR* 96 (2003): 167–80, who argues for original visionary experiences behind *4 Ezra*.

55. For the "righteous one" in the Wisdom of Solomon as a type of "the righteous," see George W. E. Nickelsburg, *Resurrection, Immortality, and Eternal Life in Intertestamental Judaism and Early Christianity* (2nd ed.; HTS 56; Cambridge: Harvard University Press, 2006), 82. Interestingly, both Wisdom 4–5 and *1 Enoch* 71 use the idea of assumption to account for the exaltation of their protagonists (*1 Enoch* 70:1-2; 71:1-5; Wisd. 4:10-15). See Daniel A. Smith, "The 'Assumption' of the Righteous Dead in the Wisdom of Solomon and the Sayings Gospel Q," *SR* 29 (2000): 287–99.

56. James M. Robinson, "Jesus—From Easter to Valentinus (or to the Apostles' Creed)," *JBL* 101 (1982): 5–37; here, 10. The other, of course, is Paul's experience, mentioned (but with no description) in 1 Cor. 9:1; 15:8. Robinson's interest in this paper was in showing that the kind of "luminous" visualization of the resurrected Jesus found in Paul (Phil. 3:21; 1 Cor. 15:40, 43; 2 Cor. 3:17-18) and in Revelation was the original way of thinking about the risen Jesus, and that the developing Christian tradition downplayed and downgraded such visualizations because of their susceptibility to Gnostic interpretations.

57. John J. Collins, "The Heavenly Representative: The 'Son of Man' in the Similitudes of Enoch," in *Ideal Figures in Ancient Judaism: Profiles and Paradigms*, ed. John J. Collins and George W. E. Nickelsburg (SBLSCS 12; Missoula, Mont.: Scholars Press, 1980), 111–33; John J. Collins, *The Apocalyptic Imagination: An Introduction to Jewish Apocalyptic Literature* (2nd ed.; Grand Rapids: Eerdmans, 1998), 105–6 (on Daniel 7), 184–87 (on *1 Enoch*).

58. Mark 9:3 focuses on the glory and luminousness of Jesus, but Luke infers from Mark's narrative that "Moses and Elijah appeared in glory" (Luke 9:30-31). Both versions of the story use imagery from Exodus 24 LXX.

59. Adela Yarbro Collins, *Mark: A Commentary on the Gospel of Mark* (Hermeneia; Minneapolis: Fortress Press, 2007), 422, citing Josephus, *Ant.* 4.8.48 and 9.2.2. See further the discussion in Daniel A. Smith, *The Post-Mortem Vindication of Jesus in the Sayings Gospel Q* (LNTS 338; London and New York: T. & T. Clark, 2006), 74–77.

60. Thus Allison is correct to maintain that "we cannot assume that earlier Jewish Christians [such as those who formulated the pre-Pauline tradition in 1 Cor. 15:3-7?] shared Paul's rather sophisticated notion of a 'spiritual body'; and in any case the apostle nowhere discusses the nature of the appearances to himself or others. First Corinthians 15:3-8 says only that there were christophanies, not what their apparent origin in space was nor what Jesus looked like" (*Resurrecting Jesus*, 287).

61. See Collins, *Apocalyptic Imagination*, 2–9.

62. This is certainly true of Paul, at least (see 1 Cor. 15:20-23), and possibly of Matthew (see Matt. 27:52-53 and below, pp. 112-13). For the view that this connection originated with Paul (particularly because of his conviction that the end of the age, when the dead would be raised, was imminent), see Joost Holleman, *Resurrection and Parousia: A Traditio-historical Study of Paul's Eschatology in 1 Corinthians 15* (NovTSup 84; Leiden: Brill, 1996). Holleman argues that the belief in Jesus' resurrection originated as an instance of the belief in the resurrection of the martyr, according to which "righteous ones who die innocently for the sake of God's laws are vindicated by God who gives them a new life in heaven immediately after their deaths" (ibid., 155). The eschatological resurrection is something quite different according to Holleman.

63. Zeller, "Erscheinungen Verstorbener," 3.

64. See also Phil. 2:9-11, which uses exaltation language but not resurrection language.

65. "What really happened" is of course not directly accessible through our textual sources, but only the language used by the early followers of Jesus to express their beliefs about Jesus' ongoing postmortem existence.

66. E.g., Stephen J. Patterson argues that, given extant literary models for the vindication of the righteous, the only presupposition for a resurrection claim is that a righteous person died in faithfulness to a divine cause. See Patterson, *The God of Jesus: The Historical Jesus and the Search for Meaning* (Harrisburg, Pa.: Trinity Press International, 1998), 218–23; see also Patterson, *Beyond the Passion: Rethinking the Death and Life of Jesus* (Minneapolis: Fortress Press, 2004), 121.

67. See N. T. Wright, *The Resurrection of the Son of God* (Christian Origins and the Question of God 3; London: SPCK; Minneapolis: Fortress Press, 2003), 696: "The combination of empty tomb and appearances of the living Jesus forms a set of circumstances which is itself *both necessary and sufficient* for the rise of early Christian belief."

68. De Jonge, "Visionary Experience," 47 (emphasis in original).

69. Allison, *Resurrecting Jesus*, 321–22.

Chapter 2

1. See the discussion in Dale C. Allison, *Resurrecting Jesus: The Earliest Christian Tradition and Its Interpreters* (New York and London: T. & T. Clark, 2005), 229–30. Allison notes its similarity to standard Jewish confessional phrases, as in "I am the LORD your God, who brought you out of the land of Egypt" (Num. 15:41), citing Klaus Wengst, *Christologische Formeln und Lieder des Urchristentums* (Gütersloh: Mohn, 1972), 27–48.

2. It is disputed whether the Cephas mentioned by Paul in his letters is the Peter of the Gospels. See Bart D. Ehrman, "Cephas and Peter," *JBL* 109 (1990): 463–74; Dale C. Allison Jr., "Peter and Cephas: One and the Same," *JBL* 111 (1992): 489–95.

3. N. T. Wright, *The Resurrection of the Son of God* (Christian Origins and the Question of God 3; London: SPCK; Minneapolis: Fortress Press, 2003), 321.

4. Along similar lines, see the survey in Martin Hengel, "Das Begräbnis Jesu bei Paulus und die leibliche Auferstehung aus dem Grab," in *Auferstehung—Resurrection: The Fourth Durham-Tübingen Research Symposium*, ed. F. Avemarie and H. Lichtenberger (WUNT 1/135; Tübingen: Mohr Siebeck, 1999), 119–83, esp. 150–72. For a useful survey of different applications of resurrection language and ideas, see James H. Charlesworth, "Prolegomenous Reflections towards a Taxonomy of Resurrection Texts (1QH^a, *1En*, 4Q521, Paul, Luke, the Fourth Gospel, and Psalm 130)," in *The Changing Face of Judaism, Christianity, and Other Greco-Roman Religions in Antiquity*, ed. I. H. Henderson and G. S. Oegema (Studien zu den Jüdischen Schriften aus hellenistisch-römischer Zeit 2; Gütersloh: Gütersloher Verlagshaus, 2006), 237–64.

5. Willi Marxsen, *The Resurrection of Jesus of Nazareth* (London: SCM; Philadelphia: Fortress Press, 1970), 70; see also Adela Yarbro Collins, *The Beginning of the Gospel: Probings of Mark in Context* (Minneapolis: Fortress Press, 1992), 124–27.

6. For the view that Paul's "spiritual" approach to resurrection was the earliest formulation, which was later corrected to a more "tangible" or "material" understanding, see James M. Robinson, "Jesus—From Easter to Valentinus (or to the Apostles' Creed)," *JBL* 101 (1982): 5–37, esp. 10; Peter Carnley, *The Structure of Resurrection Belief* (Oxford: Clarendon, 1987), 58; A. J. M. Wedderburn, *Beyond Resurrection* (London: SCM; Peabody, Mass.: Hendrickson, 1999), 70–75. For a different developmental hypothesis, see James D. G. Dunn, *Jesus Remembered* (Christology in the Making 1; Grand Rapids: Eerdmans, 2003), 870–72, who proposes that Paul's view (which itself was "corrected" by later authors such as Luke) was a modification of the traditional understanding of resurrection "as a raising (restoration?) to a life just like the present (that is, physical) life but now beyond the reach of death" (ibid., 870). See also the earlier formulation of this argument in Dunn, *Jesus and the Spirit: A Study of the Religious and Charismatic Experience of Jesus and the First Christians as Reflected in the New Testament* (London: SCM, 1975), 116–17, 120–22.

7. Gerd Lüdemann, *The Resurrection of Jesus: History, Experience, Theology* (London: SCM; Minneapolis: Fortress Press, 1994), 121; see also Rudolf Bultmann, *The History of the Synoptic Tradition* (rev. ed.; Oxford: Basil Blackwell, 1963), 290. This line of argument was omitted from the second edition of Lüdemann's book: see *The Resurrection of Christ: A Historical Inquiry* (2nd ed.; Amherst, N.Y.: Prometheus, 2004), 87–88. For the view that Mark created the empty tomb story to combat (not to explain) the "apparition tradition," see John Dominic Crossan, "Empty Tomb and Absent Lord (Mark 16:1-8)," in *The Passion in Mark: Studies on Mark 14–16*, ed. Werner H. Kelber (Philadelphia: Fortress Press, 1976), 135–52, esp. 152.

8. See Dunn, *Jesus Remembered*, 840n62.

9. Burton Mack, *Rhetoric and the New Testament* (GBS; Minneapolis: Fortress Press, 1990), 56–59; so also W. Schrage, *Der erste Brief an die Korinther* (EKKNT 7; Düsseldorf: Benziger; Neukirchen-Vluyn: Neukirchener, 1991–2001), 4:17.

10. On the non-Pauline language of the formula, see Hans Conzelmann, *1 Corinthians: A Commentary on the First Epistle to the Corinthians* (Hermeneia; Philadelphia: Fortress Press, 1975), 252; Allison, *Resurrecting Jesus*, 234; and H. J. de Jonge, "Visionary Experience

and the Historical Origins of Christianity," in *Resurrection in the New Testament: Fest-schrift J. Lambrecht*, ed. R. Bieringer et al. (BETL 165; Leuven: Peeters, 2002), 35–53, who suggests that only vv. 3b-5a are traditional and that Paul was responsible for the rest as "welcome proof of the reality of Jesus' resurrection" (39). The original language (Aramaic or Greek) of the formula, once a topic of considerable debate, is entirely beside the point: see de Jonge, "Visionary Experience," 42–43, and Hengel, "Begräbnis Jesu," 125.

11. Though both Mark and Matthew call the inner circle of Jesus' disciples "apostles" (Mark 3:14; Matt. 10:2), an equation of "the apostles" with "the Twelve" (plus or minus Judas and his replacement) seems to derive from the author of Luke-Acts (see Acts 1:21-26). Paul himself does not make this equation (cf. Rom 16:7; 1 Cor. 9:1-7; 15:8-9; Gal. 1:15-17; et al.).

12. Reginald H. Fuller, *The Formation of the Resurrection Narratives* (New York: Macmillan, 1971), 13–30. Fuller argued (ibid., 13–14) that each of the clauses introduced by "that" (Gk., *hoti*) was originally an independent tradition, and that they were combined into a coherent whole for the first time by Paul. Fuller saw something similar happening in 1 Thess. 4:14-17 (three occurrences of *hoti*), where, however, only the first ("we believe *that* Jesus died and rose") seems to introduce traditional material.

13. Stephen J. Patterson, *The God of Jesus: The Historical Jesus and the Search for Meaning* (Harrisburg, Pa.: Trinity Press International, 1998), 216–18, 223.

14. Ibid., 217.

15. Ibid., 223. See also Ulrich Wilckens, "The Tradition-History of the Resurrection of Jesus," in *The Significance of the Message of the Resurrection for Faith in Jesus Christ*, ed. C. F. D. Moule (London: SCM, 1968), 51–76, esp. 59–60. Patterson notes, however, that the specific historical claims of early Christians to such transcendental experiences mean that one cannot simply account for the origin of such claims on purely form-critical grounds (that is, the need for legitimation giving rise to the claim that legitimates).

16. Patterson, *God of Jesus*, 216n7.

17. Ibid., 217.

18. William Lane Craig, "The Historicity of the Empty Tomb of Jesus," *NTS* 31 (1985): 39–67 (here, 40); along similar lines see also Wright, *Resurrection*, 321.

19. Hengel, "Begräbnis Jesu," 127–35.

20. Ibid., 132–33.

21. See Allison, *Resurrecting Jesus*, 231–32. In the Gospels, the most explicit correlation between the kerygmatic "raised on the third day" and the narrative discovery of the empty tomb on "the first day of the week" is found in Luke 24:7.

22. Hengel, "Begräbnis Jesu," 134.

23. Allison, *Resurrecting Jesus*, 232.

24. See Wilckens, "Tradition-History," 57–58, who says that "Paul obviously has no concrete knowledge about Jesus' grave, nor of the finding of the empty tomb" (58); see also Conzelmann, *1 Corinthians*, 255. However, Dunn suggests that "he was buried" in the original tradition referred to the empty tomb, so that Paul preserves a vestige of belief in "physical" resurrection even though he himself did not think along such lines (*Jesus Remembered*, 839–40 and 840n62); Hengel ("Begräbnis Jesu," 129–35) argues that Paul received from the original community (the "Urgemeinde") information about the burial of Jesus, the location of his grave, and the discovery of it empty on "the third day," and that Paul must have been in a position to answer questions about the declarations of the tradition he handed on to the Corinthians.

25. For the same logic, see Acts 13:30-31. See Wilckens, "Tradition-History," 58; Schrage, *Erste Brief*, 4.43; and the discussion on pp. 20-21 above.

26. See, e.g., Lüdemann, *Resurrection of Jesus*, 38: although he argues vv. 6-8 were not part of the original tradition, Lüdemann does think that the "formation" of all the appearances mentioned is to be dated between 30 and 33 CE.

27. Patterson suggests (tentatively) that the transfiguration was originally a story of a resurrection appearance to Peter, James, and John, and that Paul really has two different

men named James in view in Galatians: in Gal. 1:19 he refers to "James the Lord's brother," and in Gal. 2:9 he refers simply to James, the better-known James, who figures in the transfiguration story as one of the "pillars" of the Judean Jesus movement (Patterson, *God of Jesus*, 228–29 and n. 31).

28. This remains a puzzle. Dunn suggests that the experiences of figures like Peter and James were intensely personal and as such "were not (could not be) elaborated by elders and teachers because as stories they belonged first and foremost to the one(s) who witnessed the appearance" (*Jesus Remembered*, 863). But he argues this on the basis of the "very personal character" of the stories that *are* narrated in the Gospels, so that the question remains why certain "very personal" stories were narrated and others not. In any event, that a resurrection story featuring Peter in a prominent (named) role does not appear until the Johannine appendix (John 21) may be a sign of the relative conservatism of the overall appearance tradition.

Sometimes stories now found within the literary contexts of the Gospel accounts of Jesus' career are seen as good candidates for having originally been stories about the appearance of the risen Jesus to Peter and/or other disciples. The transfiguration (Mark 9:2-10 and parallels) is one popular candidate: Bultmann, *History of the Synoptic Tradition*, 259; Robinson, "Jesus—From Easter," 8–10; Patterson, *God of Jesus*, 228–29; cf. John E. Alsup, *The Post-Resurrection Appearance Stories of the Gospel Tradition* (Calwer Theologische Monographien 5; Stuttgart: Calwer; London; SPCK, 1975), 141–44. Many scholars think that an appearance story lies behind Luke 5:1-11 and John 21: Lüdemann, *Resurrection of Jesus*, 86–87, 168; Allison, *Resurrecting Jesus*, 257, who says it is "a good bet" that the underlying tradition recounted "the famous first postresurrection appearance to Peter." François Bovon, on the other hand, thinks that the Easter setting of John 21 is secondary: Bovon, *Luke 1: A Commentary on the Gospel of Luke 1:1—9:50* (Hermeneia; Minneapolis: Fortress Press, 2001), 167.

29. So, e.g., Hengel, "Begräbnis Jesu," 123–24; pace Lüdemann, *Resurrection of Jesus*, 35, 38, who argues that vv. 3b–5 are all Paul delivered to the Corinthians in his founding visit, so that vv. 6–8 become additional testimony in favor of the resurrection of Jesus. In Lüdemann's view, Paul at this point would not have left out any appearances that could have bolstered his point, so Lüdemann concludes that the appearances to the five hundred, to James and all the apostles, and to himself are the only ones of which he was aware besides those to Peter and the Twelve.

30. So, e.g., François Bovon, "Le Privilège Pascal de Marie-Madeleine," *NTS* 30 (1984): 50–62 (here, 52); Bovon notes several reasons why the appearance to Mary may have been omitted in this setting, including the tendency of ancient patriarchal cultures to denigrate women as possible witnesses; so also Wright, *Resurrection*, 326. See, however, the objections rightly raised by Carolyn Osiek against the "unexamined scholarly commonplace in Christian exegesis" that women could not serve as legal witnesses in ancient Judaism: Osiek, "The Women at the Tomb: What Are They Doing There?" *Ex Auditu* 9 (1993): 97–107, esp. 103–4.

31. Luke 24:33-34 and (possibly) Mark 16:7 suggest as much, though these references probably do not derive from independent tradition, but are the respective authors' editorial nods to the resurrection tradition in 1 Cor. 15:5. For further discussion, see below pp. 72, 80 on Mark, and pp. 79-80 on Luke.

32. Ann Graham Brock, *Mary Magdalene, the First Apostle: The Struggle for Authority* (HTS 51; Cambridge: Harvard University Press, 2003), 157–58.

33. Dunn, *Jesus Remembered*, 859, 861.

34. Wilckens, "Tradition-History," 59.

35. Wilckens refers to 1 Cor. 9:1; 15:8-10; Gal. 1:12, 15 (ibid.).

36. Allison, *Resurrecting Jesus*, 237.

37. First Corinthians 9 is really a detour from the topic at hand as an illustration: Paul would rather defer his "rights" as an apostle than use them in situations that might be problematic (9:12b-18); similarly, believers ought to defer their "right" to follow their

conscience on the question of "idol meat" when it might mean another believer could be led back into old patterns of cultic worship (10:23-30).

38. See Raymond F. Collins, *First Corinthians* (SP 7; Collegeville, Minn.: Liturgical, 1999), 537: "last of all" (Gk., *eschaton de pantōn*) here can mean simply "last in this series" or "least of all," as Paul explicitly states in 1 Cor. 15:9.

39. Similarly, when Stephen (long after the ascension) sees "the Son of Humankind standing at the right hand of God" (Acts 7:56), this is depicted as a vision of Jesus already exalted in heaven. Luke's narrations of the call of Paul seem to presume (Acts 9:17, 27; 26:16), but not to make the point emphatically by direct narration, that Paul saw *Jesus* as he himself claimed (1 Cor. 9:1; 15:8): see Wright, *Resurrection*, 389–90.

40. George W. E. Nickelsburg, *Resurrection, Immortality, and Eternal Life in Intertestamental Judaism and Early Christianity* (2nd ed.; HTS 56; Cambridge: Harvard University Press, 2006), 5–6.

41. Ibid., 5–6, 211–18.

42. On the Sadducees, see Mark 12:18-27 and parallels; Josephus, *Ant.* 18.1.4; Anthony J. Saldarini, *Pharisees, Scribes and Sadducees in Palestinian Society: A Sociological Approach* (Wilmington, Del.: Michael Glazier, 1988), 304. Wright states that "by the time of Jesus most Jews believed in resurrection" (*Resurrection*, 205).

43. C. K. Barrett, *A Commentary on the First Epistle to the Corinthians* (2nd ed.; BNTC; London: A. & C. Black, 1992), 109; see also Collins, *First Corinthians*, 187; Anthony C. Thiselton, *The First Epistle to the Corinthians: A Commentary on the Greek Text* (NIGTC; Grand Rapids: Eerdmans, 2000), 357–59.

44. Fuller, *Formation*, 30; see also Anthony C. Thiselton, "Realized Eschatology at Corinth," *NTS* 24 (1978): 510–26 (here, 524): "The question was not whether the Corinthians believed their resurrection was past, but whether they placed such weight on the experience of transformation in the past and present that when they thought about resurrection the centre of gravity of their thinking was no longer in the future."

45. Dale B. Martin, *The Corinthian Body* (New Haven, Conn.: Yale University Press, 1995), 105.

46. Ibid., 107, 108–9: according to Martin, one popular epitaph read, "I was not, I am not, I care not," with many variations and even abbreviations (*n.f.n.s.n.c.* for *non fui, non sum, non curo*).

47. Ibid., 105–7.

48. Nickelsburg, *Resurrection, Immortality, and Eternal Life*, 121.

49. For more on this, see pp. 91-96 below.

50. See, e.g., Martin, *Corinthian Body*, 115; Collins, *Beginning of the Gospel*, 126.

51. Wright, *Resurrection*, 110–13 (with literature); John Dominic Crossan, "The Resurrection of Jesus in Its Jewish Context," *Neot* 37 (2003): 29–58; Nickelsburg, *Resurrection, Immortality, and Eternal Life*, 38. John J. Collins, noting that Daniel 12:2 "does not address the form of the resurrection" but thinks "the wise in Daniel are not said to become stars but to shine like them. The Jewish apocalypticists did not simply borrow the Hellenistic belief [of astral immortality]. Nonetheless, Hellenistic influence is likely to have shaped the way in which they developed their native tradition." Collins, *Daniel: A Commentary on the Book of Daniel* (Hermeneia; Minneapolis: Fortress Press, 1993), 392, 394.

52. "And then the Lord will heal his servants. They will rise and see great peace. . . . Their bones will rest in the earth and their spirits will be very happy." Citations from *Jubilees* are taken from *The Book of Jubilees*, ed. and trans. James C. VanderKam (2 vols.; CSCO 510–11, Scriptores Aethiopici 87–88; Leuven: Peeters, 1989). For the date of *Jubilees*, see ibid., 2:v–vi.

53. Citations from *1 Enoch* are taken from George W. E. Nickelsburg and James C. VanderKam, *1 Enoch: A New Translation* (Minneapolis: Fortress Press, 2004).

54. Robinson, "Jesus—From Easter," 10–13, cites several of the Nag Hammadi Gnostic writings as describing the risen Jesus as luminous but noncorporeal.

55. Wright, *Resurrection*, 30–31; citation from Wright, "Resurrecting Old Arguments: Responding to Four Essays," *JSHJ* 3 (2005): 209–31 (here, 214).

56. Wright, *Resurrection*, 204, citing Paul Avis, "The Resurrection of Jesus: Asking the Right Questions," in *The Resurrection of Jesus Christ*, ed. Paul Avis (London: Darton Longman & Todd, 1993), 1–22 (here, 6).

57. *Transphysical* is a neologism coined by Wright, *Resurrection*, 477–78: the term "merely, but I hope usefully, puts a label on the demonstrable fact that the early Christians envisaged a body which was still robustly physical but also significantly different from the present one." See also Wright, "Resurrecting Old Arguments," 210.

58. Nickelsburg, *Resurrection, Immortality, and Eternal Life*, 4–5, mentioning Wright, *Resurrection*, specifically. Nickelsburg states that he "began with an openness to diversity and was suspicious of whether a belief in bodily resurrection was present if it was not either explicit or intertextually implied."

59. Robinson, "Jesus—From Easter," 7–17, argues that the primary visualization of the risen Jesus was "luminous"; see also Collins, *Beginning of the Gospel*, 125–26.

60. Martin, *Corinthian Body*, 108–23.

61. See Crossan, "Resurrection of Jesus," 31–34: Crossan explains that belief in the supernatural simply was a given in the ancient world: whereas since the Enlightenment a nonbeliever in Jesus' resurrection plays the "impossibility" card, and the believer the "uniqueness" card, neither would play in the ancient world.

62. Martin, *Corinthian Body*, 113.

63. Cited by Martin, *Corinthian Body*, 113–14, but given here in my translation. For this fourfold classification of rational beings, see also Plutarch, *Def. orac.* 415B, where he credits Hesiod for this.

64. See Jeffrey R. Asher, *Polarity and Change in 1 Corinthians 15: A Study of Metaphysics, Rhetoric, and Resurrection* (HUT 42; Tübingen: Mohr Siebeck, 2000), who argues that the problem is one of "polarity": "Members of the Corinthian community, who were probably conversant with a number of philosophical ideas, challenged the resurrection on philosophical grounds, namely, that it is absurd to think that a terrestrial body can be raised to the celestial realm. These two cosmic realms and the bodies that inhabit them are completely incompatible with one another" (92).

65. Cicero, fragment from *Resp.* 3, cited by Augustine, *Civ.* 22.4; cited by Hengel, "Begräbnis Jesu," 144.

66. Martin, *Corinthian Body*, 112–17. See also Plato, *Phaed.* 81, where Socrates explains that the souls of those who care too much for bodily matters in this life remain tinged with corporeality after death, and so can be dragged back into the visible world (so that they appear lurking around tombs).

67. Martin, *Corinthian Body*, 116.

68. See Asher, *Polarity and Change*, 100–106.

69. Martin, *Corinthian Body*, 113.

70. In this connection Dieter Zeller suggests that the Corinthians who did not believe in "the resurrection of the dead" may have understood Jesus' resurrection through analogy with the apotheosis and epiphanies of various heroes, as discussed in the previous chapter, as "an exceptional event, a personal exaltation" that had no ramifications for their own resurrection: see Zeller, "New Testament Christology in Its Hellenistic Reception," *NTS* 46 (2001): 312–33 (here, 318). This, however, does not explain the lengths to which Paul goes to explain the physiology of resurrection bodies in 1 Corinthians 15.

71. See Wendy Cotter, "Greco-Roman Apotheosis Traditions and the Resurrection Appearances in Matthew," in *The Gospel of Matthew in Current Study: Studies in Memory of William G. Thompson, S.J.*, ed. David Aune (Grand Rapids: Eerdmans, 2001), 127–53 (here, 147); Daniel Boyarin, *A Radical Jew: Paul and the Politics of Identity* (Berkeley: University of California Press, 1994), 59–61, on Philo and Paul on body. Philo's understanding of Moses' apotheosis is consistent with his Platonic understanding of the body as "prison" of the soul (see Philo, *Migr.* 9).

72. The final assumption of Enoch is not described in such precise terms in *2 Enoch* 67–68.

73. This takes v. 50a as synonymous with v. 50b, referring to the bodily constitution of human beings living or dead, and not (as Jeremias and others have argued) contrasting living human beings with the dead. See John Gillman, "Transformation in 1 Cor. 15,50-53," *ETL* 58 (1982): 309–33; Asher, *Polarity and Change*, 151–55; cf. Joachim Jeremias, "Flesh and Blood Cannot Inherit the Kingdom of God (1 Cor. XV.50)," *NTS* 2 (1955–56): 151–59, and more recently Andy Johnson, "On Removing a Trump Card: Flesh and Blood and the Reign of God," *BBR* 13 (2003): 175–92.

74. See Boyarin, *Radical Jew*, 57–85; James D. G. Dunn, *The Theology of Paul the Apostle* (Grand Rapids: Eerdmans, 1998), 62–73.

75. Dunn, *Theology of Paul*, 72.

76. E.g., Marxsen, *Resurrection of Jesus*, 70; Collins, *Beginning of the Gospel*, 124–27.

77. In using the language of "tent" for the physical body, Paul uses a similar expression as Wisd. 9:15, which, however, is more Platonic than Paul seems to be; Wisd. 9:15 is suggestive of Plato, *Phaed.* 81c. See T. Francis Glasson, "2 Corinthians v. 1-10 versus Platonism," *SJT* 43 (1990): 143–55, esp. 148. Note, however, that Paul longs not for the unclothed state of a soul freed from the body, but for the clothed state of a transformed bodily existence, which he calls here an eternal house not made with hands.

78. John Gillman, "A Thematic Comparison: 1 Cor 15:50-57 and 2 Cor 5:1-5," *JBL* 107 (1988): 439–54, esp. 448–54; cf. Collins, *Beginning of the Gospel*, 126–27, who argues that the tent, the earthly body, "is to be folded up and destroyed," i.e., left to decay in the tomb. In the context, however, the possibility that the earthly tent should be "destroyed" (2 Cor. 5:1) should be read as the continuing risk to the apostle that he should meet his death (see 4:7-12)—not as the eventual decomposition of his body in the tomb.

79. See Margaret E. Thrall, *A Critical and Exegetical Commentary on the Second Epistle to the Corinthians* (ICC; Edinburgh: T. & T. Clark, 1994, 2000), 1:371–73, 391–92; Jan Lambrecht, *Second Corinthians* (SP 8; Collegeville, Minn.: Liturgical, 1999), 82–85.

80. Hengel, "Begräbnis Jesu," 127–35.

81. "The Jesus-tradition, narrated (and always interpreted) under the influence of the Passion and Resurrection accounts, which indeed had these as its climax, was not only a necessary ingredient of the early Christian proclamation, but its very foundation" (ibid., 127).

82. BDAG, ad loc.; see also George D. Kilpatrick, "Galatians 1:18 ΙΣΤΟΡΗΣΑΙ ΚΗΦΑΝ," in *New Testament Essays: Studies in Memory of Thomas Walter Manson 1893-1958*, ed. A. J. B. Higgins (Manchester: Manchester University Press, 1959), 144–49; William R. Farmer, "Peter and Paul, and the Tradition concerning 'the Lord's Supper' in 1 Cor. 11:23-26," *CTR* 2 (1987): 119–40, esp. 122–30.

83. Collins, *Mark*, 799–800.

84. These possibilities for reading the end of Mark are explored in greater detail in chap. 5, but see, e.g., Donald Juel, *A Master of Surprise: Mark Interpreted* (Minneapolis: Fortress Press, 1994), 107–21.

85. Material from the reconstructed Sayings Gospel Q is cited (according to scholarly convention) according to its Lukan chapter and verse designations, without implying that Luke preserves either the wording or order of the Q document more faithfully than Matthew. Thus "Q 13:34-35" designates the Q text that was the source for Matt. 23:37-39 and Luke 13:34-35.

86. As suggested by Bultmann, *History of the Synoptic Tradition*, 290; Lüdemann, *Resurrection of Jesus*, 121.

87. Alan F. Segal, *Life after Death: A History of the Afterlife in the Religions of the West* (New York: Doubleday, 2004), 461.

88. See Dan. 2:31-45; 7:2-8, 9-14.

89. "God put all things in subjection under his feet," in Paul's citation of Ps. 8:6 LXX (1 Cor. 15:27).

90. See R. R. R. Smith, "The Imperial Reliefs from the Sebasteion at Aphrodisias," *JRS* 77 (1987): 88–138, esp. plates XIV–XVII, showing Claudius and Britannia, and Nero and Armenia.

Chapter 3

1. G. W. Bowersock, *Fiction as History: Nero to Julian* (Berkeley: University of California Press, 1994), 99.

2. N. T. Wright, *The Resurrection of the Son of God* (Christian Origins and the Question of God 3; London: SPCK; Minneapolis: Fortress Press, 2003), 71.

3. Sjef van Tilborg and Patrick Chatelion Counet, *Jesus' Appearances and Disappearances in Luke 24* (Biblical Interpretation Series 45; Leiden: Brill, 2000), 194.

4. Wright, *Resurrection*, 72, citing Bowersock, *Fiction as History*, 121–43. But G. P. Goold dates the novel (mainly on the basis of its non-Atticizing language) to between 25 BCE and 50 CE, a range that would make early Christian influence problematic. See Goold's introductory remarks in G. P. Goold, ed., *Chariton, Callirhoe* (LCL; Cambridge: Harvard University Press, 1995), 1–2; see also the discussion in Paul Fullmer, *Resurrection in Mark's Literary-Historical Perspective* (LNTS 360; London and New York: T. & T. Clark, 2007), 73–83, who on the grounds of the novel's "historiographical content" and a reference to the work by the satirist Persius (d. 62 CE) dates it to the reign of Nero, 58–64, or earlier.

5. Unless otherwise noted, dates for early Christian texts and authors are taken from F. L. Cross and E. A. Livingstone, eds., *The Oxford Dictionary of the Christian Church* (3rd ed.; Oxford: Oxford University Press, 2005).

6. It should be noted that here we are distinguishing "assumption" from temporary heavenly journeys, whether depicted realistically or as dreams or visionary experiences. For this distinction, see Gerhard Lohfink, *Die Himmelfahrt Jesu: Untersuchungen zu den Himmelfahrts- und Erhöhungstexten bei Lukas* (SANT 26; Munich: Kösel, 1971), 32–41.

7. When she revives in the tomb as the robbers are breaking in, Callirhoe herself thinks her soul is about to be carried off to the underworld: "Where is this noise coming from? Is this what usually happens to the dead—some divine being (*tis daimōn*) is coming for pitiful me?" (*Chaer.* 1.9.3).

8. Euripides, *Alcestis*, and Plato, *Symp.* 179b-c. See the discussion in Stanley E. Porter, "Resurrection, the Greeks, and the New Testament," in *Resurrection*, ed. S. E. Porter et al. (JSNTSup 186; Sheffield: Sheffield Academic Press, 1999), 52–81, esp. 77–80.

9. See D. Felton, *Haunted Greece and Rome: Ghost Stories from Classical Antiquity* (Austin: University of Texas Press, 1999), 25–29.

10. See further the discussion below, pp. 46-49.

11. See Günter Haufe, "Entrückung und eschatologische Funktion im Spätjudentum," *ZRGG* 13 (1961): 105–13, who first demonstrated the connection; see also A. W. Zwiep, *The Ascension of the Messiah in Lukan Christology* (NovTSup 87; Leiden: Brill, 1997), 76–79.

12. Lohfink, *Himmelfahrt Jesu*, 73.

13. James VanderKam notes that, according to the Hebrew of Gen. 5:22-24, Enoch walked with *ha-'elohim* (with the definite article: i.e., the angels) and then was not because *'elohim* (no definite article: i.e., God) took him. See James C. VanderKam, *Enoch: A Man for All Generations* (Studies and Personalities of the Old Testament; Columbia: University of South Carolina Press, 1995), 13–14.

14. See the complete discussions in Lohfink, *Himmelfahrt Jesu*, 57–59, and Zwiep, *Ascension*, 58–60.

15. "Adapa," *ANET* 101–2.

16. "Epic of Gilgamesh," 11.191–96, *ANET* 95.

17. "The Deluge," *ll.* 254–58, *ANET* 44.

18. The Greek can be found in Felix Jacoby, ed., *Die Fragmente der griechischen Historiker* (3 vols. in 15; Leiden: Brill, 1954–69), 3C.1:380.

19. Haufe, "Entrückung und eschatologische Funktion," 105.

20. Ibid., 110. A longer list of nine or ten individuals is found in the Talmudic tractate Derekh Eretz Zuta 1.18: Enoch, Elijah, the Messiah, Eliezer (servant of Abraham), Hiram (king of Tyre), Ebed-melech the Cushite, Jabez (son of R. Judah ha Nasi), Bithiah (daughter of Pharaoh), Serach (daughter of Asher), and, according to some, R. Joshua ben Levi;

this list is cited by Lohfink, *Himmelfahrt Jesu*, 72n247, and Zwiep, *Ascension*, 76. For most of these, no story or tradition survives about their assumption nor about any eschatological role.

21. See Adela Yarbro Collins, *Mark: A Commentary on the Gospel of Mark* (Hermeneia; Minneapolis: Fortress Press, 2007), 429–30, for discussion and literature.

22. George W. E. Nickelsburg and James C. VanderKam, *1 Enoch: A New Translation* (Minneapolis: Fortress Press, 2004), 6.

23. Ibid., 4.

24. James C. VanderKam, "Righteous One, Messiah, Chosen One, and Son of Man in 1 Enoch 37–71," in *The Messiah: Developments in Earliest Judaism and Christianity*, ed. J. Charlesworth (Minneapolis: Fortress Press, 1982), 145–68 (esp. 185), thinks that "the identification of Enoch with the son of man in 71:14 is not inconsistent with the rest of the composition." John J. Collins thinks chap. 71 is redactional: see Collins, *The Apocalyptic Imagination: An Introduction to Jewish Apocalyptic Literature* (2nd ed.; Grand Rapids: Eerdmans, 1998), 187–91.

25. Translation from James C. VanderKam, ed. and trans., *The Book of Jubilees* (2 vols.; CSCO 510–11, Scriptores Aethiopici 87–88; Leuven: Peeters, 1989).

26. From the Syriac; translation from NRSV, in text-critical footnote to 2 Esdr. 14:48. According to Michael E. Stone, *Fourth Ezra: A Commentary* (Hermeneia; Minneapolis: Fortress Press, 1990), 442, "The textual evidence is adequate to show that the conclusion of the chapter is part of the original text."

27. For discussion, see Lohfink, *Himmelfahrt Jesu*, 60–61.

28. Both Lohfink, *Himmelfahrt Jesu*, 183, and Zwiep, *Ascension*, 72, see this pattern repeated in the Lukan ascension chronology.

29. See the discussions in Lohfink, *Himmelfahrt Jesu*, 61–69; Zwiep, *Ascension*, 64–71; Daniel A. Smith, *The Post-Mortem Vindication of Jesus in the Sayings Gospel Q* (LNTS 338; London and New York: T. & T. Clark, 2006), 75–77.

30. See Lohfink, *Himmelfahrt Jesu*, 41–49, 72–74.

31. See, e.g., Dion. Hal., *Ant. rom.* 2.56; 2.63; Plutarch, *Rom.* 27–28; *Num.* 2.1-3.

32. See, e.g., Apollodorus, *Bibl.* 2.7.7, and Diodorus Siculus, *Bibl. Hist.* 4.38.3–49.1 (Herakles disappears from the funeral pyre, although other accounts, e.g., Ovid, *Metam.* 9.268-71, describe him shedding his mortal body); Dion. Hal., *Ant. rom.* 1.64.4 (Aeneas's body disappears from the battlefield); Plutarch, *Rom.* 28.6; Pausanias, *Descr.* 9.16.7; and Antoninus Liberalis, *Metam.* 33.3-4 (Alkmene's body disappears from the bier). A contrary example is found in Phlegon of Tralles (*Mirab.* 1), the story mentioned in chap. 1 about Philinnion, the young woman who returns from the dead to have sex with the visiting stranger (see above, p. 14). In that story a careful search of the tomb is undertaken, but only after the dead Philinnion has been discovered with the visitor by the maid. Here the townspeople conclude that the body (for she dies again after being discovered by her parents) must be burned and that appropriate honors and ceremonies be performed to appropriate chthonic deities—but not that Philinnion had been taken away by the gods (for she had not really "disappeared," but only had arisen from her tomb to carry out some unfinished business).

33. For Herakles, see Diodorus Siculus, *Bibl. Hist.* 4.38.3—49.1, and H. A. Shapiro, "*Hêrôs Theos*: The Death and Apotheosis of Herakles," *CW* 77 (1983): 7–18; see also the discussions of human beings made immortal in Charles Talbert, "The Concept of Immortals in Mediterranean Antiquity," *JBL* 94 (1975): 419–36, esp. 421–22, and in Arthur Stanley Pease, "Some Aspects of Invisibility," *HSCP* 53 (1942): 1–36, esp. 12–21, for a long list. For Aristeas, see Herodotus 4.14, with the discussion of J. D. P. Bolton, *Aristeas of Proconnesus* (Oxford: Clarendon, 1962), 119–20, 125–30. For Romulus, see Plutarch, *Rom.* 27–28, with Lohfink, *Himmelfahrt Jesu*, 47–48 and n. 123. Romulus is an example of a figure whose status (human or semidivine) during his earthly career is ambiguous because of his assumption.

34. Josephus, *Ant.* 4.8.48.

35. See Gunnel Ekroth, "Heroes and Hero-Cults," in *A Companion to Greek Religion*, ed. Daniel Ogden (Oxford: Blackwell, 2007), 100–114, esp. 100–103.

36. See Gregory Nagy, *The Best of the Achaeans: Concepts of the Hero in Archaic Greek Poetry* (Baltimore: Johns Hopkins University Press, 1979), 189–210; Lawrence M. Wills, *The Quest of the Historical Gospel: Mark, John, and the Origins of the Gospel Genre* (London and New York: Routledge, 1997), 48–49; cf. Peter G. Bolt, "Mark 16:1-8: The Empty Tomb of a Hero?" *TynBul* 47 (1996): 27–37.

37. Wills, *Quest of the Historical Gospel*, 49.

38. Ibid.

39. Arrian, *Anab.* 7.27.3.

40. Origen, *Cels.* 2.55-56; see also Gregory Nazianzen, *Orat.* 4.59.

41. Greek text in R. Pfeiffer, ed., *Callimachus* (Oxford: Oxford University Press, 1949), 1:218–22 (fr. 228). Shapiro also notes that material evidence (largely from vase paintings) for belief in the assumption of Herakles is later than material evidence of cult practices that venerated him not as a hero but as a god (Shapiro, "*Hêrôs Theos*," 15–17).

42. Or the poem's assumption language was intended to legitimate the cult of Arsinoë after her death: see Günther Hölbl, *A History of the Ptolemaic Empire* (London and New York: Routledge, 2001), 101–4.

43. Translation from Ralph Marcus, ed. and trans., *Philo: Questions and Answers on Genesis* (LCL; Cambridge: Harvard University Press, 1953).

44. Plato, *Phaed.* 80d-81a: the soul goes to the divine realm unless contaminated by corporeality.

45. As in, e.g., Herodian 4.2; Dio Cassius 75.4. See Lohfink, *Himmelfahrt Jesu*, 49–50; E. Bickermann, "Die römische Kaiserapotheose," *AR* 27 (1929): 1–31; Simon Price, "From Noble Funerals to Divine Cult: The Consecration of Roman Emperors," in *Rituals of Royalty: Power and Ceremonial in Traditional Societies*, ed. S. Price and D. Cannadine (Cambridge: Cambridge University Press, 1987), 56–105, esp. 76.

46. Zwiep, *Ascension*, 77.

47. See Dale C. Allison Jr., *Testament of Abraham* (CEJL; Berlin and New York: de Gruyter, 2003), 28–31: "The upshot is that the texts in our hands are Christian, and any use of them to add to our knowledge about ancient Judaism must proceed with caution" (ibid., 31).

48. A much more restrained version of the story is told in *T. Abr.* (Shorter Recension) 14:6-7.

49. For Adam, see *L.A.E.* 32:4, 37:3-6; for Moses, Clement of Alexandria, *Strom.* 6.132.2; and for Job, *T. Job* 52:1-12. For further Christian and Jewish parallels, see Allison, *Testament of Abraham*, 398.

50. See Daniel A. Smith, "The 'Assumption' of the Righteous Dead in the Wisdom of Solomon and the Sayings Gospel Q," *SR* 29 (2000): 287–99.

51. *CIG* 3, 6227; Anne-Marie Vérilhac, *Paides aōroi: Poésie funéraire* (2 vols.; Pragmateiai tēs Akadēmias Athēnōn 41; Athēnai: Grapheion Dēmosieumatōn tēs Akadēmias Athēnōn, 1978–82), no. 148.

52. *IG* 5.1, 1186; Vérilhac, *Paides aōroi*, no. 62.

53. Pfeiffer, *Callimachus*, fr. 228.7-9.

54. Earlier in the book, Job says that Satan has killed his children (*T. Job* 18:1), so this use of assumption language in *T. Job* 39–40 implies not that God rescued them from death, but rather that God took them bodily into heaven after their death.

55. Zwiep, *Ascension*, 77.

56. See above, p. 182 nn. 27-28.

57. So Pease, "Some Aspects of Invisibility," 27–28; Haufe, "Entrückung und eschatologische Funktion," 108–9; Collins, *Mark*, 422.

58. These two figures may be identified with Moses and Elijah since they have authority to turn the waters to blood, strike the earth with a plague, destroy with fire, and shut the heavens (Rev. 11:5-6).

59. Translation from Felix Scheidweiler, "The Gospel of Nicodemus, Acts of Pilate, and Christ's Descent into Hell," in *New Testament Apocrypha*, ed. Wilhelm Schneemelcher, trans. R. McL. Wilson (rev. ed.; 2 vols.; Cambridge: James Clarke & Co; Louisville:

Westminster John Knox, 1991–92), 1:501–36. This episode is not found in the Latin version. Evidently the "holy fathers" who meet Enoch and Elijah are the saints raised from the dead at the death of Jesus (Matt. 27:52-53); after their testimony to the Jews is completed, they vanish (*Acts Pil.* 27).

60. See Smith, *Post-Mortem Vindication,* 89–92.

61. Lohfink, *Himmelfahrt Jesu,* 74–78; see the summary of Lohfink's form-critical conclusions in Zwiep, *Ascension,* 22.

62. See Zwiep, *Ascension,* 25, 34; Zwiep himself thinks that Lohfink overvalued the significance of the Greco-Roman stories (ibid., 115–17).

63. Zwiep, *Ascension,* 25–26.

64. Lohfink notes that the sequence death-resurrection-assumption is unusual (*Himmelfahrt Jesu,* 59).

65. As noted (pp. 5-6; p. 176 n. 13), the longer ending of Mark (Ps.-Mark 16:9-20) is a late scribal addition and does not come from the original author. Thus Ps.-Mark 16:19 represents an early Christian reading of the Lukan ascension story.

66. Zwiep, *Ascension,* 147–63.

67. Ibid., 175–85, 197.

68. The term *spiritual* is used here guardedly, given the discussion in the previous chapter, but because Luke and Paul both focus on how the resurrection body is "spiritual" (Paul) or is not (Luke). For more on this, see below pp. 93-96.

69. Ronald F. Hock, ed. and trans., *The Infancy Gospels of James and Thomas* (Scholars Bible 2; Santa Rosa, Calif.: Polebridge, 1995), 11–12.

70. Ibid., 77.

71. Translation from Hugo Duensing and Aurelio de Santos Otero, "Apocalypse of Paul," in Schneemelcher, *New Testament Apocrypha,* 2:712–48.

72. Stephen J. Shoemaker, "Death and the Maiden: The Early History of the Dormition and Assumption Apocrypha," *SVTQ* 50 (2006): 59–97, esp. 65. For translations of select sources and bibliography, see J. K. Elliott, *The Apocryphal New Testament* (Oxford: Clarendon, 1993), 689–723; Brian E. Daley, trans., *On the Dormition of Mary: Early Patristic Homilies* (Crestwood, N.Y.: St. Vladimir's Seminary Press, 1998), esp. 1–45; and especially Stephen J. Shoemaker, *Ancient Traditions of the Virgin Mary's Dormition and Assumption* (Oxford Early Christian Studies; Oxford: Oxford University Press, 2002). For further discussion of how the Marian dormition and assumption traditions made use of motifs from the Gospel empty tomb stories, see below, pp. 145-46.

73. Translation from Daley, *Dormition,* 74. Theoteknos is unknown apart from his homily "An Encomium on the Assumption of the Holy Mother of God." Daley estimates that he was roughly contemporary with John of Thessalonica (ibid., 12–13).

74. For further sources and discussion, see Daniel A. Smith, "The Post-Mortem Vindication of Jesus in the Sayings Gospel Q," Ph.D. diss., University of St. Michael's College, Toronto (Ottawa: National Library of Canada/Bibliothèque nationale du Canada, 2001), 162–72.

75. Shoemaker, *Ancient Traditions,* 290–350 (Appendix A, "The Ethiopic *Liber Requiei*").

76. See, however, Acts 2:31 (citing Ps. 15:10 LXX); but here the bodily nature of the resurrection is at issue, not the rescue of Jesus' mortal body from decay (as seems to be the case in the later traditions about Mary). For further instances of postmortem disappearance in early Christian sources, see the discussion in Smith, *Post-Mortem Vindication,* 89–92.

Chapter 4

1. My translations of Q are based on the reconstructed Greek text of J. M. Robinson, P. Hoffmann, and J. S. Kloppenborg, eds., *The Critical Edition of Q* (Hermeneia Supplements; Minneapolis: Fortress Press; Leuven: Leuven University Press/Peeters, 2000). According to scholarly convention, material from Q is cited according to its chapter and verse location in Luke: thus "Q 13:34-35" designates the material from Q that was the source for Matt. 23:37-39 and Luke 13:34-35.

2. A good basic introduction to the Synoptic Problem is Christopher M. Tuckett, "Synoptic Problem," *ABD* 6:263–70. Accessible introductions to Q (basic insights about its reconstruction, contents, composition, and significance to Christian origins, together with a translation of Q) can be found in James M. Robinson, *Jesus: According to the Earliest Witness* (Minneapolis: Fortress Press, 2007), 235–55; and in John S. Kloppenborg, *Q, the Earliest Gospel: An Introduction to the Original Stories and Sayings of Jesus* (Louisville: Westminster John Knox, 2008). On Q as a document, see also Kloppenborg, "Variation in the Reproduction of the Double Tradition and an Oral Q," *ETL* 83 (2007): 53–80.

3. Some of this debate revolves around questions about the validity of arguments for the existence of Q as part of the solution to the Synoptic Problem: see, e.g., Mark S. Goodacre, *The Case against Q: Studies in Markan Priority and the Synoptic Problem* (Harrisburg, Pa.: Trinity Press International, 2002), and John S. Kloppenborg, "On Dispensing with Q? Goodacre on the Relation of Luke to Matthew," *NTS* 49 (2003): 210–36. Among those who accept the Q hypothesis as part of the solution to the Synoptic Problem, there is debate as to the validity of viewing Q as evidence of a distinctive moment in the development of the Jesus traditions (or movements). For more on this, see below, pp. 68-70.

4. Kloppenborg, *Q, the Earliest Gospel*, 60–61.

5. John S. Kloppenborg, *Excavating Q: The History and Setting of the Sayings Gospel* (Edinburgh: T. & T. Clark; Minneapolis: Fortress Press, 2000), 154.

6. Ibid., 154–63.

7. Migako Sato, *Q und Prophetie: Studien zur Gattungs- und Traditionsgeschichte der Quelle Q* (WUNT 2/29; Tübingen: Mohr Siebeck, 1988); summarized and evaluated briefly by Kloppenborg, *Excavating Q*, 140–43.

8. See the recent discussions in John S. Kloppenborg, "Sagesse et prophétie dans l'évangile des paroles Q," in *La source des paroles de Jésus (Q): Aux origines de christianisme*, ed. Andreas Dett-wiler and Daniel Marguerat (MdB 62; Geneva: Labor et Fides, 2008), 73–98; and Migako Sato, "Le document Q à la croisée de la prophétie et de la sagesse," in *La source des paroles*, ed. Dettwiler and Marguerat, 99–122.

9. Q 4:1-13 narrates the temptations of Jesus, and Q 7:1-9 tells a story about a healing that situates Jesus and the following sayings in Capernaum.

10. E.g., Q 7:18-19, 22-28, which uses the narrative device of a question sent from John the Baptist through his disciples, and Jesus' reply sent back to him.

11. Mark 10:45 par. Matt. 20:28; Matt. 12:40; Luke 13:31-33.

12. See, e.g., Burton L. Mack, *The Lost Gospel: The Book of Q and Christian Origins* (San Francisco: Harper, 1993), 4–5.

13. Dieter Zeller, "Entrückung zur Ankunft als Menschensohn (Lk 13,34f.; 11,29f.)," in *À Cause de l'Évangile: Études sur les Synoptiques et les Actes offertes au P. Jacques Dupont, O.S.B. à l'occasion de son 70e anniversaire* (LD 123; Paris: Saint-André/Cerf, 1985), 513–30; Kloppenborg, *Excavating Q*, 377–79; see also Daniel A. Smith, *The Post-Mortem Vindication of Jesus in the Sayings Gospel Q* (LNTS 338; London and New York: T. & T. Clark, 2006).

14. See W. D. Davies and Dale C. Allison Jr., *The Gospel according to Saint Matthew* (3 vols.; ICC; Edinburgh: T. & T. Clark, 1988–97), 3:323; Ulrich Luz, *Matthew: A Commentary* (3 vols.; Hermeneia; Minneapolis: Fortress Press, 2001–07), 3:162–64.

15. Zeller, "Entrückung," 515–19.

16. For more on this point, see C. S. Rodd, "The End of the Theology of Q?" *ExpT* 113 (2001): 5–12; Christopher M. Tuckett, "The Search for a Theology of Q: A Dead End?"

ExpT 113 (2002): 291–94; Paul Foster, "In Defence of the Study of Q," *ExpT* 113 (2002): 295–300; Rodd, "The Theology of Q Yet Again: A Reply to the Responses of Christopher Tuckett and Paul Foster," *ExpT* 114 (2002): 80–85.

17. Though an advocate of the Two Document Hypothesis, N. T. Wright is a vocal Q skeptic. See N. T. Wright, "Resurrection in Q?" in *Christology, Controversy and Community: New Testament Essays in Honour of David R. Catchpole*, ed. D. G. Horrell and C. M. Tuckett (NovTSup 99; Leiden: Brill, 2000), 85–97, esp. 86–88, 97.

18. E.g., Christopher Tuckett is reluctant to isolate compositional strata in Q: Christopher M. Tuckett, *Q and the History of Early Christianity* (Edinburgh: T. & T. Clark, 1996), 75–82; Tuckett, "Search for a Theology of Q," 294n14.

19. Tuckett notes this against points raised by Rodd ("End of the Theology of Q") on the basis of his trial "reconstruction" of "Mark" from Matthew and Luke (Tuckett, "Search for a Theology of Q," 292).

20. See above, chap. 2.

21. For differing pictures of the theology of Q, see above all Tuckett, *Q*, and Kloppenborg, *Excavating Q*, 329–444.

22. Kloppenborg, *Excavating Q*, 371.

23. See Tuckett, "Search for a Theology of Q," 292: "Claims about the possible significance of a 'Son of Man Christology,' a Wisdom Christology, wisdom ideas, the theme of judgment set within a deuteronomistic view of history, are all thought (by some) to characterize Q's 'theology' because of the material that *is* there by common consent."

24. Frans Neirynck, "Q: From Source to Gospel," *ETL* 71 (1995): 421–30; Kloppenborg, *Excavating Q*, 398–408.

25. See especially Arland J. Hultgren, *The Rise of Normative Christianity* (Minneapolis: Fortress Press, 2004), 31–41; Kloppenborg, *Excavating Q*, 353–408; and Larry W. Hurtado, *Lord Jesus Christ: Devotion to Jesus in Earliest Christianity* (Grand Rapids: Eerdmans, 2003), 217–44 (largely in dialogue with Kloppenborg).

26. It was really not until Adolf Harnack's work with Q that it came be studied in its own right: Adolf von Harnack, *The Sayings of Jesus: The Second Source of St. Matthew and St. Luke* (New York: Putnam; London: Williams & Norgate, 1908).

27. T. W. Manson, *The Sayings of Jesus* (London: SCM, 1937), 16: "There is no Passion-story because none is required, Q being a book of instruction for people who are already Christians and know the story of the Cross by heart."

28. Heinz Eduard Tödt, *The Son of Man in the Synoptic Tradition*, trans. Dorothea M. Barton (London: SCM, 1965), 268: "There are two spheres of tradition, distinguished both by their concepts and by their history. The centre of the one sphere is the passion kerygma; the centre of the other is the intention to take up again the teaching of what Jesus had taught. The Q material belongs to the second sphere."

29. Ibid., 250–53; for criticism, see Arland D. Jacobson, *The First Gospel: An Introduction to Q* (Sonoma, Calif.: Polebridge, 1992), 28–30; see also Kloppenborg, "'Easter Faith' and the Sayings Gospel Q," *Semeia* 49 (1990): 71–99, esp. 82–84; Smith, *Post-Mortem Vindication*, 10–11.

30. James M. Robinson, "Jesus—From Easter to Valentinus (or to the Apostles' Creed)," *JBL* 101 (1982): 5–37, esp. 24: "Easter is then not a point in time in Q, but rather permeates Q as the reality of Jesus' word being valid now."

31. For the view that the apocalyptic Son of Man Christology in Q is oriented to a belief in Jesus' resurrection, see Paul Hoffmann, *Studien zur Theologie der Logienquelle* (3rd ed.; NTAbh 8; Münster: Aschendorff, 1982), 141: "Within the conceptual framework of the Q group, the Easter event is of primary significance: Jesus has been given all power and has been exalted as the Son of Man."

32. See David Seeley, "Jesus' Death in Q," *NTS* 38 (1992): 222–34, esp. 226.

33. There is a similar saying in Mark 8:34, but Matthew and Luke both preserve the Q version and the Markan version of the saying (Q version, Matt. 10:38 par. Luke 14:27; Markan, Matt. 16:24 par. Luke 9:23).

34. See Leif Vaage, *Galilean Upstarts: Jesus' First Followers according to Q* (Valley Forge, Pa.: Trinity Press International, 1994), 94–95, who hesitates to infer a knowledge of Jesus' death from this text and cites Epictetus, *Diatr.* 2.2.20, as an alternative influence. Vaage is right that the saying implies rejection for following a certain kind of lifestyle. But that Jesus is in view here is, in my opinion, unavoidable.

35. David Seeley, "Blessings and Boundaries: Interpretations of Jesus' Death in Q," *Semeia* 55 (1991): 131–46, esp. 131.

36. Q 11:48 is difficult to reconstruct, since the Matthean and Lukan versions differ considerably. See Robinson et al., *Critical Edition of Q*, 282–83.

37. Incidentally, this is the only actual reference to the murder of a prophet in the Hebrew Scriptures.

38. Tuckett, *Q*, 170.

39. Dale C. Allison Jr., *The Intertextual Jesus: Scripture in Q* (Harrisburg, Pa.: Trinity Press International, 2000), 40–41. Allison notes the proximity of this text to the one declaring that anyone hung on a tree is accursed (Deut. 21:22-23).

40. Seeley, "Blessings and Boundaries," 131. Seeley tries to demonstrate a gradual development in Q's understanding of the death of Jesus from the "mimetic" approach of Q 14:27 to the moderately deuteronomistic view of Q 13:34-35.

41. So Hoffmann, *Studien*, 188–89; see also Hoffmann, "The Redaction of Q and the Son of Man: A Preliminary Sketch," in *The Gospel behind the Gospels: Current Studies on Q*, ed. R. A. Piper (NovTSup 75; Leiden and New York: Brill, 1995), 159–98, esp. 192.

42. E.g., James M. Robinson, "The Sequence of Q: The Lament over Jerusalem," in *Von Jesus zum Christus: Christologische Studien. Festgabe für Paul Hoffmann zum 65. Geburtstag*, ed. U. Busse and R. Hoppe (BZNW 93; Berlin and New York: de Gruyter, 1998), 225–60.

43. See Hurtado, *Lord Jesus Christ*, 226–33, 239–44, mainly in response to Kloppenborg, *Excavating Q*, 369–74.

44. For discussion, see Kloppenborg, *Q, the Earliest Gospel*, 111–20, who notes how closely James's allusions to the Jesus tradition cohere with the contents of Q (ibid., 112) and suggests that "Q was not composed to be a *source* but a *resource*—a resource for moral exhortation and for the inculcation of an alternative *ethos*, called 'the kingdom of God'" (ibid., 120).

45. See, e.g., Tödt, *Son of Man*, 231; Norman Perrin, "The Son of Man in the Synoptic Tradition," *BR* 13 (1968): 3–25.

46. See Kloppenborg, *Excavating Q*, 374–76.

47. Wright, "Resurrection in Q?" 90; Hurtado, *Lord Jesus Christ*, 242–43. Wright ("Resurrection in Q?" 90–91) sees other indicators of an eschatological resurrection belief in Q: raising children for Abraham from stones (Q 3:8); trusting God for clothing, when the brilliantly clothed grass is burned in the oven (12:28); and eschatological or heavenly promises of feasting (13:28–30), treasure (12:33), or authority (22:28-30). Taken individually, most of these need not imply resurrection, and Wright imports the Pauline notion of bodily incorruptibility into Q 12:33 (ibid., 91 and n. 18).

48. Robinson et al., *Critical Edition of Q*, 248–51.

49. Wright, "Resurrection in Q?" 94.

50. See Douglas K. Stuart, *Hosea–Jonah* (WBC 31; Waco, Tex.: Word, 1987), 489; Jack M. Sasson, *Jonah: A New Translation with Introduction, Commentary, and Interpretation* (AB 24B; New York: Doubleday, 1990), 234–35; T. A. Perry, "Cain's Sin in Gen. 4:1-7: Oracular Ambiguity and How to Avoid It," *Proof* 25 (2005): 258–75, esp. 264. I wish to thank Philip Baldwin for drawing this reading to my attention.

51. Sasson, *Jonah*, 5.

52. See Simon Chow, *The Sign of Jonah Reconsidered: A Study of Its Meaning in the Gospel Traditions* (ConBNT 27; Stockholm: Almqvist & Wiksell, 1995).

53. Zeller, "Entrückung," 525.

54. Ibid., 524–25.

55. One other possible allusion to Jesus' resurrection is in the sequel to the Cross saying. According to the reconstructed order of Q, immediately following Q 14:27 was Q 17:33, which reads: "The one who finds his life will lose it, and the one who loses his life will find it" (Robinson et al., *Critical Edition of Q*, 456–57). After the Cross saying, this promise of "finding" one's life speaks of a reversal of death—again, with Jesus as the pattern. Resurrection, however, is not necessarily in view (pace Wright, "Resurrection in Q?" 91, on the grounds of the other references to resurrection he saw in Q, but which in my opinion strain the evidence).

56. Gerhard Lohfink, *Die Himmelfahrt Jesu: Untersuchungen zu den Himmelfahrts- und Erhohungstexten bei Lukas* (SANT 26; Munich: Kösel, 1971), 58.

57. Ibid., 59–61, 74.

58. The sequel line implies that the house whose abandonment is pronounced in Q 13:35a will be the location in which the speaker will be blessed again (v. 35b), although the Greek "you" in Ps. 117:26b LXX is plural.

59. Zeller, "Entrückung," 516–17.

60. "I will not die, but I will live / and I will recount in full the works of the Lord. The Lord has disciplined me / but he has not handed me over to death. . . . I will confess you, that you have heeded me / and have become a salvation for me. A stone which the builders rejected / this has become the head of the corner; this has come about through the Lord's action / and it is a marvel in our eyes" (Ps. 117:17-18, 21-23 LXX).

61. Zeller thinks Jesus was not specifically mentioned in Q 13:34 because Q intended to bypass the problem of Jesus' death and affirm his assumption along the lines of an escape from death. See Zeller, "Entrückung," 517–18; also in personal communication with me dated November 3, 2001.

62. The relevant portion reads: "For he will honor the devout upon the throne of eternal royalty, freeing prisoners, giving sight to the blind, straightening out the twisted. . . . He will heal the badly wounded and will make the dead live, he will proclaim good news to the meek, give lavishly to the needy, lead the exiled and enrich the hungry" (4Q521 fr. 2.2.7–8, 12–13). Translation from Florentino García Martínez, *The Dead Sea Scrolls in English: The Qumran Texts in English* (2nd ed.; Leiden: Brill; Grand Rapids: Eerdmans, 1996), 394–95.

63. John J. Collins, *The Scepter and the Star: The Messiahs of the Dead Sea Scrolls and Other Ancient Literature* (ABRL; New York: Doubleday, 1995), 121–22.

64. Kloppenborg, *Excavating Q*, 123–24. For Elijah bringing repentance, see Mal. 4:5-6 and Sir. 48:10, and for the "coming messenger" bringing judgment, see Mal. 3:1-2 (with Q 13:35).

65. See Allison, *Intertextual Jesus*, 142–45; Kloppenborg, *Q, the Earliest Gospel*, 50; cf. Robinson et al., *Critical Edition of Q*, 156–57.

66. Allison, *Intertextual Jesus*, 143.

67. See Daniel A. Smith, "Revisiting the Empty Tomb: The Post-Mortem Vindication of Jesus in Mark and Q," *NovT* 45 (2003): 123–37, esp. 126; Smith, *Post-Mortem Vindication*, 123–30.

68. Heinz Schürmann, "Observations on the Son of Man Title in the Speech Source," in *The Shape of Q: Signal Essays on the Sayings Gospel*, ed. John S. Kloppenborg (Minneapolis: Fortress Press, 1994), 74–97, esp. 87–88.

69. It is interesting that the author of Luke intensifies the idea of "not seeing" in Q 17:23 by adding Luke 17:22 (not in Q): "Then he said to the disciples: 'Days are coming when you will desire to see one of the days of the Son of Man, and you will not see (Gk., *kai ouk opsesthe*).'"

70. See *4 Ezra* 14:8-9, 13 and the conclusion to *4 Ezra* 14 in the non-Latin versions; see also *2 Baruch* 76. For further discussion, see above, p. 46.

71. Another example is the Tabitha of Acts 9, who appears in the Coptic *Apocalypse of Elijah* alongside Enoch and Elijah as the third witness against the Antichrist (*Apoc. El. [C]* 4:1-6; cf. Rev. 11:3-13), and who is likewise credited with an assumption in a later Coptic

Enoch apocryphon text. See Birger A. Pearson, "The Pierpont Morgan Fragments of a Coptic Enoch Apocryphon," in *Studies on the Testament of Abraham*, ed. G. Nickelsburg (Septuagint and Cognate Studies 6; Missoula, Mont.: Scholars, 1976), 227–83, esp. 235, 242, 271.

72. See, e.g., Tödt, *Son of Man*, 268; Hoffmann, *Studien*, 142; Perrin, "Son of Man." On Perrin and others taking his view, see Kloppenborg, *Excavating Q*, 376–77.

73. Kloppenborg, *Excavating Q*, 376–77 and nn. 29–30; see also Kloppenborg, "Easter Faith," 84.

74. For discussion, see above, pp. 47-49.

75. As suggested by E. Bickermann, "Das leere Grab," *ZNW* 23 (1924): 281–92, esp. 290–92; Georg Bertram, "Die Himmelfahrt Jesu vom Kreuz aus und der Glaube an seine Auferstehung," in *Festgabe für Adolf Deissmann zum 60. Geburtstag*, ed. K. L. Schmidt (Tübingen: Mohr Siebeck, 1927), 187–217 (see the brief discussion in Zwiep, *Ascension*, 7); Dieter Georgi, "Der vorpaulinische Hymnus Phil 2,6-11," in *Zeit und Geschichte: Dankesgabe an Rudolf Bultmann zum 80. Geburtstag*, ed. E. Dinkler (Tübingen: Mohr Siebeck, 1964), 263–93, esp. 292. Kloppenborg implies this as well, I think: "The only text [in Q] that directly concerns vindication invokes a death-assumption-judgment scenario, not the death-resurrection pattern that *was to become common in Christian thinking after Paul* (Kloppenborg, *Excavating Q*, 378–79, emphasis added).

76. Arguing that the story originated with Mark are John Dominic Crossan, "Empty Tomb and Absent Lord (Mark 16:1-8)," in *The Passion in Mark: Studies on Mark 14–16*, ed. W. Kelber (Philadelphia: Fortress Press, 1976), 135–52, esp. 145–49; Adela Yarbro Collins, *The Beginning of the Gospel: Probings of Mark in Context* (Minneapolis: Fortress Press, 1992), 119–48, and *Mark: A Commentary* (Hermeneia; Minneapolis: Fortress Press, 2007), 781–82. Most recently Roger David Aus has suggested that Mark combined two different views of the end of Moses (first, that his body was translated; second, that he died and was buried but was spiritually exalted by God) in his new midrashic narrative about the end of Jesus: see Roger David Aus, *The Death, Burial, and Resurrection of Jesus, and the Death, Burial, and Translation of Moses in Judaic Tradition* (Studies in Judaism; Lanham, Md.: University Press of America, 2008). The following argue for a pre-Markan source: Rudolf Bultmann, *The History of the Synoptic Tradition* (rev. ed.; Oxford: Basil Blackwell, 1963), 285–86; Ludger Schenke, *Auferstehungsverkündigung und leeres Grab: eine traditionsgeschichtliche Untersuchung* (SBS 33; Stuttgart: Katholisches Bibelwerk, 1968), 53–55; Helmut Merklein, "Mk 16,1-8 als Epilog des Markusevangeliums," in *The Synoptic Gospels: Source Criticism and the New Literary Criticism*, ed. C. Focant (BETL 110; Leuven: Peeters, 1993), 209–38, esp. 226–33; Gerd Lüdemann, *The Resurrection of Jesus: History, Experience, Theology* (London: SCM; Minneapolis: Fortress Press, 1994), 111–18.

77. Bickermann, "Das leere Grab."

78. Martin Dibelius, *From Tradition to Gospel*, trans. B. L. Woolf (London: Ivor Nicholson, 1934), 139–40; Reginald H. Fuller, *The Formation of the Resurrection Narratives* (New York: Macmillan, 1971), 53; Robert H. Stein, "A Short Note on Mark XIV.28 and XVI.7," *NTS* 20 (1974): 445–52.

79. Ibid., 289–91. See also Paul Hoffmann, "Auferstehung Jesu Christi (Neues Testament)," *TRE* 4 (1979): 478–513, esp. 499, and Lüdemann, *Resurrection of Jesus*, 119–21, who cites Bickermann with general approval but without agreeing with the "sharp distinction" Bickermann drew between assumption and resurrection (ibid., 120).

80. Bultmann, *History of the Synoptic Tradition*, 287.

81. Lüdemann, *Resurrection of Jesus*, 121.

82. Ibid., 46.

83. Ibid., 121.

84. See the review of scholarship on this position in Frans Neirynck, "Les femmes au tombeau: Étude de la rédaction matthéenne (Matt. xviii.1-10)," *NTS* 15 (1968): 168–90, esp. 247–51.

85. For a discussion of some chronological problems, see Hurtado, *Lord Jesus Christ*, 229–32.

86. "Making Difference" is the title of Kloppenborg's chapter on the distinctiveness of Q and its importance to reconstructing Christian origins (*Excavating Q*, 353–408).

87. Hurtado, *Lord Jesus Christ*, 236.

88. Ibid., 237. Interestingly, the one reference to the resurrection in Hebrews uses language suggestive of assumption: "who brought up (*ho anagagōn*) from the dead the great shepherd of the sheep, our Lord Jesus . . ." (Heb 13:20). Yet Hurtado seems to overstate the case (in order to diminish the distinctiveness of the "death-ascent/assumption-future judgment" pattern) when he writes that "Hebrews is dominated throughout by a (redemptive) death-assumption/exaltation emphasis" (ibid.), since aside from Heb. 13:20 nothing suggests "assumption" per se.

89. A. W. Zwiep, *The Ascension of the Messiah in Lukan Christology* (NovTSup 87; Leiden: Brill, 1997), 34–35.

90. See above, pp. 50-51, and Zwiep, *Ascension*, 175–85, 192.

91. See Gerhard Lohfink, "Der Ablauf der Osterereignisse und die Anfänge der Urgemeinde," *TQ* 160 (1980): 162–76. As mentioned above (p. 4), according to Lohfink there were three distinct theological frameworks that early Christians could use to express their convictions about the postmortem Jesus: first, the one who had been humiliated in suffering and death was now exalted (as in Isaiah 52–53); second, an extraordinary individual had been taken away by God (as with Enoch and Elijah); and third, the eschatological resurrection had begun (ibid., 168–69).

92. For resurrection in Phil. 2:6-11, see, e.g., Ralph P. Martin, *A Hymn of Christ: Philippians 2:5-11 in Recent Interpretation and in the Setting of Early Christian Worship* (3rd ed.; Downers Grove, Ill.: InterVarsity, 1997), 239; for assumption, see Georgi, "Vorpaulinische Hymnus," 292. Phil. 2:6-11 could also imply postmortem vindication or exaltation along the lines of the assumption of the soul.

93. See Peter Oakes, "Re-mapping the Universe: Paul and the Emperor in 1 Thessalonians and Philippians," *JSNT* 27 (2005): 301–22.

94. Hurtado, *Lord Jesus Christ*, 237.

95. Hurtado misses the point when he sets out to show that "the expectation of resurrection is implicit in Q, which means that vindication by resurrection was not an unknown or unfavored category" (*Lord Jesus Christ*, 242). The point is that Q shows no evidence of resurrection applied individually to Jesus as the mode of his postmortem vindication or as the means by which his teachings are validated, despite being a known and favored category of corporate vindication.

96. Here note the linguistic similarity but theological difference between Q 11:50 ("the blood of all the prophets that has been poured out [*to haima pantōn tōn prophētōn to ekkechumenon*] from the foundation of the world will be required from this generation") and Mark 14:24 ("this is my blood of the covenant which is poured out [*to ekchunnomenon*] for many"). While both seem to allude to Isa. 53:12 LXX, the Q saying has in view corporate suffering and vindication, but the latter has in view individualized (Christologized) suffering with a kerygmatic focus ("for many" seems to echo the pre-Pauline language associated with the death of Jesus as in, e.g., Rom. 5:8).

97. See, e.g., Hans Conzelmann, *The Theology of St. Luke*, trans. G. Buswell (New York: Harper & Row, 1960), 201.

98. Recently, Melanie Johnson-Debaufre has asked, "Does Q assert and defend [Jesus'] unique and crucial—even, 'eschatological'—identity?": Johnson-Debaufre, *Jesus among Her Children: Q, Eschatology, and the Construction of Christian Origins* (HTS 55; Cambridge: Harvard University Press, 2005), 8. Johnson-Debaufre finds good warrant for more corporate readings of pivotal Q sayings (e.g., Q 11:19-20) but does not deal directly with the Q sayings for which the identity and authority of Jesus are clearly central issues (e.g., Q 4:1-13; 10:21-22; 13:34-35; etc.) and which validate, in my opinion, the view that these issues were indeed a significant part of Q's purposes and rhetorical interests.

Chapter 5

1. Verses 19b-20 are Mark's secondary addition to the original controversy story: see Rudolf Bultmann, *The History of the Synoptic Tradition* (rev. ed.; Oxford: Basil Blackwell, 1963), 92; Adela Yarbro Collins, *Mark: A Commentary on the Gospel of Mark* (Hermeneia; Minneapolis: Fortress Press, 2007), 199.

2. Joel Marcus, *Mark: A New Translation with Introduction and Commentary* (2 vols.; AB 27-27A; New York: Doubleday, 2000; New Haven, Conn.: Yale University Press, 2009), 1:237; see also Collins, *Mark*, 199, who thinks the intertext with Isaiah 62 indicates that Jesus is God's "chief agent" who "mediates the presence of God in the last days."

3. See Veronika E. Grimm, *From Feasting to Fasting, the Evolution of a Sin: Attitudes to Food in Late Antiquity* (London and New York: Routledge, 1996), 14–33.

4. Marcus, *Mark*, 1:237.

5. "He became well pleasing to God, and was beloved by him, and while living among sinners, he *was taken up*; he *was snatched away* so that evil would not alter his understanding, or deceit lead his soul astray" (Wisd. 4:10-11).

6. See Bruce M. Metzger, *A Textual Commentary on the Greek New Testament* (2nd ed.; Stuttgart: Deutsche Bibelgesellschaft / United Bible Societies, 1994), 102–7; also Collins, *Mark*, 780–81, 802–18; Marcus, *Mark*, 2:1088–96.

7. For a fuller discussion of these alternative endings, see pp. 133-35 below.

8. Sometimes scholars suggest, while granting that the text-critically suspect additional endings are secondary, that Mark must have originally had an ending that narrated an appearance in Galilee, such as the one found in Matt. 28:16-20. Robert H. Gundry, *Mark: A Commentary on His Apology for the Cross* (Grand Rapids: Eerdmans, 1993), 1021, proposes Matt. 28:9-10, 16-20; and Luke 24:9b-12 as raw materials for reconstructing the lost Markan ending (this would place the risen Jesus at the tomb, Peter at the tomb, and a resurrection appearance in Galilee all in the earliest Gospel). See also N. T. Wright, *The Resurrection of the Son of God* (Christian Origins and the Question of God 3; London: SPCK; Minneapolis: Fortress Press, 2003), 619–24, who suggests something along the lines of either Matt. 28:9-20 or the longer ending of Ps.-Mark 16:9-20 (ibid., 624). However, it must also be noted that the early Christians who copied and used manuscripts such as the fourth-century Codex Sinaiticus (whose copy of Mark ended at v. 8) must have read Mark as complete without another ending appended. (To view Codex Sinaiticus online, visit www.codexsinaiticus.org.)

9. Many assumption stories narrate not only the discovery of the disappearance, but the assumption itself; this Mark 16 (like its source narrative) does not do. As Gerhard Lohfink observed, such assumption narratives are typically told from the perspective of earth-bound observers: Lohfink, *Die Himmelfahrt Jesu: Untersuchungen zu den Himmelfahrts- und Erhohungstexten bei Lukas* (SANT 26; Munich: Kösel, 1971), 38–39. This was not possible in instances where the body disappeared from inside a tomb.

10. Bultmann, *History of the Synoptic Tradition*, 285; Reginald H. Fuller, *The Formation of the Resurrection Narratives* (New York: Macmillan, 1971), 53; Robert H. Stein, "A Short Note on Mark XIV.28 and XVI.7," *NTS* 20 (1974): 445–52, esp. 445; Andrew T. Lincoln, "The Promise and the Failure: Mark 16:7," *JBL* 108 (1989): 283–300, esp. 296–97; Pheme Perkins, *Resurrection: New Testament Witness and Contemporary Reflection* (Garden City, N.Y.: Doubleday, 1984), 116, 120–21; Gerd Lüdemann, *The Resurrection of Jesus: History, Experience, Theology* (London: SCM; Minneapolis: Fortress Press, 1994), 113.

11. Fuller, *Formation*, 53.

12. Perkins, *Resurrection*, 115–24; Lüdemann, *Resurrection of Jesus*, 115. Lüdemann's more recent book argues that Mark 16:1-8 is not based on a traditional story: cf. Gerd Lüdemann, *The Resurrection of Christ: A Historical Inquiry* (2nd ed.; Amherst, N.Y.: Prometheus, 2004), 84–87. See also Helmut Merklein, "Mk 16,1-8 als Epilog des Markusevangeliums," in *The Synoptic Gospels: Source Criticism and the New Literary Criticism*, ed. C. Focant (BETL 110; Leuven: Peeters, 1993), 209–38, esp. 226–31: Merklein reconstructs a pre-Markan narrative that describes only the discovery of the open tomb, not the women's entrance into it nor their encounter with the figure in the tomb. Merklein admits that the

story on its own could not have been an independent unit but must have been the original conclusion of the burial story, Mark 15:42-47 (ibid., 229).

13. See, e.g., Marcus, *Mark*, 1:63.

14. David Rhoads, Joanna Dewey, and Donald Michie, *Mark as Story: An Introduction to the Narrative of a Gospel* (2nd ed.; Minneapolis: Fortress Press, 1999), 118–20; Francis J. Moloney, *Mark: Storyteller, Interpreter, Evangelist* (Peabody, Mass.: Hendrickson, 2004), 76.

15. M. Eugene Boring, *Mark: A Commentary* (NTL; Louisville: Westminster John Knox, 2006), 231.

16. Ibid., 233.

17. Ibid., 247. See also C. Clifton Black, "The Face Is Familiar—I Just Can't Place It," in *The Ending of Mark and the Ends of God: Essays in Memory of Donald Harrisville Juel*, ed. Beverley Roberts Gaventa and Patrick D. Miller (Louisville: Westminster John Knox, 2005), 33–49, esp. 35–36, where Black gives six reasons why "Jesus' baptism, transfiguration, and death in Mark beg joint consideration as mutually interpretive" (35).

18. The term "Son of God" (Gk., *ho huios tou theou*) had a wide range of associations and meanings in the worlds of Mark and his readers. In the Jewish tradition the term was applied to the Israelite king (in a mythic but adoptive sense: see, e.g., 2 Sam. 7:12-16; Ps. 2:7-9), but also the people of Israel (e.g., Exod. 4:22; *Jub.* 1:24-25) and thus to ordinary people of extraordinary wisdom or piety (e.g., Wisd. 5:5; Matt. 5:9). The term would also have reminded readers familiar with the Greco-Roman literary traditions of various heroic figures who were (biologically, so to speak) the sons of divine figures such as Zeus (e.g., Herakles or Asklepios), but also of Roman emperors who claimed that title for themselves (beginning with Octavian/Augustus). The ideas of "preexistence" and "incarnation" sometimes associated with "Son of God" in later Christian trinitarian thought are not part of either associative range, however. For a full discussion of the ideas and associations the term would have evoked for Mark's readers, see Adela Yarbro Collins, "Mark and His Readers: The Son of God among Jews," *HTR* 92 (1999): 393–408; Collins, "Mark and His Readers: The Son of God among Greeks and Romans," *HTR* 93 (2000): 85–100. Moloney distinguishes between the various Jewish usages and connotations as "background" to Mark's usage, and Greco-Roman usages and connotations as "foreground" (that is, how non-Jewish readers might hear the term): Moloney, *Mark*, 137.

19. Seeing is also crucial in epiphanies that lie outside the emplotted story time of the Gospel: the risen Jesus' being seen again by the disciples in Galilee (Mark 16:7); and beyond that, his being seen when he comes as the Son of Man (13:26; 14:62).

20. John Paul Heil, *The Transfiguration of Jesus: Narrative Meaning and Function of Mark 9:2-8, Matt. 17:1-8 and Luke 9:28-36* (AnBib 144; Rome: Editrice Pontificio Istituto Biblico, 2000), 38 (with literature, 39n9).

21. Heil classifies Mark 1:9-11 and Matt. 3:16-17 as interpretive visions, since these accounts describe a private visionary experience of Jesus; Luke 3:21-22 he calls an epiphany because Luke stresses the reality of the dove's descent and because the voice is addressed to those present (ibid., 40).

22. Marcus, *Mark*, 1:165. Isa. 63:19b LXX uses *anoigō* (open), where Mark's description is more akin to Isa. 64:1 MT, which uses the Hebrew verb *qr'* (tear).

23. Ibid., 1:158; Collins; *Mark*, 148–51.

24. According to Collins, Hellenistic readers of Mark may have noted similarities between Mark's depiction of the Spirit descending like a dove and Homeric depictions of gods descending to earth: "Members of the audience familiar with Greek mythology would understand v. 10 to mean that the earthly Jesus, from the time of his baptism, was a divine being walking the earth" (Collins, *Mark*, 149).

25. The verb is suggestive of the metamorphoses (of human beings into gods, of gods into human beings) narrated by Ovid and others; a similar usage to Mark 9:2 is found in 2 Cor. 3:18, where Moses' transformation (Exodus 34) is in view, but where the transformation is internal and invisible rather than external and visible. See Boring, *Mark*, 260; Heil, *Transfiguration*, 76–77.

26. For literature, see above p. 182 nn. 27-28.

27. See M. Eugene Boring, Klaus Berger, and Carsten Colpe, eds., *Hellenistic Commentary to the New Testament* (Nashville: Abingdon, 1995), 107-8; Dieter Zeller, "Bedeutung und religionsgeschichtlicher Hintergrund der Verwandlung Jesu (Markus 9:2-8)," in *Authenticating the Activities of Jesus*, ed. B. Chilton and C. A. Evans (NTTS 28/2; Leiden: Brill, 1999), 303-22, esp. 312-15 (on the Moses typology); Heil, *Transfiguration*, 75-93; Marcus, *Mark*, 2:1108-18.

28. Heil, *Transfiguration*, 92-93; for Heil's discussion of the relevant Jewish parallels, see ibid., 76-92.

29. Collins, *Mark*, 422. Mark uses the verb *ōphthē* in v. 4 for the appearance of Elijah ("with Moses," which explains the singular verb). This is the only instance in Mark of the characteristic verb for theophanies and resurrection appearances.

30. Boring, *Mark*, 261. Marcus concludes that "in the transfiguration Jesus is showing what he already *is* (cf. 1:11) rather than *becoming* something he was not before" (*Mark*, 2:1117-18; emphasis in original); see also Zeller, "Bedeutung," 318.

31. Mark 9:8 in Greek reads *ouketi oudena eidon alla ton Yēsoun monon*; 2 Kings 2:12 LXX reads *kai ouk eiden auton eti*.

32. Peter G. Bolt, *Jesus' Defeat of Death: Persuading Mark's Early Readers* (SNTSMS 125; Cambridge: Cambridge University Press, 2003), 222; citation from 224; similarly Boring, *Mark*, 261. This reading is consistent with Mark's depiction of Jesus as fully aware of his fate but willing to suffer it in obedience to the Father's will (see esp. Mark 14:35-36; also Mark 2:19-20; 8:31-33; 9:30-32; 10:32-34; 10:45).

33. Heil, *Transfiguration*, 51-73, classifies the transfiguration as a "pivotal mandatory epiphany," i.e., as an epiphany that issues in a mandate or command; he concludes that "the words of Jesus that the disciples and the audience are to heed are the words predicting his passion, death, and resurrection" (ibid., 73).

34. Collins, *Mark*, 422; see similarly Marcus, *Mark*, 2:637, who thinks this scene foreshadows Jesus' resurrection; and Heil, *Transfiguration*, 76, who suggests that it foreshadows "Jesus' future and permanent attainment of glory in heaven."

35. Boring, *Mark*, 430; Boring et al., eds., *Hellenistic Commentary*, 160-61; Collins, "Son of God among Greeks and Romans," 94.

36. Collins, *Mark*, 764.

37. Ibid., 752.

38. Boring, *Mark*, 432. For a detailed discussion of various interpretive proposals concerning the tearing of the temple veil and its significance in Mark, see Collins, *Mark*, 759-64; see also John S. Kloppenborg, "Evocatio Deorum and the Date of Mark," *JBL* 124 (2005): 419-50, on the significance of the predictions of the temple's destruction to the dating of Mark's Gospel.

39. See Collins, *Mark*, 765: "The cultural milieu of Mark supports the inference that the centurion's statement about Jesus is a response to one or more omens"; see also Bultmann, *History of the Synoptic Tradition*, 274.

40. In ancient Greek, both the subject (as in "this man") and the predicate ("God's son") occur in the same case (the nominative) when linked with a copulative verb such as "to be" (*eimi*, as here). When an author or speaker wanted to clarify which noun was the subject, they would tend to drop the predicate's definite article even when the predicate is definite ("the Son of God"). This leads to the ambiguity, since an indefinite predicate ("a son of god") would likewise lack the article. See Collins, *Mark*, 766-67 and nn. 339-44 for literature; see also BDF §273.

41. Collins, "Son of God among Greeks and Romans," 95, citing W. H. Buckler, "Auguste, Zeus Patroos," *RevPhil* 9 (1935): 177-88, esp. 179.

42. Black, "The Face Is Familiar," 44-45.

43. Collins, *Mark*, 769.

44. Boring, *Mark*, 433-34. Boring rightly notes that this "is to be understood at the level of the Markan narrative, not at the level of historical reporting" (ibid., 434). See

also Frank J. Matera, *Passion Narratives and Gospel Theologies: Interpreting the Synoptics through Their Passion Stories* (Maryknoll, N.Y.: Paulist, 1986), 58–59, 79.

45. Ulrich Luz, *Matthew: A Commentary* (3 vols.; Hermeneia; Minneapolis: Fortress Press, 2001–07), 3:596 (on the similar description in Matt. 28:5).

46. See above, chapter 3.

47. Boring, *Mark*, 445.

48. Adela Yarbro Collins, *The Beginning of the Gospel: Probings of Mark in Context* (Minneapolis: Fortress Press, 1992), 147.

49. Collins, *Mark*, 794. For resurrection as a corporate hope in early Judaism, see, e.g., Wright, *Resurrection*, 205 (emphasis in original): "Resurrection, in the world of Second-Temple Judaism, was about *the restoration of Israel* on the one hand and *the newly embodied life of all YHWH's people* on the other, with close connections between the two; and it was thought of as the great event that YHWH would accomplish at the very end of 'the present age,' the event which would constitute 'the age to come.'"

50. As seen above (p. 25), Paul used the idea that Christ was the "first fruits" of the resurrection from the dead (1 Cor. 15:20-23) to deal with this problem.

51. On the connection between Son of God and Son of Man in Mark, see the important study of George W. E. Nickelsburg, "Son of Man," *ABD* 6:137–50; now reprinted in Nickelsburg, *Resurrection, Immortality, and Eternal Life in Intertestamental Judaism and Early Christianity* (2nd ed.; HTS 56; Cambridge: Harvard University Press, 2006), 281–314, esp. 300, where he suggests that Mark overlays two paradigms, namely, "1 Enoch's preexistent and exalted son of man, and Wisdom of Solomon's persecuted and exalted righteous man/ son of God," with the result that Mark's composite picture of Jesus as Son of God and Son of Man is a "three-stage pattern of preexistence, incarnation, and exaltation." Thus, in Nickelsburg's view, Son of God is not only a messianic title but also one that designates Jesus "as a unique divine being" (ibid.).

52. In Q 13:35 it is "the Coming One," but see also Q 12:39-40, 42-46; 17:23-24, 26-30; 19:12-26.

53. This narrative list of Jesus' activities in Mark 1–8 is strikingly similar to the lists given in Isa. 61:1 (with 26:19; 42:7, 18; et al.); Q 7:22 (Matt. 11:4-5 par. Luke 7:22); and 4Q521. See further above, p. 64. On 4Q521, the Qumran "Messianic Apocalypse" (as it is called) and Q's synthesis of the Isaian texts, see John J. Collins, *The Scepter and the Star: The Messiahs of the Dead Sea Scrolls and Other Ancient Literature* (ABRL; New York: Doubleday, 1995), 117–22; John S. Kloppenborg, *Excavating Q: The History and Setting of the Sayings Gospel* (Minneapolis: Fortress Press, 2000), 123, 405 and n. 72.

54. The one exception is Mark 14:28, which uses the first person.

55. Simon Gathercole, "The Son of Man in Mark's Gospel," *ExpT* 115 (2004): 366–72 (here, 372; emphasis in original).

56. Susan Miller, *Women in Mark's Gospel* (JSNTSup 259; London and New York: T. & T. Clark, 2004), 177–78.

57. It has sometimes been suggested (without any real basis) that Mark 16:1-8 preserves a primitive liturgy ("see the place") that was celebrated at the known site of Jesus' burial in the early years of the Judean Jesus movement. See especially Ludger Schenke, *Auferstehungsverkündigung und leeres Grab: Eine traditionsgeschichtliche Untersuchung von Mk 16,1-8* (2nd ed.; SBS 33; Stuttgart: Katholisches Bibelwerk, 1969), 88, and Bas van Iersel, "The Resurrection of Jesus—Information or Interpretation?" in *Immortality and Resurrection*, ed. P. Benoît and R. Murphy (Concilium 60; New York: Herder & Herder, 1970), 54–67, esp. 62–63.

58. See also the parable of the entrusted talents in Q 19:12-13, 15-24, 26.

59. Daniel A. Smith, "Revisiting the Empty Tomb: The Post-Mortem Vindication of Jesus in Mark and Q," *NovT* 45 (2003): 123–37 (here, 134).

60. Ernst Lohmeyer, *Galiläa und Jerusalem* (Göttingen: Vandenhoeck & Ruprecht, 1936), 10–13; Willi Marxsen, *Mark the Evangelist: Studies on the Redaction History of the Gospel* (Nashville: Abingdon, 1969), 75–95. See also the thorough discussion in Collins,

Mark, 658–67, who concludes that Mark 16:7 refers not to the parousia but to appearances in Galilee (ibid., 797).

61. For full discussions, see J. Lee Magness, *Sense and Absence: Structure and Suspension in the Ending of Mark's Gospel* (SemeiaSt; Atlanta: Scholars, 1986), 92–102; Joan L. Mitchell, *Beyond Fear and Silence: A Feminist-Literary Reading of Mark* (New York and London: Continuum, 2001), 66–75.

62. Boring, *Mark*, 445n6, suggests, "The word 'angel' . . . may have been in [Mark's] source or tradition, and he has suppressed [it]."

63. For discussions, see Collins, *Mark*, 688–93; Marcus, *Mark*, 2:999–1000, 1124–25. There are numerous interpretations of the relationship between 14:51-52 and the young man at the empty tomb. On one level, the youth who leaves behind his garment in Mark 14:51-52 simply may be a realistic narrative touch, just as in 10:50 Bartimaeus throws off his cloak and runs to Jesus: so, with literature, Howard M. Jackson, "Why the Youth Shed His Cloak and Fled Naked: The Meaning and Purpose of Mark 14:51-52," *JBL* 116 (1997): 273–89. However, a number of considerations commend a more symbolic interpretation: (1) the youth was "following with" Jesus; (2) he was wearing a linen garment (*sindōn*), which is what Joseph of Arimathea purchased for the body of Jesus (15:46); (3) he "fled" without going back for his garment, which is suggestive of the eschatological flight predicted for Judean disciples in 13:14-19; (4) we see verbal parallels here with Mark 16:5 (*neaniskos*; *peribeblēmenos*) not found elsewhere in Mark; and (5) in 16:5 the young man's garments are described in similar terms to Jesus' apparel at the transfiguration (9:3). Although one popular (and traditional) symbolic reading takes the unclothing and reclothing of the young man as baptismal imagery (for discussion, see Collins, *Mark*, 690–91), Mark does not really display elsewhere an interest in Christian baptism (see how "baptism" means persecution in 10:38-39).

64. Boring, *Mark*, 445.

65. As noted above (pp. 49, 51-52), although most Jewish sources imagine assumption as an escape from death—the person is taken up while still alive at the end of his earthly life—some Jewish texts describe postmortem disappearances. As with the children of Job in *T. Job* 39–40, one taken away bodily into heaven after dying (or being killed) is thought of as restored to life in the presence of God.

66. Daniel A. Smith, *The Post-Mortem Vindication of Jesus in the Sayings Gospel Q* (LNTS 338; London and New York: T. & T. Clark, 2006), 82–83.

67. This makes the initial flight of the disciples (Mark 14:50-52) more than a little premature, yet the author knows they eventually would face their own moments of being handed over to oppression (cf. 13:9-13 with 14:41-49).

68. See above, p. 18; this reading is supported by studies that identify the corporate or representative function of various figures identified as "one like a son of man" (as in Daniel 7) or "that son of man" (as in the Similitudes of Enoch, *1 Enoch* 37–71). See John J. Collins, "The Heavenly Representative: The 'Son of Man' in the Similitudes of Enoch," in *Ideal Figures in Ancient Judaism: Profiles and Paradigms*, ed. John J. Collins and George W. E. Nickelsburg (SBLSCS 12; Missoula, Mont.: Scholars, 1980), 111–33; Collins, *The Apocalyptic Imagination: An Introduction to Jewish Apocalyptic Literature* (2nd ed.; Grand Rapids: Eerdmans, 1998), 105–6 (on Daniel 7), 184–87 (on *1 Enoch*). For this theme in Q, see Smith, *Post-Mortem Vindication*, 130–43. See also, on Mark, Gathercole, "Son of Man in Mark's Gospel," 370–71.

69. See, e.g., Matera, *Passion Narratives*, 39, 44.

70. On the architecture of first-century tombs in Palestine, see Byron R. McCane, *Roll Back the Stone: Death and Burial in the World of Jesus* (Harrisburg, Pa.: Trinity Press International, 2003), 32–37.

71. Some have interpreted this as a Markan apology for the late arrival of the story of the empty tomb (because he composed it). See, e.g., Neill Q. Hamilton, "Resurrection Tradition and the Composition of Mark," *JBL* 84 (1965): 415–21, esp. 417; Lüdemann, *Resurrection of Christ*, 87.

72. See Magness, *Sense and Absence*, 25–85, on other "suspended endings" in ancient literature. As Marcus, *Mark*, 2:1093–94, notes, Jonah and Acts are two prominent biblical examples.

73. See Matt. 28:16-20; Luke 24:44-49; John 21:15-19, 20-25; 1 Cor. 9:1; 15:5-11.

74. Donald H. Juel, "A Disquieting Silence: The Matter of the Ending," in *A Master of Surprise* (Minneapolis: Fortress Press, 1994), 107–21; now reprinted in *The Ending of Mark and the Ends of God*, 1–13 (here, 8); see also Lincoln, "The Promise and the Failure."

75. Juel, "Disquieting Silence," 11–12.

76. See Boring, *Mark*, 449, who observes that of all the characters who rejected or deserted Jesus, only one participant in the narrative has stayed with him to the end: the reader. Thus "with terrible restraint, the narrator breaks off the story, and leaves the readers, who may have thought the story was about someone else, with a decision to make."

77. Victoria Phillips, "The Failure of the Women Who Followed Jesus in the Gospel of Mark," in *A Feminist Companion to Mark*, ed. Amy-Jill Levine (Sheffield: Sheffield Academic, 2001), 222–34 (here, 233); for the observation on the "inside view," Phillips relies on Thomas E. Boomershine, "Mark 16:8 and the Apostolic Commission," *JBL* 100 (1981): 225–39, esp. 227. Lincoln ("The Promise and the Failure," 285–87) argues that there is no positive value to the women's fear, but there seems to be no contradiction between seeing their fear as an appropriate reaction to their experience and still regarding their flight and silence as inappropriate.

78. Phillips, "Failure of the Women," 234. For Mark's community, as I have suggested, flight is part of their endurance "to the end," and so is justified (13:9-23), but within the narrative itself, Phillips's reading is correct.

79. The related Markan verbs *thambeō* (Mark 1:27; 10:24, 32) and *ekthambeō* (9:15; 14:33; 16:5-6) have connotations of fear, alarm, amazement, excitement, and astonishment. See BDAG ad loc.; LSJ ad loc. seems to treat the two forms as virtual synonyms.

80. John Dominic Crossan, "Empty Tomb and Absent Lord (Mark 16:1-8)," in *The Passion in Mark: Studies on Mark 14–16*, ed. W. Kelber (Philadelphia: Fortress Press, 1976), 135–52, argues that "it was precisely to avoid and to oppose any such apparition to Peter or the Apostles that [Mark] created most deliberately a totally new tradition" (146).

81. See Collins, *Beginning of the Gospel*, 147: "If, according to Mark, Jesus was translated from the grave to heaven, then there was no period of time during which the risen Jesus walked the earth and met with his disciples." Given that Mark accepted the tradition that the risen Jesus appeared to his followers, this means, according to Collins, that "this appearance (or appearances) was probably of a more heavenly type, like the apocalyptic visions of heavenly beings" (ibid.).

Chapter 6

1. According to NA[27], this verse is absent from certain important Western witnesses— Codex Bezae (D) and various forms of the Old Latin version (it). The verse, however, shows evidence of Lukan style, is consistent with its context in Luke 24, and is extremely well supported by all other textual witnesses, so its originality to Luke is well supported. For a more detailed discussion, see the excursus at the end of this chapter.

2. The words "and he was carried up into heaven" (Gk., *kai anephereto eis ton ouranon*) are absent from Luke 24:51 in ℵ* D it syr[S] et al.; and the words "worshipping him" (*proskunēsantes auton*) are absent from Luke 24:52 in D it syr[S] et al. They should nonetheless probably be considered original. For further discussion, see the excursus at the end of this chapter.

3. See, e.g., Barbara E. Reid, *Choosing the Better Part? Women in the Gospel of Luke* (Collegeville, Minn.: Liturgical, 1996), 200–202. On the possibility of competing traditions about Peter and Mary Magdalene, see Ann Graham Brock, *Mary Magdalene, the First Apostle: The Struggle for Authority* (HTS 51; Cambridge: Harvard University Press, 2003).

4. See, e.g., Charles H. Talbert, *Reading Luke: A Literary and Theological Commentary on the Third Gospel* (New York: Crossroad, 1984), 228: "In order to be persuasive in a Jewish context, the second episode was necessary to buttress the first."

5. Typically scholars draw on Josephus, *Ant.* 4.8.15, to illustrate that women could not serve as legal witnesses, but see Carolyn Osiek, "The Women at the Tomb: What Are They Doing There?" *ExAud* 9 (1993): 97–107, esp. 104: according to the Mishnah, "women's testimony was valued and drawn upon in the sphere of private affairs, but not in public," except, apparently, when male witnesses (for whatever reason) were not present. Osiek cites Moshe Meiselman, *Jewish Women in Jewish Law* (New York: KTAV, 1978), and Judith Romney Wegner, *Chattel or Person? The Status of Women in the Mishnah* (Oxford: Oxford University Press, 1988). See also Tal Ilan, *Jewish Women in Greco-Roman Palestine* (Peabody, Mass.: Hendrickson, 1996), 163–66.

6. Michael D. Goulder, *Luke: A New Paradigm* (2 vols.; JSNTSup 20; Sheffield: Sheffield Academic Press, 1989), 2:777.

7. See, besides here, Mark 9:15 par. Luke 9:37; Mark 10:24 par. Luke 18:24; Mark 10:32 par. Luke 18:31; Mark 14:33 par. Luke 22:40. Cf. Mark 1:27 par. Luke 4:36.

8. For a similar reaction, see Dan. 10:9, 15, as noted by Joel B. Green, *The Gospel of Luke* (NICNT; Grand Rapids: Eerdmans, 1997), 837n4.

9. These words are absent from D it et al. For further discussion, see the excursus at the conclusion of this chapter.

10. See Turid K. Seim, *The Double Message: Patterns of Gender in Luke-Acts* (Nashville: Abingdon, 1994), 151; Green, *Luke*, 838.

11. Brock, *Mary Magdalene*, 35.

12. Ibid., 145–55; one exception is Acts 14:14, where *apostoloi* is applied to Saul and Barnabas, possibly in the nontechnical sense of "emissary," although this might represent Luke's concession to Paul's claims to apostleship. See James M. Robinson, "Jesus—From Easter to Valentinus (or to the Apostles' Creed)," *JBL* 101 (1982): 5–37, esp. 8.

13. For resurrection appearances as providing legitimation, see the discussion above, pp. 28-29. Luke makes the same connection between apostolic office and seeing the risen Lord Jesus (Acts 1:21-22).

14. See above, p. 28.

15. See, e.g., *Gos. Phil.* 55b; the *Gospel of Mary*. For discussion, see Mary Rose D'Angelo, "'I Have Seen the Lord': Mary Magdalen as Visionary, Early Christian Prophecy, and the Context of John 20:14-18," in *Mariam, the Magdalen, and the Mother*, ed. Deirde Good (Bloomington: Indiana University Press, 2005), 95–122.

16. See Katherine L. Jansen, "Maria Magdalena: *Apostolorum Apostola*," in *Women Preachers and Prophets through Two Millennia of Christianity*, ed. B. M. Kienzle and P. J. Walker (Berkeley: University of California Press, 1998), 57–96, who attributes (as others do) the origins of this title to Hippolytus of Rome (ibid., 58).

17. Brock, following Elisabeth Schüssler Fiorenza, argues that the early Christian writings show the marks of a struggle over who is to be considered the primary witness of the resurrection, Peter or Mary Magdalene: Brock, *Mary Magdalene*, passim; Elisabeth Schüssler Fiorenza, *In Memory of Her: A Feminist Theological Reconstruction of Christian Origins* (New York: Crossroad, 1983), 51. However, Brock finds in Luke the same tendency she finds in later apocryphal writings, namely, that texts that elevate the status of Peter (or Mary) as resurrection witness tend also to diminish the other. To claim this about Luke (Brock, *Mary Magdalene*, 40, 68), one must demonstrate that Luke knew but avoided a tradition describing an appearance of the risen Jesus to Mary, which Brock does not do (ibid., 34, 40).

18. So, e.g., Reginald H. Fuller, *The Formation of the Resurrection Narratives* (New York: Macmillan, 1971), 112; C. F. Evans, *Resurrection and the New Testament* (SBT 12; London: SCM, 1970), 106–7; Gerd Lüdemann, *The Resurrection of Jesus: History, Experience, Theology* (Minneapolis: Fortress Press, 1994), 26. See also Jean-Marie Guillaume, *Luc interprète des anciennes traditions sur la Résurrection de Jésus* (EBib; Paris: Lecoffre/Gabalda, 1979), 116–18, who argues that Luke's formulation is more primitive than Paul's

on the grounds that "and then to the Twelve" (1 Cor. 15:5b) "marks an expansion of the tradition" (ibid., 117).

19. Paul usually uses the name Cephas, and twice Peter, but never Simon; Luke never uses the name Cephas, but prefers Simon. Simon is used for Peter sixteen times in Luke-Acts. For alternative sides of the debate, see Bart D. Ehrman, "Cephas and Peter," *JBL* 109 (1990): 463–74; Dale C. Allison Jr., "Peter and Cephas: One and the Same," *JBL* 111 (1992): 489–95.

20. Allison, "Peter and Cephas," 492–93; see, for other considerations, ibid., 493–95.

21. In addition to Luke 24:34, see also Luke 24:3; Acts 1:21; 4:33; 7:59; et al. The words "of the Lord Jesus" are omitted by D it but should probably be considered original to Luke. For discussion, see the excursus at the end of this chapter.

22. Richard J. Dillon, *From Eye-Witnesses to Ministers of the Word: Tradition and Composition in Luke 24* (AnBib 82; Rome: Biblical Institute Press, 1978), 99.

23. Many scholars think that Paul's letters were known to the author of Luke-Acts. See, e.g., Wolfgang Schenk, "Luke as Reader of Paul: Observations on His Reception," in *Intertextuality in Biblical Writings: Essays in Honour of Bas van Iersel*, ed. S. Draisma (Kampen: Kok, 1989), 127–39. Schenk shows not only that Luke 24:34 is directly dependent on 1 Cor. 15:4-5, but also that Luke 24:9-10, in which figure "the Eleven," "James," and "the apostles," alludes to Gal. 1:17-19 and 1 Cor. 15:5, 7 (ibid., 136–37).

24. Fuller, *Formation*, 112; Evans, *Resurrection*, 107.

25. Dillon's view (*From Eye-Witnesses*, 62–68) is that the plural in 24:24 reflects Luke's knowledge of a tradition in which more than one disciple visited the tomb, whereas the author characteristically focuses attention on Peter. Of course, if Luke has created the visit of Peter redactionally, as appears to be the case, then the plural in v. 24 needs another explanation.

26. See above (p. 182 n. 28), on possibilities for relics of an original narrative of an appearance to Peter. As noted there, the miraculous catch of fish (Luke 5:1-11) and the transfiguration (Mark 9:2-10 par.), if these are to be seen as displaced resurrection appearances, are possibilities.

27. Lüdemann, *Resurrection of Jesus*, 85–86.

28. As noted above, the silence of the narrative tradition is a puzzle.

29. Lüdemann, *Resurrection of Christ*, 103.

30. The main reason for considering a tradition underlying Luke 24:12 is the similarities with John 20:3-10. Frans Neirynck thinks Luke wrote v. 12 and that the author or redactor of John knew and used Luke. See Neirynck, "Once More Luke 24,12," *ETL* 70 (1994): 319–40, esp. 339–40.

31. See Frans Neirynck, "Luke 24,12: An Anti-Docetic Interpolation?" in *New Testament Textual Criticism and Exegesis: Festschrift J. Delobel*, ed. A. Denaux (BETL 161; Leuven: Peeters, 2002), 145–58. Neirynck cites the following Lukanisms as evidence: the participle "having got up" (*anastas*), the verb "to wonder" (*thaumazein*), and the participle "that which has happened" (*to gegonos*). Other aspects of Luke 24:12 can be explained by the influence of Mark 16:1-8 on Luke (ibid., 148–52). For further discussion, see below (p. 100). For a contrary view, see James D. G. Dunn, *Jesus Remembered* (Christology in the Making 1; Grand Rapids: Eerdmans, 2003), 833–34, who thinks that Luke 24:12 was original to Luke but based on a tradition going back to the testimony of the Beloved Disciple.

32. The words "and he said to them, 'Peace to you,'" and all of v. 40 are not present in D it. See the discussion in the excursus that concludes this chapter.

33. See above, p. 14; see the detailed analysis in Dale C. Allison, *Resurrecting Jesus: The Earliest Christian Tradition and Its Interpreters* (London and New York: T. & T. Clark, 2005), 269–99.

34. To name three: NRSV, NIV, NLT; cf. ESV. This is not only a current interpretation: Codex Bezae reads *phantasma* (ghost) instead of *pneuma* (spirit) at Luke 24:37.

35. Tertullian, *de Anima* 56 (though he tried to show that ghosts are actually deceptions perpetrated by demons, and not really manifestations of restless souls). For more on this classification, see D. Felton, *Haunted Greece and Rome: Ghost Stories from Classical*

Antiquity (Austin: University of Texas Press, 1999), 25; see also Daniel Ogden, *Magic, Witchcraft, and Ghosts in the Greek and Roman Worlds: A Sourcebook* (Oxford: Oxford University Press, 2002), 146, who adds the category of the unmarried.

36. *Aeneid* 6.430–33; Ogden, *Magic, Witchcraft, and Ghosts*, 148.

37. The verb translated here as "impale on a stake" (*anaskopolizō*) is used elsewhere by Lucian for the crucifixion of Jesus (*Peregr.* 11, 13).

38. Sarah Iles Johnston, *Restless Dead: Encounters between the Living and the Dead in Ancient Greece* (Berkeley: University of California Press, 1999), 148–51.

39. One might think that the ghosts of those who died by violence were more dangerous to those who had killed them, but they were also dangerous generally because of their inability to rest (ibid., 155–56). This perhaps is one way that the disciples' fear at the sudden appearance of Jesus (Luke 24:36) could have been understood.

40. Kathleen E. Corley, *Women and the Historical Jesus: Feminist Myths of Christian Origins* (Santa Rosa, Calif.: Polebridge, 2002), 123–28.

41. Hans Dieter Betz, "Zum Problem der Auferstehung Jesu im Lichte der griechischen magischen Papyri," in Betz, *Gesammelte Aufsätze I: Hellenismus und Urchristentum* (Tübingen: Mohr Siebeck, 1990), 230–61 (here, 246).

42. Daniel Ogden, *Greek and Roman Necromancy* (Princeton, N.J.: Princeton University Press, 2001), 220. See also Philostratus, *Vit. Apoll.* 8.12, in which Apollonius allows his followers to handle his body to show that he is not a ghost.

43. See also Virgil, *Aen.* 6.700–702.

44. Ogden, *Greek and Roman Necromancy*, 220–21, 159–60. According to Johnston, *Restless Dead*, 159–60, earlier Greek sources show that ghosts, being insubstantial, would afflict the living through the agency of divine beings or through psychological means. Later texts do not restrict the dead to such indirect tactics (Ogden, *Greek and Roman Necromancy*, 220); Gregory Riley suggests, on the basis of Virgil, *Aen.* 6 (which alludes, 6.702, to Homer, *Od.* 11.204–8), that by the first century "'life' in the underworld had . . . become far more substantial, and the dead had become correspondingly more tangible." Gregory J. Riley, *Resurrection Reconsidered: Thomas and John in Controversy* (Minneapolis: Fortress Press, 1995), 53–58, citation from 55.

45. On revenants and their unclear distinction from ghosts, see Felton, *Haunted Greece and Rome*, 25–29. It is also unclear whether stories about revenants actually represent popular beliefs about what could happen to a dead person or were just weird or spooky stories. One such story that evidently made the rounds is the story mentioned above (pp. 14, 187 n. 32) about Philinnion.

46. Eduard Schweizer, "πνεῦμα, πνευματικός, κτλ," *TDNT*, 6:332–455; citation from 6:415.

47. Felton, *Haunted Greece and Rome*, 23–25; Ogden, *Greek and Roman Necromancy*, 219–20.

48. Terence Paige, "Who Believes in 'Spirit'? Πνεῦμα in Pagan Usage and Implications for the Gentile Christian Mission," *HTR* 95 (2002): 417–36 (here, 433; emphasis in original).

49. BDAG, ad loc., suggests this meaning for *pneuma* in Luke 24, but lexicographers of the New Testament are at a loss to supply a parallel to this proposed meaning of *pneuma*: see also Ernest D. Burton, *Spirit, Soul, and Flesh: The Usage of Pneuma, Psyche, and Sarx* (Chicago: University of Chicago Press, 1918), 181; Eduard Schweizer, "πνεῦμα, πνευματικός," 6:415.

50. See Sjef van Tilborg and Patrick Chatelion Counet, *Jesus' Appearances and Disappearances in Luke 24* (Biblical Interpretation Series 45; Leiden: Brill, 2000), 180–81, who note the similarity to Acts 7:59, where the dying Stephen prays similar words to the Lord Jesus.

51. Robinson, "Jesus—From Easter to Valentinus," 11–12.

52. Ibid., 13.

53. Later heresiological literature attests to disagreements within Christianity on the physicality of the resurrection (Riley, *Resurrection Reconsidered*, 58–68).

54. The immediate context of this resurrection material in *Smyrnaeans* 3 has the whole of Jesus' life—birth, suffering, death, and resurrection—in view: "truly (*alēthōs*) from the race of David . . . truly born from a virgin . . . truly nailed for us in the flesh . . . and he truly suffered just as he truly raised himself" (*Smyrnaeans* 1–2).

55. So Philipp Vielhauer and Georg Strecker, "Jewish-Christian Gospels," in *New Testament Apocrypha*, ed. W. Schneemelcher and trans. R. McL. Wilson (2nd ed.; 2 vols.; Louisville: Westminster John Knox, 1991), 134–78 (here, 144–45); Frans Neirynck, "Lc 24, 36–43: un récit lucanien," in *À Cause de l'Évangile: Études sur les Synoptiques et les Actes offertes au P. Jacques Dupont, O.S.B. à l'occasion de son 70e anniversaire* (LD 123; Paris: Cerf, 1985), 655–80, esp. 674–75. William R. Schoedel thinks Luke and Ignatius are independent of one another and "rely on common tradition." Schoedel, *Ignatius of Antioch: A Commentary on the Letters of Ignatius of Antioch* (Hermeneia; Philadelphia: Fortress Press, 1985), 227. The same theme of the risen Jesus eating and drinking with his followers occurs in both *Smyrn.* 3:3 and Acts 10:41.

56. See, e.g., I. Howard Marshall, *The Gospel of Luke: A Commentary on the Greek Text* (NIGTC; Grand Rapids: Eerdmans, 1978), 898; Joseph A. Fitzmyer, *The Gospel according to Luke* (2 vols.; AB 28–28A; New York: Doubleday, 1981–85), 2:1568.

57. See Evans, *Resurrection*, 96: "What most distinguishes Luke's account from those of the other Gospels is that the resurrection is not an end in itself or a symbol of exaltation or parousia, but a point of transition." Answering this question depends on whether the resurrection or the ascension functions Christologically for Luke as the means of Jesus' exaltation. See Gerhard Lohfink, *Die Himmelfahrt Jesu: Untersuchungen zu den Himmelfahrts- und Erhohungstexten bei Lukas* (SANT 26; Munich: Kösel, 1971), 240, who thinks that Luke historicized kerygmatic ideas about Jesus' exaltation by using an assumption story; for the opposing view, see A. W. Zwiep, *The Ascension of the Messiah in Lukan Christology* (NovTSup 87; Leiden: Brill, 1997), esp. 196–97.

58. See A. J. M. Wedderburn, *Beyond Resurrection* (London: SCM; Peabody, Mass.: Hendrickson, 1999), 31–32.

59. Cf. E. Earle Ellis, *The Gospel of Luke* (NCB; rev. ed.; London: Oliphants, 1974), 275–76.

60. Evans, *Resurrection*, 60.

61. More usually in the New Testament, *dialogismos* is used in the sense of reasoning, intention, or inner thought, but here it is used in the sense of a "reasoning that gives rise to uncertainty" (so BDAG, ad loc.).

62. In 2 Cor. 12:9 Paul refers to someone—himself, of course—who fourteen years earlier had an *optasia*.

63. The use of *ōphthē* for the "appearance" of Moses to the two quarrelers (Acts 7:26; cf. Exod. 2:13-14 LXX) is very odd.

64. W. Michaelis, "ὁράω, εἶδον, κτλ," *TDNT*, 5:359.

65. Marcion evidently thought that Christ's body was composed of spirit, not flesh and bones, and yet was tangible, giving the appearance of being "in the likeness of sinful flesh" (Rom. 8:3; cf. Phil. 2:7). See Adolf von Harnack, *Marcion: The Gospel of the Alien God*, trans. John E. Steely and Lyle D. Bierma (Durham, N.C.: Labyrinth, 1990), 68, 83–84; see also Markus Vinzent, "Der Schluß des Lukasevangeliums bei Marcion," in *Marcion und seine kirchengeschichtliche Wirkung; Marcion and His Impact on Church History*, ed. G. May and K. Greschet (TUGAL 150; Berlin and New York: de Gruyter, 2002), 79–94, esp. 86, who uses the term "pneumatic corporeality" to describe how Marcion viewed both the body of Christ and the souls of believers. Tertullian consistently uses *phantasma* for Marcion's view of Christ's body both before and after the resurrection (e.g., *Marc.* 4.42, where he asks, discussing Luke 23:46, how a phantom can give up the spirit).

66. It should be noted here that Arie Zwiep has argued that Luke narrates the resurrection appearances as appearances from heaven; he bases this on the claim that Luke has not adapted the early Christian resurrection kerygma, which always considered resurrection and exaltation (to heaven) as one and the same (for his conclusion, see Zwiep, *Ascension*,

196–97). The narrative impression one gets from Luke 24, however, is that Jesus is able to meet up with the two disciples and join them on their journey (24:13-16) not because he has appeared to them from heaven but because he has exited the tomb. The abilities of the risen Jesus to appear and disappear suddenly and to go unrecognized may be understood as related to the concept of "polymorphism," which was a way of stressing "both lack of constraint by the mortal body and transcendence over the earthly realm" (Paul Foster, "Polymorphic Christology: Its Origins and Development in Early Christianity," *JTS* 58 [2007]: 66–99 [here, 71]).

67. B. F. Westcott and F. J. A. Hort, *The New Testament in the Original Greek* (2 vols.; New York: Harper & Bros., 1882), 2:295.

68. Bruce M. Metzger, *The Text of the New Testament: Its Transmission, Corruption, and Restoration* (3rd ed.; Oxford: Oxford University Press, 1992), 134.

69. Another candidate is Matt. 27:49: "And the rest were saying, 'Let us see whether Elijah comes and saves him.' [But another, taking a spear, pierced his side, and out came water and blood.]" Many more non-Western witnesses omit this line, however.

70. Westcott and Hort considered the Western reading here to be a secondary omission (*New Testament*, 1:183). Bart D. Ehrman, *The Orthodox Corruption of Scripture: The Effect of Early Christological Controversies on the Text of the New Testament* (Oxford and New York: Oxford University Press, 1993), 223–27, discusses the Western noninterpolations at great length but does not discuss this variant. Michael Wade Martin thinks it should be included among the Western noninterpolations: Martin, "Defending the 'Western Non-Interpolations': The Case for an Anti-Separationist *Tendenz* in the Longer Alexandrian Readings," *JBL* 124 (2005): 269–94, at 293n89.

71. See *The Greek New Testament*, ed. Barbara Aland et al. (4th rev. ed.; Stuttgart: Deutsche Bibelgesellschaft / United Bible Societies, 1993), which includes all the longer readings in the text of Luke 24 and rates their originality at {B} (a "B" rating indicates that the editors consider these longer readings almost certainly to represent the original text). See the explanations of the committee's decisions in Bruce M. Metzger, *A Textual Commentary on the Greek New Testament* (2nd ed.; Stuttgart: Deutsche Bibelgesellschaft / United Bible Societies, 1994), 156–58, 160–66.

72. See Neirynck, "Luke 24,12: An Anti-Docetic Interpolation?" in *New Testament Textual Criticism and Exegesis: Festschrift J. Delobel*, ed. A. Denaux (BETL 161; Leuven: Peeters, 2002), 145–58, at 146: "The shift from the majority opinion for inauthenticity to the new consensus [of authenticity] is due to the weight of the textual witness P[75] . . . in combination with the evidence of Lukan style."

73. Ehrman, *Orthodox Corruption of Scripture*, 221 (emphasis in original).

74. Mikeal Parsons, "A Christological Tendency in P[75]," *JBL* 105 (1986): 463–79; Martin, "Defending."

75. See J. K. Elliott, "The Case for Thoroughgoing Eclecticism," in *Rethinking New Testament Textual Criticism*, ed. David Alan Black (Grand Rapids: Baker, 2002), 101–24, esp. 116: "We should not be mesmerized by [Westcott and Hort's] blanket treatment of these nine variants," he writes, stating (as an example) that the variant readings in Luke 24:51 should not be associated with the others in Luke 24.

76. Martin, "Defending," 276–78.

77. Ehrman, *Orthodox Corruption*, 211.

78. See Neirynck's bibliography in Neirynck, "Anti-Docetic Interpolation?" 145n1.

79. Ibid., 148; see also Neirynck, "Once More Lk 24,12," *ETL* 70 (1994): 319–40, esp. 324.

80. See Ehrman, *Orthodox Corruption*, 214; Neirynck, "Anti-Docetic Interpolation?" 148–52.

81. Ehrman, *Orthodox Corruption*, 214; Neirynck, "Anti-Docetic Interpolation?" 151–52. See also Luke 16:23 ("lifting up his eyes he sees"). For the translation of *parakupsas* here as a verb of seeing (not bending), see Neirynck, "ΠΑΡΑΚΥΨΑΣ ΒΛΕΠΕΙ: Lc 24,12 et Jn 20,5," *ETL* 53 (1977): 113–52, esp. 141–48.

82. Neirynck, "Anti-Docetic Interpolation?" 152–56.

83. In Luke 24:36, the Western witnesses only support the omission of the last five words of the verse, and other similarities between Luke and John are present: *estē* with *mesos*, a genitive absolute, and the motif of fear (which characteristically in John becomes "the fear of the Jews"). This is enough to cast doubt on the theory of scribal harmonization to John.

84. Neirynck, "Once More," 330; he is referring not to Ehrman but to Anton Dauer, "Zur Authentizität von Lk 24,12," *ETL* 70 (1994): 294–318.

85. So Neirynck, "Once More," 328–29.

86. Both v. 12 and v. 24 use the aorist of *aperchomai*—although the latter uses it for the trip to the tomb and the former for the trip back.

87. John Muddiman, "A Note on Reading Luke xxiv.12," *ETL* 48 (1972): 542–48, at 547; cited by Neirynck, "Anti-Docetic Interpolation?" 158.

88. Jacob Kremer, *Die Osterevangelien: Geschichten um Geschichte* (Stuttgart: Katholisches Bibelwerk, 1977), 105–6; cited with approval by Michael D. Goulder, *Luke: A New Paradigm* (2 vols.; JSNTSup 20; Sheffield: Sheffield Academic Press, 1989), 2:776–77. Luke 24:1-12 is a resurrection story but not an appearance story.

89. For the first question, Ehrman (and more recently Martin) notes that supporters of the originality of Luke 24:12 rarely ask why a Western scribe would omit it. See Ehrman, *Orthodox Corruption*, 255n138; Martin, "Defending," 284.

90. Cf. Martin, "Defending," passim.

91. John Nolland, for instance, argues for abbreviation: "Quite a bit that did not strike the scribe as essential seems to have been deleted": Nolland, *Luke* (WBC 35A–C; Dallas, Tex.: Word, 1989–93), 3:1177. Michael Martin, on the other hand, thinks the longer readings are all "anti-separationist," by which he means in opposition to the view that the divine Christ indwelt the human Jesus but escaped prior to Jesus' suffering and death; see his "Defending," 272 and n. 13, where he depends on the definitions of Ehrman, *Orthodox Corruption*, 119–24.

92. Muddiman, "Note," 547, argues this, pointing out that had an interpolator added v. 12 in light of John 20:3-10 (and Luke 24:24), the discrepancy in number could easily have been corrected either in v. 12 or in v. 24. Martin says that it has not been argued that the shorter readings arose as the result of a "heterodox" corruptor combating the view that Jesus was raised bodily and ascended bodily because so much remains of that view in Luke 24 ("Defending," 279).

93. Ehrman, *Orthodox Corruption*, 219; Neirynck, "Anti-Docetic Interpolation?" 157.

94. Metzger, *Textual Commentary*, 156–57; Marshall, *Luke*, 884; Neirynck, "Anti-Docetic Interpolation?" 157.

95. Metzger, *Textual Commentary*, 157. Compare *ouk estin hōde, ēgerthē gar kathōs eipen* (Matt. 28:6); *ēgerthē, ouk estin hōde* (Mark 16:6); and *ouk estin hōde, alla ēgerthē* (Luke 24:6, longer reading).

96. Metzger, *Textual Commentary*, 157.

97. Richard J. Dillon, *From Eye-Witnesses to Ministers of the Word: Tradition and Composition in Luke 24* (AB 82; Rome: Biblical Institute Press, 1978), 183; Neirynck, "Anti-Docetic Interpolation?" 157.

98. Ibid., 156–57 and nn. 61–62; cf. Ehrman, *Orthodox Corruption*, 218.

99. Metzger, *Textual Commentary*, 162–63.

100. Ibid., 163; Metzger also suggests that the two words may have been omitted due to homoioteleuton, "the eye of the copyist passing from ΑΥΤΟΙ … to ΑΥΤΩΝ." On worship/veneration as a motif in assumption stories, see Gerhard Lohfink, *Die Himmelfahrt Jesu: Untersuchungen zu den Himmelfahrts- und Erhohungstexten bei Lukas* (SANT 26; Munich: Kösel, 1971), 46–49, 171–74 (who sees a Hellenistic influence on Luke), and A. W. Zwiep, *The Ascension of the Messiah in Lukan Christology* (NovTSup 87; Leiden: Brill, 1997), 93–94 (who thinks that a traditional association between the resurrection appearances and worship, as seen in Matt. 28:17, has been adapted by Luke here).

Chapter 7

1. Ulrich Luz, "Fictionality and Loyalty to Tradition in Matthew's Gospel in the Light of Greek Literature," in *Studies in Matthew*, trans. R. Selle (Grand Rapids: Eerdmans, 2005), 54–79 (here, 54). Luz's comparison of Matthew with other Greek works that use fictional pieces leads him to conclude that the author had no real awareness of the distinctions that were maintained in other similar pieces of literature (ibid., 76–79).

2. Ibid., 79.

3. Luz, "The Gospel of Matthew: A New Story of Jesus, or a Rewritten One?" in *Studies in Matthew*, 18–36, (here, 27).

4. See the discussion above, p. 47.

5. The idea that the body-theft story had originated as a response to the events at the tomb as described in Matthew 28, and the idea that the Jews could not see in their own Scriptures that Jesus would rise from the dead, were important aspects of anti-Jewish rhetoric in the second century and thereafter (see below, p. 142).

6. See W. D. Davies and Dale C. Allison Jr., *A Critical and Exegetical Commentary on the Gospel according to Saint Matthew* (3 vols.; ICC; Edinburgh; London: T. & T. Clark, 1988–97), 3:682–83; Ulrich Luz, *Matthew: A Commentary* (3 vols.; Hermeneia; Minneapolis: Fortress Press, 2001–07), 3:619.

7. There is some discussion about the meaning of Matthew's time reference, since the ideas "after the Sabbath" and "at dawn on the first day of the week" seem to be contradictory. See, e.g., Robert H. Gundry, *Matthew: A Commentary on His Handbook for a Mixed Church under Persecution* (2nd ed.; Grand Rapids: Eerdmans, 1994), 586, who takes it to mean Saturday after sunset (taking *epiphōskousē* to refer to evening twilight, not dawn). Cf. Davies and Allison, 3:663–64; Luz, *Matthew*, 3:594–95; John Nolland, *The Gospel of Matthew: A Commentary on the Greek Text* (NIGTC; Grand Rapids: Eerdmans, 2005), 1245–46.

8. Byron McCane, *Roll Back the Stone: Death and Burial in the World of Jesus* (Harrisburg, Pa.: Trinity Press International, 2003), 101–4.

9. Thomas R. W. Longstaff, "What Are Those Women Doing at the Tomb of Jesus? Perspectives on Matthew 28.1," in *A Feminist Companion to Matthew*, ed. Amy-Jill Levine and Marianne Blickenstaff (Sheffield: Sheffield Academic Press, 2001), 196–204; also Davies and Allison, *Matthew*, 3:664.

10. Longstaff, "What Are Those Women Doing . . . ?" 202.

11. Warren Carter, "'To See the Tomb': Matthew's Women at the Tomb," *ExpT* 107 (1996): 201–5 (here, 203). See also Warren Carter, *Matthew and the Margins: A Sociopolitical and Religious Reading* (Bible and Liberation; Maryknoll, N.Y.: Orbis, 2000), 544.

12. Carter, "To See the Tomb," 205.

13. Luz, *Matthew*, 3:595.

14. Davies and Allison, *Matthew*, 3:660–61, citing Dan. 10:2-14; Matt. 1:18-25; *Apoc. Abr.* 10:1-17; 12:1–13:1; and *2 Enoch* 1:3-10.

15. Gundry, *Matthew*, 588; Luz, *Matthew*, 3:596.

16. See John Dominic Crossan, *The Cross That Spoke: The Origins of the Passion Narrative* (San Francisco: Harper & Row, 1988), 352–57; Helmut Koester, *Ancient Christian Gospels: Their History and Development* (Philadelphia: Trinity Press International; London: SCM, 1990), 236–38.

17. Luz, *Matthew*, 3:592 (with n. 18 for details).

18. Ibid., 3:595.

19. See, e.g., *T. Job* 39–40, where it is assumed by Job that his children's remains will not be found (they would be under the collapsed house).

20. Davies and Allison, *Matthew*, 3.666.

21. Luz (*Matthew*, 3:596) thinks it self-evident that they were afraid, "because 'fear' is the reaction of pious people as well as to an experience of God." Kenneth L. Waters Sr., "Matthew 28:1-6 as Temporally Conflated Text: Temporal-Spatial Collapse in the Gospel of Matthew," *ExpT* 116 (2005): 295–301, makes much of this, arguing that

since the women do not swoon and require celestial strengthening to meet the angel (as in other texts such as Daniel 10), they must not have been present at the angel's descent. Waters takes this passage (along with Matt. 27:52-53) as an example of "temporal-spatial collapse," where elements of a story are told out of sensible narrative or chronological sequence particularly when the divine realm impinges upon the earthly. This seems to me a strained reading that attempts to show that "Matthew therefore agrees with the other gospel writers" (ibid., 295), despite Waters's assertion that "critical exegesis has no real reason to rule out the possibility of divergence" (296).

22. Nolland, *Gospel of Matthew*, 1248.

23. Luz notes that "the contrast 'crucified—raised' is determined by early Christian confessions of faith," citing also the importance of the proclamation of the Crucified One in Pauline circles (*Matthew*, 3:596).

24. In contrast, Nolland finds the following chiasm in vv. 5b-6a: "'[Jesus] the crucified'—'you are looking for'—'he is not here'—'he has been raised'" (*Gospel of Matthew*, 1249).

25. The sign of Jonah saying in Matthew does not explicitly predict Jesus' resurrection, but does so implicitly through the correlation to Jonah, who spent three days and three nights in the belly of the big fish, but was brought up by God (see Jonah 2:6, 10).

26. E.g., Jerome, *Epis.* 48.21, who correlates this with the birth of Christ (see below, p. 141).

27. According to Nolland, Matthew made this change "for no obvious reason" (*Gospel of Matthew*, 1250); Gundry notes that the aorist of *poreuomai* is a Matthean "favorite" (*Matthew*, 589).

28. Davies and Allison, *Matthew*, 3:667.

29. Luz, *Matthew*, 3:597: "They are *Apostolae Apostolorum* . . . but *only* that!" (ibid., n. 65; emphasis in original).

30. This is proposed on the basis of sociohistorical as well as literary connections between Q, which by all indications originated in the Galilee, and Matthew. See Luz, *Matthew*, 1:49; Luz, "Matthew and Q," in *Studies in Matthew*, 39–53, esp. 52–53; James M. Robinson, "The Matthean Trajectory from Q to Mark," in *Ancient and Modern Perspectives on the Bible and Culture: Essays in Honor of Hans Dieter Betz*, ed. Adela Yarbro Collins (SPHS 22; Atlanta: Scholars, 1998), 122–54; Robinson, "From Safe House to House Church: From Q to Matthew," in *Das Ende der Tage und die Gegenwart des Heils: Begegnungen mit dem Neuen Testament und seiner Umwelt. Festschrift für Heinz-Wolfgang Kuhn zum 65. Geburtstag*, ed. M. Becker and W. Fenske (AGJU 44; Leiden: Brill, 1999), 183–99.

31. Cf. Gundry, *Matthew*, 589 (Peter has "apostasized") with Luz, *Matthew*, 3:597 and n. 66 (there is no demotion of Peter because of his denial); Davies and Allison, *Matthew*, 3:667 (here as in 28:16-20 Peter is one of the group).

32. For discussion of this gap in the tradition, made more pronounced by 1 Cor. 15:5 and Luke 24:34, see the discussion above, p. 182 n. 28.

33. Luz, *Matthew*, 3:604.

34. E.g., see Davies and Allison, *Matthew*, 3:668, who consider Matt. 28:9-10 "a shortened version of a story which has been taken up and expanded in John 20:11-18." See similarly Luz, *Matthew*, 3:606; and Raymond E. Brown, *The Gospel according to John* (2 vols.; AB 29–29A; Garden City, N.Y.: Doubleday, 1966–70), 2:1002–4, who thought that Matt. 28:9-10; John 20:14-18; and Ps.-Mark 16:9-10 represent three independent versions of the same story.

35. Gerd Lüdemann, *The Resurrection of Jesus: History, Experience, Theology* (London: SCM; Minneapolis: Fortress Press), 131–32.

36. C. H. Dodd, "The Appearances of the Risen Christ: An Essay in Form-Criticism of the Gospels," in *Studies in the Gospels: Essays in Memory of R. H. Lightfoot*, ed. D. E. Nineham (Oxford: Basil Blackwell, 1955), 9–35 (here, 11).

37. Lüdemann, *Resurrection of Jesus*, 131–32; cf. Frans Neirynck, "Note on Mt 28,9-10," *ETL* 71 (1995): 161–65, esp. 161–63.

38. Luz, *Matthew*, 3:607.

39. See Frans Neirynck, "Les femmes au tombeau: Étude de la rédaction matthéenne (Matt. xviii.1-10)," *NTS* 15 (1968): 168–90, esp. 176–84; Neirynck, "John and the Synoptics: The Empty Tomb Stories," *NTS* 30 (1984): 161–87, esp. 166–67; Gundry, *Matthew,* 591; see also Luz, *Matthew,* 3:606: "The text is almost totally Matthean in its wording," with details, n. 5.

40. Luz, *Matthew,* 3:607.

41. Davies and Allison, *Matthew,* 3:668n39.

42. Gundry, *Matthew,* 590–91. For more detail on Gundry's lost ending theory, see further above, p. 194 n. 8.

43. Davies and Allison, *Matthew,* 3:669.

44. The combination of *proserchomai* ("draw near, approach") with *proskuneō* ("worship, venerate") occurs four times in Matthew and is a distinct example of Matthean style according to Neirynck, "Les femmes au tombeau," 178, and Gundry, *Matthew,* 591.

45. So Luz, *Matthew,* 3:607; Nolland, *Gospel of Matthew,* 1252–53; Davies and Allison, *Matthew,* 3:669, as one possibility.

46. See, e.g., R. T. France, *The Gospel of Matthew* (NICNT; Grand Rapids: Eerdmans, 2007), 1102, together with the posture of veneration; see also the brief survey in Dale C. Allison Jr., "Touching Jesus' Feet (Matt. 28:9)," in *Studies in Matthew: Interpretation Past and Present* (Grand Rapids: Baker Academic, 2005), 107–16, esp. 110–11. Allison rightly notes that a text such as this one has more than one intention or reading (ibid., 115).

47. Allison, "Touching Jesus' Feet," 113.

48. Translation from C. Detlef G. Müller, "Epistula Apostolorum," in Wilhelm Schneemelcher, ed., and R. McL. Wilson, trans., *New Testament Apocrypha* (rev. ed.; 2 vols.; Cambridge: James Clarke & Co; Louisville: Westminster John Knox, 1991–92), 1:249–84.

49. See Reginald H. Fuller, *The Formation of the Resurrection Narratives* (New York: Macmillan, 1971), 78–79: "Matthew's addition of 28:9-10 is an enhancement of the tendency already discernible in Mark's addition of 16:7 to the pre-Markan tradition, viz., a desire to link up the empty tomb and the appearance traditions."

50. See Davies and Allison, *Matthew,* 3:653.

51. See Bruce M. Metzger, "The Nazareth Inscription Once Again," in *New Testament Studies: Philological, Versional, and Patristic* (NTTS 10; Leiden: Brill, 1980), 75–92, on *SEG* 8, 13, a Greek inscription of uncertain provenance, which as an "Ordinance of Caesar" forbids the molestation of graves and tombs and the transfer of bodies "with malicious intention," on threat of capital punishment (for text and translation, ibid., 76–77). Because the date (which Caesar?) is unclear, it is uncertain that the inscription responds in any way to questions about the Christian proclamation of Jesus' resurrection, but Metzger says it is another piece of evidence adding "to what we already knew concerning the sanctity with which tombs were generally regarded in antiquity and the variety of penalties against *violatio sepulchri*" (ibid., 90).

52. See Luz, "Fictionality and Loyalty," 58–59; the second citation is from Luz, *Matthew,* 3:586, where he also says it is improbable that Matthew has inserted into his Markan base text an already well-developed guard story; he says, "I would like to rate the evangelist's own involvement in this story higher than is usually done." See also Davies and Allison, *Matthew,* 3:645; Susan E. Schaeffer, "The Guard at the Tomb (*Gos. Pet.* 8:28—11:49 and Matt. 27:62-66; 28:2-4, 11-16): A Case of Intertextuality?" *SBLSP* (1991): 499–507; and Wim J. C. Weren, "'His Disciples Stole Him Away' (Mt 28,13): A Rival Interpretation of Jesus' Resurrection," in *Resurrection in the New Testament: Festschrift J. Lambrecht,* ed. R. Bieringer et al. (BETL 165; Leuven: Peeters, 2002), 147–63, esp. 156–62, who works back to a pre-Matthean source (behind Matthew and the *Gospel of Peter*) to argue against the Matthean creation of a "polemical" rival interpretation as a foil for the correct interpretation.

53. See John Paul Heil, *The Death and Resurrection of Jesus: A Narrative-Critical Reading of Matthew 26–28* (Minneapolis: Fortress Press, 1991), 3, 6; Weren, "His Disciples Stole Him," 152–53.

54. Weren, "His Disciples Stole Him," 155.

55. Schaeffer, "The Guard at the Tomb," 502–5; Weren, "His Disciples Stole Him," 155–56.

56. This could be due to historical fact (so Davies and Allison, *Matthew*, 3:653 and n. 55) or owing to Matthew's depiction of the Pharisees as a Galilean group, as argued by J. Andrew Overman, *Matthew's Gospel and Formative Judaism: The Social World of the Matthean Community* (Minneapolis: Fortress Press, 1990), 155–56; but cf. Matt. 15:1.

57. Anthony J. Saldarini, *Matthew's Christian-Jewish Community* (Chicago: University of Chicago Press, 1994), 65. See also Adelbert Denaux, "Matthew's Story of Jesus' Burial and Resurrection (Mt 27,57—28,20)," in *Resurrection in the New Testament: Festschrift J. Lambrecht*, ed. R. Bieringer et al. (BETL 165; Leuven: Peeters, 2002), 123–45, esp. 136.

58. *Ioudaioi* occurs five times in Matthew, once here and four times in the expression "King of the Jews" (Matt. 2:2; 27:11, 29, 37).

59. Saldarini, *Matthew's Christian-Jewish Community*, 36, 46; according to Saldarini, Israel, Torah, and synagogue are part of Matthew's communal consciousness.

60. Ibid., 35. Saldarini notes a similar usage of *Ioudaioi* in Josephus, *War* 2.18.9 (ibid., 36–37).

61. Luz, "Fictionality and Loyalty," 59–60.

62. See Ronald L. Troxel, "Matt. 27.51-4 Reconsidered: Its Role in the Passion Narrative, Meaning and Origin," *NTS* 48 (2002): 30–47, esp. 31–35.

63. Davies and Allison, *Matthew*, 3:640–41, citing Maria Riebl, *Auferstehung Jesu in der Stunde seines Todes? Zur Botschaft von Mt 27,51b-53* (SBB 8; Stuttgart: Katholisches Bibelwerk, 1978), 63–67.

64. The phrase introduces the peculiar idea that the saints were raised but had the decorum to wait in their tombs until Jesus was raised—unless it is read as a subjective genitive, as in, after his raising (of them). Neither GNT[4] nor NA[27] lists the omission of this phrase *meta tēn egersin autou* as a variant reading, but Davies and Allison, *Matthew*, 3:634–35, say the phrase is missing from the Diatessaron, P.Egerton 3 fr. 1.r., and the Palestinian Syriac lectionary, and conclude that it is "secondary." See also Luz, *Matthew*, 3:568–69; Troxel, "Matt. 27.51-4 Reconsidered," 36–37. Along similar lines, see also Kenneth L. Waters, "Matthew 27:52-53 as Apocalyptic Apostrophe: Temporal-Spatial Collapse in the Gospel of Matthew," *JBL* 122 (2003): 489–515, esp. 502–5, who counsels considerable emendation.

65. Ulrich Luz, *The Theology of the Gospel of Matthew* (Cambridge: Cambridge University Press, 1995), 136; also Davies and Allison, *Matthew*, 3:639.

66. Dale C. Allison Jr., *The End of the Ages Has Come: An Early Interpretation of the Passion and Resurrection of Jesus* (Philadelphia: Fortress Press, 1985), 43, who notes that the two texts are depicted together in a panel from the Dura Europos synagogue (see also Luz, *Matthew*, 3:567). Ronald Troxel has suggested an influence from *1 Enoch* ("Matt. 27.51-4 Reconsidered," 43–44).

67. On this basis, Ronald Witherup thinks *emphanizō* indicates that they appear to "testify against Jerusalem for the rejection of Jesus": Ronald D. Witherup, "The Death of Jesus and the Raising of the Saints: Matthew 27:51-54 in Context," *SBLSP* (1987): 574–85 (here, 582). However, in the passive the verb primarily connotes appearance (Troxel, "Matt. 27.51-4 Reconsidered," 40; Luz, *Matthew*, 3:567). See also Davies and Allison, *Matthew*, 3:633, but without reference to the verb *enephanisthēsan*.

68. For the effect of this belief on the interpretation of the empty tomb story, see below, p. 140.

69. See the discussion in Davies and Allison, *Matthew*, 3:676. In an earlier work, they proposed that the original form was that of a prophetic commissioning, following the conclusion of Benjamin J. Hubbard, *The Matthean Redaction of a Primitive Apostolic Commissioning: An Exegesis of Matthew 28:16-20* (SBLDS 19; Missoula, Mont.: Scholars, 1974). See Davies and Allison, "Matt. 28.16-20: Texts behind the Text," *RHPR* 72 (1992): 89–98.

70. See again Davies and Allison, *Matthew*, 3:677–78; Luz, *Matthew*, 3:616–19.

71. Wendy Cotter, "Greco-Roman Apotheosis Traditions and the Resurrection Appearances in Matthew," in *The Gospel of Matthew in Current Study: Studies in Memory of William G. Thompson, S.J.*, ed. David E. Aune (Grand Rapids: Eerdmans, 2001), 127–53 (here, 129), summarizing the conclusions of Jane Schaberg, *The Father, the Son, and the Holy Spirit: The Triadic Phrase in Matthew 28:19b* (SBLDS 61; Chico, Calif.: Scholars, 1982), esp. 114. Luz, *Matthew*, 3:619, also delineates Danielic language and motifs.

72. Dale C. Allison Jr., *The New Moses: A Matthean Typology* (Minneapolis: Fortress Press, 1993), 262–66; Davies and Allison, *Matthew*, 3:679–80.

73. Cotter, "Greco-Roman Apotheosis Traditions," 149; Cotter refers to similar scenes describing the apotheosis of figures such as Romulus, Julius Caesar, and Caesar Augustus (ibid., 133–43), and Moses (146–48). See also Carter, *Matthew and the Margins*, 553–54.

74. Cotter, "Greco-Roman Apotheosis Traditions," 149–50.

75. Here I follow the Old Greek, rather than Theodotion, since it is closer to the language of Matthew.

76. The fourth beast, Daniel discovers, will also make war on the holy ones (Dan. 7:21-22); this situates the representative function of the one like a son of humankind in the context of a community under threat, so that the reception of authority and kingdom will be a real vindication for those the son of humankind represents; a similarly corporate conceptualization of the exalted "Son of Man" figure is also present in the Similitudes of Enoch (*1 Enoch* 37–71), where he stands for the oppressed people of God, who see in the report of the seer the judgment he will bring upon their oppressors, and in whom their own vindication is guaranteed. See, e.g., John J. Collins, *The Apocalyptic Imagination: An Introduction to Jewish Apocalyptic Literature* (2nd ed.; Grand Rapids: Eerdmans, 1998), 105–6 (on Daniel 7), 184–87 (on *1 Enoch*).

77. Cotter, "Greco-Roman Apotheosis Traditions," 151.

78. The "overthrow of Rome" here depends on a reading of this passage that takes "eagles" (24:28) as referring to the Roman military standard, and "sign of the Son of Man" (v. 30) to the standard of the coming Son of Man. See Warren Carter, "Are There Imperial Texts in the Class? Intertextual Eagles and Matthean Eschatology as 'Lights Out' Time for Imperial Rome (Matthew 24:27-31)," *JBL* 122 (2003): 467–87; Daniel A. Smith, "Matthew and Q: The Matthean Deployment of Q and Mark in the Apocalyptic Discourse," *ETL* 85 (2009): 99–116 (here, 113–14).

79. Importantly (for Q as well as for Matthew), Jesus receives this from the Father and not from Satan in return for submission to him (Matt. 4:8; Q 4:5-8).

80. See, e.g., Paul Hoffmann, *Studien zur Theologie der Logienquelle* (3rd ed.; NTAbh 8; Münster: Aschendorff, 1982), 139–42.

81. John S. Kloppenborg, "'Easter Faith' and the Sayings Gospel Q," *Semeia* 49 (1990): 71–99 (here, 90–91).

82. Christopher M. Tuckett, *Q and the History of Early Christianity* (Edinburgh: T. & T. Clark, 1996), 279.

83. See the discussion above, pp. 48-49.

84. Here I presume that the mission instructions are still valid in Q and do not archive an earlier stage of itinerancy.

85. Davies and Allison, *Matthew*, 2:279.

86. See Prov. 8:1-21. For discussion, see Luz, *Matthew*, 2:171–72; Nolland, *Gospel of Matthew*, 475–76.

87. See Smith, "Matthew and Q," 115–24.

88. Ibid., 124–25.

89. Luz, *Matthew*, 1:49.

90. Robinson, "Matthean Trajectory," 130.

91. See John S. Kloppenborg, *Excavating Q: The History and Setting of the Sayings Gospel* (Edinburgh: T. & T. Clark; Minneapolis: Fortress Press, 2000), 171–75, 214–61.

Chapter 8

1. For discussion, see Raymond E. Brown, *An Introduction to the Gospel of John*, ed. Francis J. Moloney (ABRL; New York: Doubleday, 2003), 94–104; for the idea of "secondary orality" as an influence leading to parallels with the Synoptics, see Moloney's note at ibid., 101–2n31.

2. Brown, for one, traced the origin of the Fourth Gospel back through three stages (the ministry or activity of Jesus, the proclamation of Jesus in the postresurrection context of the [Johannine] community, the composition of the gospel by the evangelist and its revision by a redactor) to the influence of the Beloved Disciple, who in his view originally was a disciple of John the Baptist and became a disciple of Jesus: Brown, *Introduction*, 62–86.

3. See R. Alan Culpepper, *Anatomy of the Fourth Gospel: A Study in Literary Design* (Philadelphia: Fortress Press, 1983), who made the critical observation of how these recognition (Gk., *anagnōrisis*) scenes are tied to the plot of John: "Not only is Jesus' identity progressively revealed by the repetitive signs and discourses and the progressive enhancement of metaphorical and symbolic images, but each episode has essentially the same plot as the story as a whole" (ibid., 84). See also now Kasper Bro Larsen, *Recognizing the Stranger: Recognition Scenes in the Gospel of John* (Biblical Interpretation Series 93; Leiden: Brill, 2008).

4. Craig Koester, "Jesus' Resurrection, the Signs, and the Dynamics of Faith in the Gospel of John," in *The Resurrection of Jesus in the Gospel of John*, ed. Craig R. Koester and Reimund Bieringer (WUNT 2/222; Tübingen: Mohr Siebeck, 2008), 47–74, esp. 52–55 (citation from 52).

5. See Martinus C. de Boer, "Jesus' Departure to the Father in John: Death or Resurrection?" in *Theology and Christology in the Fourth Gospel: Essays by the Members of the SNTS Johannine Writings Seminar*, ed. G. Van Belle et al. (BETL 184; Leuven: Peeters, 2005), 1–19.

6. A concise summary is found in John 16:28: "I came out from the Father and I have come into the world; again I am leaving the world and I am going to the Father." See also John 7:27-29 (Jesus sent by the Father; "the one who sent me" occurs 25 times in John); John 4:34; 5:30; 6:38; 9:4 (Jesus doing the will of the one who sent him); John 7:33-34; 13:1-3; 14:12; 16:5-11; 17:11, 13; 20:17 (Jesus going back to the Father who sent him).

7. For discussion, see above, pp. 59-65.

8. So Francis J. Moloney, *The Gospel of John* (SP 4; Collegeville, Minn.: Michael Glazier / Liturgical, 1998), 447–48; Andrew T. Lincoln, *The Gospel according to Saint John* (BNTC; London: Continuum; Peabody, Mass.: Hendrickson, 2005), 422.

9. De Boer, "Jesus' Departure," 4 (emphasis in original).

10. Koester, "Jesus' Resurrection," 49–50.

11. Raymond E. Brown, *The Gospel according to John: Introduction, Translation, and Notes* (2 vols.; AB 29–29A; Garden City, N.Y.: Doubleday, 1966–70), 2:984; Moloney, *Gospel of John*, 522. Without suggesting that the evangelist here has used a source (not reflected in the other Gospels, however) that originally included a saying like this, one could still read this as assuming a knowledge on the part of the reader of other versions of the story in which more than one woman went to the tomb.

12. Sandra M. Schneiders, "Touching the Risen Jesus: Mary Magdalene and Thomas the Twin in John 20," in *The Resurrection of Jesus in the Gospel of John*, ed. C. Koester and R. Bieringer, 153–76 (here, 163).

13. Frans Neirynck, "Luke 24,12: An Anti-Docetic Interpolation?" in *New Testament Textual Criticism and Exegesis: Festschrift J. Delobel*, ed. A. Denaux (BETL 161; Leuven: Leuven University Press / Peeters, 2002), 145–58, esp. 148; see also Neirynck, "Once More Lk 24,12," *ETL* 70 (1994): 319–40, esp. 324. For further detail on this issue, and for an account of the text-critical problem of the absence of Luke 24:12 from the Western witnesses, see above pp. 99-101.

14. Frans Neirynck, "John and the Synoptics: The Empty Tomb Stories," *NTS* 30 (1984): 161–87, esp. 166–67.

15. For a fuller discussion of different approaches to this question, see Reimund Bieringer, "'I Am Ascending to My Father and Your Father, to My God and Your God' (John 20:17): Resurrection and Ascension in the Gospel of John," in *The Resurrection of Jesus in the Gospel of John*, ed. C. Koester and R. Bieringer, 209–35, esp. 217–21.

16. Brown, *Gospel according to John*, 2:998–1004, sees three original stories here: (1) the discovery of the empty tomb, (2) the inspection by Peter and the Beloved Disciple, and (3) the Christophany to Mary.

17. Koester, "Jesus' Resurrection," 67. Lincoln sees here a response to the charge (as in Matt. 28:13-15) that the disciples had stolen the body—clearly in John's narrative they have no idea where it is (Lincoln, *Gospel according to Saint John*, 489).

18. So Ernst Haenchen, *John: A Commentary on the Gospel of John*, ed. and trans. Robert W. Funk and U. Busse (2 vols.; Hermeneia; Philadelphia: Fortress Press, 1984), 2:209, except Haenchen attributes their inclusion to the redactor's knowledge of the other stories.

19. Brown, *Gospel according to John*, 2:999; for discussion of the *Epistula Apostolorum*, see below, pp. 135-37.

20. Brown, *Introduction*, 196–99, considered the evangelist, the author of the epistles, and the Gospel's redactor as members of a "Johannine school" who "imbued with the spirit of the BD [Beloved Disciple] and under his guidance and encouragement . . . preached and developed his reminiscences even further, according to the needs of the community to which they ministered" (ibid., 196).

21. Brown notes this was already observed by John Chrysostom, *Hom. Joh.* 85.5 (*Gospel according to John*, 2:1007).

22. See Lincoln, *Gospel according to Saint John*, 490, also referencing John 10:18: "No one takes [my life] away from me, but I lay it down of my own accord; and I have the authority to take it back again."

23. See Byron R. McCane, *Roll Back the Stone: Death and Burial in the World of Jesus* (Harrisburg, Pa.: Trinity Press International, 2003), 32–33; for the layout John presumes, see Brown, *Gospel according to John*, 2:982–83.

24. Brown, *Gospel according to John*, 2:989; Lincoln, *Gospel according to Saint John*, 492.

25. Schneiders, "Touching the Risen Jesus," 165.

26. So Brown, *Gospel according to John*, 2:1007: "The disciple who was bound closest to Jesus in love was the quickest to look for him and the first to believe in him." Similarly also Haenchen, *John*, 2:208; Moloney, *Gospel of John*, 523, who thinks "the Scripture" refers to the Fourth Gospel itself; Lincoln, *Gospel according to Saint John*, 491.

27. See above, p. 118; Koester, "Jesus' Resurrection," 52–55.

28. This interpretation is found already in Augustine, *Tract. Ev. Ioh.* 120.9.

29. See especially John 2:22; for a more elaborate explanation of the Easter hermeneutic, see Luke 24:45-47.

30. Koester, "Jesus' Resurrection," 68–69.

31. Lincoln, *Gospel according to Saint John*, 492. Moloney claims that Mary's mistaking Jesus for the gardener here is "perhaps the earliest literary evidence of a Jewish response to the Christian story of the resurrection," for "early Christian documents report a Jewish response that the body had been stolen from the tomb by a gardener" (Moloney, *Gospel of John*, citing Tertullian, *Spect.* 30).

32. Such a demonstration seems unnecessary in a second experience of the risen Jesus (see John 21:12; but contrast 21:7).

33. Adeline Fehribach, *The Women in the Life of the Bridegroom: A Feminist Historical-Literary Analysis of the Female Characters in the Fourth Gospel* (Collegeville, Minn.: Liturgical Press, 1998), 143–67; Fehribach, "The Birthing Bridegroom: The Portrayal of Jesus in the Fourth Gospel," in *A Feminist Companion to John*, ed. Amy-Jill Levine with Marianne Blickenstaff (2 vols.; London and New York: Sheffield Academic, 2003), 2:104–29, esp. 115–19.

34. Katherine Ludwig Jansen, "Maria Magdalena: *Apostolorum Apostola*," in *Women Preachers and Prophets through Two Millennia of Christianity*, ed. Beverly Mayne Kienzle and Pamela J. Walker (Berkeley: University of California Press, 1998), 57–96 (here, 58).

35. See the concise discussion in Mary Rose D'Angelo, "'I Have Seen the Lord': Mary Magdalen as Visionary, Early Christian Prophecy, and the Context of John 20:14-18," in *Mariam, the Magdalen, and the Mother*, ed. Deirdre Good (Bloomington: Indiana University Press, 2005), 95–122, esp. 97–102. For the "competition" between Peter and Mary in these later texts, see Ann Graham Brock, *Mary Magdalene, the First Apostle: The Struggle for Authority* (HTS 51; Cambridge: Harvard University Press, 2003), 73–104.

36. See Mary Rose D'Angelo, "Reconstructing 'Real' Women in Gospel Literature: The Case of Mary Magdalene," in *Women and Christian Origins*, ed. Ross Shepard Kraemer and Mary Rose D'Angelo (Oxford: Oxford University Press, 1999), 105–28; Jane Schaberg, *The Resurrection of Mary Magdalene: Legends, Apocrypha, and the Christian Testament* (New York and London: Continuum, 2002), 65–120. A major reason for this identification is the fact that Luke, after narrating the anointing of Jesus by an unnamed woman of the city, a "sinner," mentions Mary Magdalene among the women who were ministering to Jesus and the Twelve (Luke 7:36-50; 8:1-3).

37. For discussion of various tradition-critical and redaction-critical approaches to John 20:1-18, see Bieringer, "I Am Ascending," 217–21. For the view that John 20:14-18 and Matt. 28:9-10 rely on the same earlier tradition, see Brown, *Gospel according to John*, 2:1003: "Despite the lateness of the witnesses, we are inclined to believe that the tradition of the appearance to Magdalene may be ancient." See also Barnabas Lindars, "The Composition of John 20," *NTS* 7 (1961): 142–47; D'Angelo, "I Have Seen the Lord," 109.

38. See Neirynck, "John and the Synoptics," 166–67; Bieringer, "I Am Ascending," 222–32.

39. François Bovon, "Le Privilège Pascal de Marie-Madeleine," *NTS* 30 (1984): 50–62 (here, 52).

40. Claudia Setzer, "Excellent Women: Female Witness to the Resurrection," *JBL* 116 (1997): 259–72 (here, 268).

41. Schaberg, *Resurrection of Mary Magdalene*, 295–98.

42. D'Angelo, "I Have Seen the Lord," 106–11. D'Angelo rightly notes that the influence of the plot of Luke-Acts (nonvisionary resurrection appearances over forty days followed by the ascension, which brings them to an end) has obscured the similarities between the visions of Mary and John of Patmos. As noted above (pp. 18-19), Paul likewise may not have distinguished his own vision of the risen Christ from the kind reported in Revelation 1.

43. C. H. Dodd, "The Appearances of the Risen Christ: An Essay in Form-Criticism of the Gospels," in D. E. Nineham, ed., *Studies in the Gospels: Essays in Memory of R. H. Lightfoot* (Oxford: Basil Blackwell, 1955), 9–35 (here, 11); discussed above (p. 109).

44. D'Angelo, "I Have Seen the Lord," 113.

45. D'Angelo is also correct, however, that delineating the similarities between these two vision reports does not get us any closer to a source behind John 20:14-18: she suggests that "subtle variations from the usual Johannine diction suggest that this message [may be] . . . a remnant of the inherited material on which their theology was based" ("I Have Seen the Lord," 110, citing only the explicit identification between "my Father" and "my God," terms that elsewhere in John are straightforwardly assumed as synonyms).

46. Ibid., 111. Could one even imagine her receiving a prophetic utterance such as "Thus says the Lord: 'You will not see me until you say, Blessed is the Coming One in the name of the Lord'"?

47. See Sandra M. Schneiders, "John 20.11-18: The Encounter of the Easter Jesus with Mary Magdalene—A Transformative Feminist Reading," in *"What Is John?" Readers and Readings of the Fourth Gospel*, ed. Fernando F. Segovia (SBLSS 3, 7; Atlanta: Scholars, 1996), 1:155–68, esp. 159, with examples.

48. D'Angelo, "I Have Seen the Lord," 106.

49. BDAG, ad loc.

50. See BDF §336/3: "Jn 20:17 μή μου ἅπτου (which therefore has already happened or has been attempted)."

51. Harold W. Attridge, "'Don't Be Touching Me': Recent Feminist Scholarship on Mary Magdalene," in *A Feminist Companion to John*, 2:140–66, esp. 141–42n6, citing among others Brown, *Gospel according to John*, 2:992. Attridge's essay is an excellent and comprehensive survey of recent readings of this difficult passage.

52. Attridge notes several different permutations of this reading ("Don't Be Touching Me," 148–52). See also Brown, *Gospel according to John*, 2:1014; Lincoln, *Gospel according to Saint John*, 493–94.

53. Schneiders, "Touching the Risen Jesus," 172.

54. De Boer, "Jesus' Departure," 7–10.

55. Mary Rose D'Angelo, "A Critical Note: John 20:17 and Apocalypse of Moses 31," *JTS* 41 (1990): 529–36 (here, 532).

56. Ibid., 535, citing Origen, *Comm. Joh.* 6.38; *Dial. Herac.* 138; *Comm. Joh.* 13.30. See also Wayne A. Meeks, "The Man from Heaven in Johannine Sectarianism," *JBL* 91 (1972): 44–72, esp. 66 ("sacred liminality").

57. See also George R. Beasley-Murray, *John* (2nd ed.; WBC 36; Nashville: Thomas Nelson, 1999), 377–78.

58. D'Angelo, "John 20:17," 535. Attridge is impressed by this reading ("Don't Be Touching Me," 166): "The verse does not indicate a problem with Mary, but with the situation of Jesus' transitional state. On his way back on high, he was simply not fit to be touched." Cf. Moloney, *Gospel of John*, 529.

59. The narrator does not say that Thomas touched the risen Jesus in John 20:26-29.

60. Beasley-Murray, *John*, 377–78.

61. See Haenchen, *John*, 2:210: "The Evangelist presupposes a demythized concept of the resurrection, in which Jesus returns as a spirit. Mary appears to encounter Jesus in a state in which the transition from his earthly form to a state of spirituality has not yet taken place (this is told in reliance on a crude tradition); the Evangelist also felt this state, which is impossible to our way of thinking, to be inappropriate."

62. D'Angelo, "John 20:17," 534.

63. Schaberg, *Resurrection of Mary Magdalene*, 304.

64. Ibid., 304–6.

65. Ibid., 257. Schaberg also includes here 2 Kings 2, which, however, seems more important to her reconstruction of conceptualization of death and resurrection/vindication in the *basileia* movement. Schaberg credits this movement's mysticism and exegetical creativity with the origin of the resurrection traditions along the following lines: "(1) not finding the body (as Elijah's body was not found) as the context for (2) the insight about the resurrection *having occurred*, as the context or provocation for (3) a vision of the resurrected one ascending (as Elijah ascended)" (ibid., 322).

66. Ibid., 217–19.

67. Ibid., 288.

68. D. Moody Smith, *The Theology of the Gospel of John* (New Testament Theology; Cambridge: Cambridge University Press, 1995), 108.

69. The Greek reads literally, "What sign do you show us that you are doing these things?"

70. See Sandra M. Schneiders, "The Resurrection of the Body in the Fourth Gospel: A Key to Johannine Spirituality," in *Life in Abundance: Studies of John's Gospel in Tribute to Raymond E. Brown, s.s.*, ed. John R. Donahue (Collegeville, Minn.: Liturgical, 2005), 168–98, esp. 177–79 (Schneiders also refers to John 7:37-39 in her argument for "body as temple").

71. "The preposition *eis* with the accusative suggests motion to the interior. But the interior in this text is not a physical place. It is 'where the disciples were gathered together' (20:19). Jesus arises in the midst of the community" (ibid., 185). See also Schneiders, "Touching the Risen Jesus," 165–67.

72. Jörg Frey, "Eschatology in the Johannine Circle," in *Theology and Christology in the Fourth Gospel*, ed. G. Van Belle et al., 45–82 (here, 67).

73. De Boer, "Jesus' Departure," 8–10; Frey, "Eschatology," 68.

74. So, e.g., Leon Morris, *The Gospel according to John* (rev. ed.; NICNT; Grand Rapids: Eerdmans, 1995), 623, relying mainly on *opsesthe*; Brown (*John*, 2:729) says "this was the view of most of the Greek fathers."

75. Frey, "Eschatology," 82. See also Brown, *Introduction*, 234–48, and R. Alan Culpepper, "Realized Eschatology in the Experience of the Johannine Community," in *The Resurrection of Jesus in the Gospel of John*, ed. C. Koester and R. Bieringer, 253–76.

76. So Brown, *John*, 2:730.

77. See also John 14:26-28; 16:7-16.

78. See Smith, *Theology of the Gospel of John*, 139–44.

Chapter 9

1. Translation from Kathleen E. McVey, trans., *Ephrem the Syrian: The Hymns* (CWS; New York: Paulist, 1989).

2. See the discussion in Maurice Goguel, *La foi à la Résurrection de Jésus dans le christianisme primitif* (Paris: Leroux, 1933), 213–33.

3. Goguel, *La foi à la Résurrection*, 224–26. The clearest example is found in the *Gospel of Peter*, concerning which, see below, pp. 137-39. Goguel cites (Pseudo?) Ephrem the Syrian, *Hom. Res.* 7; this text describes a gradual resuscitation or awaking, but then a sudden transformation of the terrestrial body into a spiritual body, which then exited the tomb like a bolt of lightning, without breaking the seals, and ascended into heaven unseen by the guards and accompanied by angels.

4. Unless otherwise noted, dates given for early Christian authors and their works are taken from F. L. Cross and E. A. Livingstone, eds., *The Oxford Dictionary of the Christian Church* (3rd ed.; Oxford: Oxford University Press, 2005).

5. Tertullian does, however, refer to the burial of Jesus as an argument against Marcion: if a "phantom" has "expired" (that is, given up its spirit), what can be buried in the tomb (*Marc.* 4.42)?

6. In Matthew the concern is that the disciples could be accused of stealing the body to create the illusion of a resurrection, just as in antiquity a contrived disappearance could give the illusion of a disappearance or apotheosis: see Arthur S. Pease, "Some Aspects of Invisibility," *HSCP* 53 (1942): 1–36, esp. 18–21; also Origen, *Cels.* 2.55-56; Gregory Nazianzen, *Orat.* 4.59.

7. See Pheme Perkins, *Resurrection: New Testament Witness and Contemporary Reflection* (Garden City, N.Y.: Doubleday, 1984), 331–32, who explains that in the second century Christian reflection on resurrection was oriented to two kinds of discussion: first, it had to address the claims of Gnostics and others that the body could not share in immortality; and second, it had to account for "the plausibility of resurrection language" to outsiders, just as Paul had to account for it to the Corinthians.

8. Besides Cross and Livingstone, *Oxford Dictionary of the Christian Church*, see also, for the *Gospel of Peter*, Christian Maurer and Wilhelm Schneemelcher, "The Gospel of Peter," in Wilhelm Schneemelcher, ed., and R. McL. Wilson, trans., *New Testament Apocrypha* (rev. ed.; 2 vols.; Cambridge: James Clarke; Louisville: Westminster John Knox, 1991–92), 1:216–27, esp. 1:221; and for the *Epistle of the Apostles*, see C. Detlef G. Müller, "Epistula Apostolorum," in Schneemelcher, *New Testament Apocrypha*, 1:249–84, esp. 1:251; see also Ron Cameron, *The Other Gospels: Non-canonical Gospel Texts* (Philadelphia: Westminster, 1982), 133.

9. See James A. Kelhoffer, *Miracle and Mission: The Authentication of Missionaries and Their Message in the Longer Ending of Mark* (WUNT 2/112; Tübingen: Mohr Siebeck, 2000), 169–75, who indicates that citations of the longer ending in the writings of Irenaeus (*Haer.* 3.10.5, c. 180 CE) and Justin (*1 Apol.* 45.5, c. 160) mean it must have been composed earlier than c. 150.

10. Ibid., 155 (emphasis in original).

11. Ibid., 48-122, 123-56.

12. Ibid., 150-54.

13. Simon Hornblower and Anthony Spawforth, eds., *The Oxford Classical Dictionary* (3rd ed.; Oxford: Oxford University Press, 2003), s.v. "epitome."

14. For the parallel structure of these two reports, see Adela Yarbro Collins, *Mark: A Commentary on the Gospel of Mark* (Hermeneia; Minneapolis: Fortress Press, 2007), 807.

15. As noted above (pp. 122-23), seeing the empty tomb does not lead to belief for either Peter or Mary Magdalene (20:8-9, 13, 15), but only a personal encounter (20:14-18). It leads to belief for the Beloved Disciple because only he is in a position to understand the sign apart from either a personal encounter or the testimony of the Scriptures (20:8-9).

16. The "Freer logion," which is an addition to the longer ending (after v. 14) found in the manuscript Codex Washingtonianus (W) and known to Jerome, adds an additional interchange between Jesus and the apostles in which they protest that their disbelief of the resurrection reports was due to the influence of Satan, under whose authority is "this age of lawlessness and unbelief." Jesus responds that the authority of Satan is at an end. For discussion, see Bruce M. Metzger, *The Text of the New Testament: Its Transmission, Corruption, and Restoration* (3rd ed.; Oxford: Oxford University Press, 1992), 57. As Collins (*Mark*, 806) notes, it is not an independent saying, but "was added apparently to soften the transition from v. 14 to v. 15 in the longer ending."

17. Kelhoffer, *Message and Miracle*, 245-472; summary, 476. Kelhoffer also notes, however, that apologists such as Justin Martyr and Theophilus of Antioch frequently mention Christian miracle-workers who are not presented as leading figures in the movement (ibid., 476).

18. Paul Foster, "Polymorphic Christology: Its Origins and Development in Early Christianity," *JTS* 58 (2007): 66-99 (here 70).

19. Ibid., 98.

20. Ibid., 71.

21. See above, pp. 32-34, 93-95.

22. Collins, *Mark*, 803.

23. Metzger, *Text of the New Testament*, 73.

24. The verb *surgent* here does not make sense, and various emendations have been suggested: see D. W. Palmer, "Origin, Form, and Purpose of Mark 16:4 in Codex Bobbiensis," *JTS* 27 (1976): 113-22, esp. 114-15; Bruce M. Metzger, *A Textual Commentary on the Greek New Testament* (2nd ed.; Stuttgart: Deutsche Bibelgesellschaft / United Bible Societies, 1994), 101-2; see also Goguel, *La foi à la Résurrection*, 231-32. Palmer suggests that this interpolation originally described an assumption of Jesus directly from the cross ("Mark 16:4 in Codex Bobbiensis," 116-22).

25. Citations are from Müller, "Epistula Apostolorum," following the Ethiopic version.

26. See Raymond E. Brown, *The Gospel according to John: Introduction, Translation, and Notes* (2 vols.; AB 29-29A; Garden City, N.Y.: Doubleday, 1966-1970), 2:999.

27. Cameron, *The Other Gospels*, 131-32. Simon and Cerinthus are condemned as heretics in *Ep. Apos.* 1, 7.

28. Paul Foster, "Are There Any Early Fragments of the So-Called *Gospel of Peter?*" *NTS* 52 (2006): 1-28; for the date of the Akhmîm codex, p. 1 and n. 2.

29. Eusebius, *Hist. Eccl.* 6.12.1-6. See Paul Foster, "The Gospel of Peter," *ExpT* 118 (2007): 318-25, esp. 319-20.

30. Ibid., 319; H. B. Swete, *The Akhmîm Fragment of the Apocryphal Gospel of St. Peter* (London: Macmillan, 1893), xii.

31. Foster, "Any Early Fragments," 4-19; other finds are also discussed (19-27).

32. Foster, "Gospel of Peter," 325.

33. Foster, "Polymorphic Christology," 79.

34. It could be that this is meant to represent an ascent of Jesus' soul or spirit, which then (after proclaiming to the sleepers, 10.41-42) reanimates his body, as later texts suggest. See below, p. 140.

35. See John Dominic Crossan, *The Cross That Spoke: The Origins of the Passion Narrative* (San Francisco: Harper & Row, 1988), 16–30, who argues that the *Gospel of Peter* was dependent on a pre-Markan passion narrative source (which he calls "the Cross Gospel") but was also influenced by the canonical Gospels (which had used the Cross Gospel as a source). For earlier approaches to the question, see Helmut Koester, *Ancient Christian Gospels: Their History and Development* (Philadelphia: Trinity Press International; London: SCM, 1990), 216–20. Koester's own view is that "the *Gospel of Peter*, as a whole, is not dependent upon any of the canonical Gospels," but its passion narrative was based on the pre-Markan passion narrative source used by Mark and John, and it also incorporated an earlier epiphany scene describing the raising of Jesus (ibid., 240). Koester thinks that the *Gospel of Peter* was also dependent on an earlier source text (and not Matthew) for the guard at the tomb (ibid., 234–37).

36. Alan Kirk, "Examining Priorities: Another Look at the *Gospel of Peter*'s Relationship to the New Testament Gospels," *NTS* 40 (1994): 572–95, esp. 586–94 on *Gos. Pet.* 8.28—11.49 as dependent on the canonical Gospels. See also Foster, "Gospel of Peter," 324: "The text is best understood as a reflection on canonical traditions, and it also demonstrates theological trajectories that are part of later Christianity."

37. The text says: "And he [Herod] handed him over to the people on the first day of Unleavened Bread, their feast. And those who took the Lord were shoving him along, running and saying . . ." (*Gos. Pet.* 2.5—3.6). There is no clear subject for any of the verbs until 6.23 ("And the Jews rejoiced and gave his body to Joseph"), although 5.17 ("And they fulfilled everything and brought their transgressions to completion against their heads") seems consistent with the anti-Judaism of the *Gospel of Peter.*

38. See, e.g., Melito of Sardis (d. c. 190), *Peri Pascha* 79–80, in which it is said that "Israel" made ready the implements of Jesus' torture and death, and killed the Lord at the great feast (79). For detailed discussion, see John T. Carroll, Joel B. Green, et al., *The Death of Jesus in Early Christianity* (Peabody, Mass.: Hendrickson, 1995), 183–89; also the essays in vol. 2 of Peter Richardson et al., eds., *Anti-Judaism in Early Christianity* (2 vols.; ESCJ 2–3; Waterloo, Ont.: Wilfrid Laurier University Press, 1986).

39. See Helen K. Bond, *Pontius Pilate in History and Interpretation* (SNTSMS 100; Cambridge: Cambridge University Press, 1998).

40. Byron McCane, *Roll Back the Stone: Death and Burial in the World of Jesus* (Harrisburg, Pa.: Trinity Press International, 2003), 101–4. Contrary to Ulrich Luz, *Matthew: A Commentary* (3 vols.; Hermeneia; Minneapolis: Fortress Press, 2001–07), 3:579, the fact that Jesus is buried in Joseph's new tomb does not make this a "respectable, indeed a noble burial"—a new tomb does not provide Jesus with the same communal bond as a well-used family tomb.

41. Michael A. Knibb, "Martyrdom and Ascension of Isaiah," *OTP* 2:143–76 (here, 149).

42. Translation from C. Detlef G. Müller, "The Ascension of Isaiah," in Schneemelcher, *New Testament Apocrypha*, 2:603–20.

43. Goguel, *La foi à la Résurrection*, 232.

44. For the date of the so-called *Gospel of the Hebrews*, see Philipp Vielhauer and Georg Strecker, "Jewish-Christian Gospels," in Schneemelcher, *New Testament Apocrypha*, 1:134–78, esp. 176. According to Eusebius, *Hist. Eccl.* 4.22.8, the text was known to Hegesippus (c. 180).

45. Goguel, *La foi à la Résurrection*, 232–33, referring to *Mart. Isa.* 3:15-17, Mark 16:4 (k), and *Gos. Pet.* 10.41-42; although this is not explicit in the first two texts, it is found in *Mart. Isa.* 4:21.

46. John Dominic Crossan, "Appendix: Bodily-Resurrection Faith," in *The Resurrection of Jesus: John Dominic Crossan and N. T. Wright in Dialogue*, ed. Robert B. Stewart (Minneapolis: Fortress Press, 2006), 171–86 (here, 181).

47. For a brief discussion of the earliest texts betraying a knowledge of this belief, see Jared Wicks, "Christ's Saving Descent to the Dead: Early Witnesses from Ignatius of Antioch to Origen," *ProEccl* 17 (2008): 281–309. Wicks lists (among other texts) Ignatius,

Magn. 9:2; Justin, *Dial.* 72; *Ep. Apos.* 27; *Sib. Or.* 8.310-17; *Mart. Isa.* 4:21; *Asc. Isa.* 9:15-18; *Odes Sol.* 42:11-20; Melito, *Peri Pascha* 102–3; Irenaeus, *Haer.* 4.27.2; *Dem.* 78.

48. This in spite of the fact that Luke was clearly more interested in the rescue of the flesh of Jesus from corruption than in the descent of Jesus in the spirit to the underworld: see in particular his adjustment of the citation from Ps. 15:10 LXX in Acts 2:31, in which "my flesh" from v. 9 is made the subject of "to see corruption" in v. 10.

49. See Margaret Y. MacDonald, *Early Christian Women and Pagan Opinion: The Power of the Hysterical Woman* (Cambridge: Cambridge University Press, 1996), 1–5, who points out that the word *paroistros* (which I translate here as "frenzied"), often translated as "hysterical," has the connotations of uncontrolled religious fervor; the context also adds a magical connotation.

50. Katherine Ludwig Jansen, "Maria Magdalena: *Apostolorum Apostola*," in *Women Preachers and Prophets through Two Millennia of Christianity*, ed. Beverly Mayne Kienzle and Pamela J. Walker (Berkeley: University of California Press, 1998), 57–96, esp. 58–60 (citation from 58).

51. Luz, *Matthew*, 3:602 (citing Origen and others).

52. For some early Christian authors, the doctrine of the perpetual virginity of Mary extended not only to her abstinence from intercourse after giving birth to Jesus, but also to the preservation of her hymen intact in the act of giving birth (Cross and Livingstone, *Oxford Dictionary of the Christian Church*, s.v. "Virgin Birth of Christ").

53. E.g., Augustine, *Fid. Symb.* 5.11; *Tract. Ev. Jo.* 121.4; Ephrem, *Hymn Nat.* 10.6-7; Jerome, *Epis.* 48.21.

54. See, e.g., Walter Burkert, *Greek Religion*, trans. J. Raffan (Oxford: Basil Blackwell; Cambridge: Harvard University Press, 1985), 207: "The hero cult has often been compared to the Christian cult of saints; and without doubt there is direct continuity as well as a structural parallel here."

55. Jackson P. Hershbell, "Philostratus's *Heroikos* and Early Christianity: Heroes, Saints, and Martyrs," in *Philostratus's Heroikos: Religion and Cultural Identity in the Third Century* C.E., ed. E. Bradshaw Aitken and J. K. Berenson MacLean (SBLWGRW 6; Leiden: Brill, 2004), 169–79 (here, 177–78); James C. Skedros, "The *Heroikos* and Popular Christianity in the Third Century C.E.," in *Philostratus's Heroikos: Religion and Cultural Identity*, 181–93 (here, 190).

56. Helmut Koester, "On Heroes, Tombs, and Early Christianity: An Epilogue," in *Flavius Philostratus: Heroikos*, trans. J. K. Berenson MacLean and E. Bradshaw Aitken (SBLWGRW 1; Atlanta: SBL, 2001), 257–64 (here, 257–58).

57. Ibid., 263–64.

58. See Dennis D. Hughes, "Hero Cult, Heroic Honors, Heroic Dead: Some Developments in the Hellenistic and Roman Periods," in *Ancient Greek Hero Cult: Proceedings of the Fifth International Seminar on Ancient Greek Cult*, ed. Robin Hägg (Acta Instituti Atheniensis Regni Sueciae 16; Stockholm: Svenska Institutet i Athen, 1999), 167–75; for the application of this to Christian cults of saints, Hughes cites Julian, *Epis.* 78 (ibid., 167).

59. MacLean and Aitken, *Flavius Philostratus: Heroikos*, xliv–xlv.

60. Skedros, "*Heroikos* and Popular Christianity," 190–91.

61. See *Gos. Pet.* 8–13; *Ep. Apos.* 9–10; *Mart. Paul* 11:6-7; *Acts of John (Metastasis)*; *Acts Pet.* 40–41; *Acts Thom.* 169–70; Ethiopic *Liber Requiei* 67–89 (Shoemaker, *Ancient Traditions*, 290–350); *Acts Pil.* 12–16; Leontius of Neapolis, *Life of Symeon*; Chariton, *Chaer.* 3.3.

62. J. K. Elliott, *The Apocryphal New Testament* (Oxford: Clarendon, 1993), 165.

63. Incidentally, this makes Joseph of Arimathea the first witness to the resurrection of Jesus in the *Acts of Pilate*, even before the tomb has been opened.

64. Stephen J. Shoemaker, *Ancient Traditions of the Virgin Mary's Dormition and Assumption* (Oxford Early Christian Studies; Oxford: Oxford University Press, 2002), 38–46, 146–48, 232–56; also Shoemaker, "Death and the Maiden: The Early History of the Dormition and Assumption Apocrypha," *SVTQ* 50 (2006): 59–97, esp. 65: although

early manuscript fragments in Syriac and Georgian date to the fifth century, Shoemaker argues that "this rather heterodox apocryphon is almost certainly the earliest extant narrative of the end of Mary's life, composed probably in the third century, if not perhaps even earlier."

65. Citations here and following are taken from Shoemaker, *Ancient Traditions*, 290–350 ("Appendix A: The Ethiopic *Liber Requiei*").

66. On the anti-Jewishness of ancient mariological literature, see Stephen J. Shoemaker, "'Let Us Go and Burn Her Body': The Image of the Jews in the Early Dormition Traditions," *CH* 68 (1999): 775–823.

67. See Gerhard Lohfink, *Die Himmelfahrt Jesu: Untersuchungen zu den Himmelfahrts- und Erhohungstexten bei Lukas* (SANT 26; Munich: Kösel, 1971), 38–39 (on the earthbound perspective); 42–49 (on particular motifs).

68. The empty tomb of Mary figures in, e.g., the Greek *Discourse on the Dormition* (dated to the fifth or sixth century by Shoemaker, *Ancient Traditions*, 51; translation in Elliott, *Apocryphal New Testament*, 701–8), and the so-called "Euthymiac History" (a text that survives as an interpolation in a homily of John of Damascus but whose core legend is dated to c. 550–750 CE by Shoemaker, *Ancient Traditions*, 69). A translation of the Euthymiac History can be found in Brian E. Daley, *On the Dormition of Mary: Early Patristic Homilies* (Crestwood, N.Y.: St. Vladimir's Seminary Press, 1998), 224–26.

69. Shoemaker, *Ancient Traditions*, 78–141.

70. Shoemaker, "Death and the Maiden," 60–61.

71. David Golan, "Hadrian's Decision to Supplant 'Jerusalem' by 'Aelia Capitolina,'" *HZAG* 35 (1986): 226–39 (here, 226). Golan argues that Hadrian's purpose was to undermine early Christian anti-imperialism by remaking its symbolic center, Jerusalem, as a conspicuously Roman city; the double name "Aelia Capitolina" (giving tribute first to Hadrian himself and second to Jupiter Capitolinus) was intended to broadcast to "Roman dissenters—that is, Christians of Roman stock" that the emperor was the only king of Jerusalem and that Jupiter, "the real father of gods and the patron of Rome, dwells in Jerusalem as he does on the Capitoline at Rome" (ibid., 238).

72. W. Harold Mare, *The Archaeology of the Jerusalem Area* (Grand Rapids: Baker, 1987), 206 (map), 209–11 (discussion); Colin Morris, *The Sepulchre of Christ and the Medieval West: From the Beginning to 1600* (Oxford: Oxford University Press, 2005), 18.

73. Jonathan Z. Smith, *To Take Place: Toward Theory in Ritual* (CSHJ; Chicago: University of Chicago Press, 1987), 82.

74. Morris, *Sepulchre of Christ*, 21–27.

75. Dan Bahat, "Does the Holy Sepulchre Mark the Burial Place of Jesus?" *BAR* 12/3 (1986): 26–45 (here, 30).

76. Ibid., 35, 37.

77. Bahat suggests that Hadrian used ashlars from the Herodian retaining wall of the Temple Mount in order to duplicate that wall: "Instead of a temple to Yahweh, however, Hadrian built on his raised enclosure an elaborate temple to the goddess of love, Venus/Aphrodite" (ibid., 34), but Bahat relies here on Eusebius and not on archaeological evidence (Bahat, "Holy Sepulchre," 32–35).

78. Jerome Murphy-O'Connor, *The Holy Land: An Oxford Archaeological Guide from Earliest Times to 1700* (4th ed.; Oxford: Oxford University Press, 1998), 45, as part of the basis for his claim that the Church of the Holy Sepulchre is in the right place: "Is this the place where Christ died and was buried? Very probably, Yes." Murphy-O'Connor evidently has been convinced by arguments that Mark 16:1-8 preserves a primitive Christian liturgy performed at the known site of Jesus' burial. For literature, see above, p. 197 n. 57.

79. Hans Dieter Betz, "Zum Problem der Auferstehung Jesu im Lichte der griechischen magischen Papyri," in Betz, *Gesammelte Aufsätze I: Hellenismus und Urchristentum* (Tübingen: Mohr Siebeck, 1990), 230–61 (here, 246).

80. Morris, *Sepulchre of Christ*, 67–77, 120–27. Morris also indicates that the remains of a small stone model of the aedicule, dating to around 500 CE, were discovered at Narbonne in the south of France (ibid., 63).

81. Ibid., 76–77; Betz, "Zum Problem der Auferstehung," 247.

82. Morris, *Sepulchre of Christ*, 59, 76–77.

83. Smith, *To Take Place*, 86.

84. Ibid.

85. As Smith puts it, "The Church of the Holy Sepulchre (unlike the Temple) could not have been built anywhere else and still be the same. Its *locus* had to correspond fully to the *topos* of the Gospel narratives. It is tied, inextricably, to sacred biography and history" (ibid.).

86. Ibid.

87. See also Jerome, *Epis.* 108, in which he describes a pilgrim throwing herself down in front of the cross as though Christ were still hanging on it, and kissing the stone that the angel had removed from the tomb and the place where Christ had been laid. As Morris comments, "We should understand this not as a description of a single visit by a disciple of Jerome . . . but as an expression of his own ideas of devotion at the Sepulchre" (*Sepulchre of Christ*, 57).

88. See Morris, *Sepulchre of Christ*, 54; Eusebius, *Vit. Const.* 3.33.

89. Smith, *To Take Place*, 93.

90. Ibid., 92–95.

91. For a handy discussion, see William L. Petersen, "Tatian's Diatessaron," in Koester, *Ancient Christian Gospels*, 403–30.

92. Metzger, *Text of the New Testament*, 89–90, attributes this to Tatian's association with Encratism; Carmel McCarthy, *Saint Ephrem's Commentary on Tatian's Diatessaron: An English Translation of Chester Beatty MS 709 with Introduction and Notes* (JSSS 2; Oxford: Oxford University Press, 1993), 8, suggests that "the Syriac-speaking church began [in the third century] to feel the need for separate Gospels," and that the Old Syriac form of the four canonical Gospels betrays considerable Diatessaronic influence. On this latter point, see Metzger, *Text of the New Testament*, 69.

93. For discussion, see Metzger, *Text of the New Testament*, 90; Paul Foster, "Tatian," *ExpT* 120 (2008): 105–18, esp. 110–11.

94. Metzger, *Text of the New Testament*, 90.

95. Foster, "Tatian," 114.

96. For the date, see Foster, "Tatian," 110. Petersen thinks that this text is more important for "its witness to the *Diatessaron*'s sequence of the harmonization" (Petersen, "Tatian's Diatessaron," 409). A translation of this text can be found in *ANF* 10:35–130 under the title "The Diatessaron of Tatian."

97. Augustine also writes that such a coherent narrative can only be constructed "as long as the Lord is helping us" (*Cons. Ev.* 3.24.69).

Chapter 10

1. Mary Rose D'Angelo, "A Critical Note: John 20:17 and Apocalypse of Moses 31," *JTS* 41 (1990): 529–36; Origen, *Comm. Jo.* 6.37.

2. For Son of Man or other transcendent figures functioning in this corporate way in Jewish literature, see John J. Collins, "The Heavenly Representative: The 'Son of Man' in the Similitudes of Enoch," in *Ideal Figures in Ancient Judaism: Profiles and Paradigms*, ed. John J. Collins and George W. E. Nickelsburg (SBLSCS 12; Missoula, Mont.: Scholars, 1980), 111–33; John J. Collins, *The Apocalyptic Imagination: An Introduction to Jewish Apocalyptic Literature* (2nd ed.; Grand Rapids: Eerdmans, 1998), 105–6 (on Daniel 7), 184–87 (on *1 Enoch*).

3. For a fuller discussion, see Daniel A. Smith, *The Post-Mortem Vindication of Jesus in the Sayings Gospel Q* (LNTS 338; London and New York: T. & T. Clark, 2006), 130–43.

4. Translation from George W. E. Nickelsburg and James C. VanderKam, *1 Enoch: A New Translation* (Minneapolis: Fortress Press, 2004).

Bibliography

Ancient Sources: Original Language Texts

Biblia Hebraica Stuttgartensia. Edited by R. Kittel, A. Schenker, et al. 5th ed. Stuttgart: Deutsche Bibelgesellschaft, 1997.

Biblia sacra, iuxta Vulgatam versionem. Edited by B. Fischer, R. Weber, et al. Stuttgart: Württembergische Bibelanstalt, 1969.

The Greek New Testament. Edited by Barbara Aland et al. 4th rev. ed. Stuttgart: Deutsche Bibelgesellschaft / United Bible Societies, 1993.

Novum Testamentum Graece. Edited by E. Nestle, E. Nestle, K. Aland, B. Aland, et al. 27th ed. Stuttgart: Deutsche Bibelgesellschaft, 1993.

Septuaginta, id est Vetus Testamentum graece iuxta LXX interpretes. Edited by A. Rahlfs and R. Hanhart. Rev. ed. Stuttgart: Deutsche Bibelgesellschaft, 2006.

Borliffs, J. W. P., et al., eds. *Tertulliani Opera*. 2 vols. CCSL 1–2. Turnhout, Belgium: Brepols, 1954.

Borret, Marcel, ed. and trans. *Origène: Contre Celse*. 5 vols. SC 132 etc. Paris: Cerf, 1967–76.

Brock, S. P., and J.-C. Picard, eds. *Testamentum Iobi; Apocalypsis Baruchi Graece*. PVTG 2. Leiden: Brill, 1967.

Colson, F. H., G. H. Whitaker, et al., eds. and trans. *Philo: With an English Translation*. 12 vols. LCL. Cambridge: Harvard University Press, 1929–71.

Ehrman, Bart D., ed. and trans. *The Apostolic Fathers*. 2 vols. LCL. Cambridge: Harvard University Press, 2003.

Goold, G. P., ed. and trans. *Chariton, Callirhoe*. LCL. Cambridge: Harvard University Press, 1995.

Harmon, A. M., et al., eds. and trans. *Lucian*. 8 vols. LCL. London: Heinemann; New York: Putnam, 1913–67.

Hock, Ronald F., ed. and trans. *The Infancy Gospels of James and Thomas*. The Scholars Bible 2. Santa Rosa, Calif.: Polebridge, 1995.

Jacoby, Felix, ed. *Die Fragmente der griechischen Historiker*. 3 vols. in 15. Leiden: Brill, 1954–69.

Jones, Christopher P., ed. and trans. *Philostratus: The Life of Apollonius of Tyana*. 2 vols. LCL. Cambridge: Harvard University Press, 2005.

Kraus, T. J., and T. Nicklas, eds. and trans. *Das Petrusevangelium und die Petrusapokalypse: Die griechischen Fragmente*. Berlin: de Gruyter, 2004.

Labourt, Jérôme, ed. and trans. *Saint Jérôme: Lettres*. 8 vols. Collection des universités de France. Paris: 1949–63.

MacLean, Jennifer K. Berenson, and Ellen Bradshaw Aitken, trans. *Flavius Philostratus: Heroikos*. SBLWGRW 1. Atlanta: Society of Biblical Literature, 2001.

Migne, J.-P. *Patrologiae Cursus Completus*, series graeca. 162 vols. Paris: Migne, 1857–86.

———. *Patrologiae Cursus Completus*, series latina. 217 vols. Paris: Migne, 1844–55.

Perrin, Bernadette, ed. and trans. *Plutarch's Lives*. 11 vols. LCL. London: Heinemann; New York: Macmillan, 1914–26.

Pfeiffer, R., ed. *Callimachus*. 2 vols. Oxford: Oxford University Press, 1949.

Reischl, W. C., and J. Rupp, eds. *Cyrilli Hierosolymarum archiepiscopi opera quae supersunt omnia*. 2 vols. Hildesheim: Georg Olms, 1967.

Robinson, James M., Paul Hoffmann, and John S. Kloppenborg, eds. *The Critical Edition of Q: Synopsis Including the Gospels of Matthew and Luke, Mark and Thomas*. Hermeneia Supplements. Minneapolis: Fortress Press; Leuven: Peeters, 2000.

Stone, Michael E., ed. and trans. *The Testament of Abraham: The Greek Recensions*. SBLTT 2. New York: Society of Biblical Literature, 1972.

Vérilhac, Anne-Marie, ed. and trans. *Paides aōroi: Poésie funéraire*. 2 vols. Pragmateiai tēs Akadēmias Athēnōn 41. Athens: Grapheion Dēmosieumatōn tēs Akadēmias Athēnōn, 1978–82.

Ancient Sources: In Translation

Daley, Brian E., trans. *On the Dormition of Mary: Early Patristic Homilies*. Crestwood, N.Y.: St. Vladimir's Seminary Press, 1998.

Elliott, J. K. *The Apocryphal New Testament*. Oxford: Clarendon; New York: Oxford University Press, 1993.

García Martínez, Florentino, trans. *The Dead Sea Scrolls in English: The Qumran Texts in English*. 2nd ed. Leiden: Brill; Grand Rapids: Eerdmans, 1996.

Marcus, Ralph, ed. and trans. *Philo: Questions and Answers on Genesis*. LCL. Cambridge: Harvard University Press, 1953.

McCarthy, Carmel. *Saint Ephrem's Commentary on Tatian's Diatessaron: An English Translation of Chester Beatty MS 709 with Introduction and Notes*. JSSS 2. Oxford: Oxford University Press, 1993.

McVey, Kathleen E., trans. *Ephrem the Syrian: The Hymns*. CWS. New York: Paulist, 1989.

Nickelsburg, George W. E., and James C. VanderKam, trans. *1 Enoch: A New Translation*. Minneapolis: Fortress Press, 2004.

Roberts, Alexander, and James Donaldson, eds. *The Ante-Nicene Fathers: Translations of the Writings of the Fathers Down to A.D. 325*. 10 vols. Buffalo, N.Y.: Christian Literature Publishing Company, 1885–87.

Schneemelcher, Wilhelm, ed., and R. McL. Wilson, trans. *New Testament Apocrypha*. Rev. ed. 2 vols. Cambridge: James Clarke; Louisville: Westminster John Knox, 1991–92.

VanderKam, James C., ed. and trans. *The Book of Jubilees*. 2 vols. CSCO 510–11; Scriptores Aethiopici 87–88. Leuven: Peeters, 1989.

Wright, W. *Contributions to the Apocryphal Literature of the New Testament*. London: Williams & Norgate, 1865.

Works Cited

Allison, Dale C., Jr. *The End of the Ages Has Come: An Early Interpretation of the Passion and Resurrection of Jesus*. Philadelphia: Fortress Press, 1985.

———. "Peter and Cephas: One and the Same." *JBL* 111 (1992): 489–95.

———. *The New Moses: A Matthean Typology*. Minneapolis: Fortress Press, 1993.

———. *The Intertextual Jesus: Scripture in Q*. Harrisburg, Pa.: Trinity Press International, 2000.

———. *Testament of Abraham*. CEJL. Berlin and New York: de Gruyter, 2003.

———. *Resurrecting Jesus: The Earliest Christian Tradition and Its Interpreters*. New York and London: T. & T. Clark, 2005.

———. *Studies in Matthew: Interpretation Past and Present*. Grand Rapids: Baker Academic, 2005.

Alsup, John E. *The Post-Resurrection Appearance Stories of the Gospel Tradition*. Calwer Theologische Monographien 5. Stuttgart: Calwer; London; SPCK, 1975.

Asher, Jeffrey R. *Polarity and Change in 1 Corinthians 15: A Study of Metaphysics, Rhetoric, and Resurrection.* HUT 42. Tübingen: Mohr Siebeck, 2000.

Askitopoulou, Helen, et al. "Surgical Cures under Sleep Induction in the Asclepieion of Epidauros." *International Congress Series* 1242 (2002): 11–17.

Attridge, Harold W. "'Don't Be Touching Me': Recent Feminist Scholarship on Mary Magdalene." Pp. 2:140–66 in *A Feminist Companion to John*, ed. Amy-Jill Levine with Marianne Blickenstaff. 2 vols. London and New York: Sheffield Academic, 2003.

Aune, David E. "The Problem of the Genre of the Gospels: A Critique of C. H. Talbert's *What Is a Gospel?*" Pp. 2:9–60 in *Gospel Perspectives: Studies of History and Tradition in the Four Gospels*, ed. R. T. France and D. Wenham. 6 vols. Sheffield: JSOT Press, 1980–86.

———. "Heracles and Christ: Heracles Imagery in the Christology of the New Testament." Pp. 3–19 in *Greeks, Romans, and Christians: Essays in Honor of Abraham J. Malherbe*, ed. D. Balch et al. Minneapolis: Fortress Press, 1990.

Aus, Roger David. *The Death, Burial, and Resurrection of Jesus, and the Death, Burial, and Translation of Moses in Judaic Tradition.* Studies in Judaism. Lanham, Md.: University Press of America, 2008.

Bahat, Dan. "Does the Holy Sepulchre Mark the Burial Place of Jesus?" *BAR* 12/3 (1986): 26–45.

Barrett, C. K. *A Commentary on the First Epistle to the Corinthians.* 2nd ed. BNTC. London: A & C Black, 1992.

Beasley-Murray, George R. *John.* 2nd ed. WBC 36. Nashville: Thomas Nelson, 1999.

Bertram, G. "Die Himmelfahrt Jesu vom Kreuz an und der Glaube an seine Auferstehung." Pp. 187–217 in *Festgabe für Adolf Deissmann zum 60. Geburtstag*, ed. K. L. Schmidt. Tübingen: Mohr Siebeck, 1927.

Betz, Hans Dieter. "Zum Problem der Auferstehung Jesu im Lichte der griechischen magischen Papyri." Pp. 230–61 in *Gesammelte Aufsätze I: Hellenismus und Urchristentum.* Tübingen: Mohr Siebeck, 1990.

———. "Hero Worship and Christian Beliefs: Observations from the History of Religion on Philostratus's *Heroikos.*" Pp. 25–47 in *Philostratus's Heroikos: Religion and Cultural Identity in the Third Century C.E.*, ed. E. Bradshaw Aitken and J. K. Berenson MacLean. SBLWGRW 6. Leiden: Brill, 2004.

Bickermann, Elias. "Das leere Grab." *ZNW* 23 (1924): 281–92.

———. "Die römische Kaiserapotheose." *AR* 27 (1929): 1–31.

Bieringer, Reimund. "'I Am Ascending to My Father and Your Father, to My God and Your God' (John 20:17): Resurrection and Ascension in the Gospel of John." Pp. 209–35 in *The Resurrection of Jesus in the Gospel of John*, ed. C. Koester and R. Bieringer. WUNT 2/222. Tübingen: Mohr Siebeck, 2008.

Black, C. Clifton. "The Face Is Familiar—I Just Can't Place It." Pp. 33–49 in *The Ending of Mark and the Ends of God: Essays in Memory of Donald Harrisville Juel*, ed. Beverley Roberts Gaventa and Patrick D. Miller. Louisville: Westminster John Knox, 2005.

de Boer, Martinus C. "Jesus' Departure to the Father in John: Death or Resurrection?" Pp. 1–19 in *Theology and Christology in the Fourth Gospel: Essays by the Members of the SNTS Johannine Writings Seminar*, ed. G. Van Belle et al. BETL 184. Leuven: Peeters, 2005.

Bolt, Peter G. "Mark 16:1–8: The Empty Tomb of a Hero?" *TynBul* 47 (1996): 27–37.

———. *Jesus' Defeat of Death: Persuading Mark's Early Readers.* SNTSMS 125. Cambridge: Cambridge University Press, 2003.

Bolton, J. D. P. *Aristeas of Proconnesus.* Oxford: Clarendon, 1962.

Bond, Helen K. *Pontius Pilate in History and Interpretation.* SNTSMS 100. Cambridge: Cambridge University Press, 1998.

Bookidis, Nancy. "Religion in Corinth: 146 BCE to 100 CE." Pp. 141–64 in *Urban Religion in Roman Corinth: Interdisciplinary Approaches*, ed. D. Schowalter and S. Friesen. HTS 53. Cambridge: Harvard University Press, 2005.

Boomershine, Thomas E. "Mark 16:8 and the Apostolic Commission." *JBL* 100 (1981): 225–39.

Boring, M. Eugene. *Mark: A Commentary.* NTL. Louisville: Westminster John Knox, 2006.

Boring, M. Eugene, Klaus Berger, and Carsten Colpe, eds. *Hellenistic Commentary to the New Testament.* Nashville: Abingdon, 1995.

Bovon, François. "Le Privilège Pascal de Marie-Madeleine." *NTS* 30 (1984): 50–62.

———. *Luke 1: A Commentary on the Gospel of Luke 1:1–9:50.* Hermeneia. Minneapolis: Fortress Press, 2001.

Bowersock, G. W. *Fiction as History: Nero to Julian.* Berkeley: University of California Press, 1994.

Boyarin, Daniel. *A Radical Jew: Paul and the Politics of Identity.* Berkeley: University of California Press, 1994.

Brock, Ann Graham. *Mary Magdalene, The First Apostle: The Struggle for Authority.* HTS 51. Cambridge: Harvard University Press, 2003.

Brown, Raymond E. *The Gospel according to John: Introduction, Translation, and Notes.* 2 vols. AB 29–29A. Garden City, N.Y.: Doubleday, 1966–70.

———. "The Burial of Jesus (Mark 15:42-47)." *CBQ* 50 (1988): 233–45.

———. *An Introduction to the Gospel of John.* Edited by Francis J. Moloney. ABRL. New York: Doubleday, 2003.

Buckler, W. H. "Auguste, Zeus Patroos." *RevPhil* 9 (1935): 177–88.

Bultmann, Rudolf. *The History of the Synoptic Tradition.* Translated by John Marsh. Rev. ed. Oxford: Blackwell, 1963.

Burkert, Walter. *Greek Religion: Archaic and Classical.* Translated by J. Raffan. Oxford: Blackwell; Cambridge: Harvard University Press, 1985.

Burton, Ernest D. *Spirit, Soul, and Flesh: The Usage of Pneuma, Psyche, and Sarx.* Chicago: University of Chicago Press, 1918.

Cameron, Ron. *The Other Gospels: Non-Canonical Gospel Texts.* Philadelphia: Westminster, 1982.

Carnley, Peter. *The Structure of Resurrection Belief.* Oxford: Clarendon, 1987.

Carroll, John T., Joel B. Green, et al. *The Death of Jesus in Early Christianity.* Peabody, Mass.: Hendrickson, 1995.

Carter, Warren. "'To See the Tomb': Matthew's Women at the Tomb." *ExpT* 107 (1996): 201–5.

———. *Matthew and the Margins: A Sociopolitical and Religious Reading.* Bible and Liberation. Maryknoll, N.Y.: Orbis, 2000.

———. "Are There Imperial Texts in the Class? Intertextual Eagles and Matthean Eschatology as 'Lights Out' Time for Imperial Rome (Matthew 24:27–31)." *JBL* 122 (2003): 467–87.

Cartlidge, David R., and J. Keith Elliott. *Art and the Christian Apocrypha.* London and New York: Routledge, 2001.

Charlesworth, James H. "Prolegomenous Reflections towards a Taxonomy of Resurrection Texts (1QH^a, *1En*, 4Q521, Paul, Luke, the Fourth Gospel, and Psalm 130)." Pp. 237–64 in *The Changing Face of Judaism, Christianity, and Other Greco-Roman Religions in Antiquity,* ed. I. H. Henderson and G. S. Oegema. Studien zu den Jüdischen Schriften aus hellenistisch-römischer Zeit 2. Gütersloh: Gütersloher Verlagshaus, 2006.

Chow, Simon. *The Sign of Jonah Reconsidered: A Study of Its Meaning in the Gospel Traditions.* ConBNT 27. Stockholm: Almqvist & Wiksell, 1995.

Ciraolo, Leda Jean. "Supernatural Assistants in the Greek Magical Papyri." Pp. 279–95 in *Ancient Magic and Ritual Power,* ed. M. Meyer and P. Mirecki. RGRW 129. Leiden: Brill, 1995.

Collins, Adela Yarbro. *The Beginning of the Gospel: Probings of Mark in Context.* Minneapolis: Fortress Press, 1992.

———. "Mark and His Readers: The Son of God among Jews." *HTR* 92 (1999): 393–408.

———. "Mark and His Readers: The Son of God among Greeks and Romans." *HTR* 93 (2000): 85–100.

————. *Mark: A Commentary on the Gospel of Mark.* Hermeneia. Minneapolis: Fortress Press, 2007.

Collins, John J. "The Heavenly Representative: The 'Son of Man' in the Similitudes of Enoch." Pp. 111–33 in *Ideal Figures in Ancient Judaism: Profiles and Paradigms*, ed. J. J. Collins and G. W. E. Nickelsburg. SBLSCS 12. Missoula, Mont.: Scholars Press, 1980.

————. *Daniel: A Commentary on the Book of Daniel.* Hermeneia. Minneapolis: Fortress Press, 1993.

————. *The Scepter and the Star: The Messiahs of the Dead Sea Scrolls and Other Ancient Literature.* ABRL. New York: Doubleday, 1995.

————. *The Apocalyptic Imagination: An Introduction to Jewish Apocalyptic Literature.* 2nd ed. Grand Rapids: Eerdmans, 1998.

Collins, Raymond F. *First Corinthians.* SP 7. Collegeville, Minn.: Liturgical Press, 1999.

Conzelmann, Hans. *The Theology of St. Luke.* Trans. G. Buswell. New York: Harper & Row, 1960.

————. *1 Corinthians: A Commentary on the First Epistle to the Corinthians.* Hermeneia. Philadelphia: Fortress Press, 1975.

Corley, Kathleen E. *Women and the Historical Jesus: Feminist Myths of Christian Origins.* Santa Rosa, Calif.: Polebridge, 2002.

Cotter, Wendy. "Greco-Roman Apotheosis Traditions and the Resurrection Appearances in Matthew." Pp. 127–53 in *The Gospel of Matthew in Current Study: Studies in Memory of William G. Thompson, S.J.*, ed. David E. Aune. Grand Rapids: Eerdmans, 2001.

Craig, William Lane. "The Historicity of the Empty Tomb of Jesus." *NTS* 31 (1985): 39–67.

Cross, F. L., and E. A. Livingstone, eds. *The Oxford Dictionary of the Christian Church.* 3rd ed. Oxford: Oxford University Press, 2005.

Crossan, John Dominic. "Empty Tomb and Absent Lord (Mark 16:1-8)." Pp. 135–52 in *The Passion in Mark: Studies on Mark 14–16*, ed. W. Kelber. Philadelphia: Fortress Press, 1976.

————. *The Cross That Spoke: The Origins of the Passion Narrative.* San Francisco: Harper & Row, 1988.

————. *Who Killed Jesus? Exposing the Roots of Anti-Semitism in the Gospel Story of the Death of Jesus.* San Francisco: HarperSanFrancisco, 1995.

————. "The Resurrection of Jesus in Its Jewish Context." *Neot* 37 (2003): 29–58.

————. "Appendix: Bodily-Resurrection Faith." Pp. 171–86 in *The Resurrection of Jesus: John Dominic Crossan and N. T. Wright in Dialogue*, ed. Robert B. Stewart. Minneapolis: Fortress Press, 2006.

Culpepper, R. Alan. *Anatomy of the Fourth Gospel: A Study in Literary Design.* Philadelphia: Fortress Press, 1983.

————. "Realized Eschatology in the Experience of the Johannine Community." Pp. 253–76 in *The Resurrection of Jesus in the Gospel of John*, ed. Craig R. Koester and Reimund Bieringer. WUNT 2/222. Tübingen: Mohr Siebeck, 2008.

D'Angelo, Mary Rose. "A Critical Note: John 20:17 and Apocalypse of Moses 31." *JTS* 41 (1990): 529–36.

————. "Reconstructing 'Real' Women in Gospel Literature: The Case of Mary Magdalene." Pp. 105–28 in *Women and Christian Origins*, ed. Ross Shepard Kraemer and Mary Rose D'Angelo. Oxford: Oxford University Press, 1999.

————. "'I Have Seen the Lord': Mary Magdalen as Visionary, Early Christian Prophecy, and the Context of John 20:14-18." Pp. 95–122 in *Mariam, the Magdalen, and the Mother*, ed. Deirde Good. Bloomington: Indiana University Press, 2005.

Dauer, Anton. "Zur Authentizität von Lk 24,12." *ETL* 70 (1994): 294–318.

Davies, W. D., and Dale C. Allison Jr. *The Gospel according to Saint Matthew.* 3 vols. ICC. Edinburgh: T. & T. Clark, 1988–97.

———. "Matt 28.16-20: Texts behind the Text." *RHPR* 72 (1992): 89–98.

Denaux, Adelbert. "Matthew's Story of Jesus' Burial and Resurrection (Mt 27,57–28,20)." Pp. 123–45 in *Resurrection in the New Testament: Festschrift J. Lambrecht*, ed. R. Bieringer et al. BETL 165. Leuven: Peeters, 2002.

Dibelius, Martin. *From Tradition to Gospel*. Translated by B. L. Woolf. London: Ivor Nicholson, 1934.

Dillon, Richard J. *From Eye-Witnesses to Ministers of the Word: Tradition and Composition in Luke 24*. AnBib 82. Rome: Biblical Institute Press, 1978.

Dodd, C. H. "The Appearances of the Risen Christ: An Essay in Form-Criticism of the Gospels." Pp. 9–35 in *Studies in the Gospels: Essays in Memory of R. H. Lightfoot*, ed. D. E. Nineham. Oxford: Blackwell, 1955.

Dunn, James D. G. *Jesus and the Spirit: A Study of the Religious and Charismatic Experience of Jesus and the First Christians as Reflected in the New Testament*. London: SCM, 1975.

———. *The Theology of Paul the Apostle*. Grand Rapids: Eerdmans, 1998.

———. *Jesus Remembered*. Volume 1 of *Christology in the Making*. Grand Rapids: Eerdmans, 2003.

Edelstein, Emma J., and Ludwig Edelstein. *Asclepius: A Collection and Interpretation of the Testimonies*. 2 vols. Baltimore, Md.: Johns Hopkins University Press, 1945.

Ehrman, Bart D. "Cephas and Peter." *JBL* 109 (1990): 463–74.

———. *The Orthodox Corruption of Scripture: The Effect of Early Christological Controversies on the Text of the New Testament*. Oxford and New York: Oxford University Press, 1993.

Elliott, J. K. "The Case for Thoroughgoing Eclecticism." Pp. 101–24 in *Rethinking New Testament Textual Criticism*, ed. David Alan Black. Grand Rapids: Baker, 2002.

Ellis, E. Earle. *The Gospel of Luke*. NCB. Rev. ed. London: Oliphants, 1974.

Eitrem, Samson. "Zu Philostrats *Heroikos*." *Symbolae Osloenses* 8 (1929): 1–56.

Ekroth, Gunnel. *The Sacrificial Rituals of Greek Hero-Cults in the Archaic to the Early Hellenistic Periods*. Kernos Supplement 12. Liège: Centre international d'étude de la religion grecque antique, 2002.

———. "Heroes and Hero-Cults." Pp. 100–114 in *A Companion to Greek Religion*, ed. Daniel Ogden. Oxford: Blackwell, 2007.

Evans, C. F. *Resurrection and the New Testament*. SBT 12. London: SCM, 1970.

Farmer, William R. "Peter and Paul, and the Tradition concerning 'the Lord's Supper' in 1 Cor 11:23-26." *CTR* 2 (1987): 119–40.

Fehribach, Adeline. *The Women in the Life of the Bridegroom: A Feminist Historical-Literary Analysis of the Female Characters in the Fourth Gospel*. Collegeville, Minn.: Liturgical Press, 1998.

———. "The Birthing Bridegroom: The Portrayal of Jesus in the Fourth Gospel." Pp. 2:104–29 in *A Feminist Companion to John*, ed. Amy-Jill Levine with Marianne Blickenstaff. 2 vols. London and New York: Sheffield Academic, 2003.

Felton, D. *Haunted Greece and Rome: Ghost Stories from Classical Antiquity*. Austin: University of Texas Press, 1999.

Fitzmyer, Joseph A. *The Gospel According to Luke*. 2 vols. AB 28–28A. New York: Doubleday, 1981–85.

Foster, Paul. "In Defence of the Study of Q." *ExpT* 113 (2002): 295–300.

———. "Are There Any Early Fragments of the So-Called *Gospel of Peter*?" *NTS* 52 (2006): 1–28.

———. "The Gospel of Peter." *ExpT* 118 (2007): 318–25.

———. "Polymorphic Christology: Its Origins and Development in Early Christianity." *JTS* 58 (2007): 66–99.

———. "Tatian." *ExpT* 120 (2008): 105–18.

France, R. T. *The Gospel of Matthew*. NICNT. Grand Rapids: Eerdmans, 2007.

Frey, Jörg. "Eschatology in the Johannine Circle." Pp. 45–82 in *Theology and Christology in the Fourth Gospel: Essays by the Members of the SNTS Johannine Writings Seminar*, ed. G. Van Belle et al. BETL 184. Leuven: Peeters, 2005.

Fuller, Reginald H. *The Formation of the Resurrection Narratives*. New York: Macmillan, 1971.

Fullmer, Paul. *Resurrection in Mark's Literary-Historical Perspective*. LNTS 360. London and New York: T. & T. Clark, 2007.

Gathercole, Simon. "The Son of Man in Mark's Gospel." *ExpT* 115 (2004): 366–72.

Georgi, Dieter. "Der vorpaulinische Hymnus Phil 2,6-11." Pp. 263–93 in *Zeit und Geschichte: Dankesgabe an Rudolf Bultmann zum 80. Geburtstag*, ed. E. Dinkler. Tübingen: Mohr Siebeck, 1964.

Gillman, John. "Transformation in 1 Cor 15,50-53." *ETL* 58 (1982): 309–33.

———. "A Thematic Comparison: 1 Cor 15:50-57 and 2 Cor 5:1-5." *JBL* 107 (1988): 439–54.

Glasson, T. Francis. "2 Corinthians v. 1-10 versus Platonism." *SJT* 43 (1990): 143–55.

Goguel, Maurice. *La foi à la Résurrection de Jésus dans le christianisme primitif*. Paris: Leroux, 1933.

Golan, David. "Hadrian's Decision to Supplant 'Jerusalem' by 'Aelia Capitolina.'" *HZAG* 35 (1986): 226–39.

Goodacre, Mark S. *The Case against Q: Studies in Markan Priority and the Synoptic Problem*. Harrisburg, Pa.: Trinity Press International, 2002.

Goulder, Michael D. *Luke: A New Paradigm*. 2 vols. JSNTSup 20. Sheffield: Sheffield Academic Press, 1989.

Green, Joel B. *The Gospel of Luke*. NICNT. Grand Rapids: Eerdmans, 1997.

Grimm, Veronika E. *From Feasting to Fasting, the Evolution of a Sin: Attitudes to Food in Late Antiquity*. London and New York: Routledge, 1996.

Guillaume, Jean-Marie. *Luc interprète des anciennes traditions sur la Résurrection de Jésus*. Ebib. Paris: Lecoffre/Gabalda, 1979.

Gundry, Robert H. *Mark: A Commentary on His Apology for the Cross*. Grand Rapids: Eerdmans, 1993.

———. *Matthew: A Commentary on His Handbook for a Mixed Church under Persecution*. 2nd ed. Grand Rapids: Eerdmans, 1994.

Guthrie, W. K. C. *The Greeks and Their Gods*. Boston: Beacon, 1985.

Haas, N. "Anthropological Observations on the Skeletal Remains from Giv'at ha-Mivtar." *IEJ* 20 (1970): 38–59.

Haenchen, Ernst. *John: A Commentary on the Gospel of John*. Edited and translated by Robert W. Funk and U. Busse. 2 vols. Hermeneia. Philadelphia: Fortress Press, 1984.

Hamilton, Neill Q. "Resurrection Tradition and the Composition of Mark." *JBL* 84 (1965): 415–21.

Harnack, Adolf von. *The Sayings of Jesus: The Second Source of St. Matthew and St. Luke*. New York: Putnam; London: Williams & Norgate, 1908.

———. *Marcion: The Gospel of the Alien God*. Translated by John E. Steely and Lyle D. Bierma. Durham, N.C.: Labyrinth, 1990.

Haufe, Günter. "Entrückung und eschatologische Funktion im Spätjudentum." *ZRGG* 13 (1961): 105–13.

Heil, John Paul. *The Death and Resurrection of Jesus: A Narrative-Critical Reading of Matthew 26–28*. Minneapolis: Fortress Press, 1991.

———. *The Transfiguration of Jesus: Narrative Meaning and Function of Mark 9:2-8, Matt 17:1-8 and Luke 9:28-36*. AnBib 144. Rome: Editrice Pontificio Istituto Biblico, 2000.

Hengel, Martin. "Das Begräbnis Jesu bei Paulus und die leibliche Auferstehung aus dem Grab." Pp. 119–83 in *Auferstehung—Resurrection: The Fourth Durham-Tübingen Research Symposium*, ed. F. Avemarie and H. Lichtenberger. WUNT 1/135. Tübingen: Mohr Siebeck, 1999.

Hershbell, Jackson P. "Philostratus's *Heroikos* and Early Christianity: Heroes, Saints, and Martyrs." Pp. 169–79 in *Philostratus's Heroikos: Religion and Cultural Identity in the Third Century C.E.*, ed. E. Bradshaw Aitken and J. K. Berenson MacLean. SBLWGRW 6. Leiden: Brill, 2004.

Hoffmann, Paul. "Auferstehung Jesu Christi (Neues Testament)." *TRE* 4 (1979): 478–513.

———. *Studien zur Theologie der Logienquelle*. 3rd ed. NTAbh 8. Münster: Aschendorff, 1982.

———. "The Redaction of Q and the Son of Man: A Preliminary Sketch." Pp. 159–98 in *The Gospel behind the Gospels: Current Studies on Q*, ed. R. A. Piper. NovTSup 75. Leiden: Brill, 1995.

Hölbl, Günther. *A History of the Ptolemaic Empire*. London and New York: Routledge, 2001.

Holleman, Joost. *Resurrection and Parousia: A Traditio-Historical Study of Paul's Eschatology in 1 Corinthians 15*. NovTSup 84. Leiden: Brill, 1996.

Hornblower, Simon, and Anthony Spawforth, eds. *The Oxford Classical Dictionary*. 3rd ed. Oxford: Oxford University Press, 2003.

Hubbard, Benjamin J. *The Matthean Redaction of a Primitive Apostolic Commissioning: An Exegesis of Matthew 28:16-20*. SBLDS 19. Missoula, Mont.: Scholars Press, 1974.

Hughes, Dennis D. "Hero Cult, Heroic Honors, Heroic Dead: Some Developments in the Hellenistic and Roman Periods." Pp. 167–75 in *Ancient Greek Hero Cult: Proceedings of the Fifth International Seminar on Ancient Greek Cult*, ed. Robin Hägg. Acta Instituti Atheniensis Regni Sueciae 16. Stockholm: Svenska Institutet i Athen, 1999.

Hultgren, Arland J. *The Rise of Normative Christianity*. Minneapolis: Fortress Press, 2004.

Hurtado, Larry W. *Lord Jesus Christ: Devotion to Jesus in Earliest Christianity*. Grand Rapids: Eerdmans, 2003.

Ilan, Tal. *Jewish Women in Greco-Roman Palestine*. Peabody, Mass.: Hendrickson, 1996.

Jackson, Howard M. "Why the Youth Shed His Cloak and Fled Naked: The Meaning and Purpose of Mark 14:51-52." *JBL* 116 (1997): 273–89.

Jacobson, Arland D. *The First Gospel: An Introduction to Q*. Sonoma, Calif.: Polebridge, 1992.

Jansen, Katherine L. "Maria Magdalena: *Apostolorum Apostola*." Pp. 57–96 in *Women Preachers and Prophets through Two Millennia of Christianity*, ed. B. M. Kienzle and P. J. Walker. Berkeley: University of California Press, 1998.

Jeremias, Joachim. "Flesh and Blood Cannot Inherit the Kingdom of God (1 Cor. XV.50)." *NTS* 2 (1955–56): 151–59.

Johnson, Andy. "On Removing a Trump Card: Flesh and Blood and the Reign of God." *BBR* 13 (2003): 175–92.

Johnson-Debaufre, Melanie. *Jesus among Her Children: Q, Eschatology, and the Construction of Christian Origins*. HTS 55. Cambridge: Harvard University Press, 2005.

Johnston, Sarah Iles. *Restless Dead: Encounters between the Living and the Dead in Ancient Greece*. Berkeley: University of California Press, 1999.

de Jonge, H. J. "Visionary Experience and the Historical Origins of Christianity." Pp. 35–53 in *Resurrection in the New Testament: Festschrift J. Lambrecht*, ed. R. Bieringer et al. BETL 165. Leuven: Peeters, 2002.

Juel, Donald. *A Master of Surprise: Mark Interpreted*. Minneapolis: Fortress Press, 1994.

Kee, Howard C. *Miracle in the Early Christian World: A Study in Sociohistorical Method*. New Haven, Conn.: Yale University Press, 1983.

Kelhoffer, James A. *Miracle and Mission: The Authentication of Missionaries and Their Message in the Longer Ending of Mark*. WUNT 2/112. Tübingen: Mohr Siebeck, 2000.

Kilpatrick, George D. "Galatians 1:18 ΙΣΤΟΡΗΣΑΙ ΚΗΦΑΝ." Pp. 144–49 in *New Testament Essays: Studies in Memory of Thomas Walter Manson 1893-1958*, ed. A. J. B. Higgins. Manchester: Manchester University Press, 1959.

Kirk, Alan. "Examining Priorities: Another Look at the *Gospel of Peter*'s Relationship to the New Testament Gospels." *NTS* 40 (1994): 572–95.

Kitzinger, Ernst. *Byzantine Art in the Making: Main Lines of Stylistic Development in Mediterranean Art, 3rd–7th Century.* Cambridge: Harvard University Press, 1995.

Kloppenborg, John S. "'Easter Faith' and the Sayings Gospel Q." *Semeia* 49 (1990): 71–99.

———. *Excavating Q: The History and Setting of the Sayings Gospel.* Edinburgh: T. & T. Clark; Minneapolis: Fortress Press, 2000.

———. "On Dispensing with Q? Goodacre on the Relation of Luke to Matthew." *NTS* 49 (2003): 210–36.

———. "Evocatio Deorum and the Date of Mark." *JBL* 124 (2005): 419–50.

———. "Variation in the Reproduction of the Double Tradition and an Oral Q?" *ETL* 83 (2007): 53–80.

———. *Q, The Earliest Gospel: An Introduction to the Original Stories and Sayings of Jesus.* Louisville: Westminster John Knox, 2008.

———. "Sagesse et prophétie dans l'évangile des paroles Q." Pp. 73–98 in *La source des paroles de Jésus (Q): Aux origines de christianisme*, ed. Andreas Dettwiler and Daniel Marguerat. MdB 62. Geneva: Labor et Fides, 2008.

Knibb, Michael A. "Martyrdom and Ascension of Isaiah." Pp. 2:143–76 in *The Old Testament Pseudepigrapha*, ed. James H. Charlesworth. 2 vols. New York: Doubleday, 1983–85.

Koester, Craig. "Jesus' Resurrection, the Signs, and the Dynamics of Faith in the Gospel of John." Pp. 47–74 in *The Resurrection of Jesus in the Gospel of John*, ed. Craig R. Koester and Reimund Bieringer. WUNT 2/222. Tübingen: Mohr Siebeck, 2008.

Koester, Helmut. *Ancient Christian Gospels: Their History and Development.* Philadelphia: Trinity Press International; London: SCM, 1990.

———. "On Heroes, Tombs, and Early Christianity: An Epilogue." Pp. 257–64 in *Flavius Philostratus: Heroikos*, ed. J. Berenson MacLean and E. Bradshaw Aitken. SBLWGRW 1. Atlanta: SBL, 2001.

Kremer, Jacob. *Die Osterevangelien: Geschichten um Geschichte.* Stuttgart: Katholisches Bibelwerk, 1977.

Lambrecht, Jan. *Second Corinthians.* SP 8. Collegeville, Minn.: Liturgical Press, 1999.

Lang, Mabel. *Cure and Cult in Ancient Corinth: A Guide to the Asklepieion.* Princeton: American School of Classical Studies at Athens, 1977.

Larsen, Kasper Bro. *Recognizing the Stranger: Recognition Scenes in the Gospel of John.* Biblical Interpretation Series 93. Leiden: Brill, 2008.

Lincoln, Andrew T. "The Promise and the Failure: Mark 16:7, 8." *JBL* 108 (1989): 283–300.

———. *The Gospel according to Saint John.* BNTC. London and New York: Continuum; Peabody, Mass.: Hendrickson, 2005.

Lohfink, Gerhard. Die Himmelfahrt Jesu: Untersuchungen zu den Himmelfahrts- und Erhöhungstexten bei Lukas. SANT 26. Munich: Kösel, 1971.

———. "Der Ablauf der Osterereignisse und die Anfänge der Urgemeinde." *TQ* 160 (1980): 162–76.

Lohmeyer, Ernst. *Galiläa und Jerusalem.* Göttingen: Vandenhoeck & Ruprecht, 1936.

Longstaff, Thomas R. W. "What Are Those Women Doing at the Tomb of Jesus? Perspectives on Matthew 28.1." Pp. 196–204 in *A Feminist Companion to Matthew*, ed. Amy-Jill Levine and Marianne Blickenstaff. Sheffield: Sheffield Academic Press, 2001.

Lüdemann, Gerd. *The Resurrection of Jesus: History, Experience, Theology.* London: SCM; Minneapolis: Fortress Press, 1994.

———. *The Resurrection of Christ: A Historical Inquiry.* 2nd ed. Amherst, N.Y.: Prometheus, 2004.

Luz, Ulrich. *The Theology of the Gospel of Matthew.* Cambridge: Cambridge University Press, 1995.

———. *Matthew: A Commentary.* 3 vols. Hermeneia. Minneapolis: Fortress Press, 2001–07.

──────. *Studies in Matthew.* Translated by R. Selle. Grand Rapids: Eerdmans, 2005.
MacDonald, Margaret Y. *Early Christian Women and Pagan Opinion: The Power of the Hysterical Woman.* Cambridge: Cambridge University Press, 1996.
Mack, Burton L. *Rhetoric and the New Testament.* GBS. Minneapolis: Fortress Press, 1990.
──────. *The Lost Gospel: The Book of Q and Christian Origins.* San Francisco: Harper, 1993.
Magness, J. Lee. *Sense and Absence: Structure and Suspension in the Ending of Mark's Gospel.* SemeiaSt. Atlanta: Scholars Press, 1986.
Manson, T. W. *The Sayings of Jesus.* London: SCM, 1937.
Marcus, Joel. *Mark: A New Translation with Introduction and Commentary.* 2 vols. AB 27–27A. New York: Doubleday, 2000; New Haven, Conn.: Yale University Press, 2009.
Mare, W. Harold. *The Archaeology of the Jerusalem Area.* Grand Rapids: Baker, 1987.
Marshall, I. Howard. *The Gospel of Luke: A Commentary on the Greek Text.* NIGTC. Grand Rapids: Eerdmans, 1978.
Martin, Dale B. *The Corinthian Body.* New Haven, Conn.: Yale University Press, 1995.
Martin, Michael Wade. "Defending the 'Western Non-Interpolations': The Case for an Anti-Separationist *Tendenz* in the Longer Alexandrian Readings." *JBL* 124 (2005): 269–94.
Martin, Ralph P. *A Hymn of Christ: Philippians 2:5-11 in Recent Interpretation and in the Setting of Early Christian Worship.* 3rd ed. Downers Grove, Ill.: InterVarsity, 1997.
Marxsen, Willi. *Mark the Evangelist: Studies on the Redaction History of the Gospel.* Nashville: Abingdon, 1969.
──────. *The Resurrection of Jesus of Nazareth.* London: SCM; Philadelphia: Fortress Press, 1970.
Matera, Frank J. *Passion Narratives and Gospel Theologies: Interpreting the Synoptics through Their Passion Stories.* Maryknoll, N.Y.: Paulist, 1986.
Maurer, Christian, and Wilhelm Schneemelcher. "The Gospel of Peter." Pp. 1:216–27 in Wilhelm Schneemelcher, ed., and R. McL. Wilson, trans., *New Testament Apocrypha.* Rev. ed. 2 vols. Cambridge: James Clarke; Louisville: Westminster John Knox, 1991–92.
McCane, Byron. *Roll Back the Stone: Death and Burial in the World of Jesus.* Harrisburg, Pa.: Trinity Press International, 2003.
Meeks, Wayne A. "The Man from Heaven in Johannine Sectarianism." *JBL* 91 (1972): 44–72.
Meiselman, Moshe. *Jewish Women in Jewish Law.* New York: KTAV, 1978.
Merklein, Helmut. "Mk 16,1-8 als Epilog des Markusevangeliums." Pp. 209–38 in *The Synoptic Gospels: Source Criticism and the New Literary Criticism*, ed. C. Focant. BETL 110. Leuven: Peeters, 1993.
Metzger, Bruce M. "The Nazareth Inscription Once Again." Pp. 75–92 in *New Testament Studies: Philological, Versional, and Patristic.* NTTS 10. Leiden: Brill, 1980.
──────. *The Text of the New Testament: Its Transmission, Corruption, and Restoration.* 3rd ed. Oxford: Oxford University Press, 1992.
──────. *A Textual Commentary on the Greek New Testament.* 2nd ed. Stuttgart: Deutsche Bibelgesellschaft / United Bible Societies, 1994.
Michaelis, Wilhelm. "ὁράω, εἶδον, κτλ." Pp. 5:315–82 in *Theological Dictionary of the New Testament*, ed. G. Kittel and G. Friedrich. 10 vols. Grand Rapids: Eerdmans, 1964–76.
Miller, Susan. *Women in Mark's Gospel.* JSNTSup 259. London and New York: T. & T. Clark, 2004.
Mimouni, S. C. *Dormition et assomption de Marie: histoire des traditions anciennes.* Théologie historique 98. Paris: Beauchesne, 1995.
Mitchell, Joan L. *Beyond Fear and Silence: A Feminist-Literary Reading of Mark.* New York and London: Continuum, 2001.

Moloney, Francis J. *The Gospel of John.* SP 4. Collegeville, Minn.: Liturgical Press, 1998.
———. *Mark: Storyteller, Interpreter, Evangelist.* Peabody, Mass.: Hendrickson, 2004.
Morris, Colin. *The Sepulchre of Christ and the Medieval West: From the Beginning to 1600.* Oxford: Oxford University Press, 2005.
Morris, Leon. *The Gospel according to John.* Rev. ed. NICNT. Grand Rapids: Eerdmans, 1995.
Muddiman, John. "A Note on Reading Luke xxiv.12." *ETL* 48 (1972): 542–48.
Müller, C. Detlef G. "Epistula Apostolorum." Pp. 1:249–84 in Wilhelm Schneemelcher, ed., and R. McL. Wilson, trans., *New Testament Apocrypha.* Rev. ed. 2 vols. Cambridge: James Clark; Louisville: Westminster John Knox, 1991–92.
Murphy-O'Connor, Jerome. *The Holy Land: An Oxford Archaeological Guide from Earliest Times to 1700.* 4th ed. Oxford: Oxford University Press, 1998.
Nagy, Gregory. *The Best of the Achaeans: Concepts of the Hero in Archaic Greek Poetry.* Baltimore: Johns Hopkins University Press, 1979.
Neirynck, Frans. "Les femmes au tombeau: Étude de la rédaction matthéenne (Matt. xviii.1-10)." *NTS* 15 (1968): 168–90.
———. "ΠΑΡΑΚΥΨΑΣ ΒΛΕΠΕΙ: Lc 24,12 et Jn 20,5." *ETL* 53 (1977): 113–52.
———. "John and the Synoptics: The Empty Tomb Stories." *NTS* 30 (1984): 161–87.
———. "Lc 24,36-43: un récit lucanien." Pp. 655–80 in *À Cause de l'Évangile: Études sur les Synoptiques et les Actes offertes au P. Jacques Dupont, O.S.B. à l'occasion de son 70e anniversaire.* LD 123. Paris: Saint-André/Cerf, 1985.
———. "Once More Lk 24,12." *ETL* 70 (1994): 319–40.
———. "Q: From Source to Gospel." *ETL* 71 (1995): 421–30.
———. "Luke 24,12: An Anti-Docetic Interpolation?" Pp. 145–58 in *New Testament Textual Criticism and Exegesis: Festschrift J. Delobel,* ed. A. Denaux. BETL 161. Leuven: Peeters, 2002.
Nickelsburg, George W. E. "Son of Man." Pp. 6:137–50 in *The Anchor Bible Dictionary,* ed. David Noel Freedman. New York: Doubleday, 1992.
———. *Resurrection, Immortality, and Eternal Life in Intertestamental Judaism and Early Christianity.* 2nd ed. HTS 56. Cambridge: Harvard University Press, 2006.
Nickelsburg, George W. E., and James C. VanderKam. *1 Enoch: A New Translation.* Minneapolis: Fortress Press, 2004.
Nisetich, F. *The Poems of Callimachus.* Oxford: Oxford University Press, 2001.
Nock, A. D. "The Cult of Heroes." *HTR* 37 (1944): 141–74.
Nolland, John. *The Gospel of Matthew: A Commentary on the Greek Text.* NIGTC. Grand Rapids: Eerdmans, 2005.
Oakes, Peter. "Re-mapping the Universe: Paul and the Emperor in 1 Thessalonians and Philippians." *JSNT* 27 (2005): 301–22.
Ogden, Daniel. *Greek and Roman Necromancy.* Princeton, N.J.: Princeton University Press, 2001.
———. *Magic, Witchcraft, and Ghosts in the Greek and Roman Worlds: A Sourcebook.* Oxford: Oxford University Press, 2002.
Osiek, Carolyn. "The Women at the Tomb: What Are They Doing There?" *Ex Auditu* 9 (1993): 97–107.
Overman, J. Andrew. *Matthew's Gospel and Formative Judaism: The Social World of the Matthean Community.* Minneapolis: Fortress Press, 1990.
Paige, Terence. "Who Believes in 'Spirit'? Πνεῦμα in Pagan Usage and Implications for the Gentile Christian Mission." *HTR* 95 (2002): 417–36.
Palmer, D. W. "Origin, Form, and Purpose of Mark 16:4 in Codex Bobbiensis." *JTS* 27 (1976): 113–22.
Parsons, Mikeal. "A Christological Tendency in P75." *JBL* 105 (1986): 463–79.
Patterson, Stephen J. *The God of Jesus: The Historical Jesus and the Search for Meaning.* Harrisburg, Pa.: Trinity Press International, 1998.
———. *Beyond the Passion: Rethinking the Death and Life of Jesus.* Minneapolis: Fortress Press, 2004.

Pearson, Birger A. "The Pierpont Morgan Fragments of a Coptic Enoch Apocryphon." Pp. 227–83 in *Studies on the Testament of Abraham*, ed. G. Nickelsburg. SBLSCS 6. Missoula, Mont.: Scholars Press, 1976.

Pease, Arthur Stanley. "Some Aspects of Invisibility." *HSCP* 53 (1942): 1–36.

Perkins, Pheme. *Resurrection: New Testament Witness and Contemporary Reflection*. Garden City, N.Y.: Doubleday, 1984.

Perrin, Norman. "The Son of Man in the Synoptic Tradition." *BR* 13 (1968): 3–25.

Perry, T. A. "Cain's Sin in Gen. 4:1-7: Oracular Ambiguity and How to Avoid It." *Proof* 25 (2005): 258–75.

Pesch, Rudolf. "Zur Entstehung des Glaubens an die Auferstehung Jesu." *TQ* 153 (1973): 201–28.

———. "Zur Entstehung des Glaubens an die Auferstehung Jesu: Ein neuer Versuch." *Freiburger Zeitschrift für Philosophie und Theologie* 30 (1983): 73–98.

Petersen, William L. "Tatian's Diatessaron." Pp. 403–30 in Helmut Koester, *Ancient Christian Gospels: Their History and Development*. Philadelphia: Trinity Press International; London: SCM, 1990.

Phillips, Victoria. "The Failure of the Women Who Followed Jesus in the Gospel of Mark." Pp. 222–34 in *A Feminist Companion to Mark*, ed. Amy-Jill Levine. Sheffield: Sheffield Academic, 2001.

Porter, Stanley E. "Resurrection, the Greeks, and the New Testament." Pp. 52–81 in *Resurrection*, ed. S. Porter et al. JSNTSup 186. Sheffield: Sheffield Academic Press, 1999.

Price, Simon. "From Noble Funerals to Divine Cult: The Consecration of Roman Emperors." Pp. 56–105 in *Rituals of Royalty: Power and Ceremonial in Traditional Societies*, ed. S. Price and D. Cannadine. Cambridge: Cambridge University Press, 1987.

Prince, Deborah Thompson. "The 'Ghost' of Jesus: Luke 24 in Light of Ancient Narratives of Post-Mortem Apparitions." *JSNT* 29 (2007): 287–301.

Reid, Barbara E. *Choosing the Better Part? Women in the Gospel of Luke*. Collegeville, Minn.: Liturgical Press, 1996.

Rhoads, David, Joanna Dewey, and Donald Michie. *Mark as Story: An Introduction to the Narrative of a Gospel*. 2nd ed. Minneapolis: Fortress Press, 1999.

Richardson, Peter, et al., eds. *Anti-Judaism in Early Christianity*. 2 vols. ESCJ 2–3. Waterloo, Ont.: Wilfrid Laurier University Press, 1986.

Riebl, Maria. *Auferstehung Jesu in der Stunde seines Todes? Zur Botschaft von Mt 27,51b-53*. SBB 8. Stuttgart: Katholisches Bibelwerk, 1978.

Riley, Gregory J. *Resurrection Reconsidered: Thomas and John in Controversy*. Minneapolis: Fortress Press, 1995.

Robinson, James M. "Jesus—From Easter to Valentinus (or to the Apostles' Creed)." *JBL* 101 (1982): 5–37.

———. "The Matthean Trajectory from Q to Mark." Pp. 122–54 in *Ancient and Modern Perspectives on the Bible and Culture: Essays in Honor of Hans Dieter Betz*, ed. Adela Yarbro Collins. SPHS 22. Atlanta: Scholars Press, 1998.

———. "The Sequence of Q: The Lament over Jerusalem." Pp. 225–60 in *Von Jesus zum Christus: Christologische Studien. Festgabe für Paul Hoffmann zum 65. Geburtstag*, ed. U. Busse and R. Hoppe. BZNW 93. Berlin and New York: de Gruyter, 1998.

———. "From Safe House to House Church: From Q to Matthew." Pp. 183–99 in *Das Ende der Tage und die Gegenwart des Heils: Begegnungen mit dem Neuen Testament und seiner Umwelt. Festschrift für Heinz-Wolfgang Kuhn zum 65. Geburtstag*, ed. M. Becker and W. Fenske. AGJU 44. Leiden: Brill, 1999.

———. *Jesus: According to the Earliest Witness*. Minneapolis: Fortress Press, 2007.

Rodd, C. S. "The End of the Theology of Q?" *ExpT* 113 (2001): 5–12.

———. "The Theology of Q Yet Again: A Reply to the Responses of Christopher Tuckett and Paul Foster." *ExpT* 114 (2002): 80–85.

Saldarini, Anthony J. *Pharisees, Scribes and Sadducees in Palestinian Society: A Sociological Approach*. Wilmington, Del.: Michael Glazier, 1988.

——. *Matthew's Christian-Jewish Community*. Chicago: University of Chicago Press, 1994.

Sasson, Jack M. *Jonah: A New Translation with Introduction, Commentary, and Interpretation*. AB 24B. New York: Doubleday, 1990.

Sato, Migako. *Q und Prophetie: Studien zur Gattungs- und Traditionsgeschichte der Quelle Q*. WUNT 2/29. Tübingen: Mohr Siebeck, 1988.

——. "Le document Q à la croisée de la prophétie et de la sagesse." Pp. 99–122 in *La source des paroles (Q): Aux origines du christianisme*, ed. Andreas Dettwiler and Daniel Marguerat. MdB 62. Geneva: Labor et Fides, 2008.

Schaberg, Jane. *The Father, the Son, and the Holy Spirit: The Triadic Phrase in Matthew 28:19b*. SBLDS 61. Chico, Calif.: Scholars Press, 1982.

——. *The Resurrection of Mary Magdalene: Legends, Apocrypha, and the Christian Testament*. New York; London: Continuum, 2002.

Schaeffer, Susan E. "The Guard at the Tomb (*Gos. Pet.* 8:28–11:49 and Matt 27:62-66; 28:2-4, 11-16): A Case of Intertextuality?" *SBLSP* (1991): 499–507.

Schenk, Wolfgang. "Luke as Reader of Paul: Observations on His Reception." Pp. 127–39 in *Intertextuality in Biblical Writings: Essays in Honour of Bas van Iersel*, ed. S. Draisma. Kampen: Kok, 1989.

Schenke, Ludger. *Auferstehungsverkündigung und leeres Grab: eine traditionsgeschichtliche Untersuchung*. SBS 33. Stuttgart: Katholisches Bibelwerk, 1968.

Schneiders, Sandra M. "John 20.11-18: The Encounter of the Easter Jesus with Mary Magdalene—A Transformative Feminist Reading." Pp. 1:155–68 in *"What Is John?" Readers and Readings of the Fourth Gospel*, ed. Fernando F. Segovia. SBLSS 3, 7. Atlanta: Scholars Press, 1996–98.

——. "The Resurrection of the Body in the Fourth Gospel: A Key to Johannine Spirituality." Pp. 168–98 in *Life in Abundance: Studies of John's Gospel in Tribute to Raymond E. Brown, S.S.*, ed. John R. Donahue. Collegeville, Minn.: Liturgical Press, 2005.

——. "Touching the Risen Jesus: Mary Magdalene and Thomas the Twin in John 20" Pp. 153–76 in *The Resurrection of Jesus in the Gospel of John*, ed. C. Koester and R. Bieringer. WUNT 2/222. Tübingen: Mohr Siebeck, 2008.

Schoedel, William R. *Ignatius of Antioch: A Commentary on the Letters of Ignatius of Antioch*. Hermeneia. Philadelphia: Fortress Press, 1985.

Schrage, W. *Der erste Brief an die Korinther*. EKKNT 7. 4 vols. Düsseldorf: Benziger; Neukirchen-Vluyn: Neukirchener, 1991–2001.

Schürmann, Heinz. "Observations on the Son of Man Title in the Speech Source." Pp. 74–97 in *The Shape of Q: Signal Essays on the Sayings Gospel*, ed. John S. Kloppenborg. Minneapolis: Fortress Press, 1994.

Schüssler Fiorenza, Elisabeth. *In Memory of Her: A Feminist Theological Reconstruction of Christian Origins*. New York: Crossroad, 1983.

——. *Jesus, Miriam's Child, Sophia's Prophet: Critical Issues in Feminist Christology*. New York: Continuum, 1995.

Schweizer, Eduard. "πνεῦμα, πνευματικός, κτλ." Pp. 6:332–455 in *TDNT*, ed. G. Kittel and G. Friedrich; trans. G. W. Bromiley. 10 vols. Grand Rapids: Eerdmans, 1964–76.

Seeley, David. "Blessings and Boundaries: Interpretations of Jesus' Death in Q." *Semeia* 55 (1991): 131–46.

——. "Jesus' Death in Q." *NTS* 38 (1992): 222–34.

Segal, Alan F. *Life after Death: A History of the Afterlife in the Religions of the West*. New York: Doubleday, 2004.

Seim, Turid K. *The Double Message: Patterns of Gender in Luke-Acts*. Nashville: Abingdon, 1994.

Setzer, Claudia. "Excellent Women: Female Witness to the Resurrection." *JBL* 116 (1997): 259–72.

Shapiro, H. A. "*Hêrôs Theos*: The Death and Apotheosis of Herakles." *CW* 77 (1983): 7–18.

Shoemaker, Stephen J. "'Let Us Go and Burn Her Body': The Image of the Jews in the Early Dormition Traditions." *CH* 68 (1999): 775–823.

———. *Ancient Traditions of the Virgin Mary's Dormition and Assumption.* Oxford Early Christian Studies. Oxford: Oxford University Press, 2002.

———. "Death and the Maiden: The Early History of the Dormition and Assumption Apocrypha." *SVTQ* 50 (2006): 59–97.

Skedros, James C. "The *Heroikos* and Popular Christianity in the Third Century C.E." Pp. 181–93 in *Philostratus's Heroikos: Religion and Cultural Identity in the Third Century C.E.*, ed. E. Bradshaw Aitken and J. K. Berenson MacLean. SBLWGRW 6. Leiden: Brill, 2004.

Smith, D. Moody. *The Theology of the Gospel of John.* New Testament Theology. Cambridge: Cambridge University Press, 1995.

Smith, Daniel A. "The 'Assumption' of the Righteous Dead in the Wisdom of Solomon and the Sayings Gospel Q." *SR* 29 (2000): 287–99.

———. "The Post-Mortem Vindication of Jesus in the Sayings Gospel Q." Ph.D. dissertation, University of St Michael's College, Toronto. Ottawa: National Library of Canada/Bibliothèque nationale du Canada, 2001.

———. "Revisiting the Empty Tomb: The Post-Mortem Vindication of Jesus in Mark and Q." *NovT* 45 (2003): 123–37.

———. *The Post-Mortem Vindication of Jesus in the Sayings Gospel Q.* LNTS 338. London and New York: T. & T. Clark, 2006.

———. "Matthew and Q: The Matthean Deployment of Q and Mark in the Apocalyptic Discourse." *ETL* 85 (2009): 99–116.

Smith, Jonathan Z. *To Take Place: Toward Theory in Ritual.* CSHJ. Chicago: University of Chicago Press, 1987.

Smith, R. R. R. "The Imperial Reliefs from the Sebasteion at Aphrodisias." *JRS* 77 (1987): 88–138.

Stein, Robert H. "A Short Note on Mark XIV.28 and XVI.7." *NTS* 20 (1974): 445–52.

———. *Studying the Synoptic Gospels: Origin and Interpretation.* 2nd ed. Grand Rapids: Baker, 2001.

Stone, Michael E. *Fourth Ezra: A Commentary.* Hermeneia. Minneapolis: Fortress Press, 1990.

———. "A Reconsideration of Apocalyptic Visions." *HTR* 96 (2003): 167–80.

Stuart, Douglas K. *Hosea–Jonah.* WBC 31. Waco, Tex.: Word, 1987.

Sullivan, Kevin P. *Wrestling with Angels: A Study of the Relationship between Angels and Humans in Ancient Jewish Literature and the New Testament.* AGJU 55. Leiden: Brill, 2004.

Swete, H. B. *The Akhmîm Fragment of the Apocryphal Gospel of St Peter.* London: Macmillan, 1893.

Talbert, Charles H. "The Concept of Immortals in Mediterranean Antiquity." *JBL* 94 (1975): 419–36.

———. *Reading Luke: A Literary and Theological Commentary on the Third Gospel.* New York: Crossroad, 1984.

———. *What Is a Gospel? The Genre of the Canonical Gospels.* Philadelphia: Fortress Press, 1977; repr., Macon, Ga.: Mercer University Press, 1985.

Thiselton, Anthony C. "Realized Eschatology at Corinth." *NTS* 24 (1978): 510–26.

———. *The First Epistle to the Corinthians: A Commentary on the Greek Text.* NIGTC. Grand Rapids: Eerdmans, 2000.

Thrall, Margaret E. *A Critical and Exegetical Commentary on the Second Epistle to the Corinthians.* 2 vols. ICC. Edinburgh: T. & T. Clark, 1994–2000.

Tödt, Heinz Eduard. *The Son of Man in the Synoptic Tradition.* Translated by Dorothea M. Barton. London: SCM, 1965.

Troxel, Ronald L. "Matt 27.51-4 Reconsidered: Its Role in the Passion Narrative, Meaning and Origin." *NTS* 48 (2002): 30–47.

Tuckett, Christopher M. "Synoptic Problem." Pp. 6:263–70 in *The Anchor Bible Dictionary*, ed. David Noel Freedman. New York: Doubleday, 1992.

———. *Q and the History of Early Christianity*. Edinburgh: T. & T. Clark, 1996.

———. "The Search for a Theology of Q: A Dead End?" *ExpT* 113 (2002): 291–94.

Vaage, Leif. *Galilean Upstarts: Jesus' First Followers according to Q*. Valley Forge, Pa.: Trinity Press International, 1994.

van Esbroeck, Michel. *Aux origines de la Dormition de la Vierge: études historiques sur les traditions orientales*. Collected Studies 472. Brookfield, Vt.: Variorum, 1995.

van Iersel, Bas. "The Resurrection of Jesus—Information or Interpretation?" Pp. 54–67 in *Immortality and Resurrection*, ed. P. Benoît and R. Murphy. Concilium 60. New York: Herder & Herder, 1970.

van Tilborg, Sjef, and Patrick Chatelion Counet. *Jesus' Appearances and Disappearances in Luke 24*. Biblical Interpretation Series 45. Leiden: Brill, 2000.

VanderKam, James C. "Righteous One, Messiah, Chosen One, and Son of Man in 1 Enoch 37–71." Pp. 145–68 in *The Messiah: Developments in Earliest Judaism and Christianity*, ed. J. Charlesworth. Minneapolis: Fortress Press, 1982.

———. *Enoch: A Man for All Generations*. Studies and Personalities of the Old Testament. Columbia: University of South Carolina Press, 1995.

Vielhauer, Philipp, and Georg Strecker. "Jewish-Christian Gospels." Pp. 1:134–78 in Wilhelm Schneemelcher, ed., and R. McL. Wilson, trans., *New Testament Apocrypha*. Rev. ed. 2 vols. Cambridge: James Clarke; Louisville: Westminster John Knox, 1991–92.

Vögtle, Anton. "Wie kam es zum Osterglauben?" Pp. 9–131 in Rudolf Pesch and Anton Vögtle, *Wie kam es zum Osterglauben?* Düsseldorf: Patmos-Verlag, 1975.

Volbach, Wolfgang Fritz. *Elfenbeinarbeiten der Spätantike und des frühen Mittelalters*. 3rd ed. Mainz: Von Zabern, 1976.

Waters, Kenneth L. "Matthew 27:52-53 as Apocalyptic Apostrophe: Temporal-Spatial Collapse in the Gospel of Matthew." *JBL* 122 (2003): 489–515.

———. "Matthew 28:1-6 as Temporally Conflated Text: Temporal-Spatial Collapse in the Gospel of Matthew." *ExpT* 116 (2005): 295–301.

Wedderburn, A. J. M. *Beyond Resurrection*. London: SCM; Peabody, Mass.: Hendrickson, 1999.

Wegner, Judith Romney. *Chattel or Person? The Status of Women in the Mishnah*. Oxford: Oxford University Press, 1988.

Weitzmann, Kurt. *Age of Spirituality: Late Antique and Early Christian Art, Third to Seventh Century*. New York: Metropolitan Museum of Art, 1979.

Wengst, Klaus. *Christologische Formeln und Lieder des Urchristentums.*Gütersloh: Mohn, 1972.

Weren, Wim J. C. "'His Disciples Stole Him Away' (Mt 28,13): A Rival Interpretation of Jesus' Resurrection." Pp. 147–63 in *Resurrection in the New Testament: Festschrift J. Lambrecht*, ed. R. Bieringer et al. BETL 165. Leuven: Peeters, 2002.

Westcott B. F., and F. J. A. Hort. *The New Testament in the Original Greek*. 2 vols. New York: Harper & Bros., 1882.

Wicks, Jared. "Christ's Saving Descent to the Dead: Early Witnesses from Ignatius of Antioch to Origen." *ProEccl* 17 (2008): 281–309.

Wilckens, Ulrich. "The Tradition-History of the Resurrection of Jesus." Pp. 51–76 in *The Significance of the Message of the Resurrection for Faith in Jesus Christ*, ed. C. F. D. Moule. London: SCM, 1968.

Wills, Lawrence M. *The Quest of the Historical Gospel: Mark, John, and the Origins of the Gospel Genre*. London and New York: Routledge, 1997.

Winkler, Jack. "Lollianos and the Desperadoes." *JHS* 100 (1980): 155–81.

Witherup, Ronald D. "The Death of Jesus and the Raising of the Saints: Matthew 27:51-54 in Context." *SBLSP* (1987): 574–85.

Wright, N. T. "Resurrection in Q?" Pp. 85–97 in *Christology, Controversy and Community: New Testament Essays in Honour of David R. Catchpole*, ed. D. G. Horrell and C. M. Tuckett. NovTSup 99. Leiden: Brill, 2000.

———. *The Resurrection of the Son of God*. Volume 3 of *Christian Origins and the Question of God*. London: SPCK; Minneapolis: Fortress Press, 2003.

———. "Resurrecting Old Arguments: Responding to Four Essays." *JSHJ* 3 (2005): 209–31.

Zeller, Dieter. "Entrückung zur Ankunft als Menschensohn (Lk 13,34f.; 11,29f.)." Pp. 513–30 in *À Cause de l'Évangile: Études sur les Synoptiques et les Actes offertes au P. Jacques Dupont, O.S.B. à l'occasion de son 70e anniversaire.* LD 123. Paris: Saint-André/Cerf, 1985.

———. "Bedeutung und religionsgeschichtlicher Hintergrund der Verwandlung Jesu (Markus 9:2-8)." Pp. 303–22 in *Authenticating the Activities of Jesus*, ed. B. Chilton and C. A. Evans. NTTS 28/2. Leiden: Brill, 1999.

———. "New Testament Christology in Its Hellenistic Reception." *NTS* 46 (2001): 312–33.

———. "Erscheinungen Verstorbener im griechisch-römischen Bereich." Pp. 1–19 in *Resurrection in the New Testament: Festschrift J. Lambrecht*, ed. R. Bieringer et al. BETL 165. Leuven: Peeters, 2002.

Zias J., and E. Sekeles. "The Crucified Man from Giv'at ha-Mivtar: A Reappraisal." *IEJ* 35 (1985): 22–27.

Zwiep, A. W. *The Ascension of the Messiah in Lukan Christology*. NovTSup 87. Leiden: Brill, 1997.

Index of Selected Subjects

expectation of return, 50–51; eschatological role, 57–58; at transfiguration, 15, 22, 57–58, 87; as paradigm in Q, 73, 148–49

Emperor, Roman, as son of god, 88, 91, 95, 209; funerals of, 55, 95

empty tombs, ancient interpretations of, 47–49, 60–61

empty tomb of Jesus, earliest tradition concerning, 76–78, 84–85; presence of women at, 9–10, 89, 92, 94–95, 101–2, 121–23, 138, 140–41, 158–59, 162; guard at, 120, 121, 122, 123–124, 125, 128–29, 130, 131, 161, 162, 163, 165, 166, 168, 174, 176 ; appearances of risen Jesus at, 126–31, 137–38, 162–63, 179–82; apostolic inspection of, 6, 8, 93, 101, 106, 107–8, 112, 119, 138, 140–42, 145, 149–50, 173–75, 181; exit of Jesus from, 160, 162–64

empty tomb story, origins of, 3, 9–10, 76–77, 148–49; earliest significance of, 76–77, 92–98; needing apologetic support, 100–1, 113, 120, 128–31, 134–35, 155

Enoch, assumption of, 4, 40, 49–50, 52–53, 55, 198–99; preserved for eschatological role, 51–52, 57–58; identified with Son of Man, 21, 52, 73, 184

epiphanies, of heroes, etc., 17–20, 132, 189; of angels, 15, 20–22, 112; in Mark, 85–89

epitaphs, ancient, use of assumption language in, 56, 76

eschatology, realized, 36, 151–52, 195

Ezra, assumption of, 51. 52–53, 73, 75–76

ghosts, ancient, 16, 20, 107–8; varieties of embodied states of, 16, 107–8, 215–16; ancient terminology for, 108. *See also* apparitions, postmortem

Hell, harrowing of, 131, 163

Herakles, postmortem assumption of, 19, 53, 75, 199

heroes, ancient, 38; veneration of, 49, 53, 91, 219; apparitions of, 16–20, 132, 188; *anabiōsis* and, 17–18, 54, 61, 189; early Christology and, 19, 23, 190; saints and, 166–67, 190, 232

historical arithmetic and the origins of Easter faith, 23–24

Holy Sepulchre, Church of the, 170–73, 233

James, brother of the Lord, as resurrection witness, 3, 14, 27, 30, 32–33, 163, 193–10

Job, children of, postmortem assumption of, 56–57, 216, 212

Marcion, 108–9, 114, 154, 157, 217, 229

Mark 16, additions to: Longer Ending, 6, 58, 145, 155–58, 159, 161, 186, 201, 208, 229; Shorter Ending, 158, 186, 176; Freer Logion, 230; Codex Bobbiensis interpolation, 158

Mary Magdalene, at tomb of Jesus, 1, 121, 138; appearance of risen Jesus to, 10, 33, 100, 103, 126–27, 139, 144–49, 156–57, 158, 161, 174–75; as *apostolorum apostola*, 144; reputation as visionary, 127, 144;

misrepresentations of, 144–45. *See also* women

Mary, Mother of Jesus, dormition/assumption of, 60, 169–70; compared to Enoch and Elijah, 60; perpetual virginity of, 155

mē mou haptou ("Do not touch me"), 137, 146–47

Moses, death/assumption/ apotheosis of, 22, 40, 51, 53–54, 55, 57–58, 86–87, 206; at transfiguration, 15, 22, 57, 86–87

necromancy, 16, 107

ōphthē (he appeared to/was seen by), 3, 14–16, 20, 22–23, 34, 104, 112–13, 187, 210, 217

Paul, call/conversion of, 3–4, 34–35; as apostle/ resurrection witness, 10, 13–15, 21–22, 34–35; downgraded by Luke, 35, 112–13; knowledge of disappearance tradition, 28–29, 40–45, 77; theology of resurrection bodies, 35–40

Peter, appearance of the risen Jesus to, 3, 11, 13–14, 105, 111, 112, 125–26, 193–94; inspects empty tomb, 6, 100–1, 106, 107, 141–43, 150, 174, 181; priority of as resurrection witness, 33, 85, 93, 100, 142

Philinnion, postmortem noctural adventures of, 17, 215

pneuma/pneumatikon (spirit/spiritual), 14, 38, 106–11; contrasted with *psychikon* (soulish/ natural), 28, 29, 183; contrasted with *sarx* (flesh), etc., 39, 40, 41, 43, 108

Protesilaos, embodied apparitions of, 17, 23, 167, 189; *anabiōsis* of, 17, 54

Q, and Synoptic Problem, 5–6, 63; genre of, 63–64; as "gospel," 63; theology of, 67; significance to descriptions of Christian origins, 66–67; postmortem vindication of Jesus in, 67–76

representative figures, in early Jewish and Christian writings, 21, 95, 147, 183–84, 212

resurrection of the dead, as eschatological, 23–24, 43, 61, 90, 130, 183; as corporate, 61, 80, 90, 130, 163, 183; as recompense for martyrdom, 36–37; as bodily, 3, 14, 22, 37–40, 43; as nonbodily, 37–38; in Q, 4, 4, 71–72, 79

resurrection proclamation, controlling disappearance narrative, 6, 28, 90–91, 124–25, 152

Romulus, assumption of, 19, 39, 55, 90, 190, 199; postmortem apparition of, 13, 20, 97

saints, raising of in Matthew, 122–23, 130–31; veneration of in early Christianity, 166–70

Son of God, meanings of, 209; in Paul, 27, 44; in Mark, 87–98; in Roman imperial theology, 88, 90, 91, 95, 209

Son of Man, in Daniel 7, 21, 44, 92, 132, 183; Enoch as, 21, 51–52, 73, 184; Jesus as, 4, 11, 61, 64–65, 67–76, 89–95, 132–35

spirit/spiritual. See pneuma/pneumatikon

visionary experience, early Christian, 10, 15, 18, 21–22, 35, 109, 112–13, 145–47

Western non-interpolations, 115–18

women, attending the burial and tomb of Jesus, 8, 92–93, 96, 101, 121–22, 161; witnesses to empty tomb, 9–10, 89, 92, 94–95, 101–2, 121–23, 138, 140–41, 158–59, 162; commissioned by angels, 96, 125, 131; not commissioned by angels, 100, 103, 141, 162; encountered and commissioned by risen Jesus, 126–27, 144–47, 158–59; disbelieved by other disciples, 6, 101, 105–6, 154, 156–57, 159–60. See also Mary Magdalene

Xisouthros (Ziusudra), assumption of, 50, 53, 65

Zechariah (murdered prophet), 59, 69, 70

Zechariah (father of John the Baptist), murder and postmortem assumption of, 59; appearance in heaven, 59

Index of Modern Authors

Eitrem, Samson, 189
Ekroth, Gunnel, 189, 200
Evans, Christopher F., 111, 214, 215, 217
Farmer, William R., 197
Fehribach, Adeline, 226
Felton, D., 188, 198, 215–32
Fitzmyer, Joseph A., 217
Foster, Paul, 157, 160, 174, 203, 218, 230, 231, 234
France, R. T., 190, 222
Frey, Jörg, 151, 229
Fuller, Reginald H., 15–16, 30, 36, 187, 193, 195, 206, 208, 214, 215, 222
Fullmer, Paul, 198
García Martínez, Florentino, 205
Gathercole, Simon, 92, 211, 212
Georgi, Dieter, 206, 207
Gillman, John, 42, 197
Glasson, T. Francis, 197
Goguel, Maurice, 8, 154, 163, 186, 229, 230, 231
Golan, David, 233
Goodacre, Mark S., 202
Goold, G. P., 198
Goulder, Michael D., 214, 219
Green, Joel B., 214, 231
Grimm, Veronika E., 208
Guillaume, Jean-Marie, 214
Gundry, Robert H., 126–27, 208, 220, 221, 222
Guthrie, W. K. C., 188
Haas, Nicu, 186
Haenchen, Ernst, 226, 228
Hamilton, Neill Q., 212
Harnack, Adolf von, 203, 217
Haufe, Günter, 51, 198, 200
Heil, John Paul, 86, 209, 210, 222
Hengel, Martin, 42, 192, 193, 196, 197
Hershbell, Jackson P., 189, 232
Hock, Ronald F., 201
Hoffmann, Paul, 133, 202, 203, 204, 206, 224
Hölbl, Günther, 200
Holleman, Joost, 191

Hornblower, Simon, 230
Hort, Fenton J. A., 115, 218
Hubbard, Benjamin J., 223
Hughes, Dennis D., 232
Hultgren, Arland J., 203
Hurtado, Larry W., 71, 78, 79–80, 204, 206, 207
Ilan, Tal, 214
Jackson, Howard M., 211
Jacobson, Arland D., 203
Jacoby, Felix, 198
Jansen, Katherine L., 164, 214, 227, 232
Joachim, Jeremias, 197
Johnson, Andy, 13
Johnson-Debaufre, Melanie, 207
Johnston, Sarah Iles, 107, 188, 216
de Jonge, Henk Jan, 24, 187, 191, 192–9
Juel, Donald, 96, 197, 213
Kee, Howard C., 189
Kelhoffer, James A., 155, 156, 157, 229, 230
Kilpatrick, George D., 197
Kirk, Alan K., 231
Kitzinger, Ernst, 186
Kloppenborg, John S., 63, 64, 66, 73–74, 76, 133, 202, 203, 204, 205, 206, 207, 210, 211, 224
Knibb, Michael A., 231
Koester, Craig A., 138, 141, 144, 225, 226, 229
Koester, Helmut, 166–67, 190, 220, 231, 232, 234
Kremer, Jacob, 117, 219
Lambrecht, Jan, 197
Lang, Mabel, 189
Larsen, Kasper Bro, 225
Lincoln, Andrew T., 142, 144, 213, 225, 226, 228
Livingstone, Elizabeth A., 198, 229, 232
Lohfink, Gerhard, 4, 49, 55, 58, 72, 186, 190, 198, 199, 200, 201, 205, 207, 208, 217, 219, 233
Lohmeyer, Ernst, 211
Longstaff, Thomas R. W., 220
Lüdemann, Gerd, 29, 77, 85, 126, 185, 187, 192, 206, 208, 214, 221

Luz, Ulrich, 119, 123, 125, 126, 127, 128, 129, 134, 164, 186, 202, 211, 220, 221, 222, 223, 224, 231, 232
MacDonald, Margaret Y., 232
Mack, Burton L., 192, 202
MacLean, Jennifer K. Berenson, 188, 189, 232
Magness, J. Lee, 212, 213
Manson, T. W., 203
Marcus, Joel, 84, 208, 209, 210, 212, 213
Marcus, Ralph, 200
Mare, W. Harold, 233
Marshall, I. Howard, 217, 219
Martin, Dale B., 36, 38, 39, 195, 196
Martin, Michael Wade, 116, 118, 218, 219
Martin, Ralph P., 207
Marxsen, Willi, 2–3, 29, 185, 192, 197, 211
Matera, Frank J., 211, 212
Maurer, Christian, 229
McCane, Byron, 9, 161, 186, 187, 212, 220, 226, 231
McCarthy, Carmel, 234
McVey, Kathleen E., 229
Meeks, Wayne A., 228
Meiselman, Moshe, 214
Merklein, Helmut, 206, 208
Metzger, Bruce M., 118, 208, 218, 219, 222, 230, 234
Michaelis, Wilhelm, 113, 185, 187, 217
Michie, Donald, 209
Miller, Susan, 211
Mitchell, Joan L., 212
Moloney, Francis J., 209, 225, 226, 228
Morris, Colin, 233, 234
Morris, Leon, 229
Muddiman, John, 117, 219
Müller, C. Detlef G., 222, 229, 231
Murphy-O'Connor, Jerome, 172, 233
Nagy, Gregory, 200

Index of Ancient Texts

Philostratus, *Life of Apollonius of Tyana*

Phlegon of Tralles, *Book of Marvels*

Plato, *Phaedo*

Plato, *Symposium*

Plutarch, *Numa*

Plutarch, *On the Failure of Oracles*

Plutarch, *Romulus*

Plutarch, *Themistocles*

Syncellus, *Ecloga Chronographica*

Virgil, *Aeneid*

Ancient Inscriptions

CIG

IG